The Interaction between World Trade Organisation (WTO) Law and External International Law

International legal scholarship is concerned with the fragmentation of international law into specialised legal systems such as trade, environment and human rights. Fragmentation raises questions about the inter-systemic interaction between the various specialised systems of international law. This study conceptually focuses on the interaction between World Trade Organisation (WTO) law and external international law. It introduces a *legal* theory of WTO law, *constrained openness*, as a way to understand that interaction. The idea is that WTO law, from its own internal point of view, constructs its own law. The effect is that external international law is not incorporated into WTO law wholesale, but is (re)constructed as WTO law. It follows that legal systems do not directly communicate with each other. Therefore, to influence WTO law, an indirect strategic approach is required, which recognises the functional nature of the differentiated systems of the fragmented international legal system.

Ronnie R. F. Yearwood, BSc., LL.M, PhD has worked for the Prime Minister's Office (Barbados) with a special focus on the Caribbean Single Market and Economy. He has lectured in Caribbean politics and sociology in Barbados, and in law at Durham University, Newcastle University, University College London (UCL) and the School of Oriental and African Studies (SOAS), University of London.

Routledge Research in International Economic Law

Available:

Recognition and Regulation of Safeguard Measures Under GATT/WTO
Sheela Rai

The Interaction between World Trade Organisation (WTO) Law and External International Law
The constrained openness of WTO law (A prologue to a theory)
Ronnie R. F. Yearwood

Forthcoming:

Foreign Investment and Dispute Resolution Law and Practice in Asia
Vivienne Bath and Luke Nottage (eds.)

Improving International Investment Agreements
Armand De Mestral and Céline Lévesque (eds.)

Law and Power in Foreign Investment in Africa
Shades of grey in the shadow of the law
Lorenzo Cotula

The Domestic Politics of International Trade
Intellectual property rights in US-Colombia and US-Peru Free Trade Agreements
Johanna von Braun

Trade Remedies
A development perspective
Asif Qureshi

The Interaction between World Trade Organisation (WTO) Law and External International Law

The constrained openness of WTO law (a prologue to a theory)

Ronnie R. F. Yearwood

Routledge
Taylor & Francis Group
LONDON AND NEW YORK

First published 2012
by Routledge
2 Park Square, Milton Park, Abingdon, Oxon OX14 4RN

Simultaneously published in the USA and Canada
by Routledge
711 Third Avenue, New York, NY 10017

Routledge is an imprint of the Taylor & Francis Group, an informa business

British Library Cataloguing in Publication Data
A catalogue record for this book is available from the British Library

Library of Congress Cataloging in Publication Data
Yearwood, Ronnie R.F.
The interaction between WTO law and external international law : the constrained openness of WTO law / Ronnie R.F. Yearwood.
p. cm. — (Routledge research in international economic law)
ISBN 978-0-415-56516-5 (hardback)
1. World Trade Organization. 2. Foreign trade regulation.
3. Free trade. 4. International economic relations.
5. International law. I. Title.
K4610.Y43 2012
343'.087—dc22
2011003437

ISBN: 978-0-415-56516-5 (hbk)
ISBN: 978-0-203-80767-5 (ebk)

Typeset in Baskerville MT by Swales & Willis Ltd, Exeter, Devon

MIX
Paper from responsible sources
FSC® C004839
www.fsc.org

Printed and bound in Great Britain by
CPI Antony Rowe, Chippenham, Wiltshire

With love, to my 'mummy' Grace Yearwood, and my brothers Romell and Tyrone, and my 'mom' Rosalind Mayers and her family

With love to Lucy Weidner

To Denys Springer my dad and Ben Stephens my friend who left this world for another world. May they find more peace than us left behind.

'Resolving conflict with superficial means'
Mark Titchner, 2002. Concrete, carved wood, electric motor, paint.
(Courtesy the Artist and Vilma Gold, London)

Contents

Table of cases

WTO/GATT Law 1994 and GATT 1947 cases

Argentina – Footwear (EC)

Argentina – Textiles and Apparel

Australia – Salmon

Australia – Salmon (Article 21.5 – Canada)

EC – Computer Equipment

EC – Hormones

EC – Hormones (Canada)

EC – Hormones (US)

EEC – Oilseeds

EC – Poultry

Korea – Various Measures on Beef

Appellate Body Report, *Korea – Measures Affecting Imports of Fresh, Chilled and Frozen Beef*, WT/DS161/AB/R, WT/DS169/AB/R, adopted 10 January 2001 . . . . 115, 156, 164, 166–7

Mexico – Taxes on Soft Drinks

Appellate Body Report, *Mexico – Tax Measures on Soft Drinks and Other Beverages*, WT/DS308/AB/R, adopted 24 March 2006 . . . . . 199, 200, 202–4

Panel Report, *Mexico – Tax Measures on Soft Drinks and Other Beverages*, WT/DS308/R, adopted 24 March 2006, modified by Appellate Body Report, WT/DS308/AB/R 117, 199–202

US – 1916 Act

Appellate Body Report, *United States – Anti-Dumping Act of 1916*, WT/DS136/AB/R, WT/DS162/AB/R, adopted 26 September 2000 33

US – Anti-Dumping and Countervailing Duties (China)

Panel Report, *United States – Definitive Anti-Dumping and Countervailing Duties on Certain Products from China*, WT/DS379/R, adopted 22 October 2010 208

US – Carbon Steel

Appellate Body Report, *United States – Countervailing Duties on Certain Corrosion-Resistant Carbon Steel Flat Products from Germany*, WT/DS213/AB/R and Corr.1, adopted 19 December 2002 . . . . 33, 62

US – Certain EC Products

Appellate Body Report, *United States – Import Measures on Certain Products from the European Communities*, WT/DS165/AB/R, adopted 10 January 2001 117

Panel Report, *United States – Import Measures on Certain Products from the European Communities*, WT/DS165/R and Add.1, adopted 17 July 2000, modified by Appellate Body Report, WT/DS165/AB/R 117

US – Cotton Yarn

Appellate Body Report, *United States – Transitional Safeguard Measure on Combed Cotton Yarn from Pakistan*, WT/DS192/AB/R, adopted 5 November 2001 136

US – Wool Shirts and Blouses

International Court of Justice cases

Permanent Court of International Justice cases

United Kingdom cases

Other cases

Preface

This book did not originate in any grand intentions to try to rewrite international trade law. It does not offer some kind of chicken soup for the international trade lawyer soul. It is not a testimony to the moral underpinnings of international trade as either good or bad. There is no penance to be had here.

My interest in law has not been a timeless and carefully nurtured development. At worse it has been haphazard, and at best some would politely call it an adventure. I was attracted to law by the precision of argument that can be displayed by a skilled legal practitioner and its supposedly superior objectivity. During working in politics the bridge between my studies and practice widened somewhat artificially. Not that I expected the real world of politics to match the order and poetic exposition of the books. But there was no, or at least no one openly displayed an affection for, theorising as practitioners. Therefore, when I was directed to carry out a task, I could not present my superiors with philosophy, even if these were the base of whatever policy opinion I expressed. I quickly realised to keep them to myself. The consequence of doing contrary would probably have been the development of a reputation as an 'academic type' with no *bona fide* value in the real world where governmental, budgetary and news cycles were perceived to matter. Worse yet as a result of such a reputation I would not be directed any 'important' tasks. Therefore, I functioned as I was expected, as a competent practitioner.

Further, politics seemed somewhat arbitrary in that I realised practitioners did not own up to the fact that on many occasions, they were simply responding to events, all the while trying to appear as if it was a faultless process of distribution of resources, give and take, and bargains where losers were treated graciously. What happens in politics is hardly ever the same thing people think is happening. The two events can often be far apart. Practitioners attempt to create narratives around which they can coalesce power. Moreover, in the office there was no way that I could expound on the merits of political inquiry, which I studied and taught in the classroom. There was sometimes simply no time and space. Something always had to be done in the policy driven world of politics. Practitioners were constantly on the move trying or at least appearing to fix one 'problem' or another, managing relations between, and delivering resources to, competing groups. It appeared like most theorising was occurring backwards, that is, in reverse of the actual process. Politics was a naked exercise in power. The rule was determined by whosoever had the most influence over other people at the time, regarding how resources were to be distributed. It was not only simply the ability to get your way. It was the ability to finesse arguments, as part of a democratic process, to acquire power to 'maintain' that way. There was no point in winning for today but losing for tomorrow. It was about locking institutions and by extension people into a way of thought and action. This was something I was later to discover was also true of law. Law after all is above the *Realpolitik*, I originally thought, otherwise what and who secures the *Republic*. I had turned to law not merely as an addendum but extension and in some way a replacement of my political thinking. I turned to law because I imagined it as an objective, impartial, formal application of rules. In the legal world, I thought that there was no way I would be confronted by the arbitrariness and indeterminacy of politics. In law, a dispute would occur over a particular rule. We would know the rule. An adjudicator would apply the rule. The parties to the dispute lived by that decision. Someone lost. Someone won. The case then served as a guide to how to respond to the rule in the future. However, the more of law I saw, the more of politics I saw. I saw in law the same indeterminacy, ambiguity and the less than formal application of the rules. In law, I was not faced with the formal comfort I expected as an escape from politics but with a feeling that law struggled with its own form of indeterminacy.

I am left to share this sentiment:

> If God offered me, in His right hand, absolute truth and,
> in His left hand, only the quest for truth, stipulating that
> I should always fail in that quest, and if He said to me
> choose! I would humbly take His left hand and say Father,
> give me this one! Absolute truth belongs only to You.[1]

1 Quote by Gotthold Ephraim Lessing, Wolffenbutter fragmente taken from Manguel A, All Men are Liars (London: Alma Books Ltd, 2010). (I thank Lucy Weidner for pointing out this book and in particular the quotation to me.)

Acknowledgements

Writing a book is difficult. Writing a book based on a doctorate makes the task more acute for the very reason it was in the first place, namely that the work begins to intertwine and cross over into all aspects of your life. The task is not a singular project even if the production of the final work is a singular task. Along the way my life has been altered. Sometimes I have questioned whether doing the doctorate and then the book has been for the better but I trust time is the only thing that can provide me with a an answer. Not necessarily a just and fair one, but perhaps I will get one.

There are many people to thank for being part of my journey because there is something intrusive about the task of the doctorate and then its post production as a book, that whether they wanted it or not as part of their lives, my family and friends were made to share the journey with me. I could not have done it without them and that is by no means an exaggeration. It is a simple unreserved fact. This book belongs to them as much as I claim any intellectual ownership of it.

I would like to thank Charanjit Singh Sandhu, Hardeep Sandhu, Rupy Sandhu, Sumeet Sandhu for making me part of their home in Durham. I would like to thank Nicholas Bernards for a summer now long past, for loaning me his place in Newcastle when many substantive ideas of this work developed. Lucy and I have fond memories there. I would like to thank Richard White for sharing his home, at that time, in Glasgow with me when I was close to quitting this project. Sometimes changing pace and scenery can make a world of difference.

I also have to thank Abigail Humphries-Robertson for her commitment to the project from the start and for all her assistance. Oliver Dearden deserves similar praise and thanks. Life often does send the person and their skill when you need it most. His keen eye and helpful comments on structure and style have been instrumental in the final stages of this book.

I have to specially thank Imran Ahmed because very few people have a heart as true. Also to Ben Stephens, my friend and housemate, who previously travelled the doctoral journey. I thank you for always telling me I could do it when I said and looked the contrary. Sadly, you passed away in the final write up of this work as a doctorate. May the Gods protect and guide you. At *22 Moorside South*, Ben, Katy Jones (now Décube), Arnaud Décube, Giles Shorter, our two special guest residents: Eri Nishikawa and Lucy, and I all shared a 'home'. It was there around the kitchen table and usually after cups of tea that we found shelter from the storms outside, and many there were. I thank you all. We can never return to the past but in our memories, though the past can be a useful guide to celebrate the present and the future.

To Jason Beckett you encouraged me never to fear my ideas. You always listened. If there is such a thing as a true academic spirit, its dwells in you. Further thanks to Jason and his family (Nancy Burn and Christopher Beckett) for sharing their home with me.

To all my friends and family, I would like to say a heartfelt thank you. To list you all and what you did for me would be the task of another book in itself, on the art of giving. The best part of all is that most of the time none of you probably realised you were helping me along this incredible journey.

I thank all the staff at the Newcastle Law School where I did my graduate work and in particular my supervisors Ilona Cheyne and Ian Ward, and also to library staff Catherine Dale, Linda Bell, and Dorothy Smith (now retired). Thanks are especially reserved to my doctoral examiners Richard Mullender and Professor Joanne Scott. Thank you for making my work better for having to put it to the test of scrutiny. I also would like to thank Gary Malkin and the staff at the library and archive of the Baltic Centre for Contemporary Art in Newcastle/Gateshead. I also thank Mark Titchner for giving me permission to reproduce his artwork in this book. He is not only a talented artist but also a gracious person.

For funding assistance for my doctorate I would like to thank my family, the Newcastle University International Postgraduate Scholarship, the Overseas Research Scholarship, and the team at the Newcastle University International Office. In particular I thank Ashley Wilton, former Head of the Newcastle Law School, for his assistance, which was always timely and straightforward.

My biggest thank you is to Lucy, who has been there along the way. When I thought things were not possible, she inspired, cared for and loved me. The last few years have been difficult for a variety of reasons and as with life, the unplanned, curved and winding road is the one you travel. The map, you make it up as you go along. The best you do is to keep walking and in moments like this, stop to take account not of the finality of the work or its worthiness, but to realise there is always more to do. Along the way Lucy and I have lost loved ones, gained loved ones, moved houses probably a few too many times, moved cities, and we have grown somewhat older individually and together, though how much wiser we can never be sure. There are many more stories to write. The plots and themes of the stories, I do not know. In the unpredictability and uncertainty that is life, I hope Lucy that you know I always love you, and not because you ever asked, but because I simply do.

To anyone who I may have inadvertently forgotten I thank you. This has been a long and what appeared as an improbable journey. I thank God to have made it to this part of the journey. Giving up looked like an option at times but my mother showed me that it is not the option you choose. Instead you choose to live the life you want, making the best of what you were given, and knowing fully that it is the difficult choice. In doing so you fight with determination and hard work, aware there is no end.

R. Yearwood
(London) United Kingdom, (Boscobel) Barbados
Two rocks in a vast ocean
Autumn/Winter 2010

Abbreviations

AB	Appellate Body
AJIL	American Journal of International Law
ASIL	American Society of International Law
BISD	Basic Instruments and Selected Documents
BYIL	British Yearbook of International Law
CITES	Convention on International Trade in Endangered Species of Wild Fauna and Flora
CUP	Cambridge University Press
DSB	Dispute Settlement Body
DSU	Understanding on Rules and Procedures Governing the Settlement of Disputes
EC	European Communities
EEC	European Economic Community
EJIL	European Journal of International Law
EU	European Union
GATS	General Agreement on Trade in Services
GATT	General Agreement on Tariffs and Trade
ICJ	International Court of Justice
ILC	International Law Commission
IMF	International Monetary Fund
JIEL	Journal of International Economic Law
JWT	Journal of World Trade
MEA	multilateral environmental agreement
MERCOSUR	Southern Common Market (Argentina, Brazil, Paraguay, Uruguay)
MFN	Most Favoured Nation
NAFTA	North American Free Trade Agreement
OUP	Oxford University Press
PCIJ	Permanent Court of International Justice
Recueil des Cours	Recueil des Cours de l'Académie de Droit International (Hague)

SPS Agreement	Agreement on the Application of Sanitary and Phytosanitary Measures
TBT Agreement	Agreement on Technical Barriers to Trade
VCLT	Vienna Convention on the Law of Treaties
WTO	World Trade Organisation

Prologue

0.1 The tragedy of choice: to write is to choose

No idea or theory can cover every possibility. As Isaiah Berlin writes,

> The belief that some single formula can in principle be found whereby all the diverse ends of men can be harmoniously realised is demonstrably false. If, as I believe, the ends of men are many, and not all of them are in principle compatible with each other, then the possibility of conflict – and of tragedy – can never wholly be eliminated from human life, either personal or social. The necessity of choosing between absolute claims is then an inescapable characteristic of the human condition.[1]

An author is faced with a 'constant tragedy of choice.'[2] From the moment he (thinks) writes a single word (creates worlds), he has already chosen ways to understand and describe what is happening around him.[3] Albert Camus in *The Rebel* illustrates this well.

> Where Stendhal describes, in one phrase, Lucien Leuwen's entrance into the room, the realistic artist ought, logically, to fill several volumes with descriptions of characters and settings, still without succeeding in exhausting every detail. Realism is indefinite enumeration . . . Realistic novels select their material, despite themselves, from reality, because the choice and the conquest of reality are absolute conditions of thought and expression. *To write is already to choose.*[4]

An idea that is useful may later fall short in explaining what is happening. An idea only gives the best account it can give, as far as it can, at a particular moment in

1 Berlin Isaiah, *Four Essays on Liberty* (Oxford: OUP, 1969) 169.
2 Ibid.
3 'He' here and subsequently throughout the book refers to both male and female authors.
4 Camus A, *The Rebel* (London: Penguin Group [1951] (2000) 235. My emphasis in italics. I would like to thank Jason Beckett for suggesting this work to me. Also see Beckett J, *The End of Customary Law: A Purposive Analysis of Structural Indeterminacy* (Saarbrücken: VDM Verlag 2008).

time.[5] Hence, an idea can never claim to be universal truth. Ideas are always subject to contestation in theory and practice. 'Since some values may conflict intrinsically, the very notion that a pattern must in principle be discoverable in which they are all rendered harmonious is founded on a false *a priori* view of what the world is like.'[6] There is no end of history because no system of logical thought is closed.[7] An author's assumptions, filters, prejudices and meanings are part of the basis of his ideas but they do not foreclose the development of further thought. An author can 'reconstitute [and] rewrite [a] narrative [idea], reversing [his] understanding of past events in the light of present responses to [his] probing.'[8] A new idea can then make sense of the past, present and future.[9] What it does is,

> enable us to understand its predecessors in a newly intelligible way. It at one and the same time, enables us to understand precisely why its predecessors have to be rejected or modified and also why, without and before its illumination, past theories could have been credible. It introduces new standards for evaluating the past.[10]

The result is 'inevitably' something other than 'unmediated access' to what an idea is attempting to capture as to have happened.[11] As a consequence the author's role is more than simply describing what they see as a matter of objective empirical fact. He must instead exhibit patience with theory, or ways of thinking. To claim that his work is empirical objective observation from which a theory can be formed is misleading. It is a dangerous masquerade for what is really choosing from among various contested interpretations of reality. 'We can no more separate our theories and concepts from our data and precepts than we can find a true Archimedean point – a god's-eye view – of ourselves and our world.'[12] If we accept that we can

5 See MacIntyre A, 'Epistemological Crises, Dramatic Narrative and the Philosophy of Science' (1977) 60(4) *Monist* 453, 455. See also generally on the point that no system can claim hierarchy so what we have are competing rationalities. Teubner G, 'How Law Thinks: Toward A Constructivist Epistemology of Law' (1989) 23(5) *Law and Society Review* 727. Rasch W, *Sovereignty and its Discontents* (London: Birkbeck Law Press, 2004).

6 Berlin *supra* note 1, at li.

7 For a discussion of the Hegelian end of history, see Fukyama F, *The End of History and the Last Man* (Free Press, 1992). *Contra*, Huntington S, *The Clash of Civilisations: Remaking of World Order* (New York: Simon and Schuster, 1998). See also Marks S, 'The End of history? Reflections on some international legal theses' (1997) 8 EJIL 449.

8 MacIntyre *supra* note 5, at 455.

9 Ibid.

10 Ibid at 460.

11 Sunstein C, 'The Idea of a Useable Past' (1995) 95 *Columbia Law Review* 601.

12 Shermer M, 'The Really Hard Science' *Scientific American*. 16 September 2007.

The Archimedean point derives from the idea attributed to Archimedes that if he were given one solid point to stand and a lever long enough he could move the entire earth. The Archimedean point is therefore an imagined point from which a person is supposedly able to objectively assess and understand something. It supposedly entails the ability to remove yourself, that is, for example prejudices, from your process of observation so that you can see the thing in its entirety as

make rational decisions from within ourselves, then there is no need to try to stand outside ourselves, in an effort at what is really false objectivity, as if doing so makes the decision better or less prone to error. The fact of the matter is that we all have a position, a view, from which we decide what to observe and what not to observe, and what those observations mean, as we make sense of what is going on around us. There is an apt and mocking illustration of this point as noted below.[13]

> The great thinker Zeno once sat a pupil of his down at a table and put a bean in front of him.
>
> 'Is this a heap?' he asked the pupil.
>
> 'No,' said the pupil, who was very smart. 'Of course it isn't, it's a bean.'
>
> Zeno placed another bean beside the first. 'Is this a heap then?'
>
> 'No.'
>
> Zeno added beans, one at a time until the pupil said, 'Yup, guess you could call that a heap.'
>
> 'Ah,' said Zeno. 'So a heap is twenty-seven, is that right? You are telling me that the word "heap" actually means twenty-seven?' At which the pupil got uncomfortable and bopped Zeno on the head with a discus.

What we realise is that difference is infinite. Something can possibly be understood and described in a countless number of ways. Consider the question posed above of how many beans make a heap? 'Further distinctions can always be made, making the task of perceiving difference paradoxical, because difference is all we have.'[14] Reality remains contested as a political pluriverse, not a universe, in that no idea can resolve all the differences between competing ideas accounting for the same thing. Zeno's student decided how many beans it took to make a heap. It does not make it correct or incorrect. It makes it a choice. Each idea 'renders some aspect of the carriage visible, while pushing other aspects into the background, preferring certain ways to deal with it at the cost of other ways.'[15] This is why it is important to put the methods of an idea in plain sight. In many respects the methods, what and how the objects of the ideas are determined, and the vocabularies and languages used to do that, should probably be more prominent than the idea itself. The lens we choose to see and explain things determines what we include and exclude as part of our ideas. *The Wonderful Wizard of Oz* provides an illustration of this. In *The Wonderful Wizard of Oz*, Dorothy is pulled into a new world by a

it exists independently of your own observation. See for a useful discussion Broackes J, 'Realism, Scepticism and the Lament for an Archimedean Point: Stroud and the Quest for Reality' (2004) 68 *Philosophy and Phenomenological Research* 415.

13 Describing Zeno's Paradox in somewhat comic terms, see Fry S, 'Think of a lobster . . .' *Rectorial Address at University of Dundee*, 29 October 1992, 1–26, 20–21.

14 Rasch W, *Sovereignty and its Discontents* (London: Birkbeck Law Press, 2004) 21.

15 Koskenniemi M, 'The Politics of International Law – 20 Years Later' (2009) 20(1) EJIL 1, 11. See also and as providing a map to Koskenniemi's work, Beckett J, 'Rebel Without a Cause? Martti Koskenniemi and the Critical Legal Project' (2006) 7(12) *German Law Journal* 1045.

tornado. In a search to find a way back home, that is, to regain her meanings of her reality and understanding of the world around her, she meets three characters: Tin Man, Scarecrow and Lion. Our four protagonists set out on a journey to find the Wizard of Oz with the view that he could give them meanings to understand their world.[16] On finding the Wizard, they come to the conclusion that he is not magical. Ironically they had the meanings they have been searching for.[17] In a telling dialogue that I think illustrates a main theme of the story, the Wizard explains to Dorothy that Oz was no greener in colour than any other city. It underlines much of what I think about objectivity being an illusion.

> '. . . I thought, as the country was so green and beautiful, I would call it the Emerald City; and to make the name fit better I put green spectacles on all the people, so that everything they saw was green.' [The Wizard of Oz]
> '*But isn't everything here green?*' asked Dorothy.
> '*No more than in any other city*,' replied Oz; '*but when you wear green spectacles, why of course everything you see looks green to you*. The Emerald City was built a great many years ago . . . But my people have worn green glasses on their eyes so long that most of them think it *really* is an Emerald City . . .'[18]

Emerald City was not necessarily green, if not for the lens its residents choose to see it through, or rather had foisted upon them, which they appear to accept somewhat unquestionably. It also shows that ideas that resist epistemological pluralism should be greeted with suspicion because no idea is inherently ontologically necessary.[19] All ideas are aleatory. We are never in a position to be able to claim we know the truth or are fully rational.[20] On these points, Shakespeare's *Hamlet* provides a significant analogy.[21] Hamlet's father, the King of Denmark

16 Baum F, *The Wonderful Wizard of Oz* (New York: The Modern Library, 2003; originally published in 1900). Dorothy's dog Toto is also pulled into Oz with her. Ironically, he is the only one who appears content with his understandings.
17 Ibid, generally but specifically chapters 15 and 16.
18 Ibid, at 130–131.
19 Rasulov A, 'International Law and the Poststructuralist Challenge' (2006) 19 *Leiden Journal of International Law* 799, 810; Darton R, *The Great Cat Massacre and Other Episodes in French Cultural History* (New York: Basic Books Inc., 1984) 191–209; MacCormick N, 'The Ethics of Legalism' (1989) 2(2) *Ratio Juris*.
20 Macintyre *supra* note 5, at 455. For a useful discussion on what is truth, see Frank H: *On Truth* (London: Pimlico, 2007); *On Bullshit* (Princeton: Princeton University Press, 2005). In *On Truth* Frank states that truth means that there is 'honesty and clarity in reporting the facts' because 'Without truth, either we have no opinion at all concerning how things are or our opinion is wrong. One way or the other, we do not know what kind of situation we are in. We don't know what's going on, either in the world around us or within ourselves' (p. 59). He argues that 'While no one has any trouble recognising that there is plenty of bullshit around, quite a few people remain stubbornly unwilling to acknowledge that there might be – even in principle – such a thing as truth'. (pp. 7–8). For a good review of both of Frank's book, see Mullender R, 'Truth, Bullshit, and Blame Culture' (2009) 11 *Legal Ethics* 272.
21 Shakespeare W, *Hamlet* (London: Yale University Press, 2003, originally written between 1564 and 1616). See Macintyre *supra* note 5.

died. The death has a Machiavellian plot about it, because in about a month, Hamlet's uncle and the dead King's brother, Claudius, ascended the throne and married Hamlet's mother, the dead King's widow, Gertrude. Hamlet's father appears as a ghost to Hamlet to tell him that Claudius murdered him and to take revenge.[22] Posner writes that Hamlet promises to do so with great enthusiasm but the mystery of the play is that he 'feigns madness – to what end is unclear . . . instead of getting about his business' of revenge.[23] There is a suggestion that by his behaviour Hamlet is trying to buy time or throw Claudius off the trail as he plots his revenge but this fails, because his behaviour is exactly what prompts Claudius' suspicions that Hamlet knows he murdered the King, Hamlet's father.[24] Hamlet can be understood as a critique of revenge, which Posner artfully discusses. However, I think that there is an additional and perhaps more important dimension to Hamlet. That is, his struggle to come to terms with a new reality. He faces a crisis to establish meanings to understand what is going in the new world he finds himself in. Without meanings to make sense of what is going on around him, his world collapses and descends into chaos, a sort of madness or struggle to keep pace with it.[25]

Perhaps Hamlet did not feign madness but experienced it, in the form of his inability to cope with the new world he found himself surrounded by. Hamlet lacked viable ways to interpret events around him, caused principally by his father's death. 'To be unable to render oneself intelligible is to risk being taken to be mad, is, if carried far enough, to be mad.'[26] Hamlet's father as a ghost was a challenge not insomuch as a ghost, similar to the monsters and strange creatures that Dorothy faced in Oz, but what it represented. The ghost presented Hamlet not only with a proposal of revenge but also with an alternative way of thinking, or more precisely a challenge to his current ways of understanding what was happening in the world around him.[27] Hamlet struggles with various ways to interpret and understand his father's death, and subsequent events.[28] Who is he to believe: his mother, former friends Rosencrantz and Guildenstern whom Claudius had sent to kill Hamlet, or his father's ghost?[29] Hamlet's problem is the one we encounter in deciding how to understand what is happening around us, especially when things change and do not necessarily or immediately come into our focus of how we see the world around us.[30] Until we adopt some way to understand the things around us, that

22 Posner R, *Law and Literature: A Misunderstood Relation* (Cambridge, MA: Harvard University Press, 1988) 54.
23 Ibid, at 54.
24 Ibid, at 52–55.
25 Darton *supra* note 19, at 193.
26 Macintyre *supra* note 5, at 455.
27 Macintyre *supra* note 5.
28 For example, Macintyre *supra* note 5, at 454 highlights the following possibilities: the revenge schema of the Norse sagas; the renaissance courtier's schema, and the Machiavellian schema about competition for power.
29 Ibid. Also see Hamlet *supra* note 21.
30 Ibid.

is, until we have a map, we do not know what to treat as important to understand those things. Until we know what to treat as things to understand the world around us, we do not know which meanings to adopt.[31]

Possessing alternative ways of assessing what is happening around us means that an author makes political choices. By that I mean the author favours for determined reasons one way over another to understand the world. In (thinking) writing the author chooses. It is an author's ability to include and to exclude things that forms his understanding, from which he can construct an idea of what is happening. There is an inability to give meaning to all things and cover all eventualities. This makes claims to universality, marginal at best, a false aspiration or an illusion at worse. 'Futures not realised are only branches of the past, dead branches', Marco Polo says in Italo Calvino's *Invisible Cities*.[32] It means that every decision 'excludes a whole range of other potential choices'. This echoes Borges' story in the *Garden and Forking Paths* where 'each time a man is confronted with several alternatives, he chooses one and eliminates the others'.[33] The effect of making a choice of one decision over another is as 'ramified time, in which each decision leaves suspended the alternatives to that choice'.[34] It means, as in the *Garden and Forking Paths*, that in one future you can be a friend and in another an enemy. Time is not as Newton thought, uniform and absolute, but as Einstein believed, relative.[35] In Newton's world 'objects acted on each other across the expanse of a neutral, undifferentiated space in an objective and knowable manner'.[36] For Einstein space and time are dynamic, and relative. The background or the space in which things interact is not neutral and objective.[37] The background cannot be abstracted from the foreground.[38] This puts an end to the idea of determinacy in that 'one cannot predict future events exactly if one can not measure the present state of the universe precisely'.[39] As Macintyre writes,

> . . . omniscience excludes the making of decisions. If God knows everything that will occur, he confronts no as yet unmade decision. He has a single will.

31 Ibid.

32 Calvino I, *Invisible Cities*, trans. W Weaver (London: Vintage, 1997) [Originally published in Italian as *Le città invisibili* [1972] 29. There is a 'latent otherness' 'constantly exerting pressure' to be realised in Calvino's fiction as noted by Jackson R, *Fantasy: The Literature of Subversion* (London: Methuen & Co Ltd, 1981) 165.

33 McLaughlin M, *Writers of Italy: Italo Calvino* (Edinburgh: Edinburgh University Press, 1998) 103.

34 Ibid, 111. See Borges J L *El jardín de los senderos que se bifurcan (The garden of forking paths)*, *Ficciones* (Grove Press, 1962). Translated by Helen Temple and Ruthven Todd.

35 Hawking S, *A Brief History of Time: From the Big Bang to Black Holes* (London: Bantam Press, 1988) chapter 2. See also for an interesting discussion on applying physics to understanding the relative nature of law, Tribe L H, 'The Curvature of Constitutional Space: What Lawyers Can Learn From Modern Physics' (1989) 103(1) *Harvard Law Review* 1.

36 Tribe *supra* note 35, at 4. Hawking *supra* note 35, at chapter 2, specifically p. 33.

37 Tribe *supra* note 35, at 7. Hawking *supra* note 35, at 33.

38 Ibid.

39 Hawking *supra* note 35, at 61.

> It is precisely insofar as we differ from God that unpredictability invades our lives. This way of putting the point has one particular merit: it suggests precisely what project those who seek to eliminate unpredictability from the social world or to deny it may in fact be engaging in.[40]

In choosing what to include and what to exclude, the foreground and background, an author renders the idea of neutral choice a falsity. A choice will privilege certain aspects of reality and de-privilege others. The 'choice is not usually seen as such – that is as a choice – by the vocabularies, but instead [as] something natural, rendering them ideological.'[41] An ideology can become a convenient way of choosing from one of the different ready-made stories: liberal, conservative, Marxist, capitalist, feminist, environmentalist, humanitarian, free trader, socialist and so on. The ease of this is transportation into a ready-made battle within and outside the ideology with sides and debates already delineated. One simply chooses analytical weapons with identified targets and enemies, both as philosophical and sometimes physical warfare. We then learn the rallying cries and language of the ideology as if we were born party to the ideology. This renders the choice a façade. We form allegiances to these ideologies from which to engage in a phoney war, example, liberals versus conservatives, without questioning whether the ideology is the best way to see the world, or the effects of seeing the world in this or that way.[42]

0.2 There is no magic but in the pretence

As Dorothy, Lion, Scarecrow, and Tin Man discovered in *The Wonderful Wizard of Oz*, behind the screen in *Emerald City* they did not confront an abstract being or idea capable of representing everything they each imagined, and with the ability give their world meanings. There was no Wizard. Instead, what Dorothy and the others found was a representation of humanity's – an old man's – desperation not to be caught out in his hunt for a perpetual peace or coherence of all ideas that offered solutions to everything.

> As [the screen] fell with a crash they looked that way, and the next moment all of them were filled with wonder. For they saw, standing in just the spot the screen had hidden, a little old man, with a bald head and a wrinkled face, who seemed to be as much surprised as they were. The Tin Woodman, raising his axe, rushed toward the little man and cried out, 'Who are you?'
>
> 'I am Oz, the Great and Terrible,' said the little man, in a trembling voice.

40 Macintyre A, *After Virtue, A Study in Moral Theory* (London: Gerald Duckworth & Co. Ltd., 1985, 2nd Edition) 96–97.

41 Koskenniemi *supra* note 15, at 11.

42 For example see Kennedy David, *The Dark Sides of Virtue: Reassessing International Humanitarianism* (Oxford: Princeton University Press, 2005).

> 'But don't strike me – please don't – and I'll do anything you want me to.'
> Our friends looked at him in surprise and dismay.
> '*I thought* Oz was a great Head,' said Dorothy.
> 'And *I thought* Oz was a lovely Lady,' said the Scarecrow.
> 'And *I thought* Oz was a terrible Beast,' said the Tin Woodman.
> 'And *I thought* Oz was a Ball of Fire,' exclaimed the Lion.
> 'No, you are all wrong,' said the little man meekly. 'I have been making believe.'
> 'Making believe!' cried Dorothy. 'Are you not a Great Wizard?'
> 'Hush, my dear,' he said. 'Don't speak so loud, or you will be overheard-- and I should be ruined. I'm supposed to be a Great Wizard.'
> 'And aren't you?' she asked.
> 'Not a bit of it, my dear; I'm just a common man.'
> . . .
> 'But how about the voice?' she inquired.
> 'Oh, I am a *ventriloquist*,' said the little man . . .

Perhaps what the man, pretending to be the Wizard of Oz, did not realise in creating the strong-all-knowing-solving caricature of himself is that the caricature became the ventriloquist and the man the puppet. There is perhaps a lesson in this for the law. It cannot provide answers for every problem; or rather every problem need not be represented as a legal problem with a requisite legal solution.

0.3 Outline of my approach

There are three points to take away from the discussion so far that inform how I approach the study of the interaction between WTO law and external international law. Firstly we need to decide what WTO law is, and its purpose because we choose our ideas to understand that law. Without them we have no way of making sense of the world around us. It would be, analogous to Dorothy or Hamlet, to find ourselves in a world without any meanings to help us understand what is going on. Secondly, because we decide the basis and nature of our ideas there is no objective reality. The moment there is any attribution of an Archimedean point it can no longer be an Archimedean point. The law is not discovered as if by magic but is made intelligible through the ideas we choose to understand what we have defined as the law. It is a matter of being open about our ideas, and what they simultaneously bring to the foreground and push to the background. Closely related is the fact that difference is infinite as we can have varying competing meanings for what may appear as the same thing. It underlines why it is important to put forward an idea or way to explain what aspects of reality we are bringing to light. More specifically even if we agree on the general meaning, for example of what the law is, that does not preclude or foreclose discussion on the nature and purpose of that law, which actually will lead us back to questioning what the law is, because understanding law's purpose can help us to understand its meaning. Thirdly, because of infinite difference it means that there are no universal answers that cover every eventuality or situation. Every idea as much as it is an exposition of thought is also an exposition of the limitations of those thoughts. Every idea is actually a reminder of what it does not include. It is within and aware of these boundaries that I present ideas about WTO law.

I contend it is important to decide what we need to know, as there are varying interpretations of the world because there is no direct access to a pre-theoretical or *a priori* reality.[43] 'There are only competing discourses with different constructions of reality.'[44] I am reminded of Charles Darwin's response to a critique that he should have 'put the facts before us and let them rest'. The suggestion was that Darwin's work was 'too' theoretical or conceptual. In a letter to his friend Henry Fawcett, Darwin writes, 'How odd it is that anyone should not see that all observation must be for or against some view if it is to be of any service.'[45] The facts do not and cannot speak for themselves, but are made intelligible through a lens, or way of thinking. In other words, I believe that by putting forward a method and concept I can provide a way to make sense of WTO law, and more specifically its interaction with external international law. I do not pretend there is some objective truth that we discover or attempt to have the final word, as there will always be several ways to think about WTO law, which will change over time. This is because WTO law, like all law, is socially constructed.[46] It 'does not pre-exist our observation (as a new species of tree or insect, or an unexplored territory, might do) but is constituted in that original decision (now become an unarticulated and hazy assumption) to designate a specific phenomena as law: law is constituted as an object of observation by the very act of observation itself.'[47] We have control over the definition and form law should take precisely because it is a thought object and so we can alter law. Since law is not a naturally occurring phenomenon, it has 'no existence until we decide (and define) it to be'.[48] The fact that law is socially con-

43 Teubner G, 'How Law Thinks: Toward A Constructivist Epistemology of Law' (1989) 23(5) *Law and Society Review* 727. Camus *supra* note 4, at 228–237.

44 Teubner *supra* note 43, at 743.

45 Charles Darwin in a letter to Henry Fawcett (18 Sept., 1861). Fawcett at the time was defending Darwin before the British Association for the Advancement of Science against a critic who said Darwin's *On the Origin of Species* was too theoretical and that he should have 'put his facts before us and let them rest'. See Darwin F, *More Letters of Charles Darwin* Vol. 1 (New York: D. Appleton, 1903).

46 On WTO law as socially constructed see Lang A, 'Reflecting on Linkage: Cognitive and Institutional Change in the International Trading System' (2007) 70(4) *Modern Law Review* 523. On law as social constructed see Beckett J, 'Countering Uncertainty and Ending Up/Down Arguments: A Prolegomena to a Response' (2005) 16(2) *European Journal of International Law* 213–238, 214–215. For further reading on the related issue of social and institutional facts as different from brute facts see Searle J, *The Construction of Social Reality* (New York: Free Press, 1995); Specifically related to law as a social and institutional fact see MacCormick N and O Weinberger, *An Institutional Theory of Law: New Approaches to Legal Positivism* (Dordrecht: D. Reidel Pub. Co., 1986). MacCormick N, 'The Ethics of Legalism' (1989) 2 *Ratio Juris* 184, 191; Darton *supra* note 19, at 3–7, 191–209 (chapter 5: Philosophers Trim the Tree of Knowledge: The Epistemological Strategy of the Encyclopedie).
For further discussion see chapter 1.

47 Beckett *supra* note 46, at 214.

48 Ibid.

structed and is continuously being constructed 'does not mean that it is impossible to take a snapshot of where it is right now'.[49] The task is to rationally reconstruct the socially constructed (see chapter 1).

The approach here is a minimalist one, aiming to put forward a way by which we can think about the interaction between WTO law and external international law. In effect it is a theory of WTO law in that I choose ways for 'identifying, interpreting and applying the norms' of WTO law.[50] All law is contingent upon, or is rather a theory of law. 'A direct, but often overlooked – ignored, disguised or even denied – corollary . . . is that all law, even the blackest or black letter law, is always already the application of a theory of law: law does not and can not have (nor maintain) an a-theoretical existence.'[51] In WTO law there appears a vacuum of explicit theories of law that attempt to explain WTO law as a matter of law.[52] This is not only ironic but also somewhat worrying given the often rich and insightful explanations of WTO law using political science, economics and international relations.[53] In order to grasp a sense of this policy oriented approach and why international trade law may exhibit scepticism to legal theory, it is important to understand the way in which the 'founders' of WTO law broached it as a new subject.

The chief architect of international economic law is without a doubt John Jackson.[54] Jackson can be identified as 'present at the creation' of the WTO and is 'in fact' one of its creators.[55] In a tribute to Jackson, Joel Trachtman writes that Jackson, succeeded in 'establishing a dauntless empirical black letter foundation on which he has been able to build a superstructure of prescription'.[56] It is this pragmatic sensibility that was to permeate Jackson's work and also importantly the study and practice of WTO law.[57] Here, we borrow Alasdair Macintyre's definition of practice to mean the

49 Schauer F, 'The Social Construction of the Concept of Law: A Reply to Julie Dickson' (2005) *Oxford Journal of Legal Studies* 493–501, 498.

50 Beckett *supra* note 46, at 226.

51 Ibid, at 227.

52 See for fuller attempts: Carmody C, 'A Theory of WTO Law' (2008) 11(3) JIEL 527–557. Palmeter D, 'The WTO as a Legal System' (2000) *Fordham International Law Journal* 444. For a listing of some other attempts at theory in international economic law see Carmody.

53 See generally Carmody *supra* note 52, at 1–10.

54 For a well-written and highly analytical piece of work on Jackson's role in creating international economic law, see Kennedy David, 'The International Style in Postwar Law and Policy: John Jackson and the field of International Economic Law' (1994–95) 10 Am. Uni. J. Int'l L. & Policy 671.

55 Trachtman J, 'John Jackson and the founding of the World Trade Organisation: Empiricism, Theory and Institutional Imagination' (1999) *Michigan Journal of International Law* 175, 175. See Kennedy *supra* note 53 for a more critical and full explanation of how Jackson 'as a classic academic project' founded, developed and dominated the field of school of international economic law.

56 Trachtman *supra* note 55.

57 Kennedy *supra* note 54.

> coherent and complex form of socially established cooperative human activity through which goods internal to that form of activity are realised in the course of trying to achieve those standards of excellence which are appropriate to, and partially definitive of, that form of activity, with the result that human powers to achieve excellence, and human conceptions of the ends and goods involved, are systematically extended.[58]

The idea of external goods to a practice are things attached to that practice such as prestige, status and money and though the achievement of these goods are contingent upon practice, a particular kind of practice is not the only way to achieve them as alternative practices can be found.[59] What is critical for us here are goods internal to a practice, which can only be specific to the practice and can only be 'recognised by the experience of participating in the practice in question. Those who lack the relevant experience are incompetent thereby as judges of internal goods.'[60] This suggests that on entering the practice of WTO law, we accept certain standards and follow the tradition in that our performance is judged by those standards and traditions. A practice therefore has a history and for international trade lawyers a large part of the history of WTO law is intimately wrapped up in Jacksons's approach to the study of WTO law. That does not make the tradition and specifically Jackson immune from critique, but it means we appreciate that 'we cannot be initiated into a practice without accepting' the tradition of the 'best standards realized so far'.[61] To enter into a practice is not only to address and enter into a relationship with your contemporaries but your predecessors,[62] of which Jackson is preeminent in international economic law. Jackson presented a 'succinct, readable description of the various elements', which came to constitute the field of international economic law.[63] His project as Cass notes was far-sighted and radical to the extent that he conceptualised the trading system in a new by providing what was previously an international treaty (GATT) with a new constitutional legal basis.[64] It is perhaps not a stretch to say at the heart of the international trade law constitution is Jackson's constitution. However, I think there are a number of problems with the project, mainly, the empirical approach Jackson adopted for deriving the existence of a WTO constitution.[65] 'Gone' in his approach was the 'public international lawyer's elaborate speculation on the existence and nature of international law.'[66] Jackson sets aside, as Kennedy argues the procedural regime and project of international public order for a network of market relations in which

58 Macintyre *supra* note 40, at 187.
59 Ibid, at 188.
60 Ibid, at 189.
61 Ibid, at 190.
62 Ibid, at 194.
63 Kennedy *supra* note 54, at 676.
64 Cass D Z, *The Constitutionalization of the World Trade Organization: Legitimacy, Democracy, and Community in the International Trading System* (Oxford: OUP, 2005) 97.
65 Ibid, at 98.
66 Kennedy *supra* note 54, at 676.

only a few substantive rules were necessary.[67] There was a focus on institutions and the rules to govern international trade law and trade liberalisation.[68] It is at this point that we can consider that approaches that favoured legal theory to question the nature and purpose of WTO law died.[69] We could imagine the answer to a question posed about the nature and purpose of WTO law: WTO law has 'simply evolved and exists for all to see; its sources are based in fact not just law'.[70] Liberal theory and the economic justifications for trade law simply became accepted assumptions, as reflected in textbooks and courses on WTO law, which all premise discussions about WTO law by outlining the liberal economic theory of trade.[71] WTO law is presented as having no theory of law, as separate from these justifications.[72] As a pragmatist Jackson was 'deeply sceptical, even rudely dismissive of traditional distinctions', such as between economic/legal, law/politics, legal/non-legal, 'which might be thought necessary for international economic law to have an autonomous coherence'.[73] Jackson states in the *first* volume and issue of the *Journal of International Economic Law*,

> In some cases (maybe most) it would seem preferable to shape research so as to be useful for the 'active users', the legal professionals (government or private) who must regularly cope with international law concepts and legal rules. This is a 'policy research' preference rather than a 'theory' preference, although obviously there are many situations in which theory has important relevance to policy. But such theory needs to be 'good theory', and normally good theory must be tested, usually by empirical observation.[74]

This work can be seen a benchmark, in what is the highly influential journal, for how to approach the study of WTO law. Empirical analysis, seemingly void of a theory of law, not only prevailed in his work but in the journals, programmes of study and teaching of WTO law. Further by not having a clear theory of law

67 Ibid, at 678. See Jackson J, The World Trading System: Law and Policy of International Economic Relations (MIT Press, 1989) [a second edition was published in 1997].

68 Cass *supra* note 64, at 98, 99–132.

69 Kennedy *supra* note 54, at 695.

70 See Cass *supra* note 64, at 134 for that characterisation of the approach.

71 Kennedy *supra* note 54, at 679. See Jackson *supra* note 54, at 9. A cursory survey of text books on WTO would show this.

72 See a general text or course book on WTO law. For example: Jackson J, W Davey and A Sykes, *Legal Problems of International Economic Relations* (St. Paul, MN: West Group, 2002, 4th Edition). Even newer textbooks take a similar approach. See for example: Lester S and B Mercurio et al. *World Trade Law: Text, Materials and Commentary* (Oxford: Hart Publishing, 2008).

73 Kennedy *supra* note 54, at 682. This approach builds upon the elements of international policy pragmatism: a proliferation of contexts and players, an admixture of law and politics, a rejection of fetishism about sovereignty, a modesty about reform, an evolutionary progressive faith, a scepticism of grand theoretical claims or plans, a practical orientation, and a case-by-case approach. Bargaining occurs over the meaning or range of legal and political solutions, as well as over their content. [p. 695]

74 Jackson J, 'Global Economics and International Economic Law' (1998) 1 JIEL 1.

from which he was seeking to articulate the nature and purpose of WTO law, Jackson's work is not clear as to the purpose of WTO law. There is a tension in his work as to whether the WTO is a response to, or generates globalisation. As Michael Fakhri makes clear, the two purposes are not mutually exclusive but the 'result of leaving the WTO's role in globalization unclear is that [it] presents the WTO as both inevitable and desirable'.[75] Both of which are not necessarily correct. The further problem is that it makes it 'difficult to identify the legal structures that affect or construct global markets'.[76] This is central to Jackson's work given that he favours a rules-based approach over the power-based approach because it allows national governments to overcome conflicting and strong domestic interests by having appeal to WTO law.[77] Beyond this to understand WTO law, Jackson relies principally on economic theory of liberal trade, the goal of which is to 'minimise the amount of inference of governments on trade flows that cross national borders'. However, it is not clear why he thinks governments are 'trusted to negotiate' a treaty such as the WTO but the same governments are not trusted to manage domestic trade policy and thus the need for a WTO to minimise their interference in international trade.[78] Moreover he appears to think that liberal trade will create losers. However, he construes this as a political non-economic matter to be addressed domestically and not by 're-examining the international structures' that may be creating the losers in the first place.[79] But having stripped the domestic arena of its ability to manage trade, then we are left unsure as to how these 'losers' of the liberal trade system are to be addressed. This is where having a theory of law allows us to keep the debates open, and provides a space by which we can see what/who is included in an examination and what/who is excluded, and on what basis.

The critique of the Jacksonian tradition, to empirically study international trade law as not supposedly hung up on theory, is not a protest against his ideas or an attempt to validate our own, but is grounded on what I think is his misconstruction of the role of theory in international trade law. Theory is not put forward to test our observation.[80] Our observations can 'always be put to the question'.[81] 'Theory is required to support observation, just as much as observation theory.'[82] Jackson's 'no-nonsense' empirical approach hinders the debate about what WTO law is, and plasters over the value conflicts that arise from understanding the purpose and nature of WTO law differently.[83] Even the supposedly 'black letter anti-theoretical environment' of WTO law that Jackson tries to build cannot escape

75 Fakhri M, 'Reconstructing the WTO Legitimacy Debates Towards Notions of Development' (2009) 5(8) *Comparative Research in Law and Political Economy* 1–25, 8. See also Cass *supra* note 64, at chapter 4, *passim*.

76 Fakhri *supra* note 75, at 8.

77 See Jackson J, *The World Trade Organisation: Constitution and Jurisprudence* (London: Pinter, 1998).

78 Fakhri *supra* note 75, at 8–10, especially at 9. See for example Jackson J, *The World Trading System: Law and Policy of International Economic Relations*, 2nd edition (MIT Press, 1997) 122.

79 Fakhri *supra* note 75, at 8. See for example Jackson J *supra* note 77, at 24.

80 Macintyre *supra* note 40, at 81.

81 Ibid.

82 Ibid.

83 See Cass *supra* note 64 at, chapter 4, *generally*.

value conflicts as 'both free trade and social regulatory objectives are written into the WTO treaties'.[84] There is no total coherence or unity of a legal system because, as discussed earlier, competing ideas exist to create not a single view of reality but multiple views of reality.

It is also critical to realise that the Jacksonian tradition creates an artificial divide between theory and practice,[85] between *Pericles* and the *Plumber*.[86] Twining wrote that 'the image of the lawyer as a Plumber is a simple one. The lawyer is essentially someone who is a master of certain specialised knowledge, the law, and certain technical skills. What he needs is no-nonsense specialised training to make him a competent technician.'[87] The Plumber does not need to know about the history and philosophy of plumbing or matters of the aesthetics of drains for example.[88] These do not allow him to execute his immediate tasks to fix the pipes, charge his fee and leave the customer generally happier because the state of the pipes are in a better condition than prior to his appointment to the task. This image seems akin to that of the international trade lawyer where the tradition of international trade law shows an almost derisive view of theory in favour of a broad pragmatic policy oriented approach. However, like Twining I caution as to whether that the image of the plumber bears much relation to the real international trade lawyer, though earlier discussions may give strong credence to the image.[89] The other compelling image is that of the international trade lawyer as Pericles. This is the 'law-giver, the enlightened policy maker, the wise judge'.[90] Again, the caution is that the image of Pericles like that of the Plumber may not bear much relation to the real international trade lawyer.[91] 'When people articulate what they consider to be the proper objectives of legal education, are they often so modest as to equate lawyers with plumbers or so immodest as to suggest that every lawyer should be a Pericles.'[92] However, we can consider that these images strongly influence legal education in that 'much of [its] theory and practice . . . proceeds on the basis of [these] assumptions, hidden or only half-articulated.'[93] Nonetheless, I do not think that the field of international trade law has to be bound by one image as against the other image,[94] though it is difficult to deny that the image of the international trade lawyer as Plumber driven by the functional pragmatic policy approach of Jackson overshadows a field he

84 Beckett J, *supra* note 4, at 1054. For further discussion see Lang *supra* note 45, for an insightful piece of work.

85 Trachtman *supra* note 55 at 177, in what is a tribute to Jackson's pragmatism as a triumph over formalised theory in the 'social science sense' brings out this point. In fact Trachtman appears to also misconstrue the place of theory in WTO law arguing that Jackson develops his 'theory' from the empirical analysis.

86 Twining W, 'Pericles and the Plumber' (1967) 83 LQR 396.

87 Ibid, at 397.

88 Ibid, at 397–398.

89 Ibid.

90 Ibid.

91 Ibid.

92 Ibid, at 399.

93 Ibid.

94 I thank Oliver Dearden for discussions on these points about Pericles and the Plumber.

'largely invented'.[95] Knowing (theory) cannot necessarily be separated from doing (practice).[96] The international trade lawyer as a Plumber, the highly efficient practical technician is also Pericles, the thoughtful pondering legal mind. The practice of WTO law is not tested against a 'theory' but theory is used to make sense of the practice. Put differently, a theory is not made to stand 'correct', by making the practice fit to its assumption. It is one thing to have doubts about the relevance of a particular theory of law in being able to identify and explain general patterns about the practice of law. It is quite another thing to mistakenly attempt to separate theory from practice, focusing exclusively on the latter, for even black letter analysis cannot be a-theoretical. For all its promise and the institutional discipline that Jackson's pragmatic and seemingly a-theoretical approach brought to bear upon the creation and sustaining of international trade law, as a major area of study, its main shortcoming was misunderstanding the proper place of a theory of law. The tradition of international trade law thus appears to have emerged grounded in contextual policy thinking rather than the use of formalised theoretical techniques that call into question very nature, existence and purpose of WTO law.

The arguments above could be shunted aside as a fixation with definition in the field of international economic law.[97] For example, early scholars used the term 'international economic law' to distinguish it from transnational law.[98] Further distinctions were made to distinguish between private aspects of transnational law on matters such as contract law, customs law and shipping law as distinct from trade relating to governments such as WTO law, IMF and World Bank rules.[99] Public international law was not seen as central to international trade law and some attempted to label the field as international business transactions. Cass, because of this, makes the telling point that the 'self-image of the discipline is uncertain'.[100] She argues that the self-doubt is a product of the 'discipline's (relative) novelty

95 Kennedy *supra* note 54, at 672.

96 The idea is captured well in, for example, Pirsig R, *Zen and the Art of Motorcycle Maintenance: An Inquiry into Values* (London: Vintage Books [1974] 1999). The protagonist, Pirsig says, believes that the 'division of the world into parts' 'is something everyone does' but in doing that, 'something is always killed'. Fish S, 'Fathers, Sons and Motorcycles', Think Again Blog, NY Times (June 14, 2009) writes, 'what is killed is an awareness of and contact with the world before analytic thought has done its (necessarily) reductive work'. Pirsig asserts that there are two main ways to divide the world, as a classic or romantic. The classical understanding, if we think of the world as a handful of sand sorted into piles, is concerned with 'the piles and the basis for sorting and relating them'. Whereas the romantic understanding is 'directed toward the handful of sand before the sorting began.' The tension is that the 'handful of sand is only known as something that exceeds the sortings we have made of it; the world can never be grasped directly, and so we are always in danger of occupying ourselves with the wrong things.' This is partly why we should assume that our understanding is only temporary, and can always be contested and rewritten in light of new evidence. For example, Newton rewrote Aristotle and Einstein rewrote Newton and one day someone may rewrite Einstein. (See Macintyre *supra* note 5 and Hawking *supra* note 35 on this point.)

97 For example see Cass *supra* note 64, at 86–91 on the point of fixation.

98 Cass *supra* note 64, at 86–89.

99 Ibid.

100 Ibid, at 87.

compared to public international law proper, or particular aspects of international legal studies.' Cass goes on to assert that the problem of definition is also a result of the 'inherent implausibility of separating' economic and business transactions from other aspects of social life.[101] I would however add that the self-doubt is also largely a result of not having explicit theories of law. It is because of the policy oriented contextual approach bequeathed by Jackson that became the tradition of WTO law, in or as the field of international economic law, that the task of advancing any theory of WTO law is greeted with suspicion.

The anxiety and self-doubt that Cass describes thus continues with debates as to whether WTO law is part of or separate to international law; uses or does not use, external international law.[102] As Chios Charmody asserts, any discussion about a theory of WTO law 'naturally raises the issue of what a theory is and how does it differ from other concepts about law'.[103] It means that even before setting out a particular theory, we have to justify the need for theory and perhaps the best place to start is to define what it is. A theory is a tool or suggestion for the '. . . identification of valid legal norms [by] telling us what law is, what it does, and why it does so, [thus fulfilling its primary function of identifying] the legal norms applicable to the instant dispute, or the legal evaluation of particular (presumably contested) actions.'[104] The function of a theory is to provide a way to understand and evaluate practice. Essentially a theory is a set of ideas that attempt to identity, describe and explain what the law is and its purpose, and from this a theory can possess a predictive and revisionist basis to explain what has happened in the past, and what could likely happen in the future. It is not there to provide definitive final answers. Theory allows us to hold fixed in our mind, the random and constantly moving social practice of law. Theory in this way does not impose order by making the practice of law, as objects of our observation, any less random or uncertain. What it does is momentarily pause those objects for us to take a snapshot of them. A theory of law can then also tell us what the law should be.

Charmody explains five reasons for why a theory of WTO law is important. The first is descriptive. A theory can offer a descriptive explanation of WTO law. The second reason is to be analytical. This means that we can identify the key elements of the law and examine how they interact. The third reason is teleological. It allows us to move from the study of *laws* to the study of *law*.[105] This is key to creating and sustaining WTO law as a jurisprudential enterprise. We can understand what the purpose of WTO law is, what ends it serves and so will be in a position to assess whether it is serving those ends as the social phenomenon of law. Consider, how can we assess the purpose of the law if we are not clear what the law is, or how its key elements interact. This is linked to the fourth reason for a theory that is it is normative. We need to know what the law is, and so can articulate ideas of

101 Ibid, at 88.
102 See chapter 4.
103 Carmody *supra* note 52, at 10.
104 Beckett *supra* note 46, at 218.
105 Carmody *supra* note 52, at 11.

what it should be. The fifth reason is to be explanatory. Theories explain or at the least, provide a basis for us to explain what is happening around us. A theory can be the basis from which we understand and explain which ascriptions or potential ascriptions of power can be classified as law within a legal system.[106]

I would add a sixth reason for a theory of WTO law that I think Carmody only somewhat teases. Theory can provide a basis for understanding the formal existence of WTO law.[107] Discussion of WTO law occurs in non-legal terms using economics and politics, with little regard for representing WTO law as a separate legal enterprise to be held apart from politics and economics for analysis. Put another way, robbed of its formal positive existence because of a lack of a theory of law to explain WTO law as law, there is no genuine legal narrative of WTO law. This is not to deny the rich contextual analysis that can be garnered from other fields in analysing WTO law. My point is much simpler. Before that sort of analysis can occur, we need to engage with WTO law as autonomous and separate from other fields, and other types of law. The moment that analysis has to come from outside of WTO law, then WTO law loses its formal existence, its ability to be distinctive and autonomous. To (re)capture the formal existence of WTO law, there is need for a theory of law to account for what it is and what it does and in the case of this study, how it interacts with external international law. As instructive as theories of economics and politics are to understand WTO law, only a theory of law can account for the law. Otherwise, we are assessing a theory of economics or politics, not a legal theory, of WTO law. That within itself is not a dilemma, given the obvious and at times compelling need to understand WTO law using theoretical ideas from other fields because trade intersects with many issues as 'trade *and*',[108] for example, the environment, human rights, labour, migration to mention a few. This approach is not only reasonable, but also more often that not, it is essential to assess the cross relations of politics, economics, law and the numerous other fields to get a sense of the bigger picture of globalisation and modernity, where an event in one area no matter how seemingly remote can affect another area because of the interconnectedness of not only human geography but systems of politics, economics and trade.[109] However, such an approach is not legal and cannot lay authority to a legal theory of the WTO law, on which such an approach should be built on in the first place. Otherwise we may be engaging with misconceptions

106 Beckett *supra* note 46, at 215.

107 Carmody *supra* note 52, at 11.

108 See for example (2002) 96 *American Journal of International Law*. For a good critical discussion and listing of the literature, see Lang *supra* note 45.

109 See for example, Giddens A, *The Consequences of Modernity* (Cambridge: Polity Press, 1990); Castells M, *The Rise of the Network Society* (Oxford: Blackwell Publishers, 2000); Scholte J A, *Globalisation: A Critical Introduction* (Basingstoke: Macmillan, 2005, 2nd edition); Held D and A McGrew (eds) *The Global Transformations Reader: An Introduction to the Globalization Debate* (Oxford: Polity Press, 2000); Woods N (ed) *The Political Economy of Globalisation* (New York: St. Martins Press, 2000). For critiques of globalisation: Stiglitz J, *Globalisation and its Discontents* (London: Penguin Group, 2002); Dunkley G, *The Free Trade Adventure* (London: Zed Books [1997] 2000); Mertes T (ed) *A Movement of Movements: Is Another World Really Possible?* (London: Verso, 2004).

of WTO law, for having not set out firstly what it is and what we think it does, we have somehow moved on to discussing how it works with other fields, or other specialised differentiated systems of international law.

Now, we know the reasons for having a theory of law, how do we arrive at a theory, or the basis of one? At this juncture, I am not making a case for my own work or for any particular theories or ideas about WTO law. I am simply making a case for any theory of law that seeks to explain what is WTO law and so from understanding what it is and what is its purpose, we can perhaps have fuller explorations of how it interacts with external international law. The steps I identify will serve as a 'means of justifying and defending that theory'.[110] We must define WTO law[111] and postulate its purpose,[112] which includes identifying the nature of the system in which WTO law is executing this purpose.[113] We must offer an exposition of the theory itself. How does it operate and explain the nature of law.[114] In this study I focus on identifying what WTO law *is*, and explaining its interaction with external international law. Finally, we must show the effectiveness of the theory of law we choose 'in linking the empirical presuppositions' as would have been previously discussed with the 'purpose' of law.[115]

I recognise that most of the participants in the discourse have sound knowledge and practical experience of WTO law. If international trade lawyers do not believe that the current ideas that underpin international trade law are somewhat inadequate, they would be less convinced of the need for new ideas to account for *what is happening* in international trade law. The ideas I advance in this study could turn out to be my own *Emerald City*. There would be no point for me to put forward my ideas, no matter how seemingly agreeable, if they cannot come within one inch of the technical practice of varying amalgams of professionals of international trade lawyers. To reiterate, I do not think that knowing can be separated from doing. International trade lawyers would continue to believe in the existing ideas, probably because of a strong dogmatic inclination to continue to be part of the tradition on which the practice is built. This is even if those ideas no longer work in fully constructing and simultaneously understanding the world through that construction. 'A topography of critique' would focus on each steps identified previously in the negative'.[116] I must be clear that because the steps are neatly delineated here does not in any way dictate or is an indicator that they are neatly replicated as a study. What I think is important is that any critique is a disaggregation of the steps. This is because a 'composite whole critique' of a theory is near to impossible, just as a composite whole theory is impossible, as you cannot 'create an objective or even consistent inter-subjective frame of reference'.[117] Critique can be normative

110 Beckett *supra* note 46, at 227.
111 See chapter 1.
112 See chapter 4.
113 See chapters 1 and 2.
114 See chapters 1 and 2.
115 See chapters 5 and 6.
116 Beckett *supra* note 46, at 227.
117 Ibid.

or analytical, and focus on means or ends. It could be an issue of accuracy or desirability of the ideas being put forward.[118] As discussed in this Prologue, there is no foreclosure of thought and ideas remain defeasible and open to challenge. In light of this thinking, this study is to a large degree a prolegomenon. As much as I make any claims for proposing a theory of WTO law, it is also only the start of a theory, as they can never be a complete theory. My aim is to set out a lens, through which we can discuss and call into account current debates, assumptions and precepts about the interaction between WTO and external international law. In order to achieve this I go through the three steps broadly identified above. What is WTO law, what is its purpose and in what context is it operating? Next, how do I observe and evaluate WTO law? Having defined and observed WTO law, I can then analyse the practice of WTO law through that lens to realise how its purpose is realised, when it interacts with external international law.

0.4 Outline of my argument

How external international law becomes part of, or is used in WTO law is a highly contested issue among three main models.[119] I argue that the three main models: Model I (WTO law as a limited domain), Model II (WTO law as open) and Model III (WTO law as privileged), do not properly account for the interaction between WTO and external international law. I demonstrate how the debate occurring among the three models is not only a disagreement as to the basis on which WTO law can/should interact with external international law, but importantly is also structurally patterned to limit a insurgency to that debate. The aim of this study is to break into the debate instead of simply taking a side and defending WTO law as a realisation of either model. My argument is that the models and WTO law scholarship needs to be clearer about what WTO law is and what is its purpose, and do so using a theory of WTO law be able to explain the merits and demerits of their position.[120] Rather than asking questions about what WTO law is and its purpose, the discussion about the interaction between WTO and external international law appears to occur on presumptions that these matters are settled. Therefore instead of asking primary questions, they are asking secondary questions about what WTO law should be in an effort to be more legitimate and valid, whether that is as limited, open or privileged. The debate has been restrictive because WTO law is not shown as contested, though the debate appears as contested, that is, as a matter of is or is not/should or should not, the models all implicitly agree on the nature of WTO law. Commentators interjecting in the debate on the interaction between WTO and external international law therefore usually enter on the basis of one of the models, taking its presumptions, without necessarily realising, contained in the model are implicit assumptions about WTO law, which the model is attempting to

118 Ibid.
119 See chapter 4.
120 See Fakhri *supra* note 75 for a similar point.

bring to fruition in the debate and on practice of WTO law. Understanding how each model wants to use external international law in WTO law can actually show intended or otherwise, each model's view of the purpose of WTO law. The basic premise of the study is that before we can engage in a debate about how WTO law interacts with external international law, we must discuss what WTO law *is* as a key component of introducing a theory of WTO law from which to understand and rewrite the current models and debate. The basic tenets of my theory of WTO law, constrained openness, are as follows. The practice of the WTO adjudicating bodies can be understood as WTO law. These adjudicating bodies through their internal point of view produce institutional acts, which by their practice is what can be understood and observed as WTO law. In effect, WTO law constructs its own reality based on WTO law.

Chapter 1 sets out fragmentation as the context in which the debate about how WTO law interacts with external international law is taking place. Further and on the premise that law is a social construct we show how, why and what to define as WTO law. In doing so, I posit H. L. A. Hart's rule of recognition to define WTO law as the practice of the judiciary. The reason I think it is necessary to define WTO law is that there is no agreement as to what it is, which closely ties in with its purpose. Therefore when we say WTO law, there may be some sort of implicit assumption that we are talking about the same thing when in fact we are not. Is WTO law: a contract, rules, process, constitution, rights and obligations, forum for exchange of information, code of conduct for trade policy, non-discrimination, reciprocity, enforceable commitments, safety valves, transparency?[121] It is not that the method to identify WTO law should cover all of the aforementioned or even any, but the method should be open, as to what it means by WTO law. By doing this, critique of the method is readily accessible. I think that the rule of recognition provides a useful method as part of constructing a theory of WTO law. It however is only one part of a two-part puzzle, as it does not provide us with a way of examining the law once we have identified it. Therefore, we need an idea, which will provide explanations and evaluations of what we have identified as WTO law, which I set out in chapter 1.

In chapter 2, as a continuation of the discussion on fragmentation as in chapter 1, I examine the inadequacy of the professional tools of treaty interpretation, *lex specialis* and *lex posterior* to offer explanations for the interaction between WTO and external international law. Chapter 3 then discusses part two to the theory, which is to set out a way to understand what has been previously defined as WTO law in chapter 1. Using the idea that systems are operationally closed as developed by Teubner and Black I advance a framework to examine and explain WTO law. Accounting for the rule of recognition and this new framework, I call this theory of WTO law, *constrained openness*. On the basis of this I argue contrary to the assumptions of the gateway metaphor that external international law cannot be directly

121 See for a full discussion of the varying ways that WTO law can be assessed: Hoekman B and M Kostecki, *The Political Economy of the World Trading System: The WTO and Beyond* (Oxford: OUP, 2001, 2nd edition) 9–46, esp. 25–36.

incorporated into WTO law. The implication of constrained openness is that external law is (re)constructed as WTO law. Using constrained openness I return to discuss fragmentation as a *nomos* and division of labour, to continue to locate the interaction between WTO and external international law. In chapters 1, 2 and 3 having created a theory, constrained openness, to understand the interaction between WTO and external international law in the fragmented international legal system, in chapters 4, 5 and 6, I apply that theory to current discussions and practice of WTO law.

Chapter 4 explains the nature of the dispute between the three main models on how WTO law interacts with external international law. Model I is premised on the idea that WTO law is a limited domain, so WTO law can only apply WTO law. This appears as a formalist approach. Model II adopts a contrary premise that WTO law is open, so that external international law can be the basis of a defense in WTO law.[122] This appears as a somewhat anti-formalist approach. Model III, seems like an attempt to bridge the Model I and Model II, by proposing that in the event of a conflict WTO law is privileged over external international law.[123] I juxtapose the three models against each other and then as to constrained openness. I argue that there is no need to bridge the conflict between Model I and Model II, as Model III attempted because the result is a false dialectic resolution. I do not attempt using my theory of WTO law to resolve the conflicts in the debate but to make practical use of them. I show that the three models are somewhat largely prescriptive, as they do not propose a theory of law, to answer primary questions on the nature of WTO law, before engaging with more secondary questions of how it interacts with external international law. In showing the inadequacy of the three models, I do not intend to exhaust the debate but provide strategic interjection in the debate and build a theory of WTO law. From this I can make sense of the three models, and present a different way to understand WTO law and its interaction with external international law.

Chapters 5 and 6 are an examination of the practice of WTO law by which the purpose of WTO law is realised. In a continued application the theory of constrained openness, chapter 7 examines the practice of the adjudicating bodies as it specifically relates to the precautionary principle in the Agreement on Sanitary and Phytosanitary Measures (SPS Agreement). Chapter 6 examines different examples of the practice of WTO law relating to external international law, juxtaposing the three models as to each other, and to my theory constrained openness. Chapter 7 concludes that understanding WTO law is a matter of how international trade lawyers treat the practice. I argue constrained openness is one way to do that. It may not even necessarily be the most correct way but I attempt to make my assumptions clear and to show that the views of others remain as contested.

122 See chapter 4.
123 Ibid.

0.5 Mr. Palomar, Sisyphus and Alice

I remain, as the reader should be, sceptical and suspicious of my own work.[124] This book is in many ways an exploration of the limitations of the lens I choose to see WTO law. The view that a model is true, meaning it has been derived in a recognised manner from proven axioms is actually founded on incomplete experience.[125] An author should see that 'truth is limited' and 'consider the extent of its limitations'.[126] There are only competing ideas about reality. Every academic output need not conclude with the 'right policy and institutional prescription' on what the law can do. Sometimes the law may not have a role in solving a problem. International lawyers, and specifically trade lawyers for purposes of this book, should be more ready to admit when seeing something as a legal problem may not be the best way to see that thing. Also, they should be more ready to take responsibility when law fails. That does not make law impotent. It simply comes to terms with the fact that law like every other system of thought does not possess all the answers to every problem. There is no Wizard. In addition, to having no universal answer that can cover all problems, then we also realise that perhaps all we have is infinite difference. Calvino in his work *Mr. Palomar* provides a telling illustration that aptly sums up the exercise, which this study attempts, as well as the process of what it is to write and study law.

> By counting the blades of grass is futile: you never learn their number. A lawn does not have precise boundaries, there is a border where the grass stops growing but still a few scattered blades sprout farther on, then a thick green clod, then a sparser stretch: are they still part of the lawn, or not? Elsewhere the underbrush enters the lawn: you cannot tell what is lawn and what is bush. But even where there is no grass, you never know what point you can stop counting: between one little plant and the next there is always a tiny sprouting leaf that barely emerges from the earth, its root a white wisp hardly perceptible; a moment ago it could have been overlooked but soon it will also have to be counted . . . The lawn is a collection of grasses – this is how the problem must be formulated – this includes a subcollection of cultivated grasses and a subcollection of spontaneous grasses known as weeds; an intersection of the two subcollections is formed by grasses which grown spontaneously but belong to the cultivated species and are therefore indistinguishable from them. The two subcollections, in their turn, include various species, each of

124 See Macintyre *supra* note 5, esp. at 462 where he writes poignantly that: 'Doubting is a more complex activity than some sceptics have realised. To say to oneself or to someone else "Doubt all your beliefs here and now" without reference to historical or autobiographical context is not meaningless; but an invitation not to philosophy, but to mental breakdown, or rather to philosophy as a means of mental breakdown.'

125 Einstein was discussing geometry but the point is telling for all knowledge. See Einstein A, *Relativity: The Special and the General Theory*, trans. R W Lawson (London: Routledge, 2001; originally published 1916), 1–5.

126 Ibid, at 5.

> which is subcollection, or rather it is a collection that includes a subcollection or its own members, which are also of the lawn and the subcollection of those alien to the lawn. The wind blows, seeds and pollens fly, the relations among the collections are disrupted . . .[127]

As with Mr. Palomar, the futility of the exercise does not deter the exercise and an author in full knowledge of the perpetuity of writing will still write. *I have found writing difficult.* This prologue is an illustration of *how* and *why* I think about the law the way I do. The ideas that come together here as this book still cheats me because at once it represents and betrays some of my original thoughts. The text that emerges from writing is not a single conscious thought. Words like flowers do not handsomely exist in a field waiting to be picked then only to wilt and die. Language as Bakhtin argues is 'not a neutral medium that passes freely and easily into the private property of the speaker's [writer's] intention; it is populated – over populated – with the intentions of others. Expropriating it, forcing it to submit to one's own intentions and accents, is a difficult and complicated process.'[128] My role as an author has been a continuous attempt to bring my thoughts and the book closer together, knowing that no matter how much I try the fit is not and never will be perfect. Further, I do this knowing that no idea is necessary. In the realisation of this, the absurdity of the whole task becomes evident. Writing in this way can also be seen as a Sisyphean challenge. Homer tells the story of Sisyphus in the Odyssey.[129] On his visit to hell, Odysseus gives an eyewitness account of Sisyphus' suffering.

> Then I witnessed the torture of Sisyphus,[130] as he wrestled with a huge rock with both hands. Bracing himself and thrusting with hands and feet he pushed the boulder uphill on to the top. But every time, as he was about to send it toppling over the crest, its sheer weight turned it back, and once again towards the plain the pitiless rock rolled down. So once more he had to wrestle with the thing and push it up, while the sweat poured from his limbs and the dust rose high above his head.[131]

Sisyphus' punishment was 'futile and hopeless labour' because every time he thought he had achieved his task, the rock under the burden of its own weight would fall back, and he would have to start over. There was no immediate victory in his efforts, for he can never achieve the task of rolling the rock over the hill. There is also no future victory. The gods in their punishment take both the

127 Calvino I, *Mr. Palomar*, trans. W Weaver (London: Vintage, 1999) 28–29 (originally published in Italian, 1983).

128 Bakhtin M, 'The Dialogic Imagination', trans. M Holquist and C Emerson, in Morris P (ed) *The Bakhtin Reader* (London: Arnold Publishers, 1994) 74–80 *passim*, esp. 77.

129 Homer, *The Odyssey* (London: Peguin Books, 2003) (original trans. E V Rieu, 1946, revised trans. D C H Rieu, 1991, 2003) 155 Book II, paras 590–600.

130 Ibid, original footnote: 'Sisyphus was the crafty and avaricious King of Corinth, who twice tricked the god of Death, once by blinding him and once by persuading him to let him return to earth.'

131 Ibid, 155 Book II, paras 590–600.

present and future away from him for unlike them he has no objective measure of time and space. He can only repeat the same task knowing there is no final victory. Camus argues, Sisyphus is an 'absurd hero' as much through his passions as through his torture.[132] The absurdity comes because of the human desire for the 'absolute' and 'unity' of ideas is faced with the 'impossibility of reducing this world to a rational and reasonable principle'.[133] Sisyphus, like the author, becomes aware of his absurd condition, and can only roll the rock up the hill to have to fall back down. Then he has to repeat the task. It is in the realisation of this futility that Sisyphus can find contentment. 'Reason and its limits to understand must be acknowledged, without false hope' writes Camus but the 'absurd can never be accepted: it requires constant confrontation, constant revolt'.[134] Sisyphus' victory comes through scorn. 'The lucidity that was to constitute his torture at the same time crowns his victory. There is no fate that cannot be surmounted by scorn.'[135] 'I leave Sisyphus at the foot of the mountain! One always finds one's burden again .... The struggle itself toward the heights is enough to fill a man's heart. One must imagine Sisyphus happy.'[136]

I am also reminded that reading is also a difficult process. The reader enters, into what can appear to them as, a world of non-significance and non-sense. It is like *Alice* to fall down a rabbit hole or walk through a mirror into a *Wonderland*.[137] Alice in entering the new world was 'faced with semiotic chaos, and her acquired language systems cease to be of any help'.[138] Alice deprived of her normal codes and understanding of the world was faced with a crisis because her world, as she knew it, had ended.[139] The result of this deprivation for Alice, like that for a reader, is a sort of 'ontological insecurity'.[140] Alice's deprivation, like that of *Hamlet* and *Dorothy*, was less to do with the world of they found themselves, than with their actual lost of meaning. It was not the 'grotesque, grinning, apparently cruel underworld of monsters, caucuses, caterpillars, pigs, executioners, or tormenters, into which she [fell]' that contributed to Alice's uneasiness but more to do with her 'loss of identity'.[141] She was 'threatened with an immanent loss of meaning, for without language there is no differentiation of self from other.'[142] She attempts to hold onto to her name, insisting that she is *real* and *is* Alice.[143] Yet Alice is not sure what that

132 Camus A, *The Myth of Sisyphus* (London: Penguin, 2005) chapter 4, 'The Myth of Sisyphus'.
133 Ibid.
134 Ibid.
135 Ibid.
136 Ibid.
137 Carroll L: *Alice's Adventurers in Wonderland* (London: Penguin [1865] 1994); *Through the Looking-Glass and What Alice Found There* (London: Penguin Group [1872] 2003).
138 Jackson R, *supra* note 32, at 141.
139 Ibid, at 142.
140 Ibid.
141 Ibid.
142 Ibid.
143 *Supra* note 137.

means.[144] A reader is faced with something similar. He attempts to understand a book through the worlds (words) of the author, but is not always sure what they mean or, what they are suppose to mean. Simultaneously a reader is trying to escape his own world, but fully unable to do so because it is what provides him with meanings to make sense of *what is happening* around him. Without these meanings, they experience a chaos or collapse of their world.

Conceivably this study is about how to understand the interaction between World Trade Organisation (WTO) law and external international law as the title on the cover indicates, as much as it is a suggestion of *how* to think about the law. Not what to think about the law because each of us can develop our own ways to do that, but how we can go about doing that. A book constructs new worlds (words) as it attempts to deprive the reader of his own world (words). Readers therefore do not peacefully transcend the tension between their worlds (words) and that of the author. As in *Alice* 'Things slip away from words – a baby becomes a pig, a grin becomes a cat – and words assume lives of their own, "the phrase insisted on conjugating itself."'[145] Readers navigate their way among the new worlds (words) of the author using a map of their own meanings to understand and having those meanings turned upside down, for what may appear at first and sometimes for no apparently good reason. The actual space of writing becomes its reading. In the reader the competing interpretations and contestations of an author can come into focus. The book is a space where ideas mix and clash. It is a space born of, and for, contestation. The result is that both writing and reading are not neutral objective processes. We cannot stand back, or out of ourselves, marvelling upon what we have done. In the next chapter I will put forward a definitional sketch of the fragmentation of international law, in order to provide the reader with an assessment of the facts and assumptions regarding the context within which we are situating the discussion about how WTO and external international law interact. This forms the starting point for the development a theory of WTO law.

144 Jackson R *supra* note 32, at 142.
145 Ibid, at 141.

1 Introduction

The fragmented nature of international law

1.0 Introduction

The purpose of this chapter is to provide a background on the fragmentation of international law. It is also to discuss some ideas underpinning fragmentation and how we perceive them affecting the interaction between WTO and external international law. In light of this, I importantly advance a method by which to define WTO law. After all, the argument could run counter, that we all know what WTO law is: the covered agreements and possibly some secondary law making within the WTO, from for example, WTO Committees. However, the fact is that if we all agreed on what WTO law was, then much if not all the discussion to follow on the disagreements that exists among commentators on what WTO law is and on what basis external international law may or not become part of WTO law, would be *non-sequitur*. By virtue of these debates, at least one thing is clear, we all do not agree on what is WTO law. Discussion on the nature of the law does not assume we all know or share a common understanding as to what the law is and its purpose. Consider this simple analogy: if we all identify and define something as a table, then the argument could possibly follow that by common understanding we all know what a table is. How could there be disagreement as to what is a table, this most basic everyday staple in human life? But then what kind of table? Is it round, square, how many legs, is it made of wood, metal, stone or plastic, do you write on it, eat on it, sleep on it, stand on it? What is the purpose of the table? We can all agree to have a general understanding of something but then can correctly and logically disagree about the specifics of what that something looks like, how it is constituted and what purpose(s) it serves. What does WTO law look like, what purpose(s) does it serve, how are we able to know something is WTO law and something else is not WTO law. Essentially this chapter is an exercise in defining what WTO law is, within the context of a fragmented international legal system.[1] Hart in writing on the use of definitions states that,

> Sometimes . . . a definition of word can supply . . . a map: at one and the same time it may make explicit the latent principle which guides our use of the

1 I discuss the purpose of WTO law in chapter 4. The task here and perhaps no less controversial is to put forward a definition of what law is.

> word, and may exhibit relationships between the type of phenomena to which we apply the word and other phenomena. It is sometimes said that definition is 'merely verbal' or 'just about words'; but this may be most misleading where the expression defined is one in current use.[2]

The purpose to defining WTO law is not purely about being more linguistically specific.[3] In fact the concern is more to do with attempting to understand what can count as WTO law and in that way we are able to arrive at an understanding of what does not count as WTO law. The definitional exercise therefore serves two purposes. Firstly, in defining WTO law we can also know what does not constitute WTO law, for as we know and discussed in the Prologue, every definition carries its exclusion. Secondly, providing a definition of WTO law lays the basis for advancing a legal theory of WTO law, which we can use to help us understand how it interacts with external international law. In the Prologue, we argued that in order to discuss the interaction between WTO and external international law, that we must define what WTO law is, making our claims about it open to critique. Further, we emphasised that there is no objective Archimedean point from which to engage with reality. We determine what the thing is and then apply ways to understand it, always doing so from some position as to another. The role of the author is to work out as best as possible what that position is without engaging in guises of pure objective thinking where facts can speak for themselves as if magically discovered.[4]

There are several reasons for my approach of setting out a method to determine what WTO law is. Firstly, by openly defining what counts as the law I am able to decide the data that forms a basis of intelligibility for what to observe as the law. Consequently, in defining what counts as law, I am proposing that the framework for assessing that law will be more open to critique. This as will be explored, in chapter 4, is dissimilar to the dominant models on WTO law, which in their pattern of argument, counter-argument potentially shut out external critique and creates a superficial commensurable middle ground. Secondly, by defining what I see or count as the law will enable consistent analysis. There can be no unconstrained choices as to what is WTO law. Otherwise the result of the permissive empirical Jacksonian tradition of WTO law (see Prologue) may imply an ever-widening sphere of what is WTO law. Without a clear and open method, it would mean that whatever I wanted as the law could be the law, for political expediency. In laying out a method, apart from showing when our ideas can make sense of reality, we can critically show when they do not capture or make sense of all the data before them. This provides an opportunity for the improvement of those ideas through

2 Hart HLA, *The Concept of Law* (Oxford: Clarendon Press, 1961) 14. All references shall be to the 1961 edition, unless otherwise stated as the Hart HLA, *The Concept of Law, Second edition* (Oxford: OUP, 1997).

3 Stravropoulos N, 'Hart's Semantics' in *Hart's Postscript: Essays on the Postscript to the Concept of Law* (ed) Jules Coleman (Oxford: OUP, 2001) 59–98, 63–64.

4 See the Prologue.

internal and external critique. Thirdly, determining what WTO law is supports the premise as introduced in the Prologue and further explored in this chapter that law has no natural existence. Law exists because we believe it to exist. This means that law is not a brute fact. It is a thought object and only gains currency because we create and embody it as the law. As a consequence, there can be no investigation of and conclusions about the law until we determine what the law is.

Section 1.1 provides a definitional sketch of fragmentation to frame the context in which the interaction between WTO and external international law occurs. Section 1.2 then sets out rational reconstruction as the means by which I can posit an organising norm – Hart's the rule of recognition – as a method to select the data to observe as WTO law, within the context of a fragmented international legal system. Sections 1.3–1.3.3 describe and assess the merits of Hart's rule of recognition as a method for defining WTO law. The purpose of this chapter is not to comprehensively assess Hart's *The Concept of Law*[5] in which he proposed and discussed the rule of recognition. I do not offer a *de novo* interpretation of Hart's broader legal project. The purpose of this chapter is somewhat more restrained and precise. It necessary here to discuss and emphasise the elements of Hart's work, his legal method, which are relevant to defining WTO law. The task is therefore to isolate Hart's municipal rule of recognition in order to apply it to WTO law. In section 1.4, I apply Hart's rule of recognition to WTO law. This involves separating the rule of recognition as Hart's conceptual commitment to law as fact from Hart's method of the rule of recognition as the practice of the judiciary. This makes the rule of recognition counterfactual and supports the conclusion that the rule of recognition is not transposable wholesale to the discourse of WTO law, as was attempted by international trade law theorist David Palmeter.[6] Moreover, it supports the approach considered in the Prologue and taken here in this chapter that WTO law must initially be defined before it is investigated because law is a thought-object. In section 1.5, I conclude that having applied the rule of recognition to WTO law to define what counts as WTO law, it does not provide a way to describe what we have defined. In chapter 3, I consider the second part of the theory of WTO law, which is to add conceptually flesh to what we have identified as WTO law in this chapter.

1.1 Definitional sketch of fragmentation

The International Law Commission (ILC) as part of its 'long-term' work programme conducted a study entitled 'Fragmentation of International Law: Difficulties arising from the Diversification and Expansion of International Law'.[7] This is an indication

5 See *supra* note 2. For an broad and critical assessment of Hart's postscript version of the Concept of Law (1997) see Coleman J (ed) *Hart's Postscript: Essays on the Postscript to the Concept of Law* (Oxford: OUP, 2001).

6 Palmeter D, 'The WTO as a Legal System' (2000) *Fordham International Law Journal*, 444–480.

7 Koskenniemi M, 'Fragmentation of International Law: Difficulties Arising from the Diversification and Expansion of International Law' UN Doc. International Law Commission A/CN.4/L.682 13 April 2006, paras. 1–4 [hereinafter ILC Study Group Report on Fragmentation].

that contemporary international legal scholarship is concerned about the fragmentation of international law into specialised rationalities such as trade, environment and human rights.[8] 'Without attempting to add yet another sociology of globalisation, it may be accepted that political communities have become more heterogeneous, their boundaries much more porous, than assumed by the received images of sovereignty and the international order.'[9] Alongside differentiation based on the territoriality of the nation state is the emergence of a social differentiation of rationalities, which are non-territorially functional.[10] These differentiated rationalities of international law are functional detailed specialised systems of international law. Each fragmented system regulates a specific set of ideas, values and corresponding institutional practice of professional experts knowledgeable in the language and vocabulary of the specialisation. This makes them appear autonomous from the system of general international law and, importantly for the study, each other. There is a concern that irresolvable systemic conflicts may arise if the broader and general international legal system does not support or provide normative context for the interaction between these differentiated international legal systems.[11]

A debate between international trade lawyers emerged around the 'labels' attached to the ILC Study Group on Fragmentation. Joel Trachtman in a post on the International Economic Law and Policy Blog argues that Joost Pauwelyn's characterisation of the Study as the work of the ILC is somewhat misleading because strictly speaking the report is not of the ILC. In that that ILC has not adoped the report, and 'mislabelling the study and conclusions as the product of the ILC, or as approved by the ILC, would have a tendency to end the dialogue' (posted Sept. 29 2006 at 05:49 AM and Oct. 30 2006 at 01:03 PM). For the blog see 'ILC Report on Fragmentation is Out and Favours Close WTO-International Law Link' at <http://worldtradelaw.typepad.com/ielp-blog/2006/09/ilc_report_on_f.html> (Accessed 11 April 2008).

8 For example, the World Trade Organisation (WTO), European Court of Justice (ECJ), European Court of Human Rights (ECHR), United Nations Convention on the Law of the Seas (UNCLOS).

9 Koskenniemi M and P Leino, 'Fragmentation of International Law? Postmodern Anxieties' (2002) 15 *Leiden Journal of International Law*, 553, 557.

10 ILC Study Group on Fragmentation *supra* note 7, at para 133, footnote 168.

Teubner G and A Fischer-Lescano, 'Cannibalizing Epistemes: Will Modern Law Protect Traditional Cultural Expressions?', in Christoph Graber (ed) *Traditional Cultural Expressions in a Digital Environment* 2008). Teubner G and P Korth, 'Two Kinds of Legal Pluralism: Collision of Laws in the Double Fragmentation of World Society' trans. Anna Furness, revised by Anne Emert (to appear in: Margret Young (ed) *Regime Interaction in International Law: Theoretical and Practical Challenges*, 2009), Section IV (1). It is important to emphasise, as did Teubner and Korth, that the fragmentation of global society into autonomous functional global systems 'does not mean that the nation state will be disposed of in the course of globalisation. One kind of internal differentiation is not replaced with the other, rather two different principles overlap: territorial-segmental and thematic-functional differentiation.'

11 There is a large body of literature on the subject of the fragmentation of international law. I only reproduce a sample of here. See for example: Koskenniemi M, 'The Fate of Public International Law: Between Technique and Politics' (2007) 70(1) *Modern Law Review* 1–30; Slaughter-Burley A, 'International Law and International Relations Theory: A Dual Agenda' (1993) *American Journal of International Law* 205–239. Simma B and A Paulus, 'The International Community: Facing the Challenge of Globalisation' (1998) 9 *European Journal of International Law* 266; Dupy P, 'International Law: Torn between Coexistence, Cooperation and Globalisation: General Conclusions' (1998) 9 *European Journal of International Law* 278; Weil P, 'Towards Relative Normativity in International Law' (1983) *American Journal of International Law* 413–442; Charney J, 'Universal International Law'

Fragmentation implies that faced with two reasons or norms to apply to a single decision, neither reason nor norm can claim 'hierarchical superiority'.[12] This situation is made more acute in international law as there is no obvious vertical hierarchical structure of norms because different systems exist on a horizontal plane of mutual equality.[13] This suggests multiple sovereigns each with their own structures of internal hierarchy. None of the systems submit to an overall legislative and executive structure, as there is no single sovereign in international law.[14] In such a situation where different international legal systems are organised horizontally with no concrete rules for an overall hierarchy of norms or legal systems, there is no easy or obvious answer to fragmentation.[15] Although each different system

(1998) 87 *American Journal of International Law* 492–551; Symposium: 'Diversity or Cacophony?: New Sources of Norms in International Law' (2004) 25 *Michigan Journal of International Law*; Symposium: 'Is the Proliferation of International Courts and Tribunals a Systemic Problem?' (1999) 31(4) *New York University Journal of International Law and Politics* 679. Simma B and D Pulkowski, 'Of Planets and the Universe: Self-Contained Regimes in International Law' (2006) 17 *European Journal of International Law* 483–529. Pauwelyn J, *Conflict of Norms in Public International Law: How WTO Law Relates to Other Rules of International Law* (Cambridge: CUP, 2003).

12 See for example, Gardner J, 'Concerning Permissive Sources and Gaps' (1988) 8(3) *Oxford Journal of Legal Studies* 457–461, 460.

13 There is however, an exception to the horizontal structure of the norms of international law, which are *jus cogens* norms. It is also understood in international law with the exception of *jus cogens* that countries can agree between themselves for international law not to apply as in a treaty. For example see *North Sea Continental Shelf Case*, 1969 ICJ Rep. 4, para 4.72.

Jus cogens as set out in Article 53, 'Treaties conflicting with a peremptory norm of general international law' of the Vienna Convention on the Law of the Treaties 1969, states : 'A treaty is void if, at the time of its conclusion, it conflicts with a peremptory norm of general international law. For the purposes of the present Convention, a peremptory norm of general international law is a norm accepted and recognised by the international community of States as a whole as a norm from which no derogation is permitted and which can be modified only by a subsequent norm of general international law having the same character.'

However, the ascension of a norm to *jus cogens* status is not something taken lightly. *Jus cogens* is limited to a few areas, so even if a norm were *jus cogens*, this would not affect the overall fragmentation of international. Furthermore, it is still contentious as to what determines *jus cogens* norms, and what norms can actually qualify as *jus cogens*. What happens if two norms that overlap are both *jus cogens*? The point is that with *jus cogens* there is still no obvious hierarchal of structure of norms in international law. Moreover *jus cogens* itself is a contested idea.

For further discussion on hierarchy in international law, see Teubner and Fischer-Lescano, 'Regime-Collisions: The Vain Search for Legal Unity in the fragmentation of global law' (2004) *Michigan Journal of International Law* 999. Weiler JHH and AL Paulus, 'The Structure of Change in International Law or Is there a Hierarchy of Norms in International Law?' (1997) 8(4) *European Journal of International Law* 545. Weil 'Towards Relative Normativity in International Law' *supra* note 11. Shelton D, 'International Law and Relative Normativity', in Evans M, *International Law* (London: OUP, 2006) 164–173. Koskenniemi, *From Apology to Utopia: The Structure of the International Legal Argument* (Helsinki: Finnish Lawyers' Publishing Company, 1989) 280–281. [See also revised edition with an extended Prologue, 2006.]

14 See for example, Teubner and Fischer-Lescano, 'Regime-Collisions: The Vain Search for Legal Unity in the fragmentation of global law' *supra* note 13.

15 The classic understanding of international law as based on the sovereign equality of countries, which are only limited by the rules they accept is expressed in the *Lotus Judgement*, 1927, PCIJ Rep. at para 18. It states 'restrictions upon the independence of the state . . . can not be presumed.' For

maintains its own rule of law, fragmentation does not mean that the international legal system has collapsed into chaos of anything goes. It is a suggestion of the impossibility of a universal system to cohere all the fragmented systems.[16] There are no King's horses to put Humpty Dumpty back together again.[17]

'There is no escape' from the 'ambivalence' fragmentation may cause for international lawyers. It is one, if not the 'most worrying of modernity's concerns' for international lawyers[18] though it can probably be best seen as the fruition of access to varying legal arguments. However, it is somewhat perplexing that international lawyers are anxious about fragmentation having to function over the course of the history of international law with the absence of a single authority as compared to domestic legal systems.[19] Koskenniemi and Leino state that perhaps the anxiety arises from the past strategy of international lawyers to defend international not on its own terms but by domestic analogy. Treaties were similar to legislation, peaceful settlement of disputes similar to adjudicating and war and countermeasures similar to a primitive form of enforcement.[20] The situation was fuelled by Hart's famous dicta that international law move nearer the structure of a municipal system if it was to constitute a proper legal system.[21] Indeed as discussed below, international trade lawyers, such as David Palmeter appeared susceptible to this, in trying to apply Hart to WTO law to show its validity as a legal system as compared to a domestic legal system. But this approach is mistaken and misses an important point that international law, like all forms of law, can support contesting arguments deriving from the same law, but producing equally contesting answers to questions of legality.[22]

'It is possible to defend any course of action – including deviation from a clear rule – by professionally impeccable legal arguments that look from rules to their underlying reasons, make choices between several rules as well as rules and exceptions, and interpret rules in the context of evaluative standards.'[23] It is this rationale that reinforces the ambivalence international lawyers may feel towards fragmentation. Not only are they varying systems, that is, different ideas about how to organise different parts of international law, the point is that each lawyer knows that both he and his professional counterpart can create equally compelling

further discussion on fragmentation having no easy answer because of its horizontal organisation, see Weiler and Paulus *supra* note 13. Shelton *supra* note 13, at 183–184.

16 See Beckett J, 'Rebel Without a Cause? Martti Koskenniemi and the Critical Legal Project' (2006) 7(12) *German Law Journal*, 1045 esp. 1050, 1058, 1054, 1052.

17 This is a reference to the fictional character Humpty Dumpty that Alice encountered in her adventures. Carroll L, *Through the Looking-Glass and What Alice Found There* (London: Penguin Group, [1872] 2003). See Prologue for more discussion.

18 Koskenniemi M, 'Hierarchy in International Law: A Sketch' (1997) 8(4) *European Journal of International Law* 566–582, sec. 3.

19 Koskenniemi and Leino *supra* note 9, at 558.

20 Ibid.

21 Ibid. See Hart *supra* note 2 at, chapter 10.

22 Beckett *supra* note 16.

23 Koskenniemi (revised edition 2006) *supra* note 13, at 591. See also Beckett *supra* note 16, at 1053–1052.

but competing legal ideas from the same cases, texts, and practice of law. In this context, a coherence of the fragmented international legal system is unlikely, as is a hierarchy, as the very point of fragmentation is that the system of general international law was somehow unable to regulate what became differentiated technical specialism of international law.[24] In the international legal system, not only are they multiple and competing systems of international law, but also sovereign states. To compound matters, the same state will have multiple and sometimes conflicting commitments to these different specialist legal systems, which belong to the same international legal system. The fragmentation of international law casts a picture of a schizophrenic globalised system of law[25] when 'systematic practical thought offers no method' for reducing and rendering two norms or reasons commensurable.[26] The result is that in the fragmented international legal system, the application of one norm over another could produce an opposite and contradictory result.[27]

This raises questions about intra- and inter-systemic interaction among the various specialised systems of international law, and the general rules.[28] Intra-systemic interaction between the specialised systems of law such as the WTO and general international law is different to the inter-systemic interaction between the specialised systems themselves. Intra-systemic interaction focuses on conflicts, potential or real, between a specialised system of international law and the general system of international law.[29] This is where the specialised legal system would produce an unorthodox view of general international law or a special rule that exists as an exception to the general rule.[30] At this level the conflicts manifest itself in two ways, but both carry the same formulation as derogating from the general rule, either as a different view or exception. On the intra-systemic interaction between WTO law and general international law there is overwhelming WTO law practice. The adjudicating bodies apply rules of general international law,[31] general

24 Koskenniemi 'The Fate of Public International Law: Between Technique and Politics' *supra* note 11, at 19. See also, Pauwelyn J, 'Remarks at the Fourth Annual WTO Conference', in Andenas M and F Ortino (eds) *WTO Law and Process* (London: British Institute of International and Comparative Law, 2005) 494.

25 For a concrete analysis of globalisation on law see Twinning W, *Globalisation and Legal Theory*, (London: Butterworths, 2000) passim but esp. Chapter 8 'Globalisation, post-modernism, and pluralism: Santos, Haack, and Calvino'.

26 Gardner *supra* note 12, at 460.

27 Ibid.

28 ILC Study Group Report on Fragmentation *supra* note 7, at para 55.

29 Ibid, at para 53–54.

30 Ibid.

31 For a good survey of the general international law applied by the adjudicating bodies see: Lindross A and M Mehling, 'Dispelling the Chimera of "Self-Contained" Regimes: International Law and the WTO' (2005) 16(5) *European Journal of International Law* 857–877, 871. Hilf M, 'Power, Rules and Principles – Which Orientation for WTO/GATT LAW?' (2001) JIEL 111–130. Cameron J and K Gray, 'Principles of International in the WTO Dispute Settlement Body (2001) 50 ICLQ 248–298. Lennard M, 'Navigating by the Stars: Interpreting the WTO Agreements' (2002) JIEL 17–88. Maki P, 'Interpreting GATT using the Vienna Convention on the Law of the Treaties: A

rules of treaty interpretation[32] and general rules of treaty law[33] as their own. It is indisputable that the adjudicating bodies in the application of WTO law make use of general international law. Together the technical rules of treaty interpretation and the general rules of international law can help a legal system to function in the application of its own law, especially if the system lacks general rules of interpretation.[34] As the ILC Study Group Report on Fragmentation notes, 'None of the treaty-regimes in existence today is self-contained in the sense that the application of general international law would be generally excluded. On the contrary, treaty bodies in [trade law] make constant use of general international law in the administration of their special regimes.'[35]

Method to Increase the Legitimacy of the Dispute Settlement System' (2000) *Minnesota J. of Global Trade* 343–360.

For example, see the practice of WTO law on the following rules of general international law:

Competence de la competence: Appellate Body Report, United States – Anti-Dumping Act of 1916, WT/DS136/AB/R, WT/DS162/AB/R, adopted 26 September 2000 at para 54, note 30.

Judicial Economy: Appellate Body Report, United States – Measure Affecting Imports of Woven Wool Shirts and Blouses from India, WT/DS33/AB/R and Corr.1, adopted 23 May 1997, DSR 1997:I, 323 at 339–340.

Burden of proof: Appellate Body Report, United States – Measure Affecting Imports of Woven Wool Shirts and Blouses from India, WT/DS33/AB/R and Corr.1, adopted 23 May 1997, DSR 1997:I, 323 at 335, 337.

32 For example see the following:

Legitimate expectations: Appellate Body Report, India – Patent Protection for Pharmaceutical and Agricultural Chemical Products, WT/DS50/AB/R, adopted 16 January 1998, DSR 1998: I, 9 para 42, 45, 48. Appellate Body Report, European Communities – Customs Classification of Certain Computer Equipment, WT/DS62/AB/R, WT/DS67/AB/R, WT/DS68/AB/R, adopted 22 June 1998, DSR 1998:V, 1851, para 84, 97.

Principle of effectiveness: Appellate Body Report, United States – Standards for Reformulated and Conventional Gasoline, WT/DS2/AB/R, adopted 20 May 1996, DSR 1996:I, 3, p23. Appellate Body Report, Japan – Taxes on Alcoholic Beverages, WT/DS8/AB/R, WT/DS10/AB/R, WT/DS11/AB/R, adopted 1 November 1996, DSR 1996:I, 97, p12. Appellate Body Report, United States – Restrictions on Imports of Cotton and Man-made Fibre Underwear, WT/DS24/AB/R, adopted 25 February 1997, DSR 1997:I, 11, p. 16.

Principle of in dubio mitius: Appellate Body Report, EC Measures Concerning Meat and Meat Products (Hormones), WT/DS26/AB/R, WT/DS48/AB/R, adopted 13 February 1998, DSR 1998:I, 135 para 165 and footnote 154.

33 For example see the following WTO law practice regarding Article 31 (General rules of interpretation) of the Vienna Convention of Law of Treaties: Appellate Body Report, United States – Standards for Reformulated and Conventional Gasoline, WT/DS2/AB/R, adopted 20 May 1996, 3 at 16. Appellate Body Report, Japan – Measures Affecting Agricultural Products, WT/DS76/AB/R, adopted 19 March 1999, 97 at 122–123, Appellate Body Report, India – Patent Protection for Pharmaceutical and Agricultural Chemical Products, *supra* note 22, at para 46. Appellate Body Report, Argentina – Measures Affecting Imports of Footwear, Textiles, Apparel and Other Items, WT/DS56/AB/R and Corr.1, adopted 22 April 1998 para 42. Appellate Body Report, United States – Countervailing Duties on Certain Corrosion-Resistant Carbon Steel Flat Products from Germany, WT/DS213/AB/R and Corr.1, adopted 19 December 2002, para 61–62.

34 Lindorss and Mehling *supra* note 31, at 875–876.

35 ILC Study Group Report on Fragmentation *supra* note 7, at para 172.

Inter-systemic interaction, which is the focus on this study, examines conflict, potential or real, between two different types of special laws. WTO law features prominently in discussions about inter-systemic interaction because trade tends to cut across many other areas of regulation in international law.[36] For example, environmental legal systems may use trade restrictions in an attempt to pursue and attain their objectives to protect the environment.[37] This means that there is the potential for conflict or overlap between the WTO legal system and the other specialised international legal system, which does not have as its objective, or as a set of knowledgeable experts, pursuing the prohibition of restrictions on trade.[38] This example of interaction between trade and environment could raise many questions. Do the restrictions actually protect the environment? Should trade law be used to govern environmental issues? Can WTO law understand environmental law? The responses are 'bound to vary depending' on the legal framework that one chooses to adopt.[39] The purpose of the study is to examine the interaction or potential for conflict, between WTO law and other types of specialised non-WTO international law, which is external law to WTO law. The examination is attempting to open a space within the current debate to provide a chance and room for further debate. In the next sections, I examine how we can think about or rather rationalise the process of inter-systemic fragmentation and define what is law using the rule of recognition.

1.2 Rational reconstruction

Confronted with masses of data an author must have a way to understand that data. What this entails is the use of a method that brings order to the data. It is a matter

36 Ibid, at para 45, 165–170, 185, 306, 443–450, 472.

37 For example, the Convention on International Trade in Endangered Species of Wild Fauna and Flora (CITES) prohibits trade in endangered species; The Montreal Protocol prohibits trade in chlorofluorocarbons (CFCS) that destroy the ozone layer of the atmosphere, and the Basel Convention prohibits trade in waste. For general discussion on the interaction between trade and environment, see for example Cheyne I, 'Environmental Treaties and the GATT' (1992) 1 RECIEL 14. Dunoff J, 'Reconciling International Trade with Preservation of the Global Commons: Can We Prosper and Protect?' (1992) 49 Wash. & Lee L. Rev. 1407–1408. Jackson J, 'World Trade Rules and Environmental Policies: Congruence or Conflict' (1992) 49 Wash. & Lee L. Rev. 1228. Charnovitz S, 'The Environment vs. Trade Rules: Defogging the Debate' (1993) 23 Envtl. L. 475. Weiss E, 'Environment and Trade as Partners in Sustainable Development: A Commentary' (1992) 86 AJIL 728. Wold C, 'Multilateral Environmental Agreements and the GATT: Conflict and Resolution?' (1996) 26 Envtl. L. 843.

38 For a discussion on how the Montreal Protocol and Basel Convention noted *supra* at note 14 would potentially conflict with WTO law, see Lowenfeld A, *International Economic Law* (Oxford: OUP, 2002) 306–314. For a discussion on CITES noted *supra* at note 14, see Crawford C, 'Conflict Between CITES and the GATT in Light of Actions to Halt the Rhinoceros and Tiger Trade' (1995) 7 Geo. Int'l Envtl. L. Rev. 560, Sands P, 'Whither CITES? The Evolution of a Treaty Regime in the Borderland of Trade and Environment' (1997) 8(1) EJIL 34. For further discussion concerning treaty interpretation as a framework to address overlaps between differing systems of international law, using the example of CITES and WTO law, see chapter 3.

39 ILC Study Group Report on Fragmentation *supra* note 7, at para 55.

of imposing intelligibility on existing data to be able to put forward practical solutions to problems. This is an exercise in rational reconstruction. Neil MacCormick and Robert Summers state that rational reconstruction is the 'activity of explaining fragmentary and potentially conflicting data by reference to theoretical objects in the light of which the data are seen as relatively coherent, because presented as parts of a complex, well-ordered whole'.[40] In other words, rational reconstruction 'requires explanatory principles establishing criteria of what counts as well ordered and rational'.[41] What rational reconstruction entails is that we posit a norm, which serves as a means to determine what WTO law is. In doing so, we determine what to include and by that process exclude as representations of WTO law.[42] In essence, rational reconstruction is about imposing intelligibility to make WTO law comprehensible by reference to a posited organising norm, which in this case as discussed below is the rule of recognition. Rational reconstruction does not entail a literal 'rebuilding of the objects in the world'.[43] This however does not mean that it is not a process of imagination to describe and explain existing objects.[44] It is an intellectual exercise requiring the imagination or re-imagination of an organising norm to account for data in a systematic, ordered and factual manner.[45] Rational reconstruction is also a 'descriptive account of normative material'.[46] The process is descriptive in that we attempt to stay close to the data defined as the law and normative in that we are proposing a method and a concept to understand the data.[47] The point is that any definition of law comes from somewhere. Objectivity does not mean concealing that method or claiming to be detached from the data of observation but making the method open to political debate. Positing, as done in the next sections, the rule of recognition as a method to define WTO law, is simply a practical way to identify the law. In the next section, we lay out the nature and terms of the rule of recognition as the norm that we posit to define WTO law. We will indentify what is the rule of recognition, the problems of applying it to international law, and suggest a way to overcome these problems to make it applicable to WTO and external international law.

40 MacCormick N and RS Summers, *Interpreting Statutes: A Comparative Study* (Vermont: Dartmouth Publishing Co., 1991) 19. See also MacCormick N: 'Reconstruction after Deconstruction: A Response to CLS' (1990) 10(4) *Oxford Journal of Legal Studies* 539–558, 555–558. 'The Ethics of Legalism' (1989) 2(2) *Ratio Juris* 184–193, 190–199. 'The Concept of Law and "The Concept of Law"' (1994) 14(1) *Oxford Journal of Legal Studies* 1–23, 12. Mullender R, 'Parliamentary Sovereignty, the Constitution, and the Judiciary' (1998) 49(2) *Northern Ireland Legal Quarterly*, 138–166, 145.

41 MacCormick N: 'Reconstruction after Deconstruction: A Response to CLS' *supra* note 40, at 556. See also MacCormick and Summers *supra* note 40, at 19. MacCormick: 'The Ethics of Legalism' *supra* note 40. 'The Concept of Law and "The Concept of Law"' *supra* note 40. Mullender *supra* note 40.

42 See Prologue for discussion of my approach.

43 MacCormick and Summers *supra* note 40 at 19. Mullender *supra* note 40, at 145.

44 MacCormick *supra* note 40, at 19. See Lang who talks about the re-imagination of trade law. Lang A, 'Reflecting on Linkage: Cognitive and Institutional Change in the International Trading System' (2007) 70(4) *Modern Law Review* 523–549.

45 MacCormick and Summers *supra* note 40, at 19.

46 MacCormick and Summers *supra* note 40, at 21.

47 Ibid, at 22.

1.3 The rule of recognition

Hart does not hypothesise the rule of recognition, as a particular rule, preferring to locate it in the practice of the judiciary.[48] This assumes that the rule of recognition as the practice of a centralised judiciary is directly observable.[49] The rule of recognition is an empirical observable fact as the practice of the judicial officials of the legal system.[50] Thus for Hart legal theory was mainly descriptive and empirical rather than normative.[51] Hart states that in the 'day-to-day life of a legal system its rule of recognition is very seldom expressly formulated as a rule' where 'for the most part' its 'existence is *shown* in the way in which particular rules are identified, either by courts or other officials or private persons or their advisers.'[52] The rule does not take on a specific content because it is the practice of a judiciary, which could differ from legal system to legal system. This supposes that the rule is not conceptually limited to the law but is potentially applicable to any system.[53] The result is that the rule of recognition as an idea could remain fixed from system to system but because it identified the practice of the authoritative arbitrator or judicial officials of that system, its 'observable' content could vary from system to system.[54] This made the rule of recognition generic and not specific. Hart was not 'predicting the outcomes of particular cases in particular courts, but instead developing the concept of a legal system (*in abstracto*)'.[55] By focusing on what the judiciary or legal officials in a system did rather than how law could be derived from morals or dogmatic definitions such as Austin's definition of law as commands, Hart was attempting to examine law as is, not as it should be.[56]

Hart appears to be pointing towards sources of law, as the rule of recognition is what the judges say, suggesting that its content is declared on observation. This makes the rule potentially applicable to any normative system, provided it possessed a centralised authoritative arbitrator because Hart attributed 'special authoritative status' to the courts or officials of a legal system.[57] This would explain Hart's preference for locating the rule of recognition in the practice of the judiciary. The 'common practice of officials of recognising certain things and not others as constituting valid law is thus necessary in order for the rule of recognition to exist, and is a vitally important aspect of that rule'.[58] By defining the rule of recognition

48 Hart *supra* note 2, at 97–99.

49 Ibid.

50 Ibid, at 98. See also MacCormick N, *Legal Reasoning and Legal Theory* (Oxford: Clarendon Press, 1978) 229. Shapiro S, 'On Hart's Way Out', Coleman J (ed) *Hart's Postscript: Essays on the Postscript to the Concept of Law* (Oxford: OUP, 2001) 149–191, 154.

51 Beckett J, *The End of Customary Law: A purposive analysis of Structural Indeterminacy* (Germany: 2008).

52 Hart *supra* note 2, at 98–99.

53 Ibid, at 98–99.

54 Ibid, at 99.

55 Beckett *supra* note 51, at 13.

56 Ibid.

57 Hart *supra* note 2, at 98.

58 Dickson J, 'Is the Rule of Recognition Really a Conventional Rule' 2007 27(3) *Oxford Journal of Legal Studies* 373–402, 375.

as the practice of the judiciary, Hart presupposes that the institution in a system applying the rules is the judiciary. There are two points to be made here. The first is that like Julie Dickson, I can ask why the rule of recognition as what the Queen enacts in Parliament is valid law.[59] According to Hart the point concerning validity is reached where for the rule of recognition unlike any other rule in the legal system there is 'no rule providing criteria for the assessment of its own legal validity.'[60] This leads to the second point that the rule of recognition as Hart identifies as what the Queen in Parliament enacts is valid law only on acceptance by the judiciary.[61] Consider that even if the legislature has institutional prominence in a legal system it would be because the judiciary allows this. The meaning is that the judiciary is the *bona fide* location of the rule of recognition. Hart posits the rule of recognition as the basic and 'ultimate' norm of the legal system. This would make law, for Hart, an empirical observable fact in the practice of the judiciary.[62] As examined next, the internal point of view provides the basis for rule of recognition.[63]

1.3.1 The internal point of view

The internal point of view for Hart is necessary to determine the content of the rule of recognition, which is critical to the existence of a legal system.[64] 'The internal point of view is the committed point of view.'[65] Sometimes a rule is action-guiding. This is because it is viewed by those to whom it applies as reason-giving.[66] Coleman writes that those 'who accept rules from an internal point of view see the rules as reason-giving in virtue of their being rules rather than in virtue of the sanction that might attend non-compliance' with the rule.[67] Law was not simply a description of what people actually did but a 'description of what people are legally obliged to do, as understood by the rules against which legal officials will judge the conduct of others'.[68] This creates, Beckett argues, a distinction

59 Ibid, at 377.

60 Ibid, at 377. Hart *supra* note 2, at 107.

61 Hart *supra* note 2, at 103–105.

62 Hart *supra* note 2, at 103–104, 107. This would suggest that a commitment to rule of recognition as a fact leads to a commitment to law as rules. See Dworkin R, *Taking Rights Seriously* (London: 1977) on this point where he argues that the rule of recognition does not recognise principles.

63 Campbell CM, 'The Career of the Concept', in Leith P and P Ingram, *The Jurisprudence of Orthodoxy: Queens University Essays on H.L.A Hart* (London: Routledge, 1998) 11.

64 See Hart *supra* note 2, at 86 making this point. Furthermore he says that the internal point of view is critical not only for understanding law but the structure of 'any' society. For a similar idea to the internal point of view, see Cover R, 'Foreword: Nomos and Narrative' (1983) 97 *Harvard Law Review* 4, 41–46.

65 Coleman J, 'Incorporationism, Conventionality, and the Practical Difference Thesis' (ed) Coleman J *Hart's Postscript: Essays on the Postscript to the Concept of Law* (Oxford: OUP, 2001) 99–147, 110.

66 Ibid.

67 Ibid.

68 Beckett *supra* note 51, at 14.

between conduct and legal obligation, and between legal duty and habit explained only by the distinction between the internal and external aspects of a rule.[69] The external point of view is an empirical point of observation from those outside the system and for Hart is of limited value in understating the system.[70] The internal point of view is critical because we can draw a distinction between the judicial officials and the subjects of the legal system. The officials require an internal point of view while the subjects obey the law.[71] The rule of recognition as the 'ordered distillation of the pronouncements' of officials determines the law and the legal system, if it is assumed to come from a single source, which is constant over time. This translates into a presumption of convergence by judicial officials as to what determines rules as valid law, which is the internal point of view. It gives predictably and stability, to the way we see and understand, the legal system in that past decisions inform the current ones and so forth. The result is legal precedent.[72] This is also the factual aspect of official acceptance of the internal point of view. The 'content of the rule [of recognition] is what was in *fact* accepted in the past by [judicial] officials as constituting its content.'[73] For the legal system to exists according to Hart judicial officials 'accept as binding and follow' the rule of recognition in 'identifying valid law'.[74] The acceptance and following by judicial officials of the criteria laid down by the rule of recognition for identifying 'certain things as constituting valid law as binding upon themselves and other officials' is the internal point of view.[75]

Judicial officials according to Hart also have a duty to criticise deviations from the rule of recognition. This implies that the rule is somewhat shut off from critique because Hart represents it as a fact of the practice of judicial officials that determines whether a rule was valid law in a legal system.[76] The statements of the judicial officials in Hart's system automatically have greater authority than any others because the rule of recognition is located in the practice of the judiciary. If judicial officials recognise what they designate, through the rule of recognition, as valid law has been violated then their judgements have special authoritative status as to what are the rules of that legal system.[77] If the judicial officials accept that past

69 Ibid.

70 Ibid, at 14–15. See Hart *supra* note 2, at 86–87. He writes that the external point of view can be seen as the perspective of a visitor observing the practice of drivers stopping at a red light. The visitor 'treats the light merely as a natural sign that people will behave in certain ways, as clouds are a sign that rain will come. In doing so he will miss out a whole dimension of the social life of those whom he is watching, since for them the right light is not merely a sign that others will stop: they look upon it as a signal for them to stop, and so a reason for stopping in conformity to rules which make stopping when the light is red a standard of behaviour and an obligation.'

71 Ibid. See also Beckett *supra* note 51, at 15.

72 See MacCormick *Legal Reasoning and Legal Theory supra* note 50, at 133–134.

73 Dyzenhaus D, 'Positivism's Stagnant Research Programme' (2000) *Oxford Journal of Legal Studies* 703–722, 704–705. My emphasis in italics.

74 Dickson *supra* note 58, at 375.

75 Ibid.

76 See Dyzenhaus *supra* note 69, at 70. See also Hart *supra* note 2, at 56, 105–107.

77 Hart *supra* note 2, at 94–95.

practice is binding as constituting the content of the rule of recognition then there is a normative aspect to the official acceptance of the internal point of view.[78] From that position, Hart appears to conceive that the judicial officials have an obligation to follow and criticise deviations from the rule of recognition as the 'ultimate rule' that determines other rules as valid law.[79] The normative and factual aspects of the internal point of view is what therefore keeps the content of the rule of recognition stable or similar from one determination of what is valid law to another.

If Hart does not assume that the rule of recognition is the ultimate rule with no other rules and legal reasons for justifying others rules as valid law then it would be difficult to determine the content of the rule of recognition.[80] No other rule can confer authority on the rule of recognition. Otherwise, that rule would be the rule of recognition. For the rule of recognition to confer recognition on the law of a system as valid, it has to be the ultimate rule. Hart could not locate the rule of recognition's authority in morality given his work to separate law and morality.[81] The authoritative status of the rule of recognition could only be a self-referential 'matter of fact'.[82] The law is the law because it is the law.[83] There is no external validation of the rule of recognition. The validity is based on the internal point of view of the system, which is contingent upon the rule of recognition itself. As mentioned earlier Hart states that the rule of recognition 'provides criteria for the assessment of the validity of other rules but it is also unlike them in that there is no rule providing criteria for the assessment of its own legal validity.'[84] This is an indication of the self-referencing manner of a legal system.[85] If Hart did not posit the rule of recognition in this manner, the law in his definition would have to be the law because of an exogenous force or agent. In positing the rule of recognition as self-referential, Hart was able to defend the rule of recognition against infinite regression. There is a comic analogy to illustrate the point.

> What if I asked the question, 'What holds up the earth', and the reply was that 'a *turtle* holds the earth up'.
>
> To which I proposed a supplementary question, 'What held up the turtle because the earth from appearances was in outer space?'
>
> The reply to which was that it was 'Turtles all the way down.'[86]

78 Dyzenhaus *supra* note 73, at 703–722, 704–705. My emphasis in italics.
79 Ibid, at 704. Dickson *supra* note 58 at 375.
80 Dickson *supra* note 58 at 379 puts it best when she says that to 'say that there are no further legal reasons for accepting the rule of recognition as binding as not to say that there are no further reasons, tout court, for accepting it.' The point is that there may be non-legal reasons for accepting the rule of recognition but that is not a discussion I have here. See Dickson for further reading.
81 Hart HLA, 'Positivism and the Separation of Law and Morals' (1958) 71 *Harvard Law Review* 593. Additionally if he had located the rule of recognition in morality he would look like a natural lawyer and not a positivist.
82 Hart *supra* note 2, at 104, 107.
83 See chapter 2 for further discussion.
84 Hart *supra* note 2, at 104.
85 See chapter 2 for further discussion
86 Popular tale referenced by Hawking S, *A Brief History of Time* (London: Bantam, 1988) 1.

Hart therefore had to posit the rule of recognition as having no other ultimate rule but reference to itself. The internal point of view of the judicial officials essentially guarantees the consistency of the rule of recognition over time.[87] That suggests that the judicial officials are committed to the internal point of view. That does not mean that the assumption of stability of the rule of recognition is an equation of stagnation or sterility because Hart suggests that the rule of recognition can change.[88] Moreover, Hart importantly asserted that propositions carry a penumbra of doubt and therefore cannot cover or account for all situations.[89] However, his inference to the internal point of view seems like an attempt to homogenise or at the least impose a uniform comprehension, on the different levels of commitment to the law and legal system; as well as the different levels of understanding of the law and legal system not only among the judicial officials, but also between the users of the legal system and the judicial officials.[90] Nevertheless, acceptance of the internal point of view is not 'blind datum, a pure brute fact' as there are reasons legal and non-legal as to why citizens and judges accept the rule of recognition.[91] These reasons whatever we suppose them to be, determine the content of the internal point of view, which informs the rule of recognition.

1.3.2 Hart's circularity

According to the rule of recognition, in the absence of any others rules conferring power on it as a legal rule, it is not necessary for the judiciary to have some sort of 'pre-authorised' legal or moral rule by which to generate their authority as a legal rule in the legal system.[92] The judiciary creates its own rules of recognition because the rule of recognition was the practice of the judiciary. The judiciary generates these rules not out of strength or because of habitual obedience but because of their 'capacity to guide their behaviour by a rule'.[93] However, there is seemingly an immediate problem. The rule of recognition, in identifying the judicial officials who then identify the rules that are valid law in their practice, appears to be circular.[94] This means that the rule of recognition would have to identify the judicial officials before its own establishment as practice. Would not these judicial officials

87 Hart *supra* note 2, at 111–114. However, Hart was also willing to accept a distinction between cases within the core and penumbra of legal rules. See Hart *supra* note 2, at 119–120, 144–150.

88 See Hart *supra* note 2, at 93–96 on rules of change.

89 Hart *supra* note 2, at 12, 119–120. See Prologue and chapter 2 for further discussion.

90 Wood M, 'Rule, Rules and Law', in Leith P and P Ingram, *The Jurisprudence of Orthodoxy: Queens University Essays on H.L.A. Hart* (London: Routledge, 1998) 46. See MacCormick *Legal Reasoning and Legal Theory supra* note 50, at 63–64.

91 See MacCormick *Legal Reasoning and Legal Theory supra* note 50, at 63–64. See Dickson *supra* note 58, at 376–381.

92 Shapiro *supra* note 50, at 155.

93 Ibid.

94 See Kramer M, 'The Rule of Misrecognition in the Hart of Jurisprudence' (1988) *Oxford Journal of Legal Studies* 8(3) 410–433, 407. Bayles MD, *Hart's Legal Philosophy: An Examination* (London: Kluwer Academic Publishers, 1992) 81.

have to identify the valid law that includes the rules of change, which identifies the persons, institutions, and procedures that can institute change of the law?[95] Judges or judicial officials would then have to pre-exist the rule of adjudication but the rule of adjudication needs to recognise them, otherwise the judges would not be known.[96] We would then have to assume that judges are 'under a duty' to apply the law as recognised by the rule of recognition to be valid, which is what judges determine in their practice to be law in the first place.[97] The rule of recognition as the practice of judicial officials would be 'understood' 'presumably with the benefit of hindsight' by examining what judicial officials do in referring to valid law.[98] 'We should not, therefore, confuse Hart's claim that the [judiciary] have the authority to generate rules of the legal systems with the false claim that they have this *authority by virtue of their being the [judiciary] of those systems.*'[99] The circularity only exists if we retain a desire for 'valid' legislators or judiciary. That is, the legal rules of a legal system exist as a precursor to the rule of recognition, which is what gives the judiciary exclusive authority to create the rule of recognition in the first place.[100] Hart does not retain this desire but appears willing to breach the duality of is and ought so that might makes right. It is a matter of determining that certain institutions, example the judiciary make and sustain the rules of the legal system that makes them the judiciary. Hart's legal system appears more of an *ex post facto* rationalisation of institutional power than as a claim that the judiciary have power by virtue of them being the judiciary of a legal system, given Hart's definition of law *per* the rule of recognition as an 'official monopoly of sanctions'.[101] Hart presents a definition of law that the rule of recognition as the empirical observable practice of judicial officials. Inherently there is nothing incorrect or even implausible about advancing a definition of law. This is what I do. I argue that we all do it, either explicitly or implicitly in order to understand the law. The point is that we do not know what to understand as the law until we have determined what the law is. No assumption of neutrality exists in any definition of the law that Hart or anyone including myself chooses.[102] However, Hart cannot make pure claims about the rule of recognition, as I cannot in my later adoption of it to understand WTO law. The definition of the law is a decision about what data to delimit which excludes and reduces for purposes of observation vast amounts and varying forms of data that could be considered law. To represent the rule of recognition as the practice of the judiciary, that is, what the judicial officials say, Hart has 'decided' what to observe and why he has decided to observe what he observes. As Kramer argues,

95 Hart *supra* note 2, at 89–95.

96 See Kramer *supra* note 94, at 419–422.

97 Campbell *supra* note 63, at 11.

98 Ibid.

99 Shapiro *supra* note 50, at 155–156, esp. 156.

100 Ibid, at 156.

101 Hart *supra* note 2, at 91.

102 See Wood *supra* note 90; Campbell *supra* note 63; Jackson J, 'Hart and the Concept of Fact', in Leith P and P Ingram, *The Jurisprudence of Orthodoxy: Queens University Essays on H.L.A Hart* (London: Routledge, 1998) 61–84.

> . . . what Hart deems to be the foundation of any legal system turns out to presuppose that a legal regime exits already. In describing whose behaviour is shaped by the rule of recognition, Hart claims that the foundational rule is immanent in official practices. However, 'officials' can be identified as such only when a structure of laws has come into existence already.[103]

Even the judicial officials who have adopted a single internal point of view would do so on some criteria agreed beforehand for the rule of recognition to come into being. Hart cannot '. . . seize on [the rule of recognition] as a ground for deductive argument, since he will inevitably presuppose what he imagines himself to be explaining.'[104] 'The view of an egalitarian, consensual legal order, containing clear law interpreted by value neutral officials and internalised as common standards by the populace [is] [a]t best . . . an idealisation of what the legal system ought to be. At worst it is ideological rhetoric.'[105] It is unlikely that a single rule that combines all the criteria to validate other rules as valid law in a legal system exists, as judges may not be able to formulate a single standard for their practice of the law.[106] When I think about international law, this is particularly acute considering as I have discussed earlier, that fragmentation reflects the specialised systems in international law that have become differentiated from the general system of international law.[107] Even if I accept, as Hart appears to have conceived, that there was a consensual homogeneous legal order in Britain where, what the Queen in Parliament enacts is valid law, the same situation is now somewhat doubtful. The rule of recognition that what the Queen in Parliament enacts is valid law, based on the implicit supremacy of the judiciary to accept this as tenable, could be seen as challenged when it confronts the 'direct effect' of European law.[108] Arguably, this could be seen as a change of the understanding of the rule of recognition as the practice of the British judiciary. It would now be extended to include the practice of other European judicial institutions, though understanding that judicial practice would still

103 Kramer *supra* note 94, 407.

104 Ibid, at 409.

105 Wood *supra* note 90, at 29, 30–31, 55. See also Campbell *supra* note 63, at 42.

106 Bayles *supra* note 94, at 80.

107 See also chapter 2.

108 Campbell *supra* note 63, at 13–14. Wood *supra* note 86 at 37. Article 249 (ex Article 189) of the EC Treaty provides that regulations are directly applicable to in all Member States, which means that regulations are directly part of the Member States law without any legislative process of that State. Treaty articles also have direct effect subject to the conditions that they are clear, unconditional and do not need any further action for implementation in the Member State. However, in both situations, courts in the Member State would still have to make sense, from their internal point of view, of the EC regulation or treaty. (For further discussion on the idea that there is no direct incorporation of law from one system to another, see chapter 2.) For discussion of direct effect in EU law, see Fenwick and Phillipson, *Text, Cases and Materials on Public Law and Human Rights*, 2nd Ed. (London: Cavendish Publishing Limited, 2003) 187–238. Horspool and Humphreys, *European Union Law* (Oxford: OUP, 2008) chapter 7. Craig and De Burca, *EU Law: Text, Cases and Materials*, 4th Ed. (Oxford: OUP, 2007) chapter 8.

rest on the UK courts in a dispute in the UK courts.[109] Nevertheless, in presenting the internal point of view as a stable consistent determinant of the rule of recognition Hart is able to make the legal system appear 'more tidy' than in practice.[110] 'Lest one gets carried away with excessive criticism, there is an element of common sense in Hart's analysis'.'[111] Hart created a rule of recognition, which was not grounded in anything but itself.[112] Shapiro offers a technical illustration of this.[113]

> For a legal norm r_n to govern a situation, it has to be created by someone who is engaging in norm-governed behaviour. We might then ask who created the legal norm r_{n-1} that is to govern the creation of r_n? Surely not someone who governed r_n because r_n does not exist before r_{n-1} does. The only possible candidate is someone whose activities are governed by a legal norm $r_{n-2.}$ But who created $r_{n-2.}$

By making the foundation of all legal authority social practice, the practice of the judiciary Hart stopped the infinite regression, in that 'norms that create legal authority are themselves created by the fact that certain members of the group are guided by the rule that treats these norms as authoritative.'[114] For a legal system to exist there must be some convergence of standards among its judicial officials or what Hart calls the internal point of view.[115] Judicial officials must share some common standard and reason for making a particular rule valid law, which means that it 'satisfies all the criteria provided by the rule of recognition'.[116] It either is explicit or remains an implicit part of their argumentation and interpretation of law.[117] That standard or reason is the internal point of view.

1.3.3 Dworkin's challenge to Hart

The rule of recognition cannot and does not necessarily tell us what to define as the law. Hart presupposed the definition for law as the practice of the judiciary. Hart, therefore, chooses to focus on the judiciary and to call their practice law. This was a definitional exercise. Law inherently or conceptually need not be the practice of the judiciary, so that law was defined as rules.[118] For Hart, law was about what the law

109 See for example, how the UK courts on the basis of their internal point of view have gone about addressing human rights law, as to Human Rights Act 1998 which 'incorporates' the European Convention of Human Rights (ECHR). For discussion of this contentions area, see Fenwick and Phillipson, *supra* note 108, at 839–946.
110 Bayles *supra* note 94, at 73.
111 Wood *supra* note 90, at 31.
112 Shapiro *supra* note 50, at 154.
113 Ibid.
114 Ibid.
115 Bayles *supra* note 94.
116 Hart *supra* note 2, at 100.
117 See MacCormick *Legal Reasoning and Legal Theory supra* note 50, at esp. Chapter VI.
118 Beckett *supra* note 51, at 26.

is, not what the law *should* be. Essentially it was about what the judiciary did, and not about what it should do. None of this made his definition necessary or correct but what it did was it provided a way by which we could examine and understand some things about the law. For Dworkin, Hart's definition by focusing on rules ignored an important set of norms. These were principles.[119] However, the same is true of Dworkin as it is of Hart, in that nothing makes his definition correct or even necessary and he too made choices as to what the law was. As much as his critique of Hart reveals misgivings about Hart, it also shows some of Dworkin's choices and that he may not have been that far removed from Hart.[120] Dworkin criticised Hart for focusing exclusively on rules which he deemed were 'all or nothing' to the detriment of realising that in a legal system there were principles which he characterised as having dimension and weight. Rules provided conclusive reasons for action and principles were non-conclusive allowing action to be based on either side of the argument.[121] Law properly understood contained rules and principles.[122] Dworkin challenged the 'truthfulness' of Hart's rule of recognition to able to put law in its 'best light', that is, a theory of law must 'seek to present legal practice at its most desirable – and the more desirable, the truer the theory is'.[123] However, Dworkin's claim that 'legal theory is true by virtue of its desirability' must be rejected.[124] A theory of law as advocated in the Prologue and throughout the study 'will not be fully determinate: good legal theory must either give up its aspiration to apply to all legal questions, or else it must give up the aspiration to point to unique legal answers for all or even most of these questions.'[125] The important thing for the purpose of distilling the rule of recognition, and understanding its main critique in Dworkin, is to realise that he was doing to Hart what Hart did to Austin in criticising his theory of law, in that it did not capture reality properly in its narrow focus on rules.[126] Hart criticised Austin idea for not capturing reality properly on its narrow focus on law as commands.[127] Moreover, Dworkin was not criticising Hart's method, as Hart was not criticising Austin's method, in so much as they were criticising the failure of each other's method to capture 'more' of the law. They were all offering definitions of law while not offering understandings as to the purpose of the law. The

119 Dworkin *supra* note 62, at 22–28.

120 Beckett *supra* note 51, at 26–31.

121 Dworkin *supra* note 62, at 22–28. See also Shapiro *supra* note 50, at 159.

122 Ibid. However, according to Hart, judges could use their discretion when faced with a case that fell outside the core of legal rules. (Hart *supra* note 2, at 141–147) Therefore Hart's understanding of a legal rule was probably more flexible than Dworkin provided for. However, Dworkin notes that this understanding of discretion would mean that rules were ambiguous. (Dworkin *supra* note 62, at 31–33; see also Shapiro *supra* note 50, at 163.) But by Dworkin's own understanding of principles as having weight and dimension, they were also ambiguous.

123 Raban O, 'Dworkin's "Best Light" Requirement and the Proper Methodology of Legal Theory' (2003) 23(2) *Oxford Journal of Legal Studies*, 243.

124 Ibid.

125 Ibid, at 264; esp. 244–247.

126 Beckett *supra* note 51, at 27.

127 Hart *supra* note 2.

disagreement between Hart and Dworkin was not about how to theorise the law but what data to claim as the law.[128] The disagreement is over how to identify the rules and the criteria for identifying the rules, which means the dispute focuses on the institutional behaviour of the judiciary. They both agree that the law is 'subject to factual observation and is to be found in the actions and rhetoric of legal officials'. For Hart, legal practitioners were bound by shared criteria whereas for Dworkin legal practitioners 'habitually disagreed' about which rights and duties were legally valid.[129] The dispute was about what comprised those observations and how they were to be classified and described.[130] However, the fact is that understanding the law is precisely about ascertaining what the law is, while making normative claims for what the law is about, its purpose.[131] Beckett writes that the

> social practice of law relies on the understanding of law as a category (e.g. the decisions of central institutions; the pursuit of coherence or justice through hermeneutics; or the speech of competent lawyers) to structure and understand a 'reality' of law as a social practice. The cognition of reality is only possible because the data privileged for abstraction from reality is sufficiently similar to this ideal image to be recognisable as a member of that category.

To observe the social practice of law we must have identified or at least presumed what that practice was and in order to have done that, we would have made implicit or explicit definitions of that practice.[132] It is our act of defining what law is (should be) which constitute the practice as an object capable of being subjected to analysis.[133]

1.4 The counter-factual rule of recognition: the beginnings of a theory of WTO law

The rule of recognition exists as an accepted 'fact' of the legal system used by the judiciary in the operations of the legal system to identify law in their own practice.[134] As Hart writes,

> The case for calling the rule of recognition 'law' is that the rule of providing criteria for the identification of other rules of the system may well be thought a defining feature of a legal system, and so itself worth calling 'law'; the case for calling it 'fact' is that to assert that such a rule exists is indeed to make an

128 Beckett *supra* note 51, at 28.
129 Raban *supra* note 122, at 244. See also Dworkin R, *Law's Empire* (London: Fontana Press, 1986) esp. 1–44.
130 Beckett *supra* note 51, at 29.
131 Raban *supra* note 122, at 261–262.
132 Beckett *supra* note 16, at 1074.
133 Ibid.
134 Hart *supra* note 2, at 117. My emphasis in italics.

> external statement of an actual fact concerning the manner in which the rules of an 'efficacious' system are identified.[135]

What this says is that law in Hart's definition is not only the observation of the official conduct of the judiciary but that it can only be observed if the institution exists as a fact, and has a monopoly on decision-making and force. Not only may Hart appear Hobbesian from this angle but also importantly it shows that Hart cannot escape Austin's method, which he criticises, for proposing a definition of law in advance.[136] Austin sought to define law to establish the province of jurisprudence.[137] This was an attempt to distinguish law from non-law to make law 'proper' in scientific terms.[138] Austin's approach meant that he had to posit a definition of law that he believed could capture as many things that were law and exclude others that he considered were not law.[139] He defined law as the 'rule laid down for the guidance of an intelligent being by an intelligent being having power over him'.[140] Given that, for Austin, law was a 'species of commands', this leads him to propose a sanction based model of duty that 'being liable to evil from you if I comply not with a wish which you signify, I am bound or obliged by your command, or I lie under a duty to obey it'.[141] In this definition, the sovereign as the supreme and final authority would not be subject to any other sovereign. Austin wrote that the sovereign 'is not in a habit of obedience to a determinate human superior'.[142] This supposed that law was factual as a habit of obedience owed to a sovereign. Austin's definition of law is problematic for international law. Under this definition, international law would not be law because there is no centralised single sovereign to owe an obligation towards a command. Multiple lawmakers and routes of enforcement constitute international law with no central adjudicator that could resolve a potential conflict arising from the different subsystems of international law.[143]

Adherence to international law is not owed to a sovereign as in Austin's definition of law or to rules *per se* in Hart's because unlike municipal law with a hierarchal structure and final adjudicator, international law is a decentralised fragmented political process with a complex structure of enforcement.[144] There is no adjudicator, which could determine a winner and a loser between competing judicial decisions from different international specialised legal systems. International law in not coming from a single sovereign source cannot be, as Austin understood law, a command. Sanctions for non-compliance do not meet all breaches of international law so that international law under Austin's definition would not be law.

135 Hart *supra* note 2, at 108. Original emphasis in inverted commas.
136 Beckett *supra* note 51, at 25, 17.
137 Austin J, *The Province of Jurisprudence Determined* (London: Weidenfeld and Nicolson, 1971 [1832]).
138 Ibid.
139 Ibid, 18–24.
140 Ibid, at 10.
141 Ibid, at 22.
142 Austin *supra* note 136, at 194–195.
143 See also chapter 2.
144 Ibid.

Nonetheless, Austin is correct in his method for positing a definition of law to distinguish it from other normative orders. We can agree with his method but not the definition. His definition is not accurately transposable to international law, which distinctively lacks the sovereign executive, legislature and centralised judiciary of municipal law to which Austin applied his definition. Austin is correct but only within his definition of law.

The application of the rule of recognition to WTO law does not appear as a simple direct transposition to WTO law but means that I understand it counter-factually. Hart in putting forward the rule of recognition sought to employ a method that was broad enough to capture more aspects than Austin's command method to distinguish law from non-law.[145] For Hart, not all law came from a command such as law based on custom and that law not only imposes a duty of obedience but can also create powers.[146] Hart focused not on proposing a definition of the law but on the empirical observable practice of the judiciary. He wrote that his 'purpose is not to provide a definition of law, in the sense of a rule by reference to which the correctness of the use of the word [law] can be tested'.[147] Hart in the *Concept of Law* states that its purpose was 'not to provide a definition of law'.[148] However, Hart posits a definition of law, if only indirectly, to decide that the practice of the judicial officials of a centralised judiciary, was to be observed as the law. Macintyre states, 'what each observer takes himself or herself to perceive is identified and has to be identified by theory-laden concepts.'[149] Although Hart presented the rule of recognition as an empirical fact, behind that was a definition of the facts, chosen to identify what was the law. The 'recognition of legal norms is impossible without a definition of law.'[150]

Hart similarly to Austin not only posits a method to define law but also establishes that law has a factual existence.[151] Whereas Austin's definition focuses on persons as the basis of authority within the legal system, Hart locates that authority in the rules *à la* the rule of recognition. Hart like Austin believed that legal authority could be created or more specifically was presumed to be created *ex nihilo*.[152] Hart's definition of law as the practice of a centralised judiciary meant that international law in lacking a centralised judiciary could not be a legal system proper like a municipal system. This is similar to Austin's definition as discussed earlier, which would bar international law as law because it lacks a single sovereign as in a municipal legal system. This however tells us more about Hart's definition and decision as to what counts as law than it does about international law. Hart was correct but only within

145 Hart *supra* note 2, at 18–23 for critique of Austin.

146 Hart *supra* note 2, at 77–78, 135.

147 Hart *supra* note 2, at 16–17.

148 Hart *supra* note 2, at 15.

149 Macintyre A, *After Virtue: A Study in Moral Theory*, 2nd edition (London: Duckworth, 1985) 79.

150 Beckett J, 'Countering Uncertainty and Ending Up/Down Arguments: A Prolegomena to a Response' (2005) 16(2) *European Journal of International Law* 213–238, 217.

151 Bayles *supra* note 94, at 73.

152 Shapiro *supra* note 50, at 155.

his definition of a legal system as based on a rule of recognition. The rule of recognition, that is, the practice of the judiciary leads Hart to conceive law as an observable fact. However, that does not preclude the use of the rule of recognition as a method for defining international law because of its fragmented nature, as discussed earlier, in lacking a centralised judiciary as similar to municipal law which can demonstrate law as an observable fact of the practice of a judiciary. What it does mean is that I will have to transpose the rule of recognition from municipal law to international law, more specifically WTO law. Ironically, the WTO does possess a centralised judicial system, as close as any in international law to the common law systems that Hart designed the rule of recognition to understand. However, if I am to conceptually design a method that seeks to examine the interaction between WTO and external international law, it must be applicable to defining the law in both systems. The criteria of what is law must be the same, even if the nature of the law in the differentiated specialised systems of international law is different.

International trade law theorist David Palmeter attempted to apply Hart's definition of law as rule of recognition to WTO law to demonstrate that the WTO was a legal system.[153] This was in the sense of a municipal system and not a primitive legal system. Hart attributed the latter status to international law because of its lack of a rule of recognition. Hart states that,

> There is something comic in the efforts made to fashion a basic rule for the most simple forms of social structure which exist without one. It is as if we were to insist that a naked savage *must* really be dressed in some invisible variety of modern dress . . . we must emancipate ourselves from the assumption that international law must contain a basic rule . . .[154]

He argues that the idea that international law is a proper legal system as is a municipal system should be abandoned because international law lacked the rule of recognition.[155] International law for Hart was a primitive legal system.[156] However, for Palmeter the rules-based WTO, as opposed to the diplomatic nature that embodied its predecessor GATT, showed that international trade law was now a legal system in possession of a rule of recognition.[157] Given that the WTO was a new organisation at the time, Palmeter's assertions appear underlined by a sense of urgency to define and ensure that international trade law scholarship proved systematically that WTO law was a legal system. Palmeter's approach was to put forward a definition of Hart's rule of recognition and then turn to the WTO treaty to match to that definition. He states that,

153 Palmeter *supra* note 6.

154 Hart *supra* note 2, at 230. (Original emphasis for the word 'must'.)

155 Ibid.

156 Ibid.

157 Palmeter *supra* note 6.

> In the WTO, as in GATT and all treaties, the basic rule of recognition is the treaty text itself. The Members view this text from an internal perspective. They see the text as applicable to them, as providing a reason for their behaviour and as providing justification for their expectations concerning the behaviour of other Members. Their view differs radically from the external view of a non-Member.[158]

It appears that in applying Hart's rule of recognition, Palmeter by locating the rule of recognition in the text of international treaties is trying to escape Hart's commitment to the rule as the practice of the judiciary, because he is aware that international law lacks a centralised judiciary, which grounds Hart's understanding of the rule of recognition. Hart states that the existence of the rule of recognition would be 'manifest in general practice, on the part of officials or private persons, of identifying the rules [of the legal system] by this criterion'.[159] The text of a treaty as Palmeter identifies will obviously inform what judges or judicial officials do. However, Hart's formulation of the rule of recognition is not located in the text but is essentially an expression of the practice of the judiciary of those texts as the law. The rule of recognition supposes that the practice of the judiciary is the law, which means that the texts of a treaty cannot be held as law if it conflicts with the judges. It is not the text but the interpretation held by the judges or judicial officials that constitute what determines the law. Palmeter misrepresents Hart's rule of recognition because it is not the text of WTO law but it is an empirical observable fact as the practice of the judicial officials of the legal system.

A legal system produces different data for different reasons. Different people produce this data at different times and it can mean different things to different people, because there is no *One* mind to make sense of the data, unless it is assumed and posited as Hart does through the internal point of view. We can imagine a norm to tell us from among the varying bits of data we confront what counts as law, as is the rule of recognition. In other words, we create and put forward a method to understand the data by imposing patterns on the data. Take the rule of recognition, in that as a method it defines law as the practice of the judiciary. This allows me to be able to make sense of what I have determined to be the law by observing this practice. Hart would have law as the factual practice of the judiciary; however law is not a brute or plain fact.[160] As Alistair Mcintyre says it is not a fact that could 'be gathered in with the same kind of enthusiasm that at other times has informed the collection of Spode china or the numbers of railway engines'.[161]

158 Ibid, at 467. See also 455 where he notes, that 'In GATT, as in any treaty regime, the ultimate rule of recognition is the text of the treaty itself. The treaty is the source of legal rights and obligations relating to the regime it establishes.'

159 Hart *supra* note 2, at 98.

160 MacCormick, 'The Ethics of Legalism' *supra* note 40, at 191. See also Searle J, *The Construction of Social Reality* (New York: Free Press, 1995). See also chapter 2.

161 Macintyre *supra* note 149, at 79.

It only exists because we want it to exist. It does not exist, *a priori*, independently of our thought, subsequent observation and imposition of a method to identify it as law and a way to understand it.[162]

The 'normative order [of law] is not a natural datum of human society but a hard won production of organising intelligence.'[163] Law comes into being the moment it is defined as the law.[164] 'Hence the task of producing a rationally coherent view' of the international legal system calls for 'imaginative insight into the possibility of a principled and structured ordering of material which is potentially chaotic despite itself, in each fragmentary part, the output of intrinsically rational activity.'[165] Since rational reconstruction is an imaginative process, it is a hermeneutic method.[166] However, it is not closed, because as discussed in the next section, I can deploy Hart's rule of recognition without sharing his commitment to law as fact. As a 'mode of practical reasoning' I can rationally reconstruct the rule of recognition[167] as the practice of the WTO adjudicating bodies to understand its interaction with external law. Doing this allows me to realise that Hart's commitment to conceive of the rule of recognition and law as fact and rules is nothing more than that. It need not exist or even be necessary, so it is not a brute fact but a method of organising data.

The rule of recognition is simply a method for organising data as law. The definition of law is what 'we' determine it to be for law has '. . . no natural existence, no set form, and no fixed ontology; law has no natural role, because law is *not* a brute fact.'[168] The existence and use of the rule of recognition is a decision. In what is an amusing but effective analogy, Darton employs Foucault's analysis of Borges encyclopaedia of imagined animals to make a similar point regarding categories.[169] Consider Borges' encyclopaedia that categorised animals in which he sets out some of the following: '(a) belonging to the Emperor, (b) embalmed, (c) tame, (d) sucking pigs, (e) sirens, (f) fabulous, (g) stray dogs, (h) included in the present classification, (i) frenzied, (j) innumerable, (k) drawn with a very fine camelhair brush, (l) et cetera, (m) having just broken the water pitcher, (n) that from a long way look like flies.'[170] What I can realise is that the categories are not only *arbitrary* but they have a meaning to the community that uses them and may appear meaningless to an outsider. This is reminiscent of the internal point of view and allows the

162 Beckett *supra* note 150, at 214–219.

163 MacCormick 'Reconstruction After Deconstruction' *supra* note 3, at 557. Also, MacCormick and Summers *supra* note 3, 20 write that 'Normative order as order is not a natural datum of human society but a hard-won production of organising intelligence.'

164 Ibid.

165 MacCormick and Summers *supra* note 3, at 20.

166 Ibid, at 20.

167 Ibid, at 21.

168 Beckett *supra* note 150, at 214.

169 Darton R, *The Great Cat Massacre and Other Episodes in French Cultural History* (New York: Basic Books Inc., 1984) 192–194, and also 3–7, 191–209 (Chapter 5: Philosophers Trim the Tree of Knowledge: The Epistemological Strategy of the Encyclopedie).

170 Ibid, at 192.

community to make sense of the data before them by imposing some sort of pattern on that data. Methods of organising the data into certain categories in the imagined encyclopedia 'occupy an epistemological space that is prior to thought'.[171] The rule of recognition does not pre-exist our observation of data though the actual data that it organises may pre-exist our observation. If a categorisation of a brute fact collapses, that material thing would still factual exist, though the intelligible order it represents would collapse. The existence of a brute fact is not dependent on social (human) agreement and opinion[172] even if human intelligibility is dependeant upon the methods and categories we set up to make sense of that brute fact. This contrasts with law, which as an institutional fact or idea is the creation of our imagination and whose existence is dependent on social agreement.[173] The law as a thought object 'exists by being believed in, rather than being believed in by virtue of [its] existence.'[174] Law is not a brute fact though there are expressions of it such as the practice of the judiciary, which can form factual points of references. The methods and ways of understanding the law are constitutive of the law, whereas if law were a brute fact, then these methods and ways of understanding would not affect it beyond categorising it to make sense of it from other data, or to impose function upon it.[175]

Understanding the rule of recognition counter-factually means that law does not have a direct existence but exists indirectly through the recognition by the authoritative institutions of the legal system.[176] The rule of recognition has a real existence in the practice of the judiciary as supported by observation. It is not merely a premise as it represents an actual feature of the legal system.[177] It is this real existence and the centralised authority it presupposes that 'creates and sustains the counter-factual existence of legal norms', whether or not the rules are obeyed. As law exists as a thought object, then the rule of recognition would lose its counter-factual existence if judicial officials failed to recognise and implement a rule.[178] Therefore as Beckett rightly argues, the data observed is institutional and not legal in nature.[179] The data we define and question, as the law is essentially the institutional output as the practice of the judiciary.

To locate the rule of recognition in the text of the WTO treaty, as did Palmeter, would deny the usefulness of the rule of recognition, especially to international law. The rule makes the judge not just a critical institutional part of the legal

171 Ibid, at 192.

172 See Searle *supra* note 160.

173 Ibid.

174 See MacCormick 'Ethics of Legalism', *supra* note 40, at 191. See also Bos M, 'Will and Order in the Nation–State System: Observations on Positivism and Positive International Law', in MacDonald R St. J and DM Johnston (eds) *The Structure and Process of International Law* (Hague: Martinus Nijhoff Publishers, 1983) 50–78, 67–68.

175 Searle *supra* note 160, at 33.

176 Beckett *supra* note 51, at 15–16.

177 Hart *supra* note 2, at 231. See also Beckett *supra* note 51, at 23–24.

178 See Beckett *supra* note 51, at 24.

179 Beckett *supra* note 51, at 24.

system but because the rule defines law by his practice, I can also see the judge as an institutional idea or expression within the legal system.[180] By that the internal point of view of the judiciary of a legal system not only constitutes the rule of recognition but also has existence because of the institutional idea of the judiciary. In indicating that the rule of recognition was the text of the treaty and not the practice of the judiciary, Palmeter would actually restrict the method of the rule to determine the law as the observable empirical practice of the judiciary. This is particularly important in international law, which lacks a centralised judiciary as an institutional structure to situate the rule of recognition. The more diminished the institutional role of the judge as a structure in the legal system becomes, such as in international law where in many cases the practice of a centralised judiciary is not observable, then the more the judge as an institutional idea or perspective becomes critical.[181] In international law the focus is on the actions of the 'authoritative decision makers' of the differentiated specialised fragmented legal systems. In the case of the WTO, those decision makers are the adjudicating bodies. The rule of recognition is not the law. It 'projects' what the law is or what data has been determined as law.[182] The rule of recognition as a factual point of reference could identify the criteria for recognised manifestations of law, example the WTO treaty. In short, the rule of recognition provides a point by which we could observe what the judges see as recognised manifestations of international law, such as a treaty or custom.[183]

The application of the rule of recognition does not appear directly transferable to WTO law as Palmeter seems to assume to avoid the fact that international law unlike municipal law lacks a single-centralised-hierarchical-judicial system, which is critical to Hart's rule of recognition. Seeing the rule of recognition as a 'schematic representation of reality',[184] I can apply Hart's method but not way of thinking to international law because in Hart's definition the rule can only exist as the actual practice of the judiciary. In order to apply the rule of recognition to international law I see it as the product of a counter-factual and not as Hart does of a factual, legal system. The rule can then recognise what the adjudicators in international law ought to see as law but because it is counter-factual, there is no need as with Hart to hold to the commitment that law is the actual practice of a centralised judiciary.[185] In international law the rule of recognition can serve to identify law where there is the actual practice of a centralised judiciary but because I can see law as counter-factual, it can also recognise law where there is no centralised judiciary.

To propose an account of the interaction between WTO law and external law, the method for defining what counts as law for WTO law and external law should

180 This view is somewhat expressed in Chapter 1. See generally Beckett *supra* note 51.
181 Ibid.
182 Bos *supra* note 174, at 71–72.
183 See Bos *supra* note 174.
184 Ibid, at 54.
185 See Beckett *supra* note 51, generally.

be the same. Otherwise, any assessment of the interaction between the two forms of law would be somewhat inadequate in not providing a standard basis for intelligibility. There cannot be one method for WTO law and another for external law. The rule of recognition can provide the same method to tell us what counts as law in the international legal system. The content of the rule of recognition may be different in the different fragmented systems of international law but the meaning of the rule of recognition as signifying a factual reference point for the counter-factual existence of the law is the same. Hart's focus on the judiciary was generic, as is here, because a counter-factual understanding of the rule of recognition must not only have observational and predictive value for WTO law but also for external international law as we are using the same abstract concept of the rule of recognition. That each fragmented system in international law will have its own normative content as to rule of recognition, because there is no ultimate rule of recognition, does not deny that conceptually and empirically I use the same rule to define law, whether as WTO or external international law.

1.5 Conclusion

The aim of this chapter was to situate the analysis of the interaction between WTO and external international law within fragmentation and devise a way to understand what law was. We used the rule of recognition as counter-factually understood to provide a way to determine that the practice of the adjudicating bodies, counted as WTO law. The rule of recognition provides the method that can tell us what counts as WTO law but it does not provide a way to observe and make sense of that law. Luhmann whose idea of operational closure (that systems operate from their own internal point of view to construct their own reality) we use to advance a way to think about WTO law chapter 2 captures it best in writing that,

> Acceptable legal reasoning has to restrict itself to legal norms . . . professionally sound practice, and so on. This is how closure is recognised – or 'observed' in the system (every legal theorist will immediately recognise H. L. A. Hart's secondary rules of recognition). However, this does not quite satisfactorily explain how closure is produced in the first place.[186]

In other words, the rule of recognition as a method discussed in this chapter can provide a way to select what we will observe and analyse as WTO law in this study, but to analyse that law we also need a concept, to understand the law. Together the concept and method will constitute my theory of WTO law, constrained openness, as discussed in chapter 3. Having decided upon the method as the rule of recognition, we determined that WTO law is the actual and rhetorical practice of the adjudicating bodies. We partly illustrate this in chapter 3 by examining the way in

186 Luhmann N, 'Operational Closure and Structural Coupling: The Differentiation of the Legal System' (1992) 13 *Cardozo Law Review* 1419, 1427. See chapter 2.

which the adjudicating bodies develop and remain committed to an internal point of view, which points to the rule of recognition, and in chapters 5 and 6 by examining the practice of the adjudicating bodies. In chapter 2, I continue to lay the ground for the need for a theory of WTO law, by examining how specific methods of treaty interpretation are inadequate to offer a way to systemically integrate the differentiated parts of a fragmented international legal system.

2 The inadequacy of the professional tool box of treaty interpretation as an account of fragmentation

2.0 Introduction

The International Law Commission (ILC) Study Group Report on Fragmentation proposes that treaty interpretation could provide a 'professional toolbox' for addressing fragmentation. Treaty interpreters according to the Report would be required to situate the claims of conflicting or overlapping laws within the broader normative system of international law.[1] The purpose of this chapter is to challenge the idea that we can use general international law to account for and manage the interaction between specialised legal systems. In this chapter, I examine treaty interpretation techniques such as *lex specialis*, *lex posterior* and the Vienna Convention on the Law of Treaties (VCLT) demonstrating that they are somewhat unsatisfactory in accounting for the fragmentation of international law into specialised legal systems such as the WTO. In addition, following on from chapter 1, in this chapter I continue to build the arguments for the fragmentation of international law. It provides a basis to further show why a theory of WTO law is needed to start to think about the interaction between WTO law and external law.

2.1 *Lex specialis* as an account of fragmentation and WTO law

The image of WTO law as a self-contained legal system appears to persist in the thought and practice of trade lawyers,[2] especially because WTO law is *lex specialis derogat legi generali*.[3] WTO law as self-contained would be a sign that it was a 'closed

1 Koskenniemi M, 'Fragmentation of International Law: Difficulties Arising from the Diversification and Expansion of International Law', UN Doc. International Law Commission A/CN.4/L.682 13 April 2006, paras 1–4 [hereinafter ILC Study Group Report on Fragmentation], para 170.

2 For a similar point see Lindross A and M Mehling, 'Dispelling the Chimera of "Self-Contained Regimes": International Law and the WTO' (2005) 16(5) *European Journal of International Law* 857.

3 Crawford J, *The International Law Commission's Articles on State Responsibility: Introduction, Text and Commentaries* (Cambridge: CUP, 2002) 306. Article 55 (*lex specialis*) of the ILC Articles on State Responsibility, state that 'These articles do not apply where and to the extent that the conditions for the existence of an internationally wrongful act or the content or implementation of the international responsibility of a State are governed by special rules of international law.' See the commentary para 3 at 307 discussing the WTO as *lex specialis*.

legal circuit' with a full set of its own law to apply with no need to interact outside its system.[4] *Lex specialis* means that a specific rule prevails over a general rule.[5] It emphasises that WTO law is 'special' in that the rules of general international law 'do not apply where and to the extent' that the 'special rules' of WTO law governs the area of international law.[6] It is apparent that the rationale for a self-contained regime and *lex specialis* is similar in that it reflects the want for regulation of a particular concern by a specific legal institution and not that of general international law.[7] It can also explain the understanding of fragmentation (see chapters 1 and 3). The differentiated systems of international law seem to have been created to be specific and exempt from what were deemed an ineffectual system of general international law.[8] WTO law, however, lacks some general procedural rules that would make the application of its specific rules practicably workable, so it can source these from general international law.[9] WTO law has demonstrated through its application of general international law, *lex specialis* does not equate self-containedness or being entirely sealed off from international law (see chapters 1 and 3). The ILC Study Group Report on Fragmentation stated, 'No firm exclusion is implied; the significance of this being that it points to factors and practices that may have more or less relevance depending on how the problem is described (is it a 'trade law' problem, [is] it a problem in 'humanitarian law' or in human rights law?)'.[10]

For further discussion about the WTO as *lex specialis*: Marceau G, 'WTO Dispute Settlement and Human Rights' (2002) 13 *European Journal of International Law* 753–814, 765–773. Cass D, 'The Constitutionalisation of International Trade Law: Judicial Norm-Creation as the Engine of Constitutional Development in International Trade' (2001) 12 *European Journal of International Law* 65–66. Simma B and D. Pulkowski, 'Of Planets and the Universe: Self-Contained Regimes in International Law' (2006) 17 *European Journal of International Law* 483–529, 485–490. Lennard M, 'Navigating by the Stars: Interpreting the WTO Agreements' (2002) *Journal of International Economic Law*, 70–72. ILC Study Group Report on Fragmentation *supra* note 1, at paras 165–171.

4 For discussion on the issue of self-contained systems, see ILC Study Group Report on Fragmentation *supra* note 1, at paras 123–194. See also Simma B, 'Self-Contained Regimes' (1985) 16 *Netherlands Yearbook of International Law* 111–136.

Concerning WTO law see Geping R, 'The Law as Applied by WTO Panels' (2003) 17 Temp. Int'l & Comp. L.J. Nichols P, 'GATT Doctrine' (1996) 36 Va. J. Int'l Law. Kuyper P, 'The Law of GATT as a Special Field of International Law' (1994) 25 Neth. YIL. Cameron Pauwelyn J, 'The Role of Public International Law in the WTO: How Far Can We Go?' (2001) 95(3) AJIL 535–578 [Hereinafter 'The Role of Public International Law in the WTO']. Marceau G, 'A Call for Coherence in International Law' (1999) 33(5) JWT 87. Palmeter D and P Mavroidis, 'The WTO Legal System: Sources of Law' (1998) 92 AJIL. McRae D, 'The Contribution of International Trade Law to the Development of International Law' (1996) T-260 *Recueil de Cours* 99. McRae D, 'The WTO in International law: Tradition continued or new frontier?' (2000) JIEL.

5 See Article 55 on rules of state responsibility at note 3 *supra*.

6 Ibid.

7 ILC Study Group Report on Fragmentation *supra* note 1 para 191.

8 Koskenniemi M, 'The Fate of Public International Law: Between Technique and Politics' (2007) 70 (1) *Modern Law Review* 1–30, 19. See also chapter 1.

9 Abi-Sabb G, 'The WTO Dispute Settlement and General International Law', in Yerxa R and B Wilson, *Key Issues in WTO Dispute Settlement: The First Ten Years* (Cambridge: CUP, 2005) 7–11, 10.

10 ILC Study Group Report on Fragmentation *supra* note 1, at para 173.

We do not think that any system of international law is self-contained and WTO law in this respect is no different. Importantly as will be discussed and shown throughout this study that does not preclude its separate or distinct nature from the general system of international law. The less likely a system is distinct, the more likely it is to use general rules of international law as a fallback.[11] That fallback to general procedural rules however would not tend to affect the application of WTO *lex specialis* rules, because the application of the general rules is about the interpretation, application and enforcement of WTO law.[12] These general rules would have little influence over the substantial outcome of disputes between WTO law and external law.[13] Knowing that the WTO adjudicating bodies apply general international law to assist in the 'administration' of WTO law does not satisfy the more specific inquiry of the study regarding the interaction between WTO law and external law.

2.1.1 The problems with lex specialis *as an account of fragmentation*

Concerning *lex specialis*, Joost Pauwelyn argues that the special norm would prevail because it was more effective or precise, and more closely reflected the will of a country.[14] The decisive element in *lex specialis* is speciality where one norm can be more special in addressing a particular subject matter.[15] Nonetheless, there are doubts as to whether *lex specialis* can address fragmentation.[16] Which norm is more 'special' and how far does that 'special' extend is problematic to ascertain.[17] This is particularly so when we consider that the reason behind the special systems of international law is to address a particular concern in a specific manner. As I discussed, 'Fragmentation is, after all, the result of a conscious *challenge* to the unacceptable features of that general law and the powers of the institutions that apply it. This is why there will be no hierarchy between the various legal regimes in the near future'.[18] Each system is *lex specialis* as to the next system because the purpose of each system is to regulate a specific concern of international law.

Consider that an environmental treaty may prohibit the trade of a product to protect the environment, whereas the function of the WTO is based on free trade

11 Simma B and D. Pulkowski *supra* note 3 at 485.
12 Ibid.
13 Lindorss and Mehling *supra* note 2, at 875–876.
14 Pauwelyn, 'The role of Public International Law in the WTO' *supra* note 4, at 388–389.
15 Ibid, at 388–389.
16 Hafner G, 'Pros and Cons Ensuing from Fragmentation of International Law' *Michigan Journal of International Law* 849–863, 860.
17 Simma B and D Pulkowski *supra* note 3, 488.
18 Koskenniemi *supra* note 8, at 19. Also we could realise that fragmentation as discussed in chapter 3 arises from the technical development of a discipline and bureaucracy that springs up around and is part of treaties such as the WTO which establish codes of practice, working patterns and adjudicate matters as queries between competing bureaucracies leading to fragmented approaches due to a lack of central control. (I want to thank Oliver Dearden for highlighting this alternative way of framing the point.)

of that product in order to promote economic growth. Both treaties cover the same product. A country claiming derogation for the environmental treaty signed both treaties. The point is that both treaties with different and special aims express the will of the same country that claims derogation in one treaty as to the other. There is no single or ultimate legislative and judicial will in international law that reflects these competing agendas and this explains why the same country can express different wills. Different constituents of the same country negotiate for different gains and bargains. The fact is that even the constituents in municipal law with a perceived single and ultimate legislative will (in the form of a parliament and a supreme court for example) do not have a homogeneous legal community, as they too have competing agendas and interests. The central problem with *lex specialis* is that it is 'based on a particular fiction of unified state conduct'.[19]

Moreover, with *lex specialis* there is still a choice between two norms in the non-hierarchical system of international law. We are left to wonder, as did Dirk Pulkowski, whether there is 'too heavy' a reliance on methods such as *lex specialis* and as I examine below, treaty interpretation to address fragmentation.[20] Can *lex specialis* really resolve the overlap between specialised legal systems? The overlap or conflict is not resolved if the method of *lex specialis* is to overlook one norm for the other norm on the grounds of one being more 'special' while the norm passed over is still 'special' and applicable in international law. *Lex specialis* from this viewpoint temporarily shunts the overlap aside. Given that trade potentially cuts across many areas of international law *lex specialis* would appear as a somewhat unsatisfactory resolution and account of the interaction between WTO law and external international law.

2.2 *Lex posterior* as an account of fragmentation and WTO law

Lex posterior derogat legi priori is another principle of treaty interpretation, which is put forward as a method to address overlaps between treaties because of fragmentation.[21] *Lex posterior* simply means that when two different treaties cover the same matter and there is conflict or some overlap as to which treaty should be applied, the treaty that was created later in time prevails. VCLT Articles 30(3) and 30(4) can be considered to embody the *lex posterior* principle.[22] The determinant factor for the applicability of Articles 30(3) and 30(4) according to Article 30 (1) is that the conflicting treaties cover the 'same subject-matter'.[23]

19 Simma B and D. Pulkowski *supra* note 3, 489.

20 Pulkowski D, 'Book review' *European Journal of International Law* 16 (2005) 156. See also Henckels C, 'Overcoming Jurisdictional Isolationism at the WTO-FAT Nexus: A Potential Approach for the WTO' (2008) 19(3) EJIL 571–599, 579–582, esp. 582.

21 See Pauwelyn J, *Conflict of Norms in Public International Law: How WTO Law Relates to Other Rules of International Law* (Cambridge: CUP, 2003) [hereinafter *Conflict of Norms*] 335–342, 367–374. 'The Role of Public International Law in the WTO' *supra* note 4, at 545–547.

22 Mus J B, 'Conflicts between Treaties in International Law' (1998) XLV *Netherlands International Law Review* 219–220. Borgen C J, 'Resolving Treaty Conflicts' (2005) 37 *George Washington Law Review* 603.

23 Article 30 (1) states that 'Subject to Article 103 of the Charter of the United Nations, the rights

Article 30 (3) states that,

> When all the parties to the earlier treaty are parties also to the later treaty but the earlier treaty is not terminated or suspended in operation under article 59, the earlier treaty applies only to the extent that its provisions are compatible with those of the later treaty.

Article 30 (4) states that,

> When the parties to the later treaty do not include all the parties to the earlier one:
>
> (a) as between two parties, each of which is a party to both treaties, the same rule applies as in paragraph 3 [Article 30 (3)];
> (b) as between at party to both treaties and a party to only one of the treaties, the treaty to which both are parties governs their mutual rights and obligations.

The use of *lex posterior* however may not be entirely satisfactory.[24] The constant development, application and renewal of treaties make the determination of *ratione temporis* unclear and renders *lex posterior* practically ineffective. That means the applicability of *lex posterior* is ambiguous as to what 'date' determines which expression of the will of a country prevails.[25] The *ratione materiae* of *lex posterior* can also be difficult to assess if the two treaties under dispute cover the same subject matter.[26] Consider that an issue 'related' to trade is not the equivalent of covering the 'same' subject matter, which is necessary to activate and make *lex posterior* under Article 30.4 relevant in settling a dispute.[27] Given the potential overlap of trade with many other areas of international law, it is quickly realised that the practical use of *lex posterior* is limited because everything can be somewhat trade related in the context of the globalised trading system. We are reminded by *Indonesia – Autos (Panel)* that we should presume that countries are aware of their prior commitments, which prevail unless the latter in time treaty explicitly states otherwise.[28] 'Indeed, when it

and obligations of States parties to successive treaties relating to the *same subject-matter* shall be determined in accordance with the following paragraphs [that is Articles 30 (2)–(5)].'

24 ILC Study Group Report on Fragmentation *supra* note 1, at para 250. Pauwelyn, 'The Role of Public International Law' *supra* note 4, at 545. Lindross and Mehling *supra* note 21, at 864.

25 Pauwelyn, *Conflict of Norms supra* note 21, at 370–372. 'The Role of Public International Law in the WTO' *supra* note 4 at 545–547. Pauwelyn J, 'Remarks at the Fourth Annual WTO Conference' in M Andenas and F Ortino (eds) *WTO Law and Process* (London: British Institute of International and Comparative Law, 2005) 498–500.

26 Pauwelyn, *Conflict of Norms supra* note 21, at 364–366. 'The Role of Public International Law in the WTO' *supra* note 4, at 545–547. *Remarks at the Fourth Annual WTO Conference supra* note 25, at 498–500.

27 Wold C, 'Multilateral Environmental Agreements and the GATT: Conflict and Resolution?' (1996) 26 Envtl. L. 843, 911.

28 Panel Report, *Indonesia – Certain Measures Affecting the Automobile Industry*, WT/DS54/R, WT/DS55/R, WT/DS59/R, WT/DS64/R and Corr.1, 2, 3 and 4, adopted 23 July 1998, at para14.28 and note 649.

comes to the "hard cases", Article 30 in and of itself hardly offers any solutions.'[29] To illustrate this I will apply *lex posterior* to resolve a potential overlap between an environmental treaty such as the Convention on International Trade in Endangered Species of Wild Fauna and Flora (CITES) and WTO law. This is also an illustration of the overlap that can occur between different systems of international law.

2.2.1 The problems of lex posterior *as an account of fragmentation: the example of WTO law and the Convention for International Trade in Endangered Species*

At the outset, and this is not to circumscribe the illustration, but if the potential overlap between CITES and the WTO could applicably be resolved using treaty interpretation then much of the ensuing discussion on the overlap between these differentiated systems would be irrelevant. However, this appears not to be the case. To start with, whether CITES and the WTO address the same subject matter may be contentious. CITES primarily prohibits trade in endangered species to protect them whereas the WTO safeguards free trade. Nevertheless, for deployment of the illustration we can assume that both treaties address the 'same subject matter' because this is a determinant factor for the application of Article 30 as embodying *lex posterior*.

Consider the scenario of two countries where both are parties to the WTO treaty and CITES. There is a dispute and so a need to determine which treaty will resolve the dispute. In turning to *lex posterior* it appears unclear as to the 'date' that determines which treaty as the expression of the will of the country prevails.[30] For instance, the General Agreement on Tariffs and Trade (GATT) as the predecessor to the WTO was applied from 1947 until the WTO came to being in 1994. CITES was signed in 1972 and came into force in 1975. In such a situation, CITES as the latter treaty would prevail over GATT. However, on incorporation of GATT 1947 into the WTO in 1994, CITES would revert to the status as the earlier treaty. Though the fortunes of the WTO may be reversed if the regular amendments as in the CITES Appendices are considered in determination of the date to decide which treaty takes priority. This results in incongruous administrative 'hassles'[31] and renders the rule of *lex posterior* practically inutile.[32]

I also turn to Article 30(4) as the other embodiment of *lex posterior*. Article 30(4) in stipulating which treaty both countries would be party to could prove useful in

29 Pauwelyn, 'The Role of Public International Law in the WTO' *supra* note 4, at 545. *Remarks at the Fourth Annual WTO Conference supra* note 25, at 494. See also ILC Study Group Report on Fragmentation *supra* note 1, at para 250.

30 Wold *supra* note 27, at 911.

31 Ibid, at 912.

32 Eckersley R, 'The WTO and MEAs: A Case of Disciplinary Neoliberalism?' (2003) www.utas.edu.au/gov/APSA/REckersleyfinal.pdf February 2004 p. 8. Pauwelyn, *Conflict of Norms supra* note 21, at 369–370.

locating the appropriate institution to resolve the overlap.[33] However, in this situation there appears to be some incongruence between Article 30(3) and Article 30(4). If a treaty under Article 30(3) was found to be later in time Article 30(4) would still weigh towards resolving an overlap between the two conflicting treaties under the treaty that the disputing countries are parties to. I accept that the argument could be made that the incongruence between Article 30(3) and Article 30(4) is not genuine. It would then be perhaps better to read the incongruence as simply a matter of different commitments under different parts of the VCLT. However, I believe that may appear as an attempt to paper over the difference between the Articles, which can be played off against each other. Furthermore, according to VCLT Article 34 a state cannot be bound by a treaty to which it has not consented.[34] If the treaty became customary international law as under VCLT Article 38[35] then Article 34 is reversed though the ascension of a treaty to custom is not an effortless process, or one to be taken likely.[36]

The illustration appears to show that *lex posterior*, as a means to account for the interaction between different specialised systems, may prove less than incisive. In an overlap between treaties, so much for the 'will' of the country 'logically' prevailing, as Pauwelyn asserted, if there is difficulty locating that will as to *ratione materiae* and *ratione temporis*. *Lex posterior* appears to do no better than *lex specialis* in accounting for and addressing fragmentation.[37] There are some question marks over the capacity of *lex posterior* to resolve disputes between the fragmented and specialised parts of international law. In the next section I continue with an examination of treaty interpretation, specifically VCLT Article 31(1) as a means to address fragmentation concerning the interaction between WTO law and external law.

2.3 Treaty interpretation as an account of fragmentation and WTO law

As WTO law is based on a treaty, the function of its adjudicating bodies is to interpret and apply the treaty to resolve disputes, which arise between members as to what is prohibited or not, according to the terms of the treaty. It is apparent that the terms of a treaty are words and sometimes the meanings of words can be elusive in that they can carry a penumbra of doubt.

33 The WTO has 151 parties to the treaty and 32 observer countries. See http://www.wto.org/english/thewto_e/whatis_e/tif_e/org6_e.htm CITES has 172 parties to the treaty. See http://www.cites.org/eng/disc/parties/index.shtml

34 Article 34 (General rule regarding third States) states that 'A treaty does not create either obligations or rights for a third State without its consent.'

35 Article 38 (Rules in a treaty becoming binding on third States through international custom) states that 'Nothing in articles 34 to 37 precludes a rule set forth in a treaty from becoming binding upon a third State as a customary rule of international law, recognised as such.'

36 See for example Kammerhofer J, 'The Uncertainty in the Formal Sources of International Law Customary International Law and Some of its Problems' (2004) 15(3) *European Journal of International Law* 523–553.

37 See ILC Study Group Report on Fragmentation *supra* note 1, at para 250.

Concerning the interpretation of the WTO treaty, the adjudicating bodies are directed by the Dispute Settlement Understanding (DSU) of the WTO to use the VCLT to address ambiguity within that treaty in a dispute. DSU Article 3.2 notes that members recognise that the dispute settlement system 'serves to preserve the rights and obligations of Members under the covered agreements, and to clarify the existing provisions of those agreements in accordance with customary rules of interpretation of public international law.' The reference to the 'customary rules of interpretation of public international law' in DSU Article 3.2 is understood to be a reference to the VCLT. The Appellate Body (AB) in *US – Carbon Steel* states that:

> We recall that Article 3.2 of the DSU recognises that interpretative issues arising in WTO dispute settlement are to be resolved through the application of customary rules of interpretation of public international law. It is well settled in WTO case law that the principles codified in Articles 31 and 32 of the Vienna Convention on the Law of Treaties are such customary rules.[38]

The ICJ confirmed in the *Libya* v *Chad* territorial dispute that these customary rules of treaty interpretation were embodied in VCLT Articles 31 and 32.[39] This reference to the customary rule of interpretation recognised that some members of the WTO are not party to the VCLT, but because the rules are also customary, they could be applied to those members.[40]

The adjudicating bodies in recognising, as did the ICJ, that VCLT Articles 31 and 32 had entered into custom underscored their applicability through the reference to customary rules of interpretation in DSU Article 3.2 to interpret WTO law. *US – Gasoline* stated that this 'direction reflects a measure of recognition that [WTO law] is not to be read in clinical isolation from public international law.'[41] It is the practice of the adjudicating bodies to refer to VCLT Articles 31 and 32, and other jurisprudence of the ICJ.[42]

Article 31 states that:

38 Appellate Body Report, *United States – Countervailing Duties on Certain Corrosion-Resistant Carbon Steel Flat Products from Germany*, WT/DS213/AB/R and Corr.1, adopted 19 December 2002, paras 61–62 (brackets suppressed). See also Appellate Body Report, *Argentina – Measures Affecting Imports of Footwear, Textiles, Apparel and Other Items*, WT/DS56/AB/R and Corr.1, adopted 22 April 1998, DSR, para 142, Appellate Body Report, *United States – Standards for Reformulated and Conventional Gasoline*, WT/DS2/AB/R, adopted 20 May 1996, p. 3 para 16 [hereinafter *US – Gasoline*].

39 *Libya* v *Chad*, ICJ Reports (1994), p. 4; at para 41.

40 Kuyper *supra* note 4, at 232. Lennard *supra* note 3, at 18. For an example of where VCLT can be applied to states not party to it, but because the VCLT moved into customary international, see *Asian Agricultural Products Ltd (AAPL)* v *Republic of Sri Lanka* (1992) 30 ILM 577, 594.

41 *US – Gasoline supra* note 38, at p. 17, p. 3 para 16.

42 Koskenniemi M and P Leino, 'Fragmentation of International Law? Postmodern Anxieties' (2002) 15 *Leiden Journal of International Law*, 553, 571. For a survey of the application of general rules of international law in the WTO see Lindross and Mehling *supra* note 2, at 866–873; Cameron J and K Gray, 'Principles of International Law in the WTO Dispute Settlement Body' (2001) 50 *International Comparative and Law Quarterly* 252–256; Lennard *supra* note 3.

> (1) A treaty shall be interpreted in good faith in accordance with the ordinary meaning to be given to the terms of the treaty in their context and in light of its object and purpose.
> (2) The context for the purpose of the interpretation of a treaty shall comprise, in addition to the text, including its preamble and annexes:
>
> > (a) an agreement relating to the treaty which was made between all the parties in connexion with the conclusion of the treaty;
> > (b) any instrument which was made by one or more parties in connection with the conclusion of the treaty and accepted by the other parties as an instrument related to the treaty.
>
> (3) There shall be taken into account, together with the context:
>
> > (a) any subsequent agreement between the parties regarding the interpretation of the treaty or the application of its provisions;
> > (b) any subsequent practice in the application of the treaty which establishes the agreement of the parties regarding its interpretation;
> > (c) any relevant rules of international law applicable in the relations between the parties.
>
> (4) A special meaning shall be given to a term if it is established that the parties so intended.

Article 32 states that:

> Recourse may be had to supplementary means of interpretation, including the preparatory work of the treaty and the circumstances of its conclusions, in order to confirm the meaning resulting from the application of article 31, or to determine the meaning when the interpretation according to article 31:
>
> > (a) leaves the meaning ambiguous or obscure; or
> > (b) leads to a result which is manifestly absurd or unreasonable.

Article 31 is titled the 'general rule of interpretation'. The use of the singular pronoun rule is said to be instructive of the fact that the Article contains only one rule of interpretation even though it is set out in four subsections.[43] There is no hierarchy among these subsections and Article 31(1) serves as a foundational rule that is expressed in the other three subsections.[44] Not all parts of Article 31(1) will be relevant when interpreting a treaty but, it should be read as one rule, in that when the different subsections are relevant they 'should be utilised'.[45] Article 32 is connected to Article 31(1) by the reference in Article 32 to Article 31(1). This is

43 Aust A, *Modern Treaty Law and Practice* (Cambridge: CUP, 2000) 186–187.
44 Ibid.
45 Ibid. See also, French D, 'Treaty Interpretation and the Incorporation of Extraneous Legal Rules' (2006) 55 *International and Comparative Law Quarterly*, 281, 301.

so that recourse can be had to Article 32 if Article 31(1) proves to be ineffectual to the interpreter. As discussed next, the Articles appear to lend themselves to ambiguity. The result may be the adjudicating bodies using treaty interpretation primarily to advance trade liberalisation. This is contrary to the suggestion of the ILC Study Group Report on Fragmentation to use treaty interpretation to offset the fragmented systems of international law, which is by interpreting WTO law in the context of international law.[46]

2.3.1 The problems with the Vienna Convention on the Law of Treaties Articles 31 and 32 as an account of fragmentation

The task of interpretation can be summed up as 'an exercise, which requires the court [judicial officials] to identify the meaning borne by the words in question in the particular context.'[47] This summation highlights the two approaches of literal or textual and teleological interpretation.

The textual approach is carried out according to the meanings of the text or words of the treaty.[48] Article 31, specifically paragraph (1) states that a treaty is interpreted in accordance with the 'ordinary' meanings to be given to the texts of the treaty. The teleological approach seeks to ascertain the meaning behind the text, which according to Article 31 is ascertained through determining the 'object and purpose' of the treaty. This approach is borne out in Article 32, which tells the interpreter if the ordinary meaning as according to Article 31 proves to be 'ambiguous', 'obscure' or leads to a result that is 'absurd' or 'unreasonable' then they can go beyond the texts of the treaty to find what should have been an ordinary meaning. The result is that Article 31 in embodying the textual approach tells the interpreter not to go beyond the words, but simultaneously as signifying the teleological approach, supported by Article 32 tells the interpreter to go beyond the texts. Article 31 appears as an attempt to combine the textual and teleological approaches. The obvious attraction is that the weakness of each approach is

46 ILC Study Group Report on Fragmentation *supra* note 1, at paras 170–171. *US – Gasoline supra* note 38, at p. 17, p. 3 para 16 which states that WTO law is 'not to be read in clinical isolation from public international law. For a similar assessment, see Simma and Pulkowski *supra* note 4 at 510. Trachtman J, 'Jurisdiction in WTO Dispute Settlement', in Yerxa R and B Wilson, *Key Issues in WTO Dispute Settlement: The First Ten Years* (Cambridge: CUP, 2005) 136–137 writes that 'When the Appellate Body said in *US – Gasoline* that WTO dispute settlement is not clinically separate from general international law, it did not mean that general international law is fully integrated into WTO dispute settlement. While it is correct to say that the WTO is a part of the international law system, it is an error of logic, a non-sequitur, to draw from this proposition the conclusion that general international law is applicable in WTO dispute settlement.'

47 *R* v *Secretary of State for the Environment, Transport and the Regions* ex parte Spath Holme Ltd [2001] 2 AC 349, 395 HL, 37. For a further discussion on statutory interpretation see Ingman T, *The English Legal Process* (Oxford: OUP, 2006) 140–189, esp. 140.

48 In statute interpretation for example see Lord Diplock's explanation of the literal approach in *Duport Steels Ltd* v *Sirs* [1980] 1 All ER 529, HL at 541. See also Ingman *supra* note 47, at 140–145.

cancelled by the strength in the other approach.[49] However, this could create an uncertain and ambiguous situation in that the interpreter is not to go beyond the texts to know the ordinary meanings of the text, but to find the ordinary meaning of the texts the interpreter is also instructed to go beyond the texts.

The Permanent Court of International Justice (PCIJ), the forerunner to the ICJ, *Advisory Opinion on the Interpretation of the Convention of 1919 Concerning Employment of Women During the Night* appears illustrative of the ambiguity of Article 31(1).[50] According to the Convention, women in industry were not to be employed at night, which was to protect them from exploitation.[51] What if those women were managers in the factories? The Convention was unclear as to the categories of women other than manual labourers that were not to be employed at night.[52] The Court held that the terms of Article 3 of the Convention 'gives rise to no difficulty; it is general in its terms and free from ambiguity or obscurity'.[53] The court at this point seems to be applying a textual approach. However, Judge Anzilloti stated in his dissenting opinion that 'If Article 3, according to the natural meanings of its terms, were really perfectly clear, it would be hardly admissible to endeavour to find an interpretation other than that which flows from the natural meaning of its terms.'[54]

Even if the textual approach to use the ordinary meanings of the texts is accepted as the method of interpretation, it still has to assume that the texts have one meaning and not another.[55] This highlights that the textual approach does not address the fact that to have a normal meaning already involves interpretation and ascertainment of that ordinary meaning and having a dispute proved that.[56] Interpreting Article 3 of the Convention using the textual approach would mean that female managers would be disadvantaged by a convention that was to protect women. Women could not work at night in factories but that would have included women who were managers. To get around this the Court noted that Article 3 could be 'interpreted in such a way as not to apply to women holding posts of

49 This may be similar to the Golden Rule in statute interpretation. See for example *Alder* v *George* [1964] 2 QB 7. See also Ingman *supra* note 57, at 145–150.

50 *Advisory Opinion on the Interpretation of the Convention of 1919 concerning Employment of Women during the Night*, 1932 PCIJ Series A/B No. 50.

51 Convention of 1919 Concerning Employment of Women During the Night, Article 2 (1) stated that,

'For the purpose of this Convention, the term night signifies a period of at least eleven consecutive hours, including the interval between ten o'clock in the evening and five o'clock in the morning.'

52 Article 3 of the Convention of 1919 Concerning Employment of Women During the Night stated that, 'Women without distinction of age shall not be employed during the night in any public or private industrial undertaking, or in any branch thereof, other than an undertaking in which only members of the same family are employed.'

53 ICJ Advisory Opinion on the Interpretation of the Convention of 1919 Concerning Employment of Women During the Night *supra* note 50, at p. 373.

54 Ibid, at para 1 (p. 383).

55 Koskenniemi M, *From Apology to Utopia: The Structure of the International Legal Argument*, (Helsinki: Finnish Lawyers' Publishing Company, 1989) 292.

56 Ibid.

supervision and management and not ordinarily engaged in manual work, as it is necessary to find some valid ground for interpreting the provision otherwise than in accordance with the natural sense of the words.'[57] Here the court seems to be parrying its own textual approach with a teleological approach.

The case illustrates the limitations of the textual approach but at the same time the dissenting opinion begs the question of whether a teleological approach should be allowed to take priority over what countries agree to in a treaty, as Anzilotti would prefer. 'It is doubtful whether the normal meaning approach has the 'overriding force attributed to it' because what is ordinary can not be ascertained independently of the intent of the parties to what ordinary is.[58] Put it another way, to find the ordinary meanings in a 'context is already to be and always thinking (and perceiving) with and within the norms, standards, definitions, routines, and understood goals that both define and are defined by that context.'[59] I am reminded here of Lewis Carroll's children's book *Through the Looking Glass* that chronicles the adventures of Alice in a wonderland of nursery rhyme characters.[60] The child and the adult 'can gain, potentially, radically different meanings' from reading Caroll's work which Carroll may have been 'well aware' of in 'trying to address two audiences' and even attempting to 'collapse the distinction'.[61] *Through the Looking Glass* can therefore not only serve as children's literature but also as Ward asserts it 'contain[s] passages of particular jurisprudential interest'.[62] The dialogue recounted below between Alice and Humpty Dumpty is telling of the 'symbolism of words' in that the interpreter in finding the meaning of a word has already created and chosen, not simply reflected, that meaning.[63]

> 'I don't know what you mean by "glory,"' Alice said.
>
> Humpty Dumpty smiled contemptuously. 'Of course you don't – till I tell you. I meant "there's a nice knock-down argument for you!"'
>
> 'But "glory" doesn't mean a "nice knock-down argument,"' Alice objected.
>
> 'When *I* use a word,' Humpty Dumpty said in a rather scornful tone, 'it means just what I choose it to mean – neither more nor less.'
>
> 'The question is,' said Alice, 'whether you *can* make words mean so many different things.'

57 ICJ Advisory Opinion on the Interpretation of the Convention of 1919 Concerning Employment of Women During the Night *supra* note 50, at p. 373.

58 Koskenniemi, *From Apology to Utopia: the Structure of the International Legal Argument supra* note 55, at 292–293.

59 Fish S, *Doing What Comes Naturally* (Oxford: OUP, 1989) 126–127.

60 Carroll L, *Through the Looking-Glass and What Alice Found There* (London: Penguin Group, [1872] 2003).

61 Ward I, *Law and Literature: Possibilities and Perspectives* (Cambridge: CUP, 1995) 102.

62 Ibid, at 101.

63 Ibid, at 104, and esp. Chapter 3 (Cases in the laws of reading) 43–56. See also Fish *supra* note 59, esp. chapter 'Fiss v Fish', 126. See also Prologue.

> 'The question is,' said Humpty Dumpty, 'which is to be Master – that's all.'[64]

In the dialogue, Alice claims not to know what Humpty Dumpty meant by glory. I do not think that this is an assertion not to know the meaning of the word glory. It appears more of an assertion that Alice did not understand or rather did not accept Humpty Dumpty's use of the word glory because already having her meaning of glory, she objects to his meaning of glory. There is no 'ordinary meaning' as VCLT Article 31 would direct the interpreter to find because her objection could have only been based on having a prior meaning of glory. Humpty Dumpty retorts to Alice's question as to whether words could mean many things that it was about who was Master, or put another way, the interpreter of the word. In this case, Humpty Dumpty was somehow assuming on his intellect that he was the master of the word and thereby glory meant what he wanted it to mean, which Alice was to unwittingly accept.[65] The dialogue 'represent[s] so much of the anxiety of contemporary legal discourse'[66] in that the interpreter gives meaning to text or words in the process of interpretation. The point is that even the rules of interpretation in Article 31 that were laid down as a constraint or a guide to interpretation, as we will discover below, are themselves open to interpretation.[67] Article 31 cannot constrain interpretation as the ILC Study Group Report on Fragmentation suggests through systemic interpretation by placing the specialised system in the context of international law. The WTO adjudicating bodies in addressing fragmentation would already be interpreting from their context, that is, their internal point of view of WTO law.

2.4 The interpretative approaches of the WTO adjudicating bodies

In asserting the primacy of the textual approach to interpret the texts of the WTO treaty in their ordinary meanings, the AB in *Japan – Alcoholic Beverages II* notes that VCLT Article 31 'provides that the words of the treaty form the foundation for the interpretative process' in that the process 'must be based above all upon the text of the treaty'.[68] The AB in *EC – Hormones* similarly stress that 'the fundamental rule of

64 Carroll *supra* note 60, at 87.
65 Carroll L, *supra* note 60.
66 Ward *supra* note 61, at 104.
67 Fish *supra* note 59, at 126–132.
68 Appellate Body Report, *Japan – Taxes on Alcoholic Beverages*, WT/DS8/AB/R, WT/DS10/AB/R, WT/DS11/AB/R, adopted 1 November 1996, para 105. See also Appellate Body Report, *EC Measures Concerning Meat and Meat Products (Hormones)*, WT/DS26/AB/R, WT/DS48/AB/R, adopted 13 February 1998, para 181 [hereinafter *EC – Hormones*]. Appellate Body Report, *India – Patent Protection for Pharmaceutical and Agricultural Chemical Products*, WT/DS50/AB/R, adopted 16 January 1998, DSR 1998:I, para 45. Appellate Body Report, *United States – Import Prohibition of Certain Shrimp and Shrimp Products*, WT/DS58/AB/R, adopted 6 November 1998, para 114, Appellate Body Report, *United States – Final Countervailing Duty Determination with Respect to Certain Softwood Lumber from Canada*, WT/DS257/AB/R, adopted 17 February 2004 (*US – Soft-Lumber IV*) paras 58–59.

treaty interpretation requires a treaty interpreter to read and interpret the words actually used by the agreement under examination, not the words the interpreter may feel should have been used.'[69] These cases may seem like a clear support for textual approach and a rejection of the teleological approach. However, the AB in *EC – Computer Equipment* in what appears as the teleological approach stated that the 'purpose of treaty interpretation under Article 31 of the Vienna Convention is to ascertain the common intentions of the parties. The common intentions cannot be ascertained on the basis of the subjective and unilaterally determined expectations of the parties to the treaty.'[70]

This approach is similar to the one noted earlier in the ICJ case *Qatar* v *Bahrain* where in trying deciding that the minutes of a meeting between the two states was a treaty, the Court referred to the common intentions of the parties to ascertain what was the meaning of a treaty.[71] The Court stated that 'whatever may have been the motives of each of the Parties, the Court can only confine itself to the actual terms of the Minutes as the expression of their common intentions, and to the interpretation of them which it has already given.'[72] This is supported by VCLT Article 34, as discussed above, whereby a state that is not party to a treaty cannot be held to have consented to that treaty. Both Qatar and Bahrain could be held party to the 'treaty' having agreed to the minutes.

Some have argued using the idea of 'common intention' that WTO law should account for external international law in that the common intention can be ascertained using Article 31 of the VCLT.[73] To do this, in part would require the adjudicating bodies to enforce external international law. In Pauwelyn's view, the adjudicating bodies 'would not create law but merely give effect to law created elsewhere by the WTO Member itself'.[74] I think there are a few problems with this idea. The first is that his view may have stretched the idea of common intention. Perhaps it means that the adjudicating bodies, in WTO law, and elsewhere, look for the basis of 'agreement' between parties as subject to a particular text, where one party disputes the legal force of that text as making them subject to it. The second as introduced in the Prologue (and will be further discussed in chapter 3) which affects the consequence of ascertaining the common intention, is that the adjudicating bodies do not have direct access to the external international law. They would have to figure out what that law is, its purpose and how it is to be complied with, but doing so from their internal point of view. That lends itself to the presumption that the adjudicating bodies do not start from a clean slate and in finding the

69 *EC – Hormones supra* note 68, at para 181.

70 Appellate Body Report, *European Communities – Customs Classification of Certain Computer Equipment*, WT/DS62/AB/R, WT/DS67/AB/R, WT/DS68/AB/R, adopted 22 June 1998, para 84.

71 Case Concerning Maritime Delimitation and Territorial Question (*Qatar* v *Bahrain*) (Jurisdiction and Admissibility), 1994 ICJ Rep. 112, para 22.

72 Ibid.

73 Pauwelyn, *Conflict of Norms supra* note 21, at 257. 'The Role of Public International Law in the WTO' *supra* note 4, at 575–576.

74 Pauwelyn, 'The Role of Public International Law in the WTO' *supra* note 4, at 566.

common intention of parties are already bringing a particular meaning (internal point of view) to bear as to what that is the common intention. The different approaches between *EC – Hormones* and *EC – Computer Equipment*, respectively textual and teleological is not necessarily about finding an 'objective' meaning as a preference of textual over a teleological approach. For whichever approach is used, as discussed earlier the interpreter in finding the 'objective' and ordinary meaning of words will already have and proceed from a particular meaning (see chapter 1).

EC – Computer Equipment and *Qatar* v *Bahrain* reflect the ambiguous nature of Article 31. An interpreter is not to go beyond the words of a treaty but in both cases in order to ascertain those meanings the interpreters assessed the intentions of the parties, as also provided for in Article 31. *EC – Computer* stated, that the application of Article 31 'usually allows a treaty interpreter to establish the meanings of a term' but if those terms prove less than clear then according to Article 32 the interpreter can look at 'preparatory work of the treaty and the circumstances at its conclusion'.[75] This *EC – Computer Equipment* noted was to fulfil the 'purpose of treaty interpretation [which] is to establish the *common* intention of the parties to the treaty.'[76] Though the adjudicating bodies appear as from *Japan – Alcoholic Beverages II* and *EC – Hormones* to use a textual approach according to Article 31, *EC – Computer Equipment* demonstrates that Article 31 lends itself to the opposite teleological approach of which the adjudicating bodies have also made use. The result as Margaret Young[77] describes is 'de-contextualised and arbitrary reasoning' by the adjudicating bodies as the Panel in *EC – Biotech*[78] recently demonstrates.

2.4.1 *The example of* EC – Biotech

EC – Biotech arises because the US challenged the consistency of the measures of several EC members that prohibited the marketing and sale of genetically modified (GM) products. This is after the EC had approved procedures for the import and marketing of these products in the EC. Previously, the EC suspended approval of the sale and import of GM products between 1998 and 2003 in the EC because some members did not want GM products directly imported into their markets.[79]

75 *EC – Computer supra* note 70, at para 86.

76 *EC – Computer supra* note 70, at para 92 (original italics).

77 Young M, 'The WTO's Use of Relevant Rules of International Law: An Analysis of the *Biotech* Case' (2007) 56 *International and Comparative Law Quarterly* 907, 922–925.

78 Panel Report, *European Communities – Measures Affecting the Approval and Marketing of Biotech Products*, WT/DS291/R, WT/DS292/R, Corr.1 and Add. 1, 2, 3, 4, 5, 6, 7, 8, 9, adopted 21 November 2006 [hereinafter *EC – Biotech*].

79 Denmark, Austria, UK, Belgium, Finland, Germany, Netherlands, Spain and Sweden called upon the EU Commission to prepare draft legislation for the liability that could arise from potential damages posed by the release and marketing of GM products. See 2194th Environmental Council Minutes (24/25 June, 1999) 14–15 at http://register.consilium.eu.int/. Also noted in *EC – Biotech supra* note 121, at para 7.474. For a brief overview of the background to the dispute see: Baughen S, *International Trade and the Protection of the Environment* (London: Routledge-Cavendish, 2007) 73–77. Cheyne I, 'Life after the WTO Biotech Products Panel Report' (2008) 10 *Environmental Law Review* 52–64.

During this time the EC adopted legislation requiring the labelling and traceability of GM products. GM products were allowed in the EC market when the legislation came into force in April 2004.[80]

The Panel in *EC – Biotech* according to Article 31(1) in construing the 'ordinary' meaning of the texts in Annex A of the Agreement on Sanitary and Phytosanitary Measures (SPS Agreement) appears to have expanded the interpretations of the nature of risks in the SPS Agreement. I return to this point in discussing the precautionary principle as a specific example of the interaction between WTO law and external law (see chapter 5). Here I focus on illustrating the Panel's use of the ambiguous Article 31(1) that has the potential to lead to an over-inclusiveness of external law to define the meaning of the texts of the WTO treaty.[81] The SPS Agreement provides a detailed regime to regulate measures within WTO law to protect human, animal or plant life or health against risk from the spread of diseases. The regulation is to ensure that SPS measures are aimed at protection against risk from disease and not for protectionism, contrary to the WTO treaty. SPS measures must be 'necessary for the protection of human, animal or plant life or health' (see chapter 5).

The *EC – Biotech* Panel in using Article 31 appears to turn to paragraph (1) as an alternative to paragraph (3)(c) that an interpreter should take into account any relevant rules of international law applicable in the relations between the parties. The Panel was deciding whether to classify the EC measure as to the 'ordinary' meanings of the terms in Annex A of the SPS Agreement. The Panel declined the use of Article 31(3)(c) because it could already provide for the use of external law that did not bind all parties of the WTO.[82] This would contravene Article 34 as discussed earlier in that a state is not bound by the terms of a treaty to which it has not consented to. Moreover, Article 31(3)(c) presents certain difficulties and ambiguities as to the term 'parties' and who is bound to the law considering that a state is only bound to a rule of international law it has consented to.[83] Some commentators read parties to mean parties to a dispute.[84] This suggests that it would be 'sufficient' that parties to a dispute, for example over an environmental treaty, are parties to that environmental treaty, with 'no need for all WTO Members to meet that criterion'.[85] The implication of this approach, *prima facie*, is that it opens WTO

80 The legislation was adopted and came into force in April 2004 as Regulation (EC) 1829/2003 and 1830/2003 of the European Parliament and the European Council.

81 See Peel J, 'A GMO by Any Other Name . . . Might Be an SPS Risk!: Implications of Expanding the Scope of the WTO Sanitary and Phytosanitary Measures Agreement' (2006) 17 *The European Journal of International Law* 1009. Young *supra* note 77, at esp. 922–925.

82 *EC – Biotech supra* note 68, at para 7.92. See Meltzer J, 'Interpreting the WTO Agreements – A Commentary on Professor Pauwelyn's Approach' (2004) 25 *Michigan Journal of International Law* 917–922. *Contra* Pauwelyn J, 'Reply to Joshua Meltzer' (2004) 25 *Michigan Journal of International Law* 924–926. See also Lennard *supra* note 3, at 35–39.

83 Meltzer *supra* note 82. Marceau *supra* note 4, at 123–128. Lennard *supra* note 3, at 35–38.

84 Palmeter D and P Mavroidis *supra* note 4, at 411. *Less categorically* Marceau *supra* note 4, at 125.

85 Lennard *supra* note 3, at 36. See also Meltzer *supra* note 82, at 921–922.

law to external law in that the adjudicating bodies take account of applicable law between parties in the dispute. However, as the law is only between the parties the approach would 'effectively limit' the scope of reasoning by the adjudicating bodies to the parties to the dispute.[86] This reading of parties also diminishes the 'de facto' precedential role of the adjudicating bodies' reports and affects the rights and obligations of WTO Members in that the same WTO rules may have different meanings as between different WTO Members party to different non-WTO treaties.[87]

The other reading of parties is that it refers to parties to the WTO agreement, especially give that Article 2(1)(g) of the Vienna Convention states that a party is a 'State which has consented to be bound by the treaty and for which the treaty is in force'.[88] This has the advantage of acknowledging that the WTO is part of international law, in that countries are bound by the rules they consent to.[89] However, it then limits the ability of WTO law to 'reflect and respond' to international law if parties refers to 'all' parties of the WTO having to be a party of a piece of international law for it to be applicable in WTO law.[90] Article 31(3)(c) is somewhat ambiguous lending itself two disparate readings. However, both readings as parties to the dispute and parties to the WTO seem to support the use of external law as applicable law in WTO law. It is a matter of the degree to which external law becomes applicable law in WTO law. The *EC – Biotech* Panel appears to have reasoned this in that Article 31(3)(c) would require an adjudicating body to use external law as the 'relevant rules of international law between parties' whereas Article 31(1) would see the application of external law insofar as to 'shine a light' on the ordinary meaning of the words of the treaty.[91]

The Panel claimed its approach regarding Article 31(1) was consistent with *US – Shrimp* that stated, 'the mere fact that one or more disputing parties are not parties to a convention does not necessarily mean that a convention cannot shed light on the meaning and scope of a treaty to be interpreted.'[92] However, this is questionable, as the AB in *US – Shrimp* did not refer to specific sections of Article 31 in interpreting the term of 'exhaustible natural resources'. *US – Shrimp* appears as I expressed earlier to be consistent with the status of Article 31 as a general rule rather than rules.[93] Moreover, the AB *US – Shrimp* though appearing to use a textual approach, also noted that a 'teleological interpretation should consider the provision itself being interpreted, not the whole of the WTO Agreement'.[94] Though not the stated approach, which *EC – Biotech* refers to in its application of

86 Meltzer *supra* note 82, at 921.

87 Lennard *supra* note 3, at 39. Meltzer *supra* note 82, at 921–922.

88 Lennard *supra* note 3, at 36. Pauwelyn, *Conflict of Norms supra* note 21, at 257.

89 Meltzer *supra* note 82, at 920.

90 Ibid.

91 *EC – Biotech supra note* 78, at para 7.95.

92 Ibid. See also *US – Shrimp supra note* 68, at paras 157–158.

93 Young *supra* note 77, at 920.

94 *US – Shrimp supra* note 68, at para 117.

US – Shrimp, this approach appears in line with what *EC – Biotech* does as I discuss below.

The Panel in categorising whether the EC SPS fell within the SPS Agreement stated that 'nothing in Annex A' of the agreement, which defines the scope of an SPS measure 'indicates that the potential risk to animal or plant life or health must necessarily be direct or immediate result of e.g., the spread of pest.'[95] The result is that in the 'context' of GM products, their direct potential as pests[96] and possible pests effects[97] come under the review of the SPS Agreement.[98] The EC argued that an SPS measure to reduce potential risk from GM products was not related to the spread of pests.[99] The EC stated that the term pests was defined according to the International Plant Protection Convention (IPPC) as 'any species, strain or biotype of plant, animal or pathogenic agent injurious to plant or plant products'.[100] The IPPC is listed in the SPS Agreement as a 'relevant international organisation' to which Members can harmonise their SPS measures.[101]

However, the *EC – Biotech* Panel, based on this causal relationship between pests and potential risks, construed a broad definition of pests drawing on external material according to Article 31. The Panel did not find for the IPCC definition and using the 'ordinary' meaning of the word pests according to Article 31 found for a dictionary definition of pests as 'troublesome, annoying or destructive person, animal or thing'.[102] This definition is broader than the narrow meaning of pests in the IPPC. According to the Panel, in the 'context of the SPS Agreement the term pests should be understood as referring to an animal or plant which is destructive, or causes harm to health or other animals, plants or humans, or other harm, or a troublesome or annoying animal or plant.'[103]

Pests therefore did not have to be injurious as in the IPPC but merely troublesome or annoying according to the definition of pests by the Panel construed using Article 31 to look for the ordinary meanings of the texts of the WTO treaty. GM products could be considered pests under the SPS Agreement and regulated to the disciplines of the SPS Agreement not because there were potential risks to human, animal or plant life or health but troublesome. For example, if a GM plant was growing somewhere undesired.[104] This is one example of the Panel in *EC – Biotech* using Article 31 to construct the 'ordinary' meanings of texts of the treaty.[105]

95 *EC – Biotech supra* note 78, at para 7.226.

96 For example, GM crops could escape and grow in areas to affect native plant life. See *EC – Biotech supra* note 78, at para 7.231. See also Peel *supra* note 81, at 1022–1023.

97 For example, there could be gene transfer to other pants that can reduce biodiversity. See *EC – Biotech supra* note 78, at para 7.231. See also Peel *supra* note 81, at 1022–1023.

98 Peel *supra* note 81, at 1022–1023. See chapter 5 for further discussion.

99 *EC – Biotech supra* note 78, at para 7.187.

100 International Plant Protection Convention (IPPC). See < https://www.ippc.int/IPP/En/default.jsp>

101 Preamble SPS Agreement.

102 *EC – Biotech supra* note 78, at para 7.241.

103 *EC – Biotech supra* note 78, at para 7.240. See also para 7.238.

104 Young *supra* note 77, at 923. For further discussion see chapter 5.

105 See Young *supra* note 77, at 922–925 for further discussion of other examples.

EC – Biotech illustrates two things that are relevant to the discussion here on treaty interpretation as a means to address fragmentation. Firstly, as I stated at the beginning of this chapter, though the ILC Study Group Report on Fragmentation argues that treaty interpretation provides tools to address fragmentation, it appears somewhat ineffectual concerning WTO law. The ILC Study Group Report on Fragmentation criticises *EC – Biotech* for not using other relevant treaties through Article 31(3)(c) because potentially the Panel's approach 'would be the isolation of multilateral agreements as islands permitting no reference *inter se* in their application'.[106] Further the limitations I discussed above regarding the two different textual meanings of Article 31(3)(c) may point to a problem with the VCLT rules on treaty interpretation in that the VCLT were signed in 1969. Since then international law has become more fragmented with the proliferation of varying specialised systems and as a result the VCLT 'may no longer provide adequate guidance to the [WTO adjudicating bodies] on how to deal with the interface between large multilateral treaty regimes and other international law rules.'[107] Secondly, from the discussion above I can also argue that the ambiguous nature of the Article 31 itself is what allowed the Panel to make use of paragraph (1) and not (3)(c). Under paragraph (1) as the Panel notes, it is not required to take account of external law, but for purposes of giving the 'ordinary' meaning of the texts of a treaty. Whereas under paragraph (3)(c) the Panel would have to use external law 'applicable as between the parties' which would require the WTO members in dispute to have consented to the external law, according to Article 34. Since Article 31 does not require the interpreter to refer to each paragraph the Panel may then by-pass paragraph (3)(c) and choose paragraph (1) so as to use external material on the grounds of 'informative' purposes to ascertain the ordinary meanings of the texts of the WTO treaty.

As it appears in *EC – Biotech*, the adjudicating bodies potentially can construe treaty interpretation tools to use external law, not for systemic integration of WTO law into international law as the ILC Study Group Report on Fragmentation suggests, but in a 'highly selective results-oriented way'[108] for constructing WTO law. It appears that the VCLT and other rules of treaty interpretation I examined earlier have some difficulty in addressing the interaction between WTO law and external law. The 'more mature and sophisticated the WTO gets, the more it becomes apparent that general international law is very rudimentary and sometimes outdated.'[109] As the conclusion of the ILC Study Group Report on

106 ILC Study Group Report on Fragmentation *supra* note 1, at para 471.

107 Meltzer *supra* note 82, at 922–923. Henckels *supra* note 20.

108 Greenwald J, 'WTO Dispute Settlement: An Exercise in Trade law Legislation?' (2003) 6(1) *Journal of International Economic Law*, 113–124, 119. See 118–120 for discussion of *EC – Bed Linen* [Appellate Body Report, *European Communities – Anti-Dumping Duties on Imports of Cotton-Type Bed Linen from India*, WT/DS141/AB/R, adopted 12 March 2001] to which Greenwald was attributing this description of how the adjudicating body went about finding the 'ordinary meaning' of the word 'comparable'.

109 Pauwelyn, *Remarks at the Fourth Annual WTO Conference supra* note 25, at 494. See also Meltzer *supra* note 82, at 922. Henckels *supra* note 20.

Fragmentation concedes, 'in general the VCLT gives insufficient recognition to special types of treaties and the special rules that might go to interpret and apply them. More work seems necessary here.'[110]

2.5 Conclusion

This chapter showed that no single rule whether it be *lex posterior*, *lex specialis* or treaty interpretation provides a complete, single or simple means to address fragmentation in telling us how and which law would prevail in the event of an overlap or conflict, between different legal systems. The matter is not merely a technically straightforward act of treaty interpretation. We found that the WTO adjudicating bodies apply procedural and general rules of international law. This is an indication that the WTO is part of general international law, which accounts for the intra-systemic relationship between WTO law and general international law. However, we illustrated that general rules such as treaty interpretation rules, *lex specialis* and certain basic rules on the issue of priority of treaties such as *lex posterior* do not appear entirely satisfactory in accounting for and addressing fragmentation. The WTO is not impermeable to external international law but the extent that such law may be applicable in the WTO system appears not to be a foregone conclusion. The question as this chapter demonstrated cannot be answered using the general rules for systemic interpretation as basis to cohere the competing legal rationalities of the international legal system. In the next chapter, I explore how we can think about the inter-systemic interaction between WTO and external international law, introducing key elements to form a legal theory of WTO law.

110 ILC Study Group Report on Fragmentation *supra* note 1, at para 493, p. 251.

3 The constrained openness of WTO law

3.0 Introduction

In this chapter, the aim is to flesh out the second part of a theory of WTO law having in chapter 1 set out the first part by defining WTO law as the practice of the adjudicating bodies. Further to our discussion on fragmentation in chapters 1 and 2, where I showed that the rationality of treaty interpretation might prove somewhat inadequate to address fragmentation, the purpose of this chapter is to advance another way in which we can begin to think about fragmentation. More specifically the question I ask is how might we think about the interaction between WTO and external international law in the absence of an overarching hierarchical rationality. In section 3.1, I put forward operational closure as an idea on which to continue to build a theory of WTO law, *constrained openness*. In section 3.2, I illustrate the commitment that the adjudicating bodies share to the internal point of view as discussed in chapter 1. This demonstrates the basis for the argument that external international law is not directly incorporated into but *(re)constructed* into WTO law as discussed in section 3.2.1. This has important implications for how we can conceptualise our understanding of how WTO law interacts with law outside of its immediate parameters as WTO law, and how the attendant participants to that external law may influence WTO law. Some trade lawyers for example, using the metaphor of gateways, argue the contrary that there are avenues or openings in WTO law, which can facilitate what appears as the direct *incorporation* of non-trade norms into WTO law. The difference between constrained openness and gateways is in understanding the way in which external international law is situated in WTO law. The gateway metaphor appears to be built on the assumption that the external law maintains its distinctive and differentiated norms from its systems of law in becoming part of WTO law. That way external law can make WTO law more legitimate as WTO law becomes more considerate of non-trade norms, whereas constrained openness argues that the external international law loses its character as a differentiated non-trade norm, which made it attractive to the gateway proponents in the first place, because the external law is (re)constructed to meet the purpose of WTO law as a norm of WTO law. If external international law is to influence WTO law, this leads to considerations of indirect regulation, which induces actions rather than commands. Constrained openness submits that although fragmented legal systems are capable of incorporating other external norms, this is only possible through their interpretative membrane with the implication that the legal system will develop its own (subjective) understanding of what the external norm entails. It is about recognising that direct regulation of one system by another is almost if not impossible, as thematically explored in the Prologue in that there is no single idea or system to render differing systems commensurate.

In section 3.2.2, I examine conceptual debates between Petersmann and Alston about the incorporation of external international law, human rights, into WTO law, in order to show how the current arguments are being played out in the trade law scholarship.[1] This demonstrates the inadequacies of the gateways metaphor to properly account for fragmentation, in that it misses the implications of the epistemological break between an external norm moving from its own legal system into another legal system. The original norm is not the same as what is (re)constructed in the other system. Having set out constrained openness as a theory of WTO law, in section 3.3, I re-examine fragmentation describing it as *nomos*, in that each fragmented system of international law inhabits its 'own' normative universe. I extend this argument by examining fragmentation as a division of labour, which can be characterised as a process of differentiation and the rise of a technical expert tied to each fragmented system. Building on the confluence of these ideas, I discuss how a fragmented specialised system of international law could potentially interact with another fragmented specialised system of international law, given the functional non-hierarchal basis of these differentiated systems. Therefore, in section 3.4, I surmise (with an idea I return to in chapter 6) that if external international law is to influence WTO law it has to be by way of strategic indirect political influence.

3.1 The continuation of building a theory of WTO law

In chapter 1, I situated the debate about the interaction between WTO and external international law in the context of fragmentation, defining WTO law as the practice of the adjudicating bodies. At that juncture, I made clear that this was only one part of the attempt to build a theory of WTO law, as I had a method to define WTO law but lacked conceptual tools to assess what was defined as WTO law. Here I provide those tools by advancing operational closure as an explanation of how fragmented systems of international law interaction.

What is operational closure? Operationally closed systems can be understood as 'cognitively open in that they can observe other systems and their environment, and be indirectly affected by them. However, they are normatively [operationally] closed in that they recognise no norms other than those which they produce as being valid.'[2] The idea is that a system produces its own 'constructs of

1 In chapter 4, I discuss how the debate is being played out and in chapter 6, assessing the practice of the adjudicating bodies (WTO law), I demonstrate how the debate is being played out.

2 Black: 'Constitutionalising Self-Regulation' (1996) 59(1) *Modern Law Review* 24, 44; 'Critical Reflections on Regulation' (2002) 27 *Australian Journal of Legal Philosophy* 1, 5.

reality'[3] based on its coding and in law that would be illegal/legal. The basis of validity is 'solely on legal norms' inside the legal system and not external norms.[4] For example, the code broadly for economics would be profit/loss or science true/false.[5] The norms a system produces do not depend on an external source for validation.[6] The law creates its own norm-creating structure for the identification and creation of norms. Recursively, law is law because it is law.[7] The operation of the system is not imposed from outside but from inside the system, produced as a matter of 'interplay of the components of the system.'[8] Systems are therefore self-reproducing and evolve according to their internal point of view, that is, the systems 'definition of themselves and their function.'[9] We can then distinguish its operation from that of the environment, that is, everything outside the system and thus other systems.[10] This also lends to a system's differentiation in that through its code it can decide, for example, with law what is legal and what is illegal. Only the law can do that. In its operations a system reproduces itself, making it self-referential.[11] A system can observe its environment but only cognises that environment by reference to its own operations as a system. This however does not mean that systems do not communicate with each other.[12] This does not mean that a system is isolated, hermetically sealed, exists in a vacuum or does not respond to pressure from the environment or from within the system itself.[13] What it marks is a

3 See Teubner G, 'How Law Thinks: Toward A Constructivist Epistemology of Law' (1989) 23(5) *Law and Society Review*, 727, 742 for discussion on how law produces legal acts as its elements, legal rules as its structures and legal constructs of reality. Also Rasch, W *Sovereignty and its Discontents* (London: Birkbeck Law Press, 2004) 42–43.

4 Black 'Constitutionalising Self-Regulation' *supra* note 2, at, 44. Teubner *supra* note 3. See also Hart H L A, *The Concept of Law* (Oxford: Clarendon Press, 1961) 88–91, 102–103, 115–116, 242–243 on the internal point of view. See Cover R, 'Foreword: Nomos and Narrative', (1983) 97(4) *Harvard Law Review* 4, 41–46 discussing that 'interpretation is transformed into legal meaning when there is commitment to those positions'.

5 Beckett J, 'Conflicting Orders: How Peace is Waged' (2007) 20(1) *Leiden Journal of International Law* 281–319, 310. Rasch *supra* note 3.

6 Teubner wrote Hart's secondary norms are a good example of self-reference because through these secondary norms the law 'produces an internal self-description'. See Teubner G (ed) *Autopoietic Law: A New Approach to Law and Society* (Berlin: Walter de Gruyter & Co., 1988) 224; *Law as an Autopoietic System* (Oxford: Blackwell Publishers, 1993) 10, 19–20, 39–41.

7 For a similar point, see Cover *supra* note 4, at 18–25 (section on The Thickness of Law).

8 Teubner, *Law as an Autopoietic System supra* note 6, at 20; Black, 'Constitutionalising Self-Regulation' *supra* note 2.

9 Black 'Constitutionalising Self-Regulation' *supra* note 2, at 44; Teubner, *Law as an Autopoietic System supra* note 6, at 47–53.

10 Luhmann Luhmann N, 'Law as a Social System' (1989) 83 *Northwestern University Law Review*, 136, 139–141; 'Teubner 'How Law Thinks' *supra* note 3 at, 742–743; Teubner *Law as an Autopoietic System supra* note 6, at 13–24, 25–46; Black 'Constitutionalising Self-Regulation' *supra* note 2.

11 Ibid.

12 King argues that critics interpret or perhaps it is better expressed that they misinterpret operational closure to mean that professionals from different disciplines are not able to understand each other. See King M, 'The Construction and Demolition of the Luhmann Heresy' (2001) 12 *Law and Critique* 1, 20.

13 Ziegert K A, 'The Thick Description of Law: An Introduction to Niklas Luhmann's Theory of

distinction between a system and the environment.[14] A system communicates with its external environment but the communication is only as a reference to itself. The external environment is mediated by the internal point of view. A system can learn from the environment around it, but based on its own operations as a system. This should not be confused with self-containedness[15] or a closure that suggests that communication is limited to the point of being shut off from other systems. What I am suggesting here is a system reproduces itself by focusing on its operations that it has exclusive access to creating 'its elements with its own elements'. In other words, systems 'cannot but bring into play their own operations'.[16] A system cannot communicate directly with its environment and as a corollary other systems 'but it can and must necessarily communicate about the environment'[17] of which it belongs. When a system uses norms from another system, it 'simply' has not 'reached out' of its own system into the other system[18] as a matter of seeing the norm from a 'different angle'.[19] Norms do not come into a system, 'bearing [a] label',[20] of construction. A system observes external norms as noise or irritations until it reconstructs them according to its code or its internal point of view. The external norms may then take on a different meaning from where they originally came.[21] The internal construction is the system's only reality and the external norm will continue to exist in the external environment effectively unaffected by the construction of the norm in the system. The external norm the system will use is an observation of that external norm made intelligible and valid according to the system's internal point of view. It explains how we can have multiple systems understanding the same reality, or same things, in apparently different and even competing ways.

A system has no direct access to another system, but only its observation and subsequent construction of that observation. There is 'no direct cognitive access to reality. There are only competing discourses with different constructions of reality.'[22]

Operatively Closed Systems,' in Banakar R and M Travers (eds) *An Introduction to Law and Social Theory* (Oxford: Hart Publishing, 2002) 60–61. Luhmann N, *Law as a Social System*, trans. K Ziegert (Oxford: OUP, 2004) 80; Black *supra* note 2; Teubner 'How Law Thinks' *supra* note 3, at 742–743; Teubner *Law as an Autopoietic System supra* note 6, at 13–24, 25–46, 84; Simma B and D Pulkowski, 'Of Planets and the Universe: Self-Contained Regimes in International Law' (2006) 17 *European Journal of International Law*, 483, 492.

14 Luhmann, *Law as a Social System*, trans. K Ziegert *supra* note 13, at 80.

15 For a discussion on the concept of self-contained see Simma B, 'Self-Contained Regimes', (1985) XVI *Netherlands Yearbook of International Law* 111; For a discussion of the concept regarding the WTO, see Hu J, 'The Role of International Law in the Development of WTO Law' (2004) 7 *Journal of International Economic Law* 143–167.

16 Ziegert *supra* note 13, at 61.

17 Luhmann N, 'The Unity of the Legal System', in Teubner (ed) *Autopoietic Law: A New Approach to Law and Society* (Berlin: Walter de Gruyter & Co., 1988).

18 Black, 'Constitutionalising Self-Regulation' *supra* note 2, at 45. Beckett 'Conflicting Orders: How Peace is Waged' *supra* note 5, at 310.

19 Teubner, 'How Law Thinks' *supra* note 3, at 749.

20 Ibid.

21 Ibid.

22 Ibid, 743.

That means that each system is sovereign over its particular and distinct area but 'none is sovereign over the whole [as] [t]here is no pope or emperor . . . that can subordinate the codes of one system to another.'[23] Put differently, 'No system can declare its world view as the only view and as binding on all others.'[24] Operationally closed systems 'construct their own perceptual apparatus'.[25] A system cannot stand outside of itself[26] and it is only through experiences and constructions of the environment based on its own binary code (what is/what is not part of the system) that a system cognises[27] or recognises other norms and can essentially learn. The actions of a system thus only produce the action of that system and nothing else.[28] Different systems using their own operations, that is, their vocabulary, meanings, interests, values, as a basis will interpret or are open to the world from that basis. There is no direct access to a pre-theoretical reality.[29] The system can be cognitively open from a normative basis. This can be used to explain the idea that the varying specialists see the world around them differently.[30] It also explains why there are contested rationalities in that we essentially make political choices in deciding which rationality to use to see the world, based on the normative framework we choose to inhabit. In effect each legal community even if it appears to speak with one voice is a coalition of differing voices, but all having a common characteristic that allow them to bear the label of that community. The effects of the fragmentation of international law as the growth of varying specialist affects the ability of international lawyers to share a common community, a church of reason. Instead, experts are trapped in, and, by their field, which we can understand as the operations of their systems. As discussed in the preceding sections, I can surmise that this operational closure is occurring on three levels. The first is law as a field separate and distinct from other fields. Secondly, within law, further distinctions to create more specialist fields, such as WTO law. Thirdly, within those fields even further distinctions. The next step is to discuss the implications of understanding WTO

23 Rasch *supra* note 3, at 8, 42–44 discussing Luhmann.

24 Black: 'Constitutionalising Self-Regulation' *supra* note, at 45; 'Critical Reflections on Regulation' *supra* note 2, at 7. Teubner *Law as an Autopoietic System supra* note 6, at 32–34.

25 Black, 'Critical Reflections on Regulation' *supra* note 2, at 5.

26 For a good exposition on this point of not being able to stand outside one's culture using the work of R Cover and M Bakhtin to argue for pluralism and what Bakhtin calls a heteroglossia, meaning that there are multiple narratives, see Mullender R, 'Two Nomoi and a Clash of Narratives: The Story of the United Kingdom and the European Union' (2006) 3 *Issues in Legal Scholarship* 9, 1–13. See also Morris P (ed) *The Bakhtin Reader* (London: Arnold Publishers, 1994); Dolin K, *Fiction and the Law: Legal Discourse in Victorian and Modernist Literature* (Cambridge: CUP, 1999) 1–20. For further discussion see the Prologue.

27 Black, 'Critical Reflections on Regulation' *supra* note 2, at 5. Teubner *Law as an Autopoietic System supra* note 6, at 84–85.

28 Teubner *Law as an Autopoietic System supra* note 6, at 84–85.

29 See Teubner 'How Law Thinks' *supra* note 3; Camus A, *The Rebel* (London: Penguin Group, [1951] (2000) 230–235.

30 See for example: Teubner *supra* note 3 and 6. Rasch *supra* note 3. Beckett *supra* note 5. Black 'Constitutionalising Self Regulation' *supra* note 2.

law as constructing its own reality from the basis of its own operations. This forms the basis of my theory of WTO law, *constrained openness*. In the next section I start this discussion by demonstrating the commitment to an internal point of view, as necessary to maintain the practice of the adjudicating bodies as WTO law.

3.2 The internal point of view of the WTO adjudicating bodies

Considering WTO law, there is a sense that not only is there a shared commitment to the system but importantly a shared internal point of view among the adjudicating bodies, especially the Appellate Body which can review and issue final rulings after earlier Panel proceedings. It is straightforward to see the WTO as a 'classic product of the Westphalian order' emerging from a series of long and hard fought negotiations and compromises that are part of the politics of diplomacy.[31] Article 3.2 of the Dispute Settlement Understanding (DSU) appears to embody those comprises in placing the state at the centre of the WTO in that the adjudicating bodies cannot alter the negotiated rights of Members. However, this view of the WTO does not capture the autonomous nature of the adjudicating bodies, which has been formally codified in DSU Articles 16.4, 17.14 and 23.[32] Taken together I think that these DSU articles stipulate two important things that underline the autonomous nature of WTO law, in that Members are not permitted outside the WTO legal system to address a dispute on WTO law. Firstly, Members shall only have redress to address grievances about WTO law within the DSU as managed by the Dispute Settlement Body (DSB). Secondly, the reports (judgements) of the adjudicating bodies (Panel and Appellate Body) are adopted by the DSB, that is, officially binding on the parties to that dispute, unless the DSB decided by consensus not to adopt the report. The internal point of view of the adjudicating bodies is further informed by the practice of the adjudicating bodies.[33] The first chairman of the Appellate Body Julio Lacarte notes that,

> The Appellate Body has been described as unflinching in its rulings. I believe this to be the case. We are well aware that none of our rulings is likely to be greeted with universal approval; but our function is another: to be *independent*, impartial and objective at all times. I believe this also to have been the case.[34]

Former Appellate Body Member, Claus-Dieter Ehlermann confirms this position, stating that at the start of the Appellate Body, they were 'determined to contribute

31 See Perez O, 'Purity Lost: The Paradoxical Face of the New Transnational Legal Body' (2007) 33(1) *Brooklyn Journal of International Law* 1–58, 17–18. For example Jackson, *The World Trade Organisation: Constitution and Jurisprudence* (London: Cassell Imprint, 1998). Also see Prologue for further discussion.

32 Perez *supra* note 31.

33 See chapters 5 and 6 for examples and concrete discussion of the practice of adjudicating bodies.

34 Ehlermann C, 'Reflections on the Appellate Body of the WTO' (2003) 6(3) *Journal of International Economic Law* 695–708, 696. My emphasis in italics.

to the building of a new *independent* institution.'[35] It is notable from the outset that the WTO adjudicating bodies are not only aware of their autonomous nature but are somewhat single-minded in their approach to institutionalise that commitment to their expert specialisation of WTO law as differentiated from other systems of international law. This underwrites the internal point of view that appears to emerge in WTO law. As Lacarte states:

> I don't think that any one of us [as Members of the Adjudicating Body] concerned himself to what would be the public opinion repercussions of what our rulings could lead to. We just went ahead and ruled in *terms of our own view*, of our own earnest and hopefully very honest approach and analysis of the subject matter that was submitted to us.[36]

This shows us the commitment of the WTO adjudicating bodies to their internal point of view, and explains the Appellate Body's 'attitude towards consensus as opposed to voting and individual opinions, be they dissenting or concurrent.'[37] In order to ensure this, the Appellate Body emphasised a collegiate system of dispute settlement and even where dissent was allowed, it was done anonymously.[38] At the committee level of the WTO, the Agreement on Sanitary and Phytosanitary Measures (SPS) Committee, Joanne Scott argues that the Committee presents a picture of the WTO as less to do with the adversarial politics and the pursuit of self-interests by states, but based on cooperation, peer review and an exchange of information.[39] Further, both the AB and the SPS Committee, by reference to their working procedures function on a basis of consensus, which underlines the internal point of view and the rule of recognition as the practice of the adjudicating bodies.[40]

35 Ibid.

36 *American Society of International Law* 'Proceedings of the 99th Annual Meeting of the American Society of International Law: New World Order or a World in Disorder? Testing the Limits of International Law', WTO Appellate Body Roundtable, 175–187, 177. My emphasis in italics.

37 Elhermann *supra* note 34, at 696.

38 See DSU Art 17.11 which states: 'Opinions expressed in the Appellate Body report by individuals serving on the Appellate Body shall be anonymous.' In fact, there have been very few cases with an anonymous dissenting view in WTO law so far, especially compared to the ICJ where dissenting opinions are authored, and sometimes form their own *ratio* in the cases. Even where there is dissent the dissenting AB member seems generally to be pains to stay close to the majority view, and that of the internal point of view. Dissent is usually expressed as 'concurring' or 'separate' observations. For a good overview of the dissenting views in the practice of WTO law see, Flett J, 'Collective intelligence and the possibility of dissent: anonymous individual opinions in WTO jurisprudence' (2010) 13(4) *Journal of International Economic Law* 286–320. He argues (and more in line with the view here) that adjudicating body members should tend to find 'common ground.' *Contra*, see Lewis M, 'The Lack of Dissent in WTO Dispute Settlement' (2006) 9(4) *Journal of International Economic Law* 895–931 for a view that more dissenting opinions should be expressed in WTO law.

39 Scott J, *Commentary on the Sanitary and Phytosanitary Measures Agreement* (Oxford: OUP, 2007) 49–60.

40 For example Working Procedures for Appellate Review WT/AB/WP/5 (4 Jan. 2005). Part 1, 3(2).

Moreover, the adjudicating bodies refer to themselves quoting their previous decisions as authority to a current decision, though there is no official precedent in WTO law.[41] This is an indication of a high degree of self-reference, which has the effect of not only securing an internal, but also to a large degree a single or as far as possible a homogeneous point of view. However, there appears to be division on the merits of the consensus approach to decision making by the adjudicating bodies, which stresses a single internal point of view. Donald MacRae argues that the practice of the International Tribunal of Law of the Seas and the International Court of Justice, which permits judicial officials to write separate, and dissenting opinions is 'unfavourable' as to the WTO consensus approach.[42] Conversely, John Greenwald argues that 'one of the troubling aspects of WTO panel and Appellate Body decision-making has been the general absence of dissent.'[43] Ehlermann, as a former Appellate Body Member, defends the consensus approach on the basis that critics such as Greenwald could be underestimating the 'negative consequences of individual opinions' in maintaining consensus.[44] Lacarte, another former Appellate Body Member argues that 'at the Appellate Body, we came down to [the] formula of consensus . . .'[45] This is supported by Article 3.2 of the Working Procedures for Appellate Review which notes that the 'Appellate Body and its divisions shall make every effort to take their decisions by *consensus*.' These procedures according to DSU Article 17.9 are drawn up by the 'Appellate Body in consultation with the Chairman of the DSB [Dispute Settlement Body] and the Director-General, and communicated to the Members for their information'. A similar analysis arises if we are to look at the SPS Committee. SPS Agreement Article 12:1 directs the Committee to 'reach its decisions by consensus.' The Appellate Body not only functions on consensus but it sets out the rules that direct its operations. Therefore, not only is there a sense of self-reference in the rulings of the Appellate Body but also in how it operates.[46] As Ehlermann who formerly sat as an Appellate Body Member reminds us, 'the adoption of the working procedures is thus a matter for the Appellate Body *itself*.'[47]

The same can also be said of the SPS Committee which, according to SPS Agreement Article 12:4, develops its own procedures to monitor the process of international harmonisation, and under Article 12:7 gets to review the operation

41 Greenwald J, 'WTO Dispute Settlement: An Exercise in Trade law Legislation?' (2003) 6(1) *Journal of International Economic Law* 113–124, 123–124. Pulkowski D, 'Multiple Perspectives on the Fragmentation of International Law' (2004) Paper presented at the European Society of International Law 1–6, 4. Lewis *supra* note 38.

42 McRae D, 'The WTO in International Law: Tradition Continued or New Frontier?' (2000) JIEL 39

43 Greenwald *supra* note 41, at 123.

44 Elhermann *supra* note 34, at 697.

45 WTO Appellate Body Roundtable *supra* note 36, at 183.

46 See for examples, chapters 5 and 6.

47 Ehlermann C, 'Six Years on the Bench of the "World Trade Court": Some Personal Experiences as Member of the Appellate Body of the World Trade Organization' (2002) 36(4) *Journal of World Trade* 605, 610 (my emphasis in italics).

of the SPS Agreement.[48] The SPS Agreement allows the SPS Committee like the DSU allows the Appellate Body to develop its own working procedures. The underlining instruction in both cases is to function based on consensus. This can be seen as an indication that the commitment that the adjudicating bodies share to WTO law, an internal point of view, is one that they construct and determine on their own terms. The rule of recognition does not appear externally validated but exists as the adjudicating bodies and SPS Committee here illustrate by reference to WTO law.[49] The fact is that during the first six years of the Appellate Body as Elhermann points out, the consensus approach appears to have worked as none of the reports contained a dissenting opinion and there was one anonymous concurrent opinion.[50] In order for this to be practically maintained in terms of institutional design the number of Appellate Body Members is limited to seven. This helps to promote and entrench the 'intimacy and collegiality' of the internal point of view in the application of WTO law by the adjudicating bodies.[51]

Accounting for WTO law as the practice of the adjudicating bodies raises the question: does this mean that everything the judiciary does is the law? The short answer is no. More critically, such a question misunderstands what the rule of recognition is attempting to do. Not everything a judiciary, in the case of WTO law, the adjudicating bodies does and says will be law. Is everything a common law judge does and says the law? No, it is not. It is the same with international law. From any judicial system, they will be hundreds, perhaps, thousands of utterances every day. Now, if all that was law, not only would the legal system be overloaded but also for practical purposes it would be near impossible for legal professionals in that system to know what actually is 'law' and what is 'not the law'. In reading any case from any judiciary a legal professional employs the same process of sieving through to find the *ratio(nes) decidendi* and *obiter dictum (dicta)*. Law as Hart observes is open textured[52] carrying also a penumbra of doubt.[53] Rules are inherently indeterminate in their meaning and application.[54] It is therefore not something that we can escape, for no matter how precise a rule is, it cannot cover all situations and eventualities. It is matter of attempting to address the indeterminacy, not by imposing an external order, but by having legal theories so that we can make sense of what we see at the moment but also possibly what we may be able to see in the future. This

48 SPS Agreement Art 12:4, 12:7.

49 See for examples, chapters 5 and 6.

50 Ehlermann *supra* note 47, at 614–615. The concurrent opinion was in *EC – Asbestos.*

51 Ibid, at 610, 613.

52 Hart *supra* note 4, at 124–132.

53 Ibid, at chapter 7 (generally).

54 Stravropoulos N, 'Hart's Semantics', in *Hart's Postscript: Essays on the Postscript to the Concept of Law* (ed) Jules Coleman (Oxford: OUP, 2001) 59–98, 90. I think this goes for principles as well. Dworkin defined rules as all or nothing and principles as wider. But that does not solve the problem of indeterminacy as they still also bear the process of having to be interpreted and applied. In fact principles are probably more indeterminate, because of their varying nature in trying to account for as many situations as possible. For related discussion on this point, see the Prologue, especially discussion on the task of writing as regards to interpretation.

does not make any answer we will devise correct but within its own terms, and sometimes not then. What it does is that it is an attempt to rationalise what we see before us as the law by imposing understanding as discussed in chapter 1.

By using a particular legal theory or approach, as I do here, with the rule of recognition, I exclude and include some things to constitute the information that I define as the law. That information is constitutive of the actual understanding of what I mean by law. Consider that the rule of recognition cannot include the mental, physic or psychological processes of the judiciary to define the law. We are looking at their practice, the outcomes on the assumption that those outcomes are built by a shared determination of what they observe and understand as the law. I would not perceive to know what the adjudicating bodies, or more specifically what the individual members, think. Rather it is about assessing what I observe as expressions in their practice to constitute what they think. By excluding certain information, such as the physiological processes of the adjudicating bodies, it excludes the meanings that that data carries.[55] In that way we privilege the output of the judiciary, its social practice, above other forms of what could be considered legal output. I do so because I believe the judiciary of a legal system has an internal point of view, a sort of collective intentionality. This is not simply a matter of adding the varying individual intentionality or internal point of views of members of the judiciary together to be supplanted as a collective but recognising that individual intentions derive or come from a collective intention.[56]

The collective intention or the internal point of view is related to the purpose of the legal system in that any individual intention is only executed in order to meet the aims of the collective.[57] Our understanding is that the adjudicating bodies do not simply patch together a judgment to reach a 'synchronised' position. They appears to be, as discussed earlier, 'genuine cooperative behaviour' to pursue and fulfil the aims of WTO law.[58] The internal point of view does not force us to reduce the collective behaviour of the judiciary to individual acts that have been summated. This in essence makes the rule of recognition a social fact as the practice of the judiciary, the adjudicating bodies.[59] Law is a social fact by virtue of its existence as dependant on social practice. It is the act of defining law that is constitutive of the law. The observation of the practice gives status to certain things as law. Everything a system does is not necessarily the law and depends on the assignment of the status of that practice as law. Advocating a theory of WTO law is not a reflection of the social practice of WTO law but a way to pause the dynamics of WTO law just long enough for us to capture, a temporary understanding of something that is always moving. The theory allows us to question whether the frame of the picture

55 Ibid, at 73.
56 See Searle J, *The Construction of Social Reality* (New York: Free Press, 1995) 24–25.
57 Ibid.
58 Ibid, at 25.
59 Ibid, at 26.

was the right one to use, what elements we included and excluded, foreground and background, and did we capture everything we could in the frame. It is from these snapshots that we attempt to put a map together to navigate our way through the practice. The trade off is that we get to observe some things clearly and others we do not and cannot account for.

3.2.1 The (re)construction of external international law into WTO law

On the basis of the approach discussed above, I do not dispute that a specialised legal system can observe the law of another specialised legal system, or for the matter, a different type of social system. What I do dispute is that its observations of that system will be whole. If we consider this in the context of WTO law, an observation of non-trade law can enter WTO law, and that observation is not based on the non-trade legal system but on WTO law. It is that observation which is then constructed to form the WTO's reality. WTO law only has access to reality through WTO law. Recursively WTO law is WTO law because it is WTO law. It can only observe and make use of other law based on its code of WTO legal/illegal. Norms that come in WTO law are (re)constructed based on this code. The practice of WTO law demonstrates that all questions of law before the adjudicating bodies will take the form of inquiry as to whether there has been a violation of WTO law.[60] There are no questions about the violation of other law, which also suggests the jurisdiction of WTO law to address issues pertaining to WTO law. WTO law has its own access to how it defines the world as real through the operations of WTO law, which is to prohibit discriminatory or disguised restrictions on trade in an overall effort to liberalise trade.[61] Based on its operations the WTO can observe non-trade law but it does not come directly and wholly into WTO law. A (re)constructed observation of that law enters the WTO. Cognition occurs through the WTO's operations or its internal point of view. In this way, I describe WTO law as *constrained openness*. However, this does not mean that WTO law is entirely shut off from other systems. It means that the WTO is not entirely connected to those systems either, which it will see as 'noise'. Systems make sense of the noise of other systems through what Julia Black calls the 'internal environment'.[62] A system constructs its own epistemic space, as it does not directly communicate with its environment, so much as about its environment. There is one world but varying realities of that world because each system cognises via their own internal point of view. The internal environment provides a space through which a system can act intelligibly on the 'noise' of another system. The decisions of the WTO are then decisions of the WTO. That is crucial because what it says is that the law of other systems are (re)constructed into WTO law, so that the WTO can make sense of it. The premise is that external international law is not (re)constructed on its own terms as a wholesale product from its own system.

60 See chapters 5 and 6.

61 See chapter 4. For examples see WTO/GATT Articles I, III, XI and XX.

62 Black *supra* note 2.

My ideas are at variance with some other trade lawyers. For example, Ilona Cheyne argues that there are gateway provisions in WTO law, which 'allows non-trade principles or concepts to be introduced into the WTO Agreement.'[63] According to Cheyne, gateways incorporate concepts, principles, norm or values from different international legal systems into the WTO legal system.[64] The broad meaning of the metaphor makes it applicable to a wide range of laws. Cheyne argues that there are gateways for the incorporation of international environmental law such as the precautionary principle and sustainable development into WTO law. She suggests that gateways address the 'persistent problems of the WTO' in finding an 'appropriate balance between trade rules and environmental protection measures'.[65] Joost Pauwelyn strikes a similar tone, arguing 'trade is but an instrument to achieve nobler goals' such as 'respect for human rights'.[66] His reason for this appears threefold. The first appears as a moral undertone that because 'trade is a money-making exercise' and 'at the heart' of his work as a trade lawyer he is 'inspired by a willingness to see more to life than money'.[67] The second is that he seems to, as Cho argues, see the integration of non-trade law into the WTO as a demonstration that it is 'porous via these *inter se* modifications' as the logical step in his rejection of the image of the WTO as self-contained regimes.[68] The third I would add is that he sees these gateway- type mechanisms as a tool to cohere the differentiated international legal systems as a response to fragmentation.[69]

Thus far I can surmise that both Cheyne and Pauwelyn imply three broad underlining reasons for gateways. Firstly, they privilege other international law over trade because of an implicit view that protection-based law such as human rights or the environment can make trade law better. Secondly, by incorporating external international law into WTO law, there can be a balance of the tensions, or interests between different and special systems of international law. This is related to the third reason that having external international law incorporated into WTO law ensures some sort of coherence and unity in the international legal system. In this way, the international trade lawyer is transformed into some sort of legal alchemist hunting for coherence among the specialised fragmented parts of international law, by presenting gateways to incorporate 'universally good' laws into WTO law to protect human rights and the environment.[70] Gateways

63 Cheyne I, 'Gateways to the Precautionary Principle in WTO Law' (2007) *Journal of Environmental Law* 155, 155–156. See also French D, 'Treaty Interpretation and the Incorporation of Extraneous Legal Rules' (2006) 55 *International and Comparative Law Quarterly* 281.

64 Cheyne *supra* note 63, *passim*.

65 Ibid, at 155–156.

66 Pauwelyn J, *Conflict of Norms in Public International Law: How WTO Law Relates to Other Rules of International Law* (Cambridge: 2003) xi, and reinforced at 75.

67 Ibid, at xi, and generally.

68 Cho S, 'WTO's Identity Crisis', 5 *World Trade Review* 298 (2006) [reviewing Joost Pauwelyn *supra* note 66].

69 Pauwelyn *supra* note 66, at xi, and generally.

70 Human rights and protection-based law have a tendency to categorise things in terms of universal goods and evils. For a critique, see Kennedy David, *The Dark Sides of Virtue: Reassessing International Humanitarianism* (Princeton and Oxford: Princeton University Press, 2005).

are presented as a practical way to include non-trade interests in WTO law. It is an attempt to make international trade law more morally appealing by it appearing responsive to wider non-trade interests from external international law. The WTO becomes a 'Christmas tree' from which to 'hang any and every good cause that might be secured by exercising trade power'.[71] The implication is that the metaphor is so wide, that anything can be a gateway.

The first problem is that the use of the metaphor to describe how external international law can enter WTO law is misguided in its understanding of fragmentation as discussed in chapter 1, as questions remain about how and where different norms are harmonised. The nature of fragmentation means there is no like for like matching of the norm from one system to another. The specialised systems of international law are all functionally differentiated systems, where each system is oriented towards its own binary code of legal/illegal. Instead of a generalised system of expectations by means of authoritative final decisions, each system is characterised as having its own internal point of view. Therefore the conflicts between the differentiated legal systems are not simply policy conflicts that can be overcome through interpretation but are deeper conflicts between different societal systems and their corresponding values.[72] What gateways plaster over is that the harmonisation process they envisage is all occurring in WTO law, which, whether they desired or otherwise, makes WTO law preeminent in the legal order. This however defeats the very purpose of having WTO law more inclusive of other law. Ironically in his quest to see more to life than money and trade, Pauwelyn whether conscious or not is proposing as a result on the presumption to have non-trade law integrated into WTO law that we 'turn all non-trade issues into trade variables.'[73]

This leads into the second problem, which is in the discussions on gateways there is little engagement, even when there is acknowledgment, of the – political – choice that is being made. Andrew Lang in discussing the 'trade and' debate correctly argues that both constituents within the debate are socially constructed and do not carry natural definition.[74] The debate he demonstrates defines the values as

71 Joint Statement on the Multilateral Trading System (Feb. 1, 2001), at <http://www.wto.org/english/news_e/news_e.htm>. The authors were directors-general of the General Agreement on Tariffs and Trade (GATT) of the WTO: Arthur Dunkel, Peter D. Sutherland, and Renato Ruggiero. They noted that the WTO should not become a Christmas tree for every good cause, which is essentially what gateways would potentially turn it into. Charnovitz argues that they however do not tell us 'how to ascertain the good causes that ought to be secured by trade power.' See Charnovitz S, 'Triangulating the World Trade Organisation' (2002) 96 *American Journal of International Law* 28.

72 See chapter 2 for a discussion on how interpretation is an inadequate understanding of fragmentation.

73 See Beckett, 'Fragmentation, Openness, and Hegemony: Adjudication and the WTO', in Lewis M K and S Frankel (eds) *International Economic Law and National Autonomy* (Cambridge: 2009).

74 Lang A, 'Reflecting on Linkage: Cognitive and Institutional Change in the International Trading System' (2007) 70(4) *Modern Law Review* 523–549.

either trade or non-trade values.[75] The effect, of which I agree with, is to 'reproduce and reconstitute precisely the kind of trade regime which it (simultaneously) subjects to contestation'.[76] The short of the story is that the 'trade and . . .' debate privileges WTO law in its 'structure and content' but does 'little for the external regimes whose legitimacy its recuperates' or as I would argue (re)constructs for itself.[77] To address this, Lang argues for the 're-imagination' of international trade law to account for non-trade values. This appears to hinge on the belief that trade lawyers are more equipped to do this job because of their specialised expertise as trade lawyers.[78] He contends that 'Law does not just entrench and objectify particular meanings of the liberal trade project, it also can be used in precisely the opposite way, as an imaginative resource to actually facilitate the renewing and re-imagining of that project.'[79] However, there is no explicit acknowledgement that trade lawyers have no special claim for being better at making the political choices for the more inclusive liberal trade project. WTO law and more specifically trade lawyers possess no more expertise or powers, none so more than any other legal or non-legal expert to attempt to have non-trade law influence WTO law. Further, there are no *a priori* reasons why external international law is made to accommodate to WTO law through these gateways. The same is true of the argument vice versa.

Arguments for trade lawyers to stand outside trade law to make trade law, and the liberal trade project, more open and responsive to non-trade interests are often seen as admirable and inclusive. However, it is essentially a proposal for an Archimedean point, an objective point of observation and learning, from within trade law, which I have argued in the Prologue does not exist. Gateways are not neutral fixed objective points of observations. There is an error in the metaphor to implicitly assume that the observer can 'confront a fact face-to-face without any theoretical interpretation interposing itself'.[80] There is no *a priori* reality. What trade lawyers would do is (re)construct non-trade law to make sense of it in the context and operations of WTO law. Using the gateway metaphor there is no realisation, as constrained openness highlights, that WTO law does not directly incorporate norms wholesale through gateways, but must (re)construct them as WTO, trade law, variables to make sense of them.[81] This suggest that there is an epistemological break that occurs between the norm as a norm in the external legal system and that which is incorporated, or more correctly, according to the understanding of constrained openness, (re)constructed in WTO law. Rather than

75 Ibid, at 536.

76 Ibid, at 538.

77 Ibid at 523–524. Also see Beckett *supra* note 73.

78 Lang *supra* note 74, generally and esp. 547–548.

79 Ibid, at 547.

80 Macintyre A, *After Virtue, A Study in Moral Theory* (London: Gerald Duckworth & Co. Ltd., 1985, Second Edition) 79. See generally, the Prologue.

81 See Beckett *supra* note 73, where he notes that although Cheyne is attempting to argue the opposite, the point is clearly illustrated in her work, at 160–161, 168 and openly conceded at 171.

the cosmopolitan utopia of a coherent international legal system and discourse, the result is that gateways by creating, and allowing what appears as legitimate spaces in WTO law for external international law, also determines the confines within which opposition to WTO law is occurring. It allows WTO law to remake external international law that comes into contact with WTO law in the image of WTO law, which is more acute given the boundary cutting nature of trade into other areas of law such as human rights and environmental law. Real insurgency is foreclosed, on the basis that the human rights or environmental law is not actually incorporated to displace trade law aims but are (re)constructed as part of those aims. In the next section, I examine how this debate is being played out in trade scholarship.

3.2.2 The Petersmann–Alston debate

Petersmann argues that WTO law can integrate human rights law.[82] This is to guarantee human rights and freedoms by subjecting governments to additional checks through trade law.[83] He states that certain provisions of WTO law 'reflect' human rights law.[84] He assumes that WTO law can be used to enforce human rights by 'construing' WTO law to conform to human rights law.[85] Similarly to Cheyne and Pauwelyn, this implies that the adjudicating bodies can find an objective point within WTO law from which to understand and make rulings that account for and even if need be privilege human rights law over WTO law. Alston objects to Petersmann's assessment because the 'human rights' that would become incorporated into WTO law would be a 'mirage' of human rights law.[86] Alston argues that we need to resist gateways to incorporate human rights into WTO law because these gateways actually represent the merger and acquisition of human rights by WTO law.[87] Alston states that Petersmann does not recognise the 'break' that occurs between human rights law and human rights law that WTO law reconstructs. The reconstruction of human rights law into WTO law is not a neutral objective process through a gateway. The human rights law in WTO law expands the WTO legal regime and though it appears more inclusive, the human rights regime on the outside remains 'ineffectual'.[88] The economic

82 Petersmann E, 'Time for a United Nations "Global Compact" for Integrating Human Rights into the Law of Worldwide Organizations: Lessons from European Integration' (2002) 13 *European Journal of International Law* 621. See for a good critique of Petersmann rights-based trade theory, Cass D Z, *The Constitutionalization of the World Trade Organization: Legitimacy, Democracy, and Community in the International Trading System* (Oxford: OUP, 2005) Chapter 5, 145–176.

83 Petersmann *supra* note 82, at 643–644.

84 Ibid, at 654. He states that the non-discrimination and necessity requirements in the general exceptions of WTO law (e.g. in Article XX of GATT and Article XIV of GATS) reflect these human rights principles.

85 Petersmann *supra* note 82.

86 Alston P, 'Resisting the Merger and Acquisition of Human Rights by Trade Law: A Reply to Petersmann' (2002) 13 *European Journal of International Law* 753.

87 Ibid.

88 Ibid.

market freedoms that Petersmann wishes to be seen as human rights (re)constructs human rights law as trade law.[89] In this (re)construction the conflicts and debates in human rights law are neutralised and sterilised. The human rights law that is eventually employed by the WTO will not be the same as the human rights law that is initially introduced and ushered in through the gateway. The WTO will (re)construct the human rights law to make sense of it to provide practical solutions for WTO law. Human rights law then becomes a tool in the arsenal of trade law, with the potential to lose the universal appeal, which ironically Petersmann endorses as its attractive quality.[90] When we consider that the WTO is the only compulsory adjudication system in international law, Alston's point of the epistemological break between human rights and human rights included in WTO law becomes more acute, where non-trade law concerns may be entirely ignored or effaced by the trade concerns of WTO law.[91] Gateways do not account for the difficulty of seeing WTO law as rights and the integration of market freedom as rights obscures an entire body of other rights.[92] There is no consideration of the primacy of WTO law and that based on this, other systems may start to accommodate WTO law by trying to frame their questions in trade law terms.[93] The consequence of which are the implications of (re)construction and an epistemological break when law moves from one system to another. What is an important value for one specialised fragmented system of law does not necessarily and easily translate as an important value for another specialised fragmented system of law. Concepts such as gateways may appear progressive in asserting the incorporation of external international law into WTO law to present WTO law in its *best light*.[94] However, such a trend should give cause for concern, because the core reason for gateways, is probably to validate and legitimise WTO law, whether it actually is better does not appear to be considered.[95] As Petersmann writes, 'Human rights law offers WTO rules moral, constitutional and democratic legitimacy far beyond the

89 Petersmann *supra* note 82.

90 Ibid.

91 See Cass *supra* note 82, at 173. See for example, WTO Report of Appellate Body, *Canada – Certain Measures Concerning Periodicals*, WT/DS31/AB/R (adopted 30 June 1997) I, 449 [hereinafter *Canada – Periodicals*]. See below for further discussion.

92 Cass *supra* note 82, at 154. See also, Howse R, 'Human Rights in the WTO: whose Rights, What Humanity? Comment on Petersmann' (2002) 13 EJIL 651, 658. For example Appellate Body Report, *United States – Import Prohibition of Certain Shrimp and Shrimp Products*, WT/DS58/AB/R, adopted 6 November 1998 at para 116 [hereinafter *US – Shrimp*]. Cass argues that the WTO adjudicating bodies had difficulty conceptualising a right or fundamental premise of WTO law.

93 See for example, Kelly C R, 'Power, Linkage and Accommodation: The WTO as an International Actor and its influence on other Actors and Regimes' (2006) 24 *Berkeley Journal of International Law* 79–127.

94 See Dworkin's 'best light' theory. Dworkin, *Law's Empire* (London: Fontana, 1986), esp. 51–53. For a critique of this approach see Raban O, 'Dworkin's "Best Light" Requirement and the Proper Methodology of Legal Theory' (2003) 23(2) *Oxford Journal of Legal Studies* 243, esp. 244–249. Also see Beckett J, *The End of Customary Law: A Purposive Analysis of Structural Indeterminacy* (Germany: VDM Verlag, 2008) 26–28.

95 Cass *supra* note 82, at 151 writes that 'At base, the human-rights emphasis is a means for WTO law, quite simply, to exploit the legitimacy factor of human rights.'

traditional economic and utilitarian justifications.'[96] Gateways incorporate 'good' law such as human rights law into WTO law to advance the practice of WTO law as 'worthy of being pursued', 'desirable' and 'good'. The point is that the more worthy, desirable and good the practice of WTO law appears to be, the 'truer' the concept of it as gateway is. In this view, WTO law is valid and legitimate because it incorporates external international law for the protection of human rights and the environment. However, gateways do not consider that competing values cannot be ranked, as there is no common scale.[97] What I am therefore suggesting is that while 'reason can alert us to the two sources of value it is silent on the question' of which should be 'preferred'.[98] As discussed in the Prologue, there are no universal ideas that all systems can ascribe to, making difference inevitable and infinite. The unwitting result of gateways would be hegemonic and imperialistic where WTO law as embodying all these external values have actually (re)constructed them as WTO law.

The point is that the universality and peace that gateways seek to impose on a fragmented international legal system through WTO law cannot accommodate all the experts in these specialised legal systems equally[99] or all at the same time. No matter how open the gateways by which external international law is situated into WTO law are, as I have discussed, that law is (re)constructed as WTO law which also suggests that WTO law experts in WTO law will have the upper hand over outsiders.[100] Gateways do not 'consequently provide a proceduralist escape'[101] by which we can produce a consensus and cohere the fragmented international legal system through WTO law because arguments remain defeasible. 'Whether desirable or not, conflict in inevitable, and resolution of conflict is a matter of decision, not a matter of sublation. All adjudications of disputes are simultaneously declarations of a new war [conflict].'[102] There is no synthesis of one value to another but only by privileging one set over another.[103] This recognition of plurality gives rise to the recognition of incommensurability.[104] Proponents of gateways could always argue that there is no way to demonstrate that two values are actually incommensurable, and that you can always compare values. However, that misses the mark in that I am not saying that two values cannot be compared. I am saying

96 Petersmann, 'The WTO Constitution and Human Rights' (2000) 3 JIEL 19, 24.

97 For a discussion of incommensurability, see for example Raz J, *The Morality of Freedom* (Oxford: Clarendon Press, 1986), chapter 13.

98 See for example Mullender R, 'Hegel: 'Human Rights and Particularism' (2003) 30(4) *Journal of Law and Society* 554–574; 'Human Rights: Universalism and Cultural Relativism' (2003) 6(3) *Critical Review of International Social and Political Philosophy* 70–103.

99 See for example Beckett J, 'Rebel Without a Cause? Martti Koskenniemi and the Critical Legal Project', (2006) 7(12) *German Law Journal*, 1045, 1049.

100 Ibid.

101 Ibid.

102 Rasch *supra* note 3, at 40.

103 Beckett *supra* note 94, at 1066.

104 Different groups within the same system may find they have hold incommensurable norms. See Gray J, *Two Faces of Liberalism* (Cambridge: Polity Press, 2004) 8.

that they cannot be compared on the same scale. To claim incommensurability does not mean that the two things 'cannot be compared *tout court*'.[105] 'They can be compared endlessly –but they can not be compared with one another in overall value.'[106] The significance is that instead of asking questions about the 'relative importance of two options' we look to the 'failure of comparability'.[107] I do not suggest that there can be no comparison of interests but we reject the applicability of judgements of 'relative' interests. 'A and B are incommensurate if it is neither true that one is better than the other nor true that they are of equal value'.[108] The question is *not*, as gateways pose it, about the *extent* to which WTO law can or cannot incorporate international law but whether they *can*. Changing the assumption that WTO law may not be able to incorporate external changes the question and opens new space for debate about how WTO and external international law interact. The question is about whether WTO law is actually capable of incorporating external international law. The metaphor of gateways asks the secondary question ahead of this primary question. Proponents could always retort that the metaphor is much more nuanced than I give credit, in that it reflects a two-directional process of norm construction, in that norms from the outside through provisions in WTO law can be incorporated into WTO law. Nonetheless, the metaphor would still prove inadequate to explain how different functional legal systems interaction within the context of a fragmented international legal system. Even if the metaphor can show the movement of law is not simple leapfrogging, gateways only works if we assume that law can be incorporated in the first place. That is, that we all agree to somehow share universal values about what should be incorporated, and that we can cohere the different fragmented legal rationalities.

3.3 Fragmentation reconsidered

Fragmentation, to recap earlier discussion in chapter 1, is a collision of rationalities. The differentiation of international law into specialised legal systems does not necessarily translate into a collapse of order. The technical competence of the different systems is a 'product of the social world of a particular group of professionals'.[109] A legal system exists because its members share some form of commitment to legal meaning in that legal system. Even then, we can never expect complete unity within that legal system, as much as we could expect between different systems. However, we can expect that judicial officials of a system will give effect and purpose to their system. For WTO law fragmentation as a process of differentiation has meant the emergence of a 'new specialised international bar'

105 Ibid, at 41.
106 Ibid, at 41–42.
107 Raz *supra* note 97, at 322.
108 Ibid.
109 Orford A, 'A Journal of the Voyage from Apology to Utopia' (2006) 7(12) *German Law Journal* 994–1010, 997.

which is comprised of 'specialists in WTO law and litigation'.[110] This can act as a 'constraint upon the behaviour of those who wish to enter, or be recognised as competent members of, that professional community.'[111] The division of labour can be used to explain and justify the process of fragmentation that has created specialised legal systems in international law served by a cadre of experts.

These specialist experts are supposedly more efficient than the generalist. The specialist international lawyer would be able to focus more on his area without the distractions of other areas of law. The new specialist need not know or only has to be marginally aware of what is happening outside his world. Perhaps as a result the 'problems faced by public international law today . . . result in large part from [this] strategy of becoming [too] technical.'[112] Fragmentation is not only limited to international law itself, and often neglected is the further division of labour or differentiation within the specialist systems. So that within what is already a specialised system of international law is the occurrence of more specialisation and attendant experts. It is the creation of experts within experts. Each (sub)system has the ability to create its own vocabulary and means of functioning that can divorce it from the general meanings of an already differentiated and specialised international legal system.[113] This is a process akin but perhaps not as acute as the original divorce of the specialised legal system from general international law.

The entire process of fragmentation is a technicalisation and professionalisation of international law. The expert, though highly skilled and technically competent in the language of his system may fail to speak the language or be able to engage with other systems. That expert may also fail to speak the language of the other (sub)systems within his own specialised system. This threatens the general knowledge and can result in an acute division between the various parts of the specialised legal system. WTO lawyers, for example, are not a homogeneous group as a process of specialisation takes hold with different experts for example on Agriculture, GATS, GATT, SPS, TRIPS, and developing countries. These experts hold vast knowledge in their area but may lack the same expertise in other areas of WTO law or WTO law as a whole.[114] The technical expert who emerged as an answer to the generalist, who lacked specialist knowledge to address specific legal problems, can now become a drawback in failing to have a general knowledge of the legal system. This is a result of the division of labour becoming too acute as to the maximisation of the specialist system.[115] It destroys the general picture before

110 See, e.g., Sacerdoti G, 'The Role of Lawyers in the WTO Dispute Settlement System', in Yerxa R and B Wilson, *Key Issues in WTO Dispute Settlement: The First Ten Years* (Cambridge: CUP, 2005) 125–131.

111 For a brief discussion on this point, see Orford *supra* note 109, at 997.

112 Koskenniemi M, 'The Fate of Public International Law: Between Technique and Politics' (2007) 70(1) *Modern Law Review* 1–30, 2.

113 See Fiona Smith, 'Law, Language and International Agricultural Trade' (2010) *Current Legal Problems* 448–474.

114 Ibid.

115 See chapter 2 on discussion of *EC – Biotech*.

our reductive thought slices it up into marginal bits. Our view becomes too small. Law as one lens differentiates lawyers from other specialisations such as economics, history and political science. Within law broadly there are even further specialisations such as, to name a few, laws covering the environment, international finance, and war. The fact is that we all make things more manageable by breaking them down into smaller pieces. It is an awareness of what is destroyed in the process that we need to retain in order to remember that the choices we make are essentially political ones.[116] But that I mean choices that determine what we see and through what lens we see.

The remaining question, is whether seeing fragmentation as a division of labour is helpful in understanding how to think about the interaction between WTO and external international law. We think the result of the division of labour is to realise, to borrow Robert Cover sentiment, that each fragmented system inhabits a 'nomos – a normative universe' which its participants 'constantly create and maintain'.[117] The normative universe is held together by commitments of its inhabitants to determine 'what the law means and what the law shall be.'[118] Actions of a system or a nomos can only be understood in relation to its own norms because its own normative universe is the product of a socially constructed reality.[119] This is not to say that the WTO or any other specialised legal system occupies a different physical world from the general legal system or other specialised legal systems, or that the WTO nomos changes that world. Firstly, two legal systems can occupy the same world. Secondly, a nomos does not change the existence of the physical world, as such. The point is that only through its own nomos, that is, its own descriptions and understanding of the world can any legal system assess and access the world. As Richard Rorty puts it, 'where there are no sentences, there is no truth . . . the world is out there, but descriptions of the world are not.'[120] Each system that has 'achieved law' 'has its own nomos – narratives, experiences, and visions to which its norm articulated is the right response.'[121] This means for example that the WTO adjudicating bodies may find interpretations and narratives that 'threaten to compromise the integrity of the normative world within which they adjudicate' as 'unacceptable'.[122] Norms carry a corresponding legal system, expectations and legal interpretations of what they mean, and to whom they apply. Hence, different legal systems will construct and interpret the world differently. Essentially, they create their own understanding of the world, from which to operate and interact with the broader environment.

116 See Prologue for discussion of S. Fish on *Zen and the Art of Motorcycle Maintenance.*

117 Cover *supra* note 4.

118 Ibid, at 7.

119 Ibid, at 8.

120 Rorty R, *Consequences of Pragmatism* (Minneapolis: University of Minnesota Press, 1982) 4–5.

121 Cover *supra* note 4, at 42.

122 This characterisation about judicial bodies protecting their nomos is borrowed from Mullender R, 'Two Nomoi and a Clash of Narratives: The Story of the United Kingdom and the European Union' (2006) 3 *Issues in Legal Scholarship* 3.

On the basis of nomos, we can think of WTO law as a special and differentiated system of international law. However, we could accept that 'no regime can be created outside the scope of general international law';[123] this would not prevent WTO law as nomos. This means that WTO law, like other special international legal systems, has its own distinctive normative framework and interpretations of international law. It is an implication of differentiation and specialisation from international law. Fragmentation in this view is not so much a growing pathology[124] or a mistake but is better considered as the result of the increasing specialisation of international law into different areas.[125] Fragmentation is not the result of some 'frailty of reason' but is a realisation or perhaps an actualisation of the fact that there are different reasons and ways to think about and address social problems using international law.[126] The worry is not so much the emergence of these differing laws but that the laws reflect their own nomos, that is, interpretation of international law, and its role and place in the broader rationalities of social systems.[127] In this way, fragmentation can be seen as a 'division of labour' in international law that leads to technical specialisations in varying areas of legal regulation, as a result of modernity. On this basis, we realise that new ways of thinking about how to address fragmentation are probably needed, as the traditional professional toolbox of treaty interpretation tools (see chapter 2) and gateways explored here do not prove wholly adequate.

3.4 Indirectly and strategically influencing WTO law

In this section, I will discuss how the idea of reflexive law[128] supplementing constrained openness can provide a better explanation of how we can conceptualise the interaction between WTO and external international law. Constrained openness at its premise though advancing that WTO law cannot directly incorporate external international law but would (re)construct it as argued above, is not resigned to defeatism. By that I mean that external international law can still influence WTO law and vice versa if we appreciate as discussed earlier the functional

123 Lindross A and M Mehling, 'Dispelling the Chimera of "Self-Contained Regimes": International Law and the WTO' (2005) 16(5) *European Journal of International Law* 857. Koskenniemi M, 'Fragmentation of International Law: Difficulties Arising from the Diversification and Expansion of International Law' UN Doc. International Law Commission A/CN.4/L.682 13 April 2006, para 172 (hereafter ILC Study Group Report on Fragmentation).

124 For early concern about the diversity of norms in international law, see Weil P, 'Towards Relative Normativity in International Law' (1983) 77 *American Journal of International Law* 413.

125 Koskenniemi M and P Leino, 'Fragmentation of International Law? Postmodern Anxieties' (2002) 15 *Leiden Journal of International Law* 553–579, 561. ILC Study Group Report on Fragmentation *supra* note 110, at paras 15–16.

126 Gray *supra* note 104, at 8.

127 Koskenniemi and Leino *supra* note 125, at 561. ILC Study Group Report on Fragmentation *supra* note 123, at paras 8–9, 15.

128 Teubner *Law as an Autopoietic System supra* note 6, at 74–94. Black: 'Constitutionalising Self-Regulation' *supra* note 2, at 47.

differentiated legal realities do not necessarily commensurate. The influence is indirect and strategic. Consequently, systems do not act directly upon each other because of a presumed regulatory trilemma.[129] That is, the use of law to impose rationality that is not appropriate to the 'life world' structure of the regulated social areas and which fails to achieve the desire results does so at the cost of destroying the structures, or the intervening system is destroyed.[130] This regulatory crisis was postulated as interaction between law and the social world, where law attempted to perform interventionist welfare-type functions. That however does not preclude its application to the interaction between differentiated systems as a matter of fragmentation[131] because we do not deny the need for intervention between systems, just that the gateway approach has to change, as there can be no direct intervention between the varying differentiated systems of a fragmented international legal system.[132] To demonstrate the crisis, we consider in short Cheyne's assertions of the gateway principle to incorporate the precautionary principle as discussed above.[133] Yet, we know as to constrained openness, that the precautionary principle, its meaning, purpose and corresponding institutional structures would not be examined directly by WTO law but would be effaced, (re)constructed as WTO law (see chapter 5). As to references to Cheyne's own work we see that WTO law interacts with the precautionary principle with reference to itself as WTO law, which acts as a 'gateway by incorporating its [WTO law's] own version of the precautionary principle'.[134] The precautionary principle of environmental law, as to the discussion on human rights above, is potentially effaced, bundled into a singular principle for the purposes of being 'integrated' into WTO law, which reduces its complexity as to environmental law, or its own goals are shunted aside as nothing more than noise while WTO law goals dominate.

I can further demonstrate the regulatory crisis in the practice of WTO law, with reference to *Canada – Periodicals*.[135] This case concerned a ban by Canada on the import and distribution of split-run periodicals. Split-runs are second edition magazines printed by foreign owned companies but using similar articles and advertisements from the original print. The purpose of printing a split run was for the foreign company to qualify for tax treatment as Canadian but Canada imposed a higher tax on them. The aim of the Canadian tax was to protect the national print industry by undermining split runs that were fronting as Canadian for tax purposes. The AB found that an 80 per cent tax on periodicals by Canada

129 Teubner: *Law as an Autopoietic System supra* note 6, at 72–77, 'Substantive and Reflexive Elements in Modern Law (1983) 17 *Law and Society Review* 239, 254, 273. Black: 'Constitutionalising Self-Regulation' *supra* note 2, at 47, 'Critical Reflections on Regulation', *supra* note 2, at 7.

130 Ibid.

131 Beckett *supra* note 73.

132 Teubner 'Substantive and Reflexive Elements in Modern Law' *supra* note 127 makes this point. See Black 'Constitutionalising Self-Regulation' *supra* note 2, at 48.

133 See Cheyne *supra* note 63. See chapter 6 for a full and in-depth assessment.

134 See Cheyne *supra* note 63, at 159, 171. See chapter 6.

135 See *supra* note 91.

was in violation of national treatment pursuant to Article III:2, second sentence as imported split runs and Canadian non-splitruns were 'directly competitive or substitutable' products in that they were part of the same periodical market in Canada.[136] Canada had submitted that the content of the periodicals was critical and on that basis imported split runs and Canadian non-split runs were not directly substitutable for purposes of Article III:2. From Canada's perspective, the content made the periodicals different and therefore the consumer end use different. The point being made by Canada was that a split run was not substitutable with a Canadian non-split run periodical.[137] What is important about the case for our purposes is that the AB did not directly consider the cultural concerns of Canada to protect its periodical industry but focused on the trade concerns of the matter being discriminatory. The AB went as far to state that:

> In order to avoid any misunderstandings as to the scope and implications of the findings above we would like to stress that the ability of any Member to take measures to protect its cultural identity was not an issue in he present case. The only task entrusted to this Panel was to examine whether the treatment accorded to imported periodicals under specific measures identified in the complainant's claim is compatible with the rules of GATT 1994.[138]

Culture, as Cass writes, was 'subjugated to the free trade considerations through a straightforward interpretation of "like product" for the purposes of the national treatment provision.'[139] As an example of the regulatory crisis discussed above, the AB in their mainly economic assessment of the issue before them ignored external cultural concerns to directly influence WTO law.

The central issue, from the discussion on gateways for the precautionary principle and cultural concerns, is direct regulation is difficult to achieve and so it is best to conceptualise it as reflexive law, the regulation of other systems through self-regulation.[140] The idea is to 'recognise the impossibility, which is analytical as opposed to merely practical, of regulating directly and to change regulatory strategy to regulate indirectly, to induce actions rather than command them.'[141] It is the process of the interaction between the differentiated autonomous systems that we focus on, as this provides a point at which external international law could influence WTO law and vice versa. It is about the adoption of indirect regulatory

136 For further discussion of the case, see Lester S and B Mercurio et al. *World Trade Law: Text, Materials and Commentary* (Oxford: Hart Publishing, 2008) 832–836. Trebilcock M J and R Howse, *The Regulation of International Trade* (London: Routledge, 2005, third edition) 94–95.

137 *Canada – Periodicals supra* note 91, para 3.60–3.119.

138 Ibid, at para 5.45.

139 Cass *supra* note 82, at 173.

140 Black, 'Constitutionalising Self-Regulation' *supra* note 2, at 45, notes that this is a view that not all autopoieticists share.

141 Black 'Constitutionalising Self-Regulation' *supra* note 2, at 46 and generally. Black applies reflexive law to regulating other social systems. Here I am borrowing it to apply between differentiated legal systems.

strategies. For example the aim of procedural regulation Black argues is, without controlling the substantive outcome of a decision, to structure the processes of a system so that it accounts for the impact of its operations on other systems.[142] The autonomy of each fragmented system is maintained, as reflexive intervention does not seek to resolve the conflict between the rationalities.

Instead, we accept that the rationalities cannot be made commensurate so indirect regulatory strategies seek to increase the chances of achieving purposive goals.[143] The premise is to consider the responses to interventions with the aim of refining them. It is not simply a matter of framing the questions of external international law as questions of WTO law but to focus on the interaction considering as we argued earlier that a system sees the utterances of another system as noise. The key is to sensitise WTO law to the noise of other systems of external international law, rather than a conscious alteration of WTO law.[144] The point is to utilise the resistance of a system, not destroy it. It is about creating opportunities for different legal systems to be more responsive to the noise of each other. It raises the question that Black poses of whether reflexive law is simply a technique for intervention, a 'vessel into which any substantive purpose can be poured, or does it restrict not only the means by which substantive goals can be pursued, but those that can be pursued at all?' Black does not tell us unequivocally whether reflexive law is simply a technique of intervention but she does give us an important clue from which we can say the answer is no. On the basis that there are no overall legitimating norms, the focus is on flexible procedural regulation, adapted to the regulation of each functional system as the 'only legitimate form of intervention'.[145] Systems regulate each other, only by regulating themselves, so only indirect regulation is possible.[146]

As a consequence of systems being autonomous because of fragmentation, not only is regulation an indirect process, but knowledge is also fragmented.[147] No single system as discussed in the Prologue can provide all the answers to a problem and as such no system can dominate the regulatory process as systems are restricted by their own self-referential logic and the autonomy of other systems.[148] WTO law, or external international law vice versa, need not grasp the details of the other system but need to know how it operates because as noted above this is where strategic intervention is directed. Therefore rather than direct entry of external international law into WTO law there has to be the more subtle inducement. The idea of a reflexive strategy is to induce a system to work at and hopefully achieve the values of external international law. Instead of having those values, as gateways would do, imposed from outside but only to be (re)constructed, ignored

142 Ibid.
143 Ibid, at 47.
144 Teubner *Law as an Autopoietic System supra* note 6, at 81.
145 Black 'Constitutionalising Self-Regulation' *supra* note 2, at 49–50.
146 Teubner *Law as an Autopoietic System supra* note 6, at 77–78.
147 Black 'Critical Reflections on Regulation', *supra* note 2, at 5.
148 Ibid, at 6.

or effaced as WTO law responds, the idea is to have those values internalised through a process of subtle inducement.

The lesson to draw from the discussion is that we should place an emphasis, if not more, on the techniques and procedure we use to induce the values, as to the value themselves.[149] The focus is the 'way' in which things are done rather than on 'what' is being done.[150] It is about procedural solutions as emphasised above and not so much particular outcomes,[151] as these may not even be achieved. 'What is important is who is at the table, not what they decide.'[152] WTO law can be connected to external international law, normatively and empirically[153] through proceduralism.[154] There are obvious disagreements as to the outcomes between participants because they are seeing the matters from their own rationality, with external rationalities as noise. So instead of addressing gateways and the 'trade and' issue as questions of what is good or fair, because of the incommensurate nature of these issues, the focus should be on procedural solutions.[155] *US – Shrimp*[156] and *EC – Asbestos*[157] provides us with a case in point, where there are small signs of a 'shifting emphasis away from a strictly classical economic theory'.[158]

In *US – Shrimp* the Appellate Body (AB) approved a unilateral US measure to ban the import of shrimp not caught using devices that protected endangered turtles as to Article XX(g). The decision in effect meant that an importing state could limit access to its market, based on a unilaterally adopted measure, so as long as the importing state was acting in a non-discriminatory manner pursuant to Article XX.[159] This contrasted with previous practice in *Tuna Dolphin* whereby the GATT panel supported an 'absolute rule' on national sovereignty in that states may never unilaterally impose policies on another sovereign state pursuant to social goals when those policies resulted in trade discrimination.[160] The claimant WTO Members argued that turtles were not 'exhaustible natural resources' pursuant to Article XX(g). The Article they argued covered the issue of 'finite resources such as minerals, rather than biological or renewable resources'.[161] The AB reasoned that

149 Black 'Constitutionalising Self-Regulation' *supra* note 2, at 51.
150 Cass *supra* note 82, at 84.
151 Ibid.
152 Ibid, at 85.
153 Black 'Constitutionalising Self-Regulation' *supra* note 2, at 47.
154 Cass *supra* note 82, at 85.
155 Ibid.
156 *US – Shrimp supra* note 92.
157 Appellate Body Report, *European Communities – Measures Affecting Asbestos and Asbestos-Containing Products*, WT/DS135/AB/R, adopted 5 April 2001 [hereinafter *EC – Asbestos*].
158 Cass *supra* note 92, at 175. See chapter 4 for further discussion.
159 *US – Shrimp supra* note 82, at para 121. See also Cass *supra* note 82, at 127.
160 See Cass *supra* note 82, at 127–128. For *Tuna Dolphin* cases see GATT Panel Report, *United States – Restrictions on Imports of Tuna* (not adopted, circulated on 3 Sept., 1991) [Tuna Dolphin I] 30 ILM 1594 (1991); GATT Panel Report, *United States – Restrictions on Imports of Tuna* (not adopted, circulated on 16 Jun., 1994) [Tuna Dolphin II] 33 ILM 936 (1994).
161 *US – Shrimp supra* note 92 at, para 129.

Article XX(g) was drafted fifty years prior to the case before them and as such their interpretation should reflect contemporary environmental concerns of sustainable development, such as the protection of turtles.[162] Two things stand out in this case. The first is that the AB, as Cass argues, abandons the strict rule of not allowing unilateral imposition of trade discriminatory polices.[163] The second is that the AB is making its ruling to account for 'contemporary' environmental concerns supported it legal reasoning by reference to non-WTO law, environmental treaties.[164] What both moves have in common is there appear to exemplify acts of strategic interaction between WTO law and external norms. In the first instance, it is a matter of the tension between national sovereignty and the autonomous nature of WTO law. The AB appeared aware of the subtle manoeuvre that they were making and were at pains to point out the 'boundaries of its finding' highlight what they had 'not decided'.[165] In the second instance, the AB appears to be acknowledging some sort of non-trade value in and for the enforcement of WTO law. In both instances the AB appears to focus on the 'manner' in which the regulating government executes its measures.[166] It is not concerned as a reading of case shows with the details of the US measure or of the environmental treaties it references in support of the measure. It is about strategically devising a procedural solution by which a Member can execute his desired policy, within the confines of WTO law. There is no direct integration of environmental or other legal policy concerns in WTO law.

The second example of an emphasis on procedure for strategic intervention of non-WTO law concerns in the practice of WTO law is that of *EC – Asbestos*. France implemented a measure that prohibited the manufacture, sale, distribution and import of asbestos and asbestos-containing products. The claimant WTO Member Canada argued, in the main, that the ban was a violation of GATT Article III because it discriminated against Canadian asbestos and asbestos-containing products in favour of substitute French products. France's claim was that there was no other available measure to achieve the level of protection desired, which the AB upheld because the value pursued was both 'vital and important in the highest degree.'[167] The AB accepted France's measure because of the well-known carcinogenic health concerns of asbestos that the measure was pursuant to Article XX(b) necessary to protect human life or health. Cass argues that in this case health considerations played a part in the interpretation under Article III in determining whether asbestos-containing products were 'like' non-asbestos-containing products, which had similar uses and markets.[168] In this case as in *US – Shrimp*, the

162 Ibid.
163 Cass *supra* note 82, at 127–128.
164 See chapter 4.
165 Cass *supra* note 82, at 128. See *US – Shrimp supra* note 92, at para 121.
166 Cho *supra* note 68.
167 *EC – Asbestos supra* note 157, at para 172.
168 Cass *supra* note 82, at 175.

AB does not seem directly concerned about the details of the measure to protect health as the AB noted France had a right to determine the level of protection.[169] The AB thus appeared concerned with the nature and effect of the measure and not its source.

The indirect reflexive law approach can be seen as a recognition of the politicalisation of WTO law and fragmentation. By that we mean the effect is to create credible platforms from which systems come to terms with their autonomous contested nature as to other systems. It is an argument for the primacy of politics to show that there are choices and for the professional class of international trade lawyers as counsel and jurists to show how and on what basis they make their choices as regards to how external international law may at points indirectly influence WTO law. We can also practically conceptualise the interaction between WTO and external international law as *questio iuris*. Whereby if the primary concern of a matter is WTO law, it is addressed pursuant to the substantive rules of WTO law, which would be able to claim the strongest structural connection to the issue being addressed and the strongest interest in the matter being debated.[170] The questions can equally be applied if the primary matter is of external international law. In some cases as discussed above, and as further discussed in chapter 5 and 6 in examining examples of the practice in WTO law as to external international law, this may mean non-WTO law induces strategic influence in shaping certain decisions on aspects of WTO law.

3.5 Conclusion

In this chapter, I advanced constrained openness as a theory of WTO law. This accounts for the definition of WTO law as the practice of the adjudicating bodies premised in chapter 1, using to the (counter-factual) rule of recognition. In chapter 2 regarding interpretative devices such as *lex specialis*, *lex posterior* and the VCLT and here as to the idea of gateways, we showed them as not wholly adequate to account for fragmentation. More specifically for the subject under investigation in my work, these ideas did not properly account for the interaction between WTO law and external international law. In part, this was because they failed to account for the fragmented functional *nomos* of international law, which could be understood as a result of a division of labour of international law. In this chapter, I show that the idea of constrained openness provides what I think is a better way to

169 *EC – Asbestos supra* note 157, at para 168.

170 Tuebner G and A Lescano, 'Regime-Collisions: The Vain Search for Legal Unity in the Fragmentation of Global Law' (2004) (Summer) *Michigan Journal of International Law* 999, 1030. Teubner G and P Korth, 'Two Kinds of Legal Pluralism: Collision of Laws in the double fragmentation of World society' trans. Anna Furness, revised by Anne Emert (to appear in Margaret Young (ed) *Regime Interaction in International Law: Theoretical and Practical Challenges*), Section IV (3) See also Trachtman J P, 'Institutional Linkage: Transcending 'Trade and…' (2002) 96(1) AJIL 77–93, 89–91.

conceptualise the interaction between WTO and external international law, accounting for the fragmented nature of international law. In order to understand how fragmented systems interact, we had to abandon a territorial view of international law. Rather we have to appreciate that alongside the state-centric territoriality of international law, there sat, if uncomfortably, a set of functional systems that were capable of constructing their own reality to maximise their own rationality. This does not mean that the hierarchical nation state view of international law, in which the ICJ is a court of general jurisdiction to resolve disputes between states, does not necessarily work. I simply think that it does not work for understanding fragmentation and attempts to reproduce a Hartian common law view on international law (chapter 1) does not easily, if at all, translate to international law, or WTO law. Therefore there is no avoiding or containing the conflict of the varying rationalities because fragmentation as I discussed is not just about conflict systems but a division of labour which sees different systems and their attendant constituents aiming to maximise the goals of their system as to others. We cannot wish or interpret our way out of fragmentation (chapter 2) for there is only so much understanding the 'ordinary meaning' meaning of a word can do. The point is that mechanical technical approaches to fragmentation may not work. What was needed as introduced here is a political strategy recognising that the legal systems are not simply offshoots of states, even if originally created by states in the general international legal system, but fully functioning separate systems with their own legal and political rationalities. This is why the idea of reflexive law is critical as it can facilitate this recognition, enabling us to be able to devise strategies for indirect influence of external international law in WTO law (chapter 6). In the next chapter, I explore how the three main models on the question of the interaction between WTO and external international law have eviscerated critique through the structural nature of their debate.

4 The debate on the interaction between WTO law and external international law

4.0 Introduction

The purpose of this chapter is to explore the three main models that have emerged as responses to the inter-systemic fragmentation of international law (see chapters 1 and 2). The models are as follows:

> *Model I*: the *limited domain* of WTO law. This is premised on the view that the adjudicating bodies can only use WTO law in addressing a WTO law dispute.[1]
> *Model II*: the *openness* of WTO law. This is based on the idea that as part of an inclusive international legal system the WTO adjudicating bodies should apply external international law in addressing WTO law disputes.[2]

1 Trachtman J: 'The Domain of WTO Dispute Resolution' (1999) 40 *Harvard International Law Journal* 333–377; 'The Jurisdiction of the WTO' (2004) 98 *American Society of International Law Proceedings* 139; 'Jurisdiction in WTO dispute settlement' 137 in R Yerxa and B Wilson (eds) *Key Issues in WTO Dispute Settlement: The First Ten Years* (Cambridge: CUP, 2005); 'Book Review of Conflict of Norms in Public International Law: How WTO Law Relates to Other Rules of International Law by J Pauwelyn' (2004) 98 *American Journal of International Law* 855–861 [hereinafter 'Book Review of Conflict of Norms'], 'Institutional Linkage: Transcending 'Trade and . . .' (2002) 96 *American Journal of International Law* 77–93; See also, *less categorically* Marceau G: 'A Call for Coherence in International Law' (1999) 33(5) *Journal of World Trade* 87–152; 'Conflicts of Norms and Conflicts of Jurisdictions: The Relationship between the WTO Agreement and MEAs and other Treaties' (2001) 35(6) *Journal of World Trade* 1081–1131 [hereinafter 'Conflicts of Norms and Conflicts of Jurisdictions']; 'WTO Dispute Settlement and Human Rights' (2002) 13 *European Journal of International Law* 753–814. Steger D, 'The Jurisdiction of the WTO' (2004) 98 *American Society of International Law Proceedings* 142–146. *Contra*: see *supra* note 2.

2 Pauwelyn J: *Conflict of Norms in Public International Law: How WTO Law Relates to Other Rules of International Law* (Cambridge: CUP, 2003) [hereinafter *Conflict of Norms*]. Pauwelyn 2003 *supra* note 1; Pauwelyn J: 'The Role of Public International Law in the WTO: How Far Can We Go? (2001) 95(3) *American Journal of International Law* 535–578, 536 [hereinafter 'The Role of Public International Law']; 'The Jurisdiction of the WTO' (2004) 98 *American Society of International Law Proceedings* 135–138; 'Enforcement and Countermeasures in the WTO: Rules are Rules – Towards a More Collective Approach' (2000) 94 *American Journal of International Law* 335 [hereinafter 'Enforcement and Countermeasures in the WTO']; Symposium: 'Diversity or Cacophony?: New Sources of Norms in International Law' (2004) 25 *Michigan Journal of International Law*; 'Bridging Fragmentation and Unity: International Law as a Universe of Inter-Connected Islands' (2004) 25 *Michigan Journal of International Law* 903 [hereinafter 'Bridging Fragmentation and Unity'. See also Schoenbaum T, 'WTO Dispute Settlement: Praise and Suggestions for Reform' (1998) 47 ICLQ 652–653. *Contra*: see *supra* note 1.

Model III: this is an attempt to reconcile Model I and II, by premising that WTO law is *privileged* over external international law in a dispute in WTO law because of a conflicts clause inferred in WTO law.[3]

In this chapter, I examine not only the substantive arguments but also critically the structural nature of the debate among the models. What I am attempting to discern is *why* and *how* the models conflict. This insight, using constrained openness (see chapter 3), will provide a basis from which I can structurally enter and hopefully reshape the current debate (see chapter 6). The general argument of this chapter is that the three models provide inadequate conceptual accounts of the interaction between WTO and external international law.

4.1 Model I: WTO law as a limited domain

The presumption that WTO is a limited domain is that the WTO adjudicating bodies can only apply WTO law. International external law thus cannot be used as a defence against a violation of WTO law.[4] This can be explained by the doctrine of attributed powers. It means that the intent of the drafters of the WTO treaty should be respected and protected by the adjudicating bodies.[5] The treaty sets out the powers and terms of the WTO as negotiated for and agreed to by its Members. Trachtman states that WTO law can use external international law only if incorporated into the WTO law.[6] Trachtman, states that 'while it might well be argued that the customary rules of interpretation would apply without express invocation, this would not change the fact that the drafters demonstrated an intent to exclude other international law by virtue of their decision not to mention it.'[7] The emphasis is thus on an almost sacrosanct Westphalia state-sovereignty rather

3 Bartels L, 'Applicable Law in the WTO Dispute Settlement Proceedings' (2001) 35 JWT 499–519.

4 Trachtman 'Jurisdiction in WTO Dispute Settlement' *supra* note 1, at 137 and also 'The Jurisdiction of the World Trade Organisation' *supra* note 2 at, 139 writes that 'Of course, outside the WTO dispute settlement system, general international law has the range and effect that it was intended to have. None of it was written with the expectation or intent that it would be applicable law within the WTO. It would be dangerous to disregard state's intent and expectations in order to force general international law into the WTO dispute settlement system. It is clear that for the WTO, general international law as applicable law would be an unwelcome guest, and for many exponents of environmental protection and human rights, the WTO dispute settlement system would be a Procrustean bed indeed.' *Contra* Pauwelyn *supra* note 2.

5 See *supra* note 1.

6 See Trachtman 'Domain of WTO Dispute Resolution' *supra* note 1. He writes that the circumstances are when external law is referenced as in DSU Article 3.2 to customary rules on treaty interpretation, a waiver or in WTO law such as the Agreement on Trade Related Aspects of Intellectual Property Rights (TRIPS), and as relevant facts under WTO law.

7 Trachtman: 'Jurisdiction of WTO Law' *supra* note 1, at 14 and also 'The Domain of WTO Dispute Settlement Resolution' *supra* note 1 at, 342. *Contra* Pauwelyn 'Jurisdiction of WTO Law' *supra* note 2.

than the general interests of the international legal system.[8] It appears that 'there is no room in the reasoning to imply any powers'[9] and therefore this approach looks narrow in scope and power. The adjudicating bodies would be inward looking to protect the rights and obligations of WTO Members. Consequently, WTO law explained by this model would be less likely to fall back on general international law to fill gaps or *lacunae*.[10]

4.2 Model II: WTO law as open

Contrary to the presumption of the adequacy of WTO law associated with Model I, Model II is premised on the view that as a consequence of gaps in WTO law[11] there is fall back on general international law[12] and the rules of state responsibility.[13] This is unless WTO law has specifically 'contracted out' of these rules.[14] According to the model WTO law is not viewed as a 'secluded island' but also as part of international law based on 'implied powers' that the adjudicating bodies should provide complete legal answers.[15] The result is that the adjudicating bodies could apply external international law as a defence against a violation of

8 This is a reflection of the *Lotus* doctrine whereby 'Restrictions upon the independence of the state . . . can not be presumed.' See *Lotus Case*, 1927, PCIJ Rep. para 18. For further discussion on the doctrine of attributed powers see Klabbers J, *An Introduction to International Institutional Law* (Cambridge: CUP, 2002) 63–67; Akande D, 'International Organisations', in Malcolm Evans (ed) *International Law* (London: OUP, 2006) 277–305, esp. 290–291. See also *Jurisdiction of the European Commission of the Danube between Galatz and Braila Advisory Opinion*, 1926, PCIJ Rep. 64.

9 Klabbers *supra* note 8 at 73.

10 Simma B and D Pulkowski, 'Of Planets and the Universe: Self-Contained Regimes in International Law' (2006) 17 *European Journal of International Law* 484–485; Pulkowski D, 'Book Review of Conflict of Norms in Public International Law: How WTO Law Relates to Other Rules of International Law' (2005) *European Journal of International Law* 153–160, 156.

11 Pauwelyn *Conflict of Norms supra* note 2, at 200–212, esp. 207–212; 'The Role of Public International Law' *supra* note 2, at 559–565; 'Bridging Fragmentation and Unity' *supra* note 2, at 911–916; and generally *supra* note 2. For a similar assessment, see Lindross A and M Mehling, 'Dispelling the Chimera of "Self-Contained Regimes": International Law and the WTO' (2005) 16(5) *European Journal of International Law* 857, 864–866.

12 For a good survey of the application of the general rules of international law in the WTO see: Lindross and Mehling *supra* note 11, at 866–873. Cameron J and Gray K, 'Principles of International Law in the WTO Dispute Settlement Body' (2001) 50 *International Comparative and Law Quarterly* 252. Lennard M, 'Navigating by the Stars: Interpreting the WTO Agreements' (2002) 5 *Journal of International Economic Law* 17–89.

13 See generally Crawford J, *The International Law Commission's Articles on State Responsibility: Introduction, Text and Commentaries* (Cambridge: CUP, 2002).

14 Pauwelyn *Conflict of Norms supra* note 2, at 212–220; 'The Role of Public International Law in the WTO' *supra* note 2, at 538–543, esp. 543; 'The Jurisdiction of the World Trade Organisation' *supra* note 2, at 136. For a similar assessment, see Simma and Pulkowski *supra* note 10, at 495–505, 507–509. *Contra* Trachtman *supra* note 1.

15 In *agreement* see: Pauwelyn *Conflict of Norms supra* note 2, at 447–451; 'The Role of Public International Law' *supra* note 2, at 555–559. Bartels *supra* note 3, at 505–506, Schoenbaum *supra* note 2, at 652–653. *Contra* see: Trachtman 'The Domain of WTO Law' *supra* note 1, at 342; Marceau 'A Call for Coherence in International Law' *supra* note 1, at 109–115.

WTO law.[16] The model also suggests that the WTO treaty should be interpreted to ensure its fullest effect, which may mean going beyond the strict confines of the text of the treaty. In contrast to the basis of Model I, which excludes international external law because it was not explicitly mentioned in WTO law, Pauwelyn, a proponent of Model II, promotes that 'the absence of explicit contracting out must be regarded as a continuation of implicit acceptance of the rules in question'.[17] The adjudicating bodies would be outward looking in making rulings to protect the sanctity of international law as a unitary system. This makes the model look broad in its scope.[18] The rationale is that the drafters of a treaty are not 'omniscient' as circumstances may emerge in which a system needs powers to function effectively. Accordingly, the WTO explained by Model II would be more likely to fall back on general international law, and to apply external international law.[19]

4.3 Model III: WTO law as privileged

In this model, the premise that WTO law is privileged over external law appears as an attempt to reconcile, or at least break into, the debate between Models I and II.[20] Bartels, a proponent of Model III, claims the 'large print' is to put forward a different view from that of Model I, which he argued could be 'too restrictive', 'unduly positivistic' and 'not reflecting the actual practice' of the adjudicating bodies.[21] The model suggests that WTO law is *privileged* or given priority over external international law in the event of a conflict in WTO law. The basis of the model is a conflicts clause inferred from Articles 3.2 and 19.2 of the DSU.[22] Proponents of

16 Some proponents further argue that the adjudicating bodies should apply international law when there has been no direct violation of WTO law. See for example Schoenbaum *supra* note 2 at 653, who argues that violations of public international law should be 'non-violation' or 'situation' complaint whether or not a violation of a covered agreement has occurred.

17 Pauwelyn 'The Role of Public International Law' *supra* note 2, at, 541.

18 For further discussion on the doctrine of implied powers see Klabbers *supra* note 8 at, 67–73, 78–80. Akande *supra* note 8. Marceau 'Conflicts of Norms and Conflicts of Jurisdictions' *supra* note 1, at 1082–1083. Also see cases: *Interpretation of the Greco-Turkish Agreement of December 1st, 1926 Advisory Opinion*, 1928, PCIJ Rep. 20. *Effect of Awards of Compensation Made by the United Nations Administrative Tribunal*, 1954 ICJ Rep. 57. *Certain Expenses of the United Nations (Article 17, Paragraph 2, of the Charter) Advisory Opinion*, 1962 ICJ Rep. 168.

19 Pauwelyn *Conflict of Norms supra* note 1, at 207–212.

20 Bartels *supra* note 3.

21 Bartels *supra* note 3, at 499.

22 Bartels *supra* note 3, at 506–508, passim. For discussion on conflicts clauses see Pauwelyn *Conflict of Norms supra* note 2, at 327–439, esp. 328–329, 336.

DSU Article 3.2 reads: The dispute settlement system of the WTO is a central element in providing security and predictability to the multilateral trading system. The Members recognise that it serves to preserve the rights and obligations of Members under the covered agreements, and to clarify the existing provisions of those agreements in accordance with customary rules of interpretation of public international law. Recommendations and rulings of the DSB [Dispute Settlement Body] cannot add to or diminish the rights and obligations provided in the covered agreements

DSU Article 19.2 reads: In accordance with paragraph 2 of Article 3, in their findings and recommendations, the panel and Appellate Body cannot add to or diminish the rights and obligations provided in the covered agreements.

the model would claim to escape the restrictiveness of Model I to limit the domain of WTO law[23] while appearing to temper the broad openness of Model II. The idea is that it is not a normal conflicts clause because the Articles do not as a matter of substantive law regulate conflict between the covered agreements and other agreements of WTO law. The General Interpretative Note of Annex 1A[24] and Article XVI:3 of the WTO Agreement regulates such conflict.[25] On this basis, Articles 3.2 and 19.2 limit the powers of the Dispute Settlement Body (DSB) and the adjudicating bodies, but do not directly determine the substantive law applicable in a dispute. They share the same effect as a conflicts clause in determining the primacy, though not the exclusivity of WTO law in the WTO legal system.[26] The premise of Model III that WTO law is privileged is qualified by the 'small print' that the adjudicating bodies can only hear claims based on WTO law.[27] A qualification that both Models I and II accept. The real argument emerges in deciding what law can be applicable as a claim/defense in WTO law against a violation of WTO law and so whether there can be some resort to external international law, and on what basis.

4.4 The structural nature of the debate

Do we subscribe to Model I, that international law is heterogeneous and fragmented, consisting of systems that generally apply their own law, so that WTO law does not apply law outside the WTO legal system? Alternatively, do we subscribe to Model II that international law is a unitary and homogeneous system, which generally has the same practical significance for all systems, so that external international law can be applied in WTO law? The advantages of one model reflect the disadvantages on the other, and vice versa. What emerges appears as an entrenched and implicitly agreed to pattern of debate – argument, counter-argument, argument – that shields them from critique. As I discussed in the Prologue there is no whole composite critique because it is impossible to have a basis to capture everything so we disaggregate the models. Critique can be normative, analytical, or be about the purposes of the models. Two things are important to note. The first is that I am not suggesting that

23 Bartels *supra* note 3, at 499.

24 This regulates conflict between GATT 1994 and Annex 1A Agreements, stating that, 'in the event of conflict between a provision of the General Agreement on Tariffs and Trade 1994 and a provision of another agreement in Annex 1A to the Agreement Establishing the World Trade Organization (referred to in the agreements in Annex 1A as the 'WTO Agreement'), the provision of the other agreement shall prevail to the extent of the conflict. Also see Montaguti E and Maurits Lugard, 'The GATT 1994 and other Annex 1A Agreements: Four Different Relationships?' (2000) JIEL 473–484.

25 This regulates conflict between the WTO Agreement and the multilateral agreements set out in Annex 1, 2 and 3 of the WTO Agreement. It states that 'in the event of a conflict between a provision of this Agreement and a provision of any of the Multilateral Trade Agreements, the provision of this Agreement shall prevail to the extent of the conflict.'

26 Bartels *supra* note 3, at 507–508.

27 Bartels *supra* note 3, at 499.

the models shield WTO law from a critique. It is the debate about how WTO law interacts with external international law that is shielded from critique. The second is that it is not the models that create a barrier to critique, because we know what the models, as explored above, entail. To make a claim to the contrary would be unmerited. It is actually how the models frame and shape the debate on the interaction between WTO law and external international law that creates the shield. What is important at this specific point is not the actual arguments but the guise of the debate. The debate appears to constantly move back and forth between Model I (WTO law as a limited domain) and Model II (WTO law as open). We can imagine that when the inadequacies of Model I become evident as to the idea that WTO law is a limited domain the debate shifts to Model II. When Model II inadequacies as to the idea that WTO law is open become evident the debate shifts back to Model I to compensate. This is not to suggest that by acknowledging Models I and II as nested oppositions is the only way to represent the structural patterns of the debate between them.[28] The representation is not exhaustive but simply explanatory.[29] There is nothing implausible or necessarily incorrect about viewing the structural pattern of the debate in this way.

What the pattern suggests is that questions about Model I (limited domain) are usually framed as a response or critique to Model II (openness), and questions about Model II are usually framed as a response or critique of Model I. In doing so, a reasoned critique of either model goes unaddressed, unnoticed or even stifled, whether that critique is structural as done here, or ideological, analytical, normative. The pattern of the debate makes it difficult to break the current deadlock, as Models I and II are able to sanitise dissent by allowing their own contradictions, as to each other. This creates legitimate opposition to the debate *within* the debate. It sets out the terms of what is acceptable opposition in the debate and forecloses an insurgency. In that way, the debate in its entirety appears credible, even if none of the models on its own is a wholly satisfactory explanation of the interaction between WTO law and external international law. In shifting between models, neither model realises or perhaps wants to realise its inadequacy as an entirely satisfactory explanation of the interaction. Neither model wants to yield to the other because that may compromise the integrity of its nomos, which it seeks to impose on WTO law. The models are monological, suggesting they talk past each other. This leads to a stalemate, which Model III (WTO law as privileged) attempted to solve but I am not convinced of its success for reasons I explore in the next section.

28 Balkin J: 'Nested Oppositions' (1990) 99 *Yale Law Journal* 1669–1705, esp. 1671–1677, 1683–1686; 'Being Just with Deconstruction' (1994) 3 *Social and Legal Studies* 393–404, esp. 396–398. Nested oppositions can be understood to mean that conceptually the models contain each other. That is to say, that they have a conceptual dependence upon each other. The point is that one model informs its opposite model. It does not mean that there is no difference in the models. Of course, there is a difference. Otherwise, they would not be opposites. What it does mean is that the models 'possess simultaneous relationships of difference and similarity which are manifested as we consider them in different contexts of judgement.'

29 Ibid.

4.5 Resolution of conflict by superficial means

I am doubtful of the utility of inferring a conflicts clause in Articles 3.2 and 19.2 to privilege WTO law over external international law. The Articles do not stipulate that WTO Members in their future negotiations cannot change or overrule, in essence derogate from the WTO treaty.[30] Even if the Articles were a conflicts clause, the WTO could always frame the relationship with external international law[31] through authoritative interpretations on the treaty,[32] waivers,[33] amendments[34] or adoption of guidelines by the Ministerial Council.[35] As Pauwelyn argues, a conflicts clause would be somewhat futile in regulating a conflict between WTO and external international law because *lex posterior* is not deactivated.[36] The latter treaty would prevail over the former treaty, unless the latter treaty explicitly states that it is subject to the former treaty. However, the intent or will of Members to give primacy to new areas of regulation by creating the basis for new law through a treaty or over time by custom, limits a conflicts clause (see chapter 2). Bartels, the main proponent of Model III, admits that 'in fact I myself wrote an article in which I argued that Article 3.2 DSU should be seen as a conflicts clause. But I no longer think that this is correct.'[37] He goes on to assert a new position, stating that 'I now think that the phrase "add to or diminish rights and obligations in the covered agreements" can and should be read to mean "add to or diminish *applicable* rights and obligations in the covered agreements".'[38] The 'question of applicability' is 'decided in accordance with the secondary rules of public international law' such as rules on treaty conflicts.[39] However, having explored the rules on treaty interpretation we realise that these rules can be somewhat ineffectual in addressing an

30 Bartels *supra* note 3, at 354.

31 Ibid, 344.

32 Marrakesh Agreement Establishing the World Trade Organisation Article XI (Decision-making) para 2 states that 'The Ministerial Conference and the General Council shall have the exclusive authority to adopt interpretations of this Agreement and of the Multilateral Trade Agreements . . .' See www.wto.org for the full text of the WTO Agreement.

33 Marrakesh Agreement Establishing the World Trade Organisation Article XI (Decision-making) para 3 states that 'In exceptional circumstances, the Ministerial Conference may decide to waive an obligation imposed on a Member by this Agreement or any of the Multilateral Trade Agreements . . .' See www.wto.org for the full text of the WTO Agreement.

34 Marrakesh Agreement Establishing the World Trade Organisation Article X (Amendments) para 1 states that 'Any Member of the WTO may initiate a proposal to amend the provisions of this Agreement or the Multilateral Trade Agreements in Annex 1 by submitting such proposal to the Ministerial Conference . . .' See www.wto.org for the full text of the WTO Agreement.

35 Marrakesh Agreement Establishing the World Trade Organisation Article IV (Structure of the WTO) para 1 states that '. . . the Ministerial Conference shall have authority to take decision on all matters under any of the Multilateral Trade Agreements, if so requested by a Member . . .' See www.wto.org for the full text of the WTO Agreement.
Pauwelyn *Conflict of Norms supra* note 1, at 336, 355.

36 Ibid, 336, 355.

37 Andenas M and F Ortino (eds) *WTO Law and Process* (London: British Institute of International and Comparative Law, 2005) 517.

38 Ibid.

39 Ibid, 517–518.

overlap between the laws of differing legal systems in international law (see chapter 2). What is more, Articles 3.2 and 19.2 do not have to be a conflicts clause to bring effect to Bartels's perspective. The 'winner-takes-all' adjudication system reflects the 'limited subject-matter jurisdiction' of the WTO law.[40] WTO law already prevails, and is the only law the adjudicating bodies can 'directly' address. The result is that there is 'no justification or benefit' in articulating a conflicts rule in Articles 3.2 and 19.2.[41] Further to this, having realised that Bartels moves closer to the position of Model II, what I do next is to return to a discussion on how Models I and II assess the Articles.

4.5.1 Models I and II on the purpose of Articles 3.2 and 19.2

In discussing Articles 3.2 and 19.2, Pauwelyn, a proponent of Model II (WTO law as open), argues that if the WTO applies external international law, it was not 'adding to or diminishing' the rights and obligations of WTO Members as Articles 3.2 and 19.2 articulates.[42] He argues that the phrase 'can not add to or diminish the rights and obligations' of WTO Members 'does not prevent WTO Members from consenting to other treaties that may affect their WTO obligations'.[43] Pauwelyn is of the view that Articles do not mean that the adjudicating bodies cannot 'never' add or diminish the rights and obligations of Members because occasionally the adjudicating bodies use external international law to interpret WTO law.[44] He stresses that the Articles do not address the jurisdiction or the applicable law before an adjudicating body but distinguish between the legislative and judicial function of the WTO.[45] The Articles according to Model II set out the limits of interpretation of the adjudicating body to that of the covered agreements (WTO law).[46] Therefore, in this view, Articles 3.2 and 19.2 do not mean that pre or post 1994 international law cannot influence the WTO or in the event of conflict that the WTO law must prevail over international law.[47] Pauwelyn suggests that the reference to customary rules of interpretation in Article 3.2 was *ex abundante cautela* or made out of excess caution. This means that what the law does not exclude by specific mention, the law includes.[48] Steger argues that Pauwelyn neglects the text of Articles 3.2 and 19.2 in that Article 3.2 does not require an interpreter to apply 'all' existing law between parties to determine whether a WTO Member has been consistent with WTO law.[49] McGinnis notes that Pauwelyn's suggestion

40 Palmeter D, 'The WTO as a Legal System' (2000) *Fordham International Law Journal* 480.
41 Marceau *supra* note 22, at 776–777. Pauwelyn *Conflict of Norms supra* note 1, at 355.
42 Pauwelyn 'The Jurisdiction of the WTO' *supra* note 2, at 138.
43 Ibid.
44 Ibid.
45 Pauwelyn *Conflict of Norms supra* note 1, at 353–354.
46 Ibid, at 353.
47 Pauwelyn 'The Role of Public International Law in the WTO' *supra* note 2, at 564; 'The Jurisdiction of the WTO' *supra* note 2, at 138.
48 Ibid.
49 Steger *supra* note 1, at 144.

to allow customary international law to override WTO law, 'misconceives and distorts' WTO law. In his view Article 3.2 sets out that WTO law be interpreted 'according' to customary international law and not that customary international law should 'serve as a rule of decision' in a dispute.[50]

Trachtman, the main proponent of Model I, argues contrary to Pauwelyn that Article 3.2 is more than *ex abundante cautela* because the history of the GATT does not reflect the application of general international law.[51] In other words, the fact that Article 3.2, and generally the DSU did not mention any other international law, but the customary rules of treaty interpretation is not to be taken lightly. Trachtman proposes that the principle of *effet utile* counters *ex abundante cautela*: the latter doing exactly what the former requires not be done, in that one is not to read and interpret the clauses of a treaty to redundancy.[52] He also asserts that *ex abundante cautela* could not undermine another common rule of interpretation *expressio unius est exclusio alterius* where the specific reference to customary rules does the exact opposite to what Pauwelyn proposes. As Trachtman argues, 'the drafters demonstrated intent to exclude international law by virtue of their decision not to mention it.'[53] The point is that because Article 3.2 does not positively prohibit external international law does not mean that it negatively includes it.[54] This argument between Model I (WTO law as a limited domain) and Model II (WTO law as open) over the inclusion or exclusion of external international law in the WTO through *expressio unius* and *ex abundante* illustrates two earlier points. The first is that the rules of treaty interpretation do not decisively address fragmentation (see chapter 2). The second and more pressing for this chapter is that it shows the structural nature of the debate between the models as discussed earlier.

4.5.2 The distinction between jurisdiction and applicable law

Bartels writes it is 'important' to 'recognise the distinction' between the 'subject matter of a dispute' and the 'sources of applicable law' because a court can have limited jurisdiction of the disputes it can resolve but not in the applicable law to resolve these disputes.[55] On its jurisdictional competence to apply and enforce WTO law the starting point for applicable law in the WTO is WTO law. Claims of violations in the WTO can only be made about WTO law, as set out in the covered agreements as a textual basis for WTO law.[56] Essentially considerations

50 McGinnis J, 'The Appropriate Hierarchy of Global Multilateralism and Customary International Law: The Example if the WTO' (2003) 44 *Virginia Journal of International Law* 229, 265–267.
51 Trachtman 'The Jurisdiction of the WTO' *supra* note 1, at 139–140.
52 Ibid, 140.
53 Ibid.
54 Ibid.
55 Bartels *supra* note 3, at 501–502.
56 Bartels *supra* note 3 at 503. Marceau G, 'WTO Dispute Settlement and Human Rights', *supra* note 1, at 766–767. Lindross and Mehling *supra note* 11, at 860–861. Further for example the DSU Article 2 notes that the 'rules and procedures of this Understanding shall apply subject to such special or additional rules and procedures on dispute settlement contained in the covered agreements as are identified in Appendix 2 to this Understanding.'

about jurisdiction and applicable law in the current debate about how WTO and external international law interact appear to about the *extent* to which the WTO adjudicating bodies, can or cannot apply external international law when addressing a claim/defense. A limited jurisdiction does not necessarily mean that the law the adjudicating bodies may apply when considering a claim/defense is limited.[57] Further to that, a wide jurisdiction does not necessarily mean that the law the adjudicating bodes in that jurisdiction apply when considering a claims/defense is somehow wide ranging. The distinction between jurisdiction and applicable law is no direct indicator of the law that will be applied in that jurisdiction, even if it points to a difference between the law that is part of a claim/defense and the law that can determine which law is applicable in that claim/defense.

Bartels highlights three further distinctions between applicable external international law as; an aide to the interpretation of a given provision of WTO law, evidence of a Member's compliance with WTO law, and law in a chain of legal reasoning.[58] However, my response is that the distinctions may actually be merely different ways of coming to the same conclusion that a limited jurisdiction does not equal limited applicable law. The distinctions do not affect the nature of the debate between Model I (the limited domain of WTO law) and Model II (WTO law as open), or address the fundamental concern of *how* WTO and external international law interact. Having the distinction is a matter of knowing where the external international law arises in the legal argument of a claim/defense. Important as that is, I think we are back at where we started because this does not tells us how that external international law can be applied in WTO law, and what role it serves in meeting the purpose of WTO law.

There are three things to appreciate about the conceptual shortcomings of Bartels (Model III) to break the debate between Model I (WTO law is a limited domain) and Model II (WTO law is open), which has dominated literature about the interaction between WTO and external international law. The first is that Bartels' model does not define WTO law and assumes that we have all agreed to what it is and does. As in the Prologue I think that we can only succinctly address the issue of how external international law interacts with WTO law if we decisively define and know what is WTO law. The second issue is that his model appears as part of the sanitised contradictions of WTO law as a limited domain (Model I) versus WTO law as open (Model II). As discussed earlier, the structural nature of the debate allows a space for dissent but only within the pattern of the debate, so that the same arguments are repeated as if anew as support for or against, either Model I or Model II. Bartels' model tries to make WTO law open to external international law but when that external law comes into WTO law, according to this model, WTO law is privileged in the event of a conflict between WTO law and external international law. The consequence of which would be to deny the effectiveness of external international law in WTO law. Unintended as it may be, we are then back to WTO law as a limited domain,

57 See for example, Bartels *supra* note 3, at 502.
58 Bartels *supra* note 3, at 510.

which is what he wanted to avoid. The third issue is that Model III does not tell us what happens to the external international law beyond analytically and descriptively situating it in the three ways as noted above. The question goes unanswered because his model is engaging in the terms of the debate as between Model I and Model II, about the extent to which external law can be used in WTO law, and not as the primary question if WTO law can directly respond to external international law, as constrained openness explored (see chapter 3).

4.5.3 Illustrating the debate

I believe we can visually illustrate the shortcomings of the debate and attempts to reconcile Models I and II, as Model III seems to do, using Mark Titchner's artwork *Resolving Conflict by Superficial Means*. This work shows that conflicts or opposites are not eliminated but are hidden.[59] Reminiscent of the optical illusions of Marcel Duchamp's kinetic *Rotoreliefs*, the piece comprises of a central revolving disc.[60] The result of the disc in motion was an optical illusion in which the three separate sets of circles unify into one consistent and coherent spiral. Once the motion stops the three circles return to their original and true state as separate. There was no reconciliation. This is analogous to what happens with the three models in the debate. The structural pattern of the debate essentially creates a façade in which the debate between the dominate models continues, instead of its core presumptions being called into question about what is WTO law and how does it interact with external international law.

In the next section, appreciating Bartels' attempt to break the debate between Model I and Model II, I continue advancing a theory of WTO law, constrained openness. This is not as an alternative or dialectic to either Model I or Model II, but is a way to make practical use them, which I think Model III fails to do. This is not because it was incomplete, in the sense that no idea can ever be complete to account for all eventualities as discussed in the Prologue. More conceptually, this is because Model III did not bring Model I and Model II to a new position. Instead Model III appears as an insertion into the current debate, without rearranging it,

59 Titchner M, *Resolving Conflict by Superficial Means* (2002), concrete, carved wood, electric motor, paint. For image see Artwork in the front pages of the book. For further discussion of the artwork see: Titchner M, *It Is You* (ed. M. Clarke) (Bristol: Arnolfini, 2006) 36; *British Art Show 6* (London: Hayward Gallery Publishing, 2005) 116, 119; Titchner M, 'We Were Thinking of Evolving' (Vilma Gold Gallery) at www.vilmagold.com/newpages/previous/mark3.htm (last visited January 2010). For further discussion on Titchner's work see the pamphlet *Turner Prize* (London: Tate Publishing, 2006); Titchner M, *Why and Why Not (Vibrations, Schizzes and Knots)* (London: Book Works, 2004, 2006).

60 See *supra* note 59. For further reading about Marcel Duchamp see Judovitz D, *Unpacking Duchamp: Art in Transit* (Berkeley: University of California Press, 1998) esp. 96–101; Demos T J, *The Exiles of Marcel Duchamp* (Massachusetts: MIT, 2007) esp. 43–44; Paz O, *Marcel Duchamp: Appearance Stripped Bare*, trans. Philips R and D Gardner (New York: Arcade Publishing, 1990) [Original Spanish edition, 1978] esp. 99–100; Crop C, *Marcel Duchamp: Critical Lives*, trans. V. Rehberg (London: Reaktion Books Ltd, 2006).

so that when we stop moving as shown here in Titchner's artwork, we are back to the same positions as before. The aim as discussed in the next section is to move, if I only slightly, beyond the current debate to create a space in which we can start to consider theories of WTO law, which can be used to map the interaction between WTO and external international law.

4.6 The constrained openness of WTO law: identifying the purpose of WTO law

Constrained openness as a theory of WTO law is thus far constitutive of a method (counter-factual rule of recognition) to tell us what is WTO law (chapter 1), a context (fragmentation) in which that WTO law operates (chapters 1, 2 and 3) and concepts (operational closure and reflexive law) to tell us how to understand that law (chapters 1 and 3). The task has been to understand WTO law as an autonomous and distinct legal entity. As a theory, it will importantly present a new way to understand the current models as discussed in this chapter. Thereby, recasting previous thought and providing a way to understand the practice of WTO law as explored in chapters 5 and 6. The theory of constrained openness is however not fully devised until it identifies the purpose of WTO law. As discussed in the Prologue and chapter 1, law is socially constructed meaning that the purpose of law like the definition of law is not naturally occurring but like the definition of law must also be determined. If we understand law as a socially determined tool, then law's purpose is to make what we have defined as law useful. In knowing the purpose of WTO law we can distinguish it from external international law or other social phenomenon. Until we define the purpose of WTO law, the debate over which idea best secures an understanding of how WTO law interacts with external international law is somewhat meaningless. In other words, if we do not know law's purpose how can we debate over which idea best secures an understanding of that purpose?

The main aim of WTO law is commonly understood as based on the WTO's prohibition of trade restrictive measures. This is realised through the Most-Favoured-Nation Status[61] and National Treatment,[62] which form the cornerstone

61 Article I (Most-Favoured Nation Status) of WTO/GATT states: 'With respect to customs duties and charges of any kind imposed on or in connection with importation or exportation or imposed on the international transfer of payments for imports or exports, and with respect to the method of levying such duties and charges, and with respect to all rules and formalities in connection with importation and exportation, and with respect to all matters referred to in paragraphs 2 and 4 of Article III,* any advantage, favour, privilege or immunity granted by any contracting party to any product originating in or destined for any other country shall be accorded immediately and unconditionally to the like product originating in or destined for the territories of all other contracting parties.' [Annex 1 footnotes suppressed]

See Cases: *EC – Bananas III* (European Communities – Regime for Importation, Sale and Distribution of Bananas III) 1997 WT/DS27/AB/R para 126; *Canada – Autos* [Canada – Certain Measures Affecting the Automobile Industry) 2000 WT/DS139/AB/R, WT/DS142/AB/R para 78–81, 84:

62 Article III:1 (National Treatment) states that 'The contracting parties recognize that internal taxes and other internal charges, and laws, regulations and requirements affecting the internal sale,

or heart of WTO law.[63] 'Any advantage, favour, privilege or immunity granted' by one Member 'shall be accorded immediately and unconditionally' to 'all' other Members.[64] Tariff commitments made by a Member in their Schedule pursuant to GATT/WTO Article II also 'represent a common agreement among *all* Members.'[65] The universality and scope of this central principle in WTO law that what is afforded to one Member is afforded to all Members means that all Members are afforded the same treatment as to each other concerning restrictions on their imported goods and as to domestic goods so no protection disadvantages imported goods.[66] Even when a measure is allowed to be trade restrictive and contravene WTO law as can occur primarily under Article XX,[67] the measure must still pass a 'necessity test' as the least trade restrictive of available measures.[68] Measures must also meet an overall test of not being a disguised, arbitrary or discriminatory prohibition of free trade.[69] The exceptions allowed in Article XX are only secondarily

offering for sale, purchase, transportation, distribution or use of products, and internal quantitative regulations requiring the mixture, processing or use of products in specified amounts or proportions, should not be applied to imported or domestic products so as to afford protection to domestic production.*' [Annex 1 footnotes suppressed]

See cases: *Japan – Alcoholic Beverages II* (Japan – Taxes on Alcoholic Beverages) 1996 WT/DS8/AB/R, WT/DS10/AB/R, WT/DS11/AB/R 16–18; *EC – Asbestos* (European Communities – Measures Affecting Asbestos and Products Containing Asbestos) WT/DS135/AB/R para 93. For discussion see Jackson J, W Davey and A Sykes, *Legal Problems of International Economic Relations* (St. Paul, MN: West Group, 2002, *Fourth Edition*) 479–531.

63 Jackson et al. *Legal Problems of International Economic Relations (Fourth Edition) supra* note 192, at 415, 415–446. Jackson J, *The Jurisprudence of GATT and the WTO* (Cambridge: CUP, 2000) 58–61. EC – *Tariff Preferences* (European Communities – Conditions for the Granting of Tariff Preferences to Developing Countries) WT/DS246/AB/R noted that 'It is well settled that the MFN principle embodied in Article I:1 is a 'cornerstone of the GATT' and 'one of the pillars of the WTO trading system', which has consistently served as a key basis and impetus for concessions in trade negotiations . . .'.

64 See *supra* note 61.

65 See Appellate Body Report, *EC – Customs Classification of Certain Computer Equipment*, WT/DS62/AB/R adopted 5 June 1998, para 84, 73–76.

66 See *supra* note 62.

67 WTO/GATT Article XX states that: 'Subject to the requirement that such measures are not applied in a manner which would constitute a means of arbitrary or unjustifiable discrimination between countries where the same conditions prevail, or a disguised restriction on international trade, nothing in this Agreement shall be construed to prevent the adoption or enforcement by any contracting party of measures:

(a) necessary to protect public morals;
(b) necessary to protect human, animal or plant life or health;
. . .
(g) relating to the conservation of exhaustible natural resources if such measures are made effective in conjunction with restrictions on domestic production or consumption; . . .'

For further discussion see Jackson et al. *supra* note 63, at 532–574.

68 For example, see *Korea – Various Measures on Beef* (Korea – Measures Affecting Imports of Fresh, Chilled and Frozen Beef) 2000 WT/DS161/AB/R, WT/DS169/AB/R paras 161–164, 176.

69 For example, see *United States – Gasoline supra* note 88, at 23–25; *US – Shrimp* (US – Import Prohibition of Certain Shrimp and Shrimp Products) 1998 WT/DS58/AB/R paras 150, 164–165, 177.

invoked *after* the adjudicating bodies examine the primary and substantive question of the contravention of WTO law. Every question to the adjudicating bodies is the basic form of 'Has *WTO law* been violated?'[70] The standard recommendation, judgements, in the reports of the WTO adjudicating bodies is that the Member concerned brings the measure into conformity with WTO law.[71] Disputes in WTO law are raised and settled only within WTO law.

The purpose of WTO law is to promote free trade, or specifically the liberalisation of trade. Instinctively this is correct because 'after all the origins' of WTO law 'lie in GATT, the General Agreement on Tariffs and *Trade* 1947 which is now part of the World *Trade* Organisation.'[72] There is also a more insightful point that WTO law, as Carmody states, does not 'operate directly to require specific quantities of trade as much as indirectly to maintain conditions that promote trade.'[73] The purpose of WTO law is not merely to protect individual transactions occurring here and now but about the expectations concerning trade that may have not occurred as yet. It underpins the universality principle of WTO law. As a consequence the purpose of WTO law to protect expectations of trade is unhinged from a 'frame of reference in the here and now' and abstracted to render it 'timeless'.[74] Protecting the legitimate expectations of all Members to be able to trade and have any concession extended to one Member extended to all Members means that the purpose of WTO law is to promote and regulate not only trade but everything that trade depends upon, specifically the freedom or ability to trade.[75] 'The purpose of many [GATT/WTO] disciplines, indeed one of the primary objects of the GATT/WTO as a whole, is to produce certain market conditions which would allow this individual activity to flourish.'[76] The security and predictability afforded

70 Marceau 'Conflicts of Norms and Conflicts of Jurisdictions' *supra* note 1, at 1082. Sacerdoti G, 'The Role of Lawyers in the WTO Dispute Settlement System', in Yerxa R and B Wilson, *Key Issues in WTO Dispute Settlement: The First Ten Years* (Cambridge: CUP, 2005) 27.

71 See *supra* note 22.

72 Carmody C, 'A Theory of WTO Law' (2008) 11 (3) JIEL 1–31, 14.

73 Ibid.

74 Ibid.

75 Ibid, at 15. Some may argue that a look at the preamble could highlight other purposes of WTO law, especially with regards to environmental protection. The preamble to the Marrakesh Agreement that establishes the WTO reads: 'Recognizing that their relations in the field of trade and economic endeavour should be conducted with a view to raising standards of living, ensuring full employment and a large and steadily growing volume of real income and effective demand, and expanding the production of and trade in goods and services, while allowing for the optimal use of the world's resources in accordance with the objective of sustainable development, seeking both to protect and preserve the environment and to enhance the means for doing so in a manner consistent with their respective needs and concerns at different levels of economic development . . .'
However, the short response would be that in doing all these things WTO law is still ensuring, promoting and protecting the freedom to trade.

76 See *United States – Sections 301–310 of the Trade Act 1974*, WT/DS152/R, adopted 22 December 1999, para 7.73.

by the DSU are thus vital to maintaining the purpose of WTO law, especially Article 23 on 'Strengthening of the Multilateral System'.[77] Pursuant to that Article a Member shall only seek redress for a violation of WTO law through the DSU (WTO law).[78]

Further, pursuant to Article 23, any WTO Member that considers its 'WTO benefits have been nullified or impaired as a result of a measure adopted by another Member has the right to bring the case before the WTO dispute settlement system.'[79] The consequence is that the conditions of trade are not only owed to all WTO Members but redress for those consequences are owed to the entire legal system as well. Even if a Panel were to deny jurisdiction regarding an agreement between two parties to a dispute, then at the request of another Member not party to the agreement another panel could be asked to examine the matter.[80] DSU Article 10(2) corroborates this, in that a Member with only an interest, and not a legal interest but 'substantial interest' in a matter before the WTO adjudicating bodies may become party to a dispute as third party. Furthermore as to DSU Article 10(4), if a third party considers that a matter already under adjudication by a Panel 'nullifies or impairs benefits' it has under WTO law, that Member may request a Panel to consider the matter. I think that this undermines ideas about WTO law as a contractual bilateral agreement subsisting among Members because pursuant to Article 10, obligations, rights, benefits, and any impairment or nullification is not only an issue between the parties to that dispute but to *all* WTO Members. The conditions of trade, as to the rules set out in WTO law, which the adjudicating bodies attempt to clarify in the event of dispute between Members are not narrowly confined between Members in a dispute but exist among all Members.

As discussed in chapters 1 and 3, the constrained openness of WTO law advocates that WTO law can observe external international law but only through its own primary and substantive WTO law. This underlines the purpose and operation of WTO law to liberalise trade, by the prohibiting trade restrictions and protecting expectations of trade. The adjudicating bodies are central in executing the operations of the WTO with their rulings reflecting a high degree

77 DSU Article 23(1) states that: 'When Members seek the redress of a violation of obligations or other nullification of impairments of benefits under the covered agreements or an impediment to the attainment of any objective of the covered agreements, they shall have recourse to, and abide by, the rules and procedures of this Understanding.'

78 Panel, *United States – Import measures on Certain Products from the European Communities*, WT/DS165/R and Add.1, adopted 1 July 2000, paras 16.19–16.20. Also upheld by Appellate Body, *United States – Import measures on Certain Products from the European Communities*, WT/DS165/AB/R adopted 10 January 2001, para 111.
See chapter 6 for further discussion on no recourse to countermeasures.

79 Panel Report, *Mexico – Tax Measures on Soft Drinks and other Beverages*, WT/DS308/R, 7 October 2005, para 7.9.

80 Roessler F, 'Mexico (Tax Measures on Soft Drinks and Other Beverages): prepared for the ALI project on the case law of the WTO' (2009) 8(1) *World Trade Review* 25, 27.

of self-reference.[81] The purpose of WTO law does not suggest that it is isolated from the international legal system, but it does not necessarily follow that external international law is part of WTO law or vice versa. Not being isolated does not imply a direct step to inclusion. A system does not communicate with its environment, things external to it, so much as it communicates about its environment because of pressure or irritations from that environment. On this basis, external international law, to reiterate the discussion of chapter 3, is not directly incorporated into WTO law but should seek to indirectly and strategically influence WTO law. In recognition of its central purpose to liberalise trade, reflexive interventions should bear this in mind, for failure to do so may mean being ignored, dominated or effaced by WTO law.

Having established the purpose of WTO law, as part of the theory of constrained openness, we can now critique the models, in particular Model I (WTO law as a limited domain) and Model II (WTO law as open) to show how they can be utilised in my new theory. Consider Pauwelyn's view as a proponent of Model II that the WTO should defer to a higher epistemic authority.[82] On the basis of constrained openness, what is not realised is that such a deferral can only be based on the adjudicating bodies' (re)construction of reality (see chapter 3). The WTO would not be 'directly' able to seek external advice, as Pauwelyn proposes, because WTO law would only understand that advice on its own terms and through to its operation to liberalise trade. The only way the WTO can seek the advice would be to turn the case over to the other legal authority. However, the dilemma is that when the judgment returns to WTO law, the adjudicating bodies still only understand it through a (re)construction based on purpose of WTO law. The meaning of the judgement is potentially lost and its influence on WTO law along with it. To follow through with Pauwelyn's arguments the WTO would have to turn the case and decision over to the other system. Even then, that would be occurring based on the WTO's (re)construction of reality, as to the code of WTO legal/WTO illegal. However, if the WTO does not engage with the rich complex legal environment outside its covered agreement, its ability to learn is potentially limited. A closed WTO faces criticisms[83] of being 'narrowly focused',[84] 'myopic',[85] and singularly focused on trade,[86] with the likelihood of hostile

81 Greenwald J, 'WTO Dispute Settlement: An Exercise in Trade law Legislation?' (2003) 6(1) *Journal of International Economic Law*, 113–124, 123–124. Pulkowski D, 'Multiple Perspectives on the Fragmentation of International Law' (2004) Paper presented at the European Society of International Law 1–6, 4.

82 Pauwelyn *Conflict of Norms supra* note 1, at 119–120. Mavrodis P, 'The Trade Disputes Concerning Health Policy Between the EC and the US' in E Petersmann E and M Pollack (eds) *Transatlantic Economic Disputes: The EU, the US and the WTO* (Oxford: OUP, 2003) 233–245, 244.

83 For a good overview of the literature on this point, see Lang A, 'Reflecting on Linkage: Cognitive and Institutional Change in the International Trading System' (2007) 70(4) *Modern Law Review* 523, 532–536.

84 Wai R, 'Countering, Branding, Dealing: Using Economic and Social Rights In and Around the International Trade Regime' (2003) 14 *European Journal of International Law* 59.

85 Nicholas P, 'Trade Without Values' (1996) *Northwestern University Law Review* 701.

86 Guzman A, 'Global Governance and the WTO' (2004) 45 *Harvard International Law Journal* 313. Stiglitz J, *Globalisation and its Discontents* (London: Penguin Group, 2002) 216.

responses,[87] such as the 'Seattle' or 'Cancun' protests against 'unfair' international trade practices. These protests against the WTO assumed it was closed off from international social welfare.[88] As a proponent of Model I, Trachtman's desire for a limited jurisdiction and limited applicable law to that of WTO law as a response to the fragmentation of international law seems inadequate. He correctly underscores that each system in international law is different and functional, and pays careful attention to the texts of the treaty, as a basis from which to articulate the law. Between Models I and II, Model I appears to have the 'better of the textual arguments.'[89] However, it seems self-defeating in trying to strictly contain the influence of external international law in the WTO by narrowly sticking to the texts of the WTO treaty to produce the single right answer.[90] Moreover, this could perhaps re-ignite the opinion of the WTO as 'ignorant' to international law.[91]

None of the models account for the institutional centralisation of the adjudicating bodies of WTO law, making the models somewhat unsatisfactory explanations of the complex epistemological issue of *how* the adjudicating bodies apply external international law. Additionally, the models do not appear to deal with the political effect of the application and subsequent internalisation of external international law into the WTO as the only international legal system that has a compulsory, exclusive and automatic adjudication system. The WTO can attract jurisdiction in that its dispute settlement mechanism can be set in motion if a Member shows that trade is being affected even if only nominally. Meeting the conditions for initiating the dispute settlement mechanism is somewhat easy.[92] 'Allegations that WTO trade is affected would generally suffice to trigger formally the regular WTO dis-

87 Kelly C, 'Power, Linkage and Accommodation: The WTO as an International Actor and its influence over other actors and regimes' (2006) 24 *Berkeley Journal of International Law* 79–128, 86.

88 Mertes T (ed) *A Movement of Movements: Is Another World Really Possible* (London: Verso, 2004); Njehu N, 'Cancel the Debt' 94–110, 100–101; Bove J, 'A Farmers' International?' 137–151, 143–144; Sader E, 'Beyond Civil Society' 248–261, esp. 259. See also International Centre for Trade and Sustainable Development (2003) *Bridges* 7(6) and (7) (pre and post Cancun publications) at http://www.ictsd.org/monthly/bridges/BRIDGES7-6.pdf and http://www.ictsd.org/monthly/bridges/BRIDGES7-7.pdf.
Also see International Centre for Trade and Sustainable Development (1999) *Bridges* 3(8) (pre Seattle publication) at http://www.ictsd.org/English/BRIDGES3-8.pdf.

89 Dunoff J L, 'The WTO in Transition: Of Constituents, Competence and Coherence' (2001) *George Washington International Law Review* 979, 998.

90 Howse R, 'From Politics to Technocracy – and Back Again: The Fate of the Multilateral Trade Regime' (2002) 96 *American Journal of International Law* 94, 106. Lindross and Mehling *supra* note 11, at 863.

91 Kuyper P, 'The Law of GATT as a Special Field of International Law' (1994) 25 *Netherlands Yearbook of International Law* 140. Marceau 'A Call for Coherence in International Law' *supra* note 1, at 95 argues that *US – Gasoline* changed the view of the WTO adjudicating bodies as ignorant to international law.

92 Marceau, 'WTO Dispute Settlement and Human Rights' *supra* note 1, at 757–762. For example, see the following cases: *US – Wool Shirts and Blouses* [Appellate Body Report, US – Measures Affecting Imports of Woven Shirts and Blouses from India] 1997 WT/DS33/AB/R 13; *EC–Bananas III* [EC – Regime for the Importation, Sale and Distribution of Bananas] 1997 WT/DS27/AB/R para 135.

pute settlement process through a simple request in writing for consultations, copied to the Dispute Settlement Body [DSB].'[93] The models do not account for the normative and structural impact of the primacy and power of WTO law over external international law.[94] For constrained openness every decision the WTO takes essentially remains a WTO decision, where external international law does not directly enter WTO law. In order to apply external international law, the WTO adjudicating bodies must determine what that law *is*, *where* it is found, what it *says*, and what it *means*, according to the code of WTO law, which is to liberalise trade. This is what I can call an issue of *capture* in that the WTO cannot observe and make sense of external international law but through its internal point of view. The WTO cannot stand outside itself, as it has no Archimedean point. Constituents wanting an authoritative and final judgment on external international law in a field that lacks compulsory jurisdiction may represent their claim as a WTO claim.[95] This is because a decision and enforcement of that decision[96] is ensured given the highly legalised dispute settlement mechanism of the WTO[97] that can produce 'hard law'. This is compared to the 'soft-law'[98] based dispute settlement mechanisms of other international law such as international environmental law.[99] Moreover, because of its dispute settlement mechanism, near universal Membership and exceptions to prohibition of trade in Article XX, external international

93 Marceau *supra* note 1, at 758. See DSU esp. Articles 3(7)–3(8), 4(3)–4(4).

94 See Kalderimis D, 'Problems of WTO Harmonisation and the Virtues of Shields over Swords' (2004) 13 *Minnesota Journal of Global Trade* 305–351. Simma and Pulkowski *supra* note 10, at 510. Kelly C, 'Power, Linkage and Accommodation: The WTO as an International Actor and Its Influence over Other Actors and Regimes' (2006) 24 *Berkeley Journal of International Law* 79, 86–93, 113–126 *passim*. Kelly seems to advance a similar discussion as to the one I put forward here regarding the normative and institutional impact of WTO law on external law. However, she does not go as far as I do in conceptualising the WTO as constrained openness.

95 See Pauwelyn, 'How to Win a World Trade Organisation Dispute Based on Non-World Trade Organisation Law? Questions of Jurisdiction and Merits' (2003) 37(6) *Journal of International Economic Law* 997–1030.

96 See DSU Article 21 (Surveillance of Implementation of Recommendations and Rulings) and Article 22 (Compensation and Suspension of Concessions).

97 Kelly C *supra* note 94, at 190–191.

98 There is no accepted definition of soft law. However, it can be understood as instruments other than a treaty; particularly declarations, principles or standards of expected behaviour that are not legally binding, but are more in the way of political, ethical, or economic values operating in a 'grey zone' between law and politics. Soft law is characterised by an intended vagueness regarding obligations with a weak command structure. Some commentators welcome the use of soft law whereas others see it as a pathological slip to relative normativity. For example: *In support*: Boyle A, 'Soft Law in International Law-Making' in M Evans (ed) *International Law* (London: OUP, 2006) 141–158; Shelton D, 'International Law and Relative Normativity', in Evans, ibid, 159–185. Dupuy P, 'Soft Law and the International Law of the Environment' (1991) 12 *Michigan Journal of International Law* 420.

Contra: Weil P, 'Towards Relative Normativity in International Law' (1983) *American Journal of International Law* 413–442; Arend A, *Legal Rules and International Society* (Oxford: OUP, 1999) 24–25.

99 For examples of soft law in international environmental law, see the 1992 Rio Declaration on Environment and Development. See Boyle *supra* note 98, at 142.

legal systems begin to make room for the WTO by modelling their law on WTO law.[100] This is something that should be guarded against, as it reduces the complexity of the international legal system. The point of reflexive interventions (see chapter 3) is that systems retain their critical identity and strategically attempt to influence another system, not redefine their own law as to the other system.

Consider a state challenging the environmental measures of another state. The challenging state takes the case before the adjudicating bodies to make a ruling based on a claim of a violation of WTO law. The adjudicating bodies are in effect being forced to give a ruling on what is primarily a claim of international environmental law because an environmental measure creates a trade restriction that violates WTO law.[101] Given its strong dispute settlement mechanism, pressing the WTO into addressing external international law for the sake of a united system of international law potentially expands the jurisdiction of the WTO and gives it too much arbitral power.[102] The WTO ruling on external international law looks judicially active[103] in overstepping its legal, and more specifically jurisdictional and political boundaries purposely designated to liberalise trade. The WTO would look like a potential intruder that disturbs the political balances struck by the competing constituents as the adjudicating bodies would be taking decisions on issues that were not explicitly part of WTO law. Furthermore, no tribunal generally wants to look out of step with the politics of its Membership that gives it existence, for fear of being abolished or having its power reduced by its executive.[104]

The models also seem to miss the point that the strong judicial function of the WTO adjudicating bodies is enhanced by the correspondingly weak legislative structure of the WTO.[105] The Ministerial Conference and General Council are

100 See for example, Kelly C *supra* note 94, at 113–126 discussing the effect the WTO's SPS Agreement on the Cartagena Protocol regarding risk assessment and the use of scientific evidence.

101 For a discussion on the interaction between environmental law and WTO law see chapter 2 and chapter 5 on the precautionary principle.

102 For a discussion of the 'trade and . . .' debate see Lang *supra* note 83. For further discussion about linking WTO law with international law see Symposium: 'The Boundaries of the WTO' (2002) 96 *American Journal of International Law*; Symposium: 'Linkage as Phenomenon: Linking the Trade Linkage Debate' (1998) 19 *University of Pennsylvania Journal of International Economic Law*. See also Kelly C *supra* note 94 for a discussion on the dangers of linking in that WTO law would assume normative and structural dominance over external law because of the primacy and strong legal framework of WTO law. For a similar argument regarding human rights and WTO law see Alston P, 'Resisting the Merger and Acquisition of Human Rights by Trade Law: A Reply to Petersmann' (2002) 13 *European Journal of International Law* 753–814.

103 See Kelly J, 'Judicial Activism at the WTO: Developing Principles of Self-restraint' (2002) 22 *Northwestern Journal of International Law and Business* 353, 361.

104 See for general discussion on this matter regarding how the WTO responds to environmental rules and issues: Keleman R, 'The Limits of Judicial Power: Trade–Environment Disputes in the GATT/WTO and the EU' (2001) 34(6) *Comparative Political Studies* 624. However, the adjudicating bodies possess a *de facto* power given the weak legislative part of the WTO as discussed further below, which has broader consequences for the prominence of WTO law in relation to international law.

105 On this point of the strong judicial structures of the WTO as to the weaker legislative structure see Ehlermann C: 'Tensions Between the Dispute Settlement Process and the Diplomatic and

the only bodies allowed to issue an authoritative interpretation of the treaty as specified in Article IX:2 of the WTO Agreement. This in effect means that the adjudicating bodies only decide on the cases at hand but those rulings do not bind them in the future. There is no official precedent in WTO law but the adjudicating bodies are guided by subsequent WTO practice.[106] Though Members may protest in public on issues important to their domestic constituents, there has been virtually no use of Article IX: 2 to initiate an authoritative interpretation to reverse rulings of the adjudicating bodies.[107] The process of getting a majority of three-quarters of WTO Membership standing as the Ministerial Council may also prove difficult. Whereas the adoption of the rulings of the adjudicating bodies by the DSB is automatic unless the parties to the dispute raise a consensus against its adoption.[108] Therefore, the adjudicating bodies rulings *de facto* bind Members and in effect to some degree, what may be issues for political negotiation and choice are handed over to the adjudicating bodies, under the guise of the pursuit of a false legal objectivity (see chapter 1).

Pauwelyn's desire for a 'coherent set of disciplines' as a response to fragmentation would appear as an unwitting acceptance of a hierarchical structure of international law with the WTO at the top as some sort of tribunal *maximus* which is acceptable to the rest of international law. In other words, the WTO would at best be a corrupted version of the *Philosopher King* or at worse a hegemony in international law. By that, I mean that in making use of external international law, WTO law would (re)construct it to meet the WTO's operation to liberalise trade (see chapter 3). Pauwelyn would more than likely disagree with this. The aim of his project appears to be an effort to ground WTO law within and as part of international law, as a response to the fragmentation of international law. However, in doing so on the premise of constrained openness, WTO law does not simply incorporate external international law, or embeds itself in international law (see chapter 5 and 6). The WTO would likely pass over the different constituents and agendas that represent external international law, and so homogenise it. In doing this, the fragmentation of international law remains. It is hidden as coherence in Pauwelyn's idea of systemic interpretation (see chapter 2). The other result could be that

Treaty-making Activities of the WTO' (2002) 1(3) *World Trade Review* 301, 302; 'Six Years on the Bench of the "World Trade Court": Some Personal Experiences as Member of the Appellate Body of the World Trade Organization' (2002) 36(4) *Journal of World Trade*, 605, 632.

106 *Japan – Alcoholic Beverages II supra* note 62, at para 13, 15. *Chile Price Band* [Chile – Price Band System and Safeguard Measures Relating to Certain Agricultural Products] 2002 WT/DS207/AB/R para 213–214, 272.

107 See for a generally discussion on authoritative interpretations, Van Damme I, 'Treaty Interpretation by the WTO Appellate Body' (2010) 21(3) EJIL 605.

108 The matter of adoption of reports by the adjudicating bodies by negative consensus by the DSB is considered a hallmark change from the former GATT system where Members could block reports as consensus had to be reached on adoption. The negative consensus is often considered the factor that promotes the legalistic rule-oriented nature of the WTO, from its former diplomatic-oriented nature. See generally, Jackson J, *The World Trade Organisation: Constitution and Jurisprudence* (London: Pinter, 1998).

the fragmented systems are potentially rendered impotent by WTO hegemony, in that it (re)constructs external international law as variables of WTO law.

Model I (WTO law as a limited domain) appears to makes sense if we follow through with the WTO law as defeatist and withdrawing from a system of international law constituent of different functional systems. Perhaps Model I, is also somewhat supercilious in assuming that it is sufficient unto itself. Model II (WTO law as open) if we follow through with its arguments appears workable with WTO law as hegemony in a hierarchical system of international law. Constrained openness shows that the WTO is not an open hegemonic or a limited defeatist system, but one that through its own operations 'maximise[s] [its] particular rationality of international trade'.[109]

4.6.1 Distilling the features of a theory: mapping constrained openness through Calvino's **Invisible Cities**

Calvino's *Invisible Cities* can provide illustrative currency for distilling features of constrained openness, because his work and the main protagonist exhibit a commitment towards an internal construction of reality. *Invisible Cities* is an imaginary dialogue between the Kublai Khan and Marco Polo. They converse about 'impossible places that exist within, or around, real ones' where Venice, a real city, is mentioned throughout the text but as a negative of itself.[110] The young Polo is an ambassador and 'obliging narrator at the service of the Khan'.[111] Polo relates to the ageing Khan the state of the Khan's empire as an 'endless formless ruin'.[112] In Polo's accounts, the Kahn wants 'to discern' the 'walls and towers destined to crumble, the tracery of a pattern so subtle it could escape the termites' gnawing'.[113] The Khan is trying to 'recover the ability to rule his empire if he can understand, and thus grasp, its underlying pattern'.[114] Yet, there is no necessary pattern to be discovered as we discussed in the Prologue. It is a matter of choice.

Invisible Cities is an intricate epistemological puzzle. The dialogue seems 'governed by no external logic or necessity'.[115] 'The arrangement of Calvino's cities is not one that builds up a story or anything at all except its *own* system.'[116] The structure of Calvino's dialogue is self-referential,[117] analogous to the manner in which

109 Pulkowski, 'Multiple Perspectives on the Fragmentation of International Law' *supra* note 81, at III: a.

110 Jackson R, *Fantasy: The Literature of Subversion* (London: Methuen, 1981) 165.

111 Springer C, 'Textual Geography: The Role of the Reader in Invisible Cities' (1985) 15(4) *Modern Language Studies* 289–299, 290.

112 Calvino I, *Invisible Cities*, trans. W. Weaver (London: Vintage, 1997) 5 [originally published in Italian as *Le città invisibili*, 1972].

113 Ibid, 5–6.

114 Twining W, *Globalisation and Legal Theory* (London: Butterworths, 2000) 137.

115 Springer *supra* note 111, at 290.

116 James C P, 'Seriality and Narrativity in Calvino's *Le città invisibili*' (1982) 97 (1) *Modern Language Notes* (Italian Issue), 144, 147. My emphasis in italics.

117 The fifty-five descriptions of cities divided into nine chapters with each chapter containing five descriptions of cities. The first and last chapters consist of ten descriptions of cities. The fifty-five

constrained openness describes WTO law as operating on its own internal point of view. If there is a protagonist in Invisible Cities it is not the Khan or Polo, but *Invisible Cities* (Venice). The fifty-five descriptions of the cities Calvino evokes through Marco Polo can be read in three ways. These are as accounts of fifty-five different cities, fifty-five accounts of one city or more plausibly as fifty-five accounts, 'all of which implicitly use Venice as the reference point of comparison'.[118] The following dialogue between Polo and Khan supports the last suggestion as the more plausible:

> [Polo] 'Sire, now I have told you about all the cities I know.'
> [Khan] 'There is still one of which you never speak.'
> Marco Polo bowed his head.
> 'Venice,' the Khan said.
> Marco Polo smiled. 'What else do you believe I have been talking to you about?'
> The emperor did not turn a hair. 'And yet I have never heard you mention that name.'
> And Polo said: 'Every time I describe a city I am saying something about Venice.'
> [Khan] 'When I ask about other cities, I want to hear about them. And about Venice. When I ask you about Venice.'
> [Polo] 'To distinguish the other cities' qualities, I must speak of a first that remains *implicit*. For me it is Venice.'[119]

The dialogue also re-substantiates the point that Polo in describing the cities is using his model of Venice. Venice, like constrained openness, is his method and concept to select the data he observes about the cities, and the way in which that data will make sense to him, as he tries to present a report to the Khan about the state of the empire. Marco Polo's account of a city proceeds from inside, not dictated by an external source. Polo is embedded in his assessments, which proceed from his particular (internal) point of view.[120] Another way of saying this is that systems use their internal point of view to make sense of things around them. Similarly for the assessment of constrained openness, the adjudicating bodies' account of external international law is not based on external sources, but on WTO law.

cities are divided into eleven sets of cities in order of appearance: Cities and memory, Cities and desire, Thin Cities, Trading cities, Cities and the dead, Cities and the sky, Continuous cities, Hidden cities. The cities do not correspond to the divisions of the chapters. The cities are not grouped thematically but mathematically starting in descending orders. For further discussion on the structure of the book and Calvino's work see Springer *supra* note 111; James *supra* note 116, at 144–161; Markey C, 'Calvino and the Existential Dilemma: The Paradox of Choice' (1983) 60(1) *Italica* 55–70. From a legal standpoint, see Twining *supra* note 114.

118 Twining *supra* note 114, at 212 and 213–215, suggests that there are multiple standpoints or pluralities in that 'each person draws practical lessons relevant to their respective spheres of action.'

119 Calvino *supra* note 112, at 86. My emphasis in italics.

120 For further reading on this point see chapter 3, section 3.4.

Further dialogue between Marco Polo and Kublai Khan in *Invisible Cities* illustrate this idea.

> Kublai asks Marco, 'When you return to the West, will you repeat to your people the same tales you tell me?'
>
> 'I speak and speak,' Marco says, 'but the listener retains only the words he is expecting . . . *It is not the voice that commands the story: it is the ear.*'[121]

For Polo the account of every city is 'implicit' in Venice. Like Polo, the Khan also had a model from which to distinguish the external environment, that is, other cities, as recounted in the dialogue below.

> 'From now on, I'll describe the cities to you,' the Khan had said, 'in your journeys you will see if they exist.'
>
> But the cities visited by Marco Polo were always different from those thought of by the emperor.
>
> 'And yet I have constructed in my mind a *model* city from which all possible cities can be deduced,' Kublai said. 'It contains everything corresponding to the norm. Since the cities that exit diverge in varying degree from the norm, I need only foresee the exceptions to the norm and calculate the most probable combinations.'
>
> 'I have also thought of a *model* city from which I *deduce* all the others.' Marco answered.[122]

Polo does not seek to escape *his* Venice. He realises as he tells the Khan that to make sense of other cities he must first speak of Venice. Polo could have equally told the Khan, 'there is no view from nowhere; of course we all stand somewhere.'[123] This is the idea of there being no Archimedean point. We cannot take up the standpoint to which the name *sub specie aeternitatis* is given. There is no direct access to reality as constrained openness suggests. Calvino writes that the 'cities neither interact nor refer to one another'.[124] Polo does not deny that other cities exist, as constrained openness would not to law external to WTO law, but like Polo suggests his description of the other cities only occurs through referring to his account of Venice. 'If . . . the cities seem all alike, it is not because they add up to one city but because each must create itself as the paradigm of itself.'[125] Polo (Calvino) is continuously (re)constructing his own apparatus to observe the cities.

121 Calvino *supra* note 112, at 135.

122 Calvino *supra* note 112, at 69. My emphasis in italics.

123 Sunstein C, 'The Idea of a Useable Past' (1995) 95 *Columbia Law Review* 601–608, 601. See also Cover R, 'Foreword: Nomos and Narrative' (1983) 97(4) *Harvard Law Review* 4, 4–11.

124 James *supra* note 116, at 150.

125 Ibid.

As we suggested in the Prologue, there are only competing descriptions, interpretations, pluralities, or multiple standpoints.[126] There can be fifty-five descriptions of the cities or in other words, there can be fifty-five descriptions cognised through one city. In *Invisible Cities*, as in constrained openness, there is no absolute episteme and 'the only form of knowledge implied by Calvino is the relative knowledge gained by mastering the process of reading itself'.[127] In the Prologue and chapter 1, I introduced the idea, and further discussed it in this chapter that a system engages with its own self as a way to understand other systems. This can be surmised by Polo's comment in Invisible Cities that 'Every time I describe a City I am saying something about Venice'.[128]

4.7 Conclusion

Plainly, commentators disagree on how best to describe or how best to explain WTO law and its interaction with external international law. The limitations of Model I (WTO law as limited domain) were evident as the advantages of Model II (WTO law as open), and vice versa. Model I was premised on the doctrine of attributed powers: Model II on the doctrine of implied powers. Model I was narrow: Model II was broad. Model I premised a differentiated system with specific functional systems of international law: Model II premised a unitary system of international law. Model I works based on differentiation: Model II works based on homogeneity. Each model therefore was the opposite of the other and in the pattern of their debate accepting one would mean a rejection of the other model. The model that WTO law was privileged failed because rather than recasting Models I and II as practical useful legal arguments it attempts to reconcile them but inherits the inadequacies of both. Additionally the pattern of the argument between Models I and II hides the inadequacies of each model from each other, as well as from wider critique. The issue of *how* the WTO applies or does not apply external international law remained un-explained.

Using constrained openness, we make three main observations. Firstly, no proposition is an epistemic hegemony, or in fact is even necessary. The value of a new theory is in its power to offer a more adequate explanation than the old versions. Secondly, the new theory illuminates the old models by being able to recast past premises based on present situations. Thirdly, constrained openness is revisable, as it does not claim to be universal. I do not purport to reconcile the debates, so much as to make practical use of them. I also concede that constrained openness attempts to harness a binary approach of WTO law/non-WTO law, using the rule of recognition (counter-factual) to define WTO law as the practice of the judiciary. The critique could be fostered that this confines WTO law to the adjudication process. I do not disregard this but the answer is straightforward, as discussed

126 For further discussion see Twining *supra* note 114, at 215. Springer *supra* note 111. James *supra* note 116, at 148–149, 159–160.

127 Springer *supra* note 111, at 293.

128 Calvino *supra* note 112, at 86.

in this chapter, that we need to go back to primary questions about the nature of WTO law, what it is and what purpose does it serve, before we can engage with the secondary questions about for example, non-state actors, polycentricism, unofficial influence from within in WTO law. After all, what is there to deconstruct if it was never constructed? The first task has to be, and I could not stress it enough, to define WTO law. In other words we need to devise varying and competing legal theories of WTO law. As to constrained openness, as a theory of WTO law, the anti-WTO (anti-globalisation) activists would be right to believe that, 'much of the actual balancing between different values [in the WTO] is done according to WTO rules'.[129] This however is not a negative assumption, as they may be fast to assume. The institutional nature of the WTO, as it would be for say an international environmental law institution, is to function based on its operational goals that explain and define on what basis and how the system will relate to external international law. The operation of the WTO to liberalise trade on trade and create an environment in which trade can operate delimits the basis on which WTO law functions and will address external international law. Theorising WTO law as constrained openness, *open in a closed sort of way*,[130] does not mean that the 'balance struck' between WTO law and external international law is 'off-kilter'. As to constrained openness I have advanced and laid open the basis (bias) from which I can further inquire into how the adjudicating bodies respond when faced with external international law. We do this bearing in mind that the adjudicating bodies only ask and answer *one* question: *Has WTO law been violated*?

129 Kalderimis *supra* note 94, at 315.

130 Kennealy P, 'Talking About Autopoiesis – Order From Noise' in Teubner (ed) *Autopoietic Law: A New Approach to Law and Society Autopoietic Law: A New Approach to Law and Society* (Berlin: Walter de Gruyter & Co., 1987).

5 The precautionary principle and the WTO Agreement on Sanitary and Phytosanitary Measures

5.0 Introduction

This chapter, along with chapter 6, seeks to demonstrate the applicability of constrained openness as a lens through which we can understand the interaction between WTO and external international law. It is not, nor does it intend to be, exhaustive and complete. The challenge is to re-interpret the debate between the currently entrenched models of WTO law as a limited domain and WTO law as open. This is to provide a stimulus to further enquiry and discussion. I show the usefulness of constrained openness to specifically understand the practice of the adjudicating bodies as it relates to the Agreement on Sanitary and Phytosanitary Measures (SPS Agreement) of WTO law, and the precautionary principle. The chapter is set out as follows. Section 5.1 examines the precautionary principle, to highlight the main features that construe the principle. I then use this to make the relevant comparisons of whether the notion of precaution entertained in the texts of the SPS Agreement and the practice of that Agreement point to a (re)construction or an incorporation of the principle, as proponents of gateways (chapter 2) would suggest. Section 5.2 briefly reconsiders how proponents of gateways argue for the incorporation of the precautionary principle into the SPS Agreement. In other words, how do proponents of gateways argue for external international law to be part of WTO law (chapter 2)? Section 5.3 provides an overview of, and examination of the SPS Agreement, given it is this agreement that gateway proponents argue provides gateways for the precautionary principle. Having done this, in sections 5.3–5.4 I discuss the notion of the precautionary principle in the texts of the SPS Agreement. This is to show that the structure and design of the SPS Agreement focuses on the operations of the WTO, to liberalise trade by prohibiting restrictions on trade. This provides the first basis to suggest that the precautionary principle is not incorporated into the texts of the SPS Agreement, and actually the texts shows contrary to what the principle entails. Sections 5.5–5.5.6 follow on with an examination of the practice of the adjudicating bodies on the precautionary principle. The reason is to provide a concrete examination of specific external international law, which the adjudicating bodies address. This allows us to apply the therory of constrained openness to make sense of WTO law. It provides evidence to suggest that there is no direct incorporation of external international law into WTO law, but that the WTO (re)constructs external international law into WTO law variables. In sections 5.5.7–5.6, I return to, and rethink the argument for the incorporation of the precautionary principle into WTO law.

5.1 The precautionary principle

In the later part of the twentieth century, the precautionary principle became an important part of international environmental law.[1] The maxim 'better safe than sorry' characterises the principle.[2] The precautionary principle attempts to inhibit the use of scientific uncertainty as a justification for not acting where the consequences of action could result in serious or irreversible harm to the environment or human health.[3] The principle has no single fixed

1 Cameron J and J Abouchar, 'The Status of the Precautionary Principle in International Law', in Freestone D and E Hey, *The Precautionary Principle and International Law: The Challenge of Implementation* (Hague: Kluwer Law International, 1996) 31. Freestone D and E Hey, 'Origins and Development of the Precautionary Principle', ibid, at 4. Cameron J, 'The Status of the Precautionary Principle in International Law' in O'Riordan T and J Cameron J, *Interpreting the Precautionary Principle* (London: Cameron May Ltd., 1994) 262. O'Riordan T and Cameron, 'The History and Contemporary Significance of the Precautionary Principle', ibid, at 12. Bell S and D McGillivray, *Environmental Law: The Law and Policy Relating to the Protection of the Environment* (London: Blackstone Press, 5th Edition, 2000) 48. O'Riordan, T and A Jordan, *The Precautionary Principle, Science, Politics and Ethics* (London: Centre for Social and Economic Research on the Global Environment, 1995) 2–3. Dobos D, 'The Necessity of Precaution: The Future of Ecological Necessity and the Precautionary Principle' (2002) 12 Fordham Envtl. L.J. 384. Fisher E, 'Is the Precautionary Principle Justiciable?' (2001) 13(3) JEL 315. Segger M and M Gehring, 'The WTO and Precaution: Sustainable Development Implications of the WTO Asbestos Dispute' (2003) 15(3) JEL 292, 297. Sands P D, 'The Greening of International Law: Emerging Principles and Rules' (1994) 1 Ind. J. Global Legal Studies 297 [hereinafter Sands, *Greening*]. Sands P D, *Principles of International Environmental Law* Vol. 1 (Manchester: University Press, 1995) 208–213 [hereinafter Sands, *Principles*]. Cross F, 'Paradoxical Perils of the Precautionary Principle' (1996) 53 Wash. & Lee L. Rev. 851. Weiss C, 'Scientific Uncertainty and Science-Based Precaution' (2003) 3 *International Environmental Agreements: Politics, Law and Economics* 137. Dana D, 'Behavioural Economic Defense of the Precautionary Principle' (2003) 97 Nw. U. L. Rev. 1315. Ellis J, 'The Precautionary Principle: From Paradigm to Rule of Law' (2000) 2 *International Law FORUM* 127.

2 Alder J and D Wilkinson, *Environmental Law and Ethics* (London: Macmillan, 1999) 149. Bilder R and J Brunnee, 'Book Review of The Precautionary Principle and International Law: The Challenge of Implementation' (1997) AJIL 210. Cross *supra note* 1, at 851. Cameron and Abouchar *supra note* 1, at 30. O'Riordan T, 'The politics of the precautionary principle' in Harding R and E Fisher, *Perspectives on the Precautionary Principle* (Australia: Federation Press, 1999) 283. Weiss *supra note* 1, at 139. Sunstein C, 'Beyond the Precautionary Principle' (2003) 151 U. Pennsylvania L. Rev. 1003–1004. Wiener J B, 'Precaution', in Bodansky D, J Brunnee and E Hey, *Oxford Handbook of International Environmental Law* (Oxford: OUP, 2007) 598–612, 598.

3 Grosko B, 'Genetic Engineering and International law: conflict or harmony? An Analysis of the biosafety protocol, GATT and the WTO SPS Agreement' (2001) *Virginia Environmental Law Journal* 315. Freestone and Hey *supra* note 1, at 2–12. O'Riordan and Jordan *supra* note 1, at 2–4. Alder and Wilkinson *supra* note 2, at 149. Bell and McGillivray *supra* note 1, at 47. Sands, *Greening supra* note 1, at 297. Sands, *Principles supra note* 1, at 208. Fisher *supra* note 1, at 316. Weiss *supra* note 1, at 137. Tarlock A D, 'Is there a there there in environmental law?' (2004) *Journal of Land Use and Environmental Law* 251. Bilder and Brunnee, *supra* note 2, at 210. Santillo et al. 'The Precautionary

definition,[4] and appears in various formulations in many treaties and national legislation.[5] However, for the purposes here of pointing up its main features, I can turn to the most widely cited and authoritative version in Principle 15 of the Rio Declaration.[6] What this means is that in examining the gateway arguments for incorporation of the precautionary principle in section 5.2 below, we will both be engaging with a common definition.

Principle 15 states that,

> In order to protect the environment, the precautionary approach should be widely applied by States according to their capabilities. Where there are threats of serious irreversible damage, lack of full scientific certainty shall not be used as a reason for postponing cost-effective measures to prevent environmental degradation.[7]

In short, this version of the precaution principle underscores that uncertainty does not justify inaction.[8] This means, in its simplest form, the absence of scientific proof is not sufficient to make action unnecessary.[9] It consists of three negatives:

Principle: Protecting Against Failures of Scientific Method and Risk Assessment' (1998) 36(12) *Marine Pollution Bulletin* 939–940. Cross *supra note* 1, at 851. Dana *supra* note 1, at 1315–1316. Bohanes J, 'Risk Regulation in WTO Law: A Procedure-based Approach to the Precautionary Principle' (2002) 40 Colum. J. Transnational Law 330–333. Priess and Pitschas, 'Protection of Public Health and the Role of the Precautionary Principle under WTO Law: A Trojan Horse before Geneva'a Walls? (2000) 24 Fordham International L.J. 520–521. Matthee M and D Vermersch, 'Are the Precautionary Principle and the International Trade of Genetically Modified Organisms Reconcilable?'(2000) 12 J. of Agricultural and Environmental Ethics 59–70, 60–1. Segger and Gehring *supra* note 1, at 292–293. Immordino G, 'Looking for a Guide to Protect the Environment: The Development of the Precautionary Principle' (2003) 17(5) *Journal of Economic Surveys* 630–631. Hohmann H, The Precautionary Principle: International Environmental Law: Between Exploitation and Protection (London: Kluwer Publishers, 1994) 312.

4 For example see: Sands, *Principles supra* note 1, at 212. Sands, *Greening supra* note 1, at 300. O'Riordan and Jordan *supra* note 1, at 1. Bell and McGillivray *supra* note 1, at 48. Immordino *supra* note 3, at 630.

5 See examples of the varying formulations illustrated in: Freestone and Hey *supra note* 1, at 5–12. Cameron and Abouchar *supra* note 1, at 31. Haigh N, 'The Introduction of the Precautionary Principle into the UK', in Cameron and O'Riordan *supra* note 1, at 243–251. Harding and Fisher *supra* note 2, at 299–308.

6 Hohmann *supra* note 3, at 321. Bell and McGillivray *supra* note 1, at 48. Sands, *Greening supra note* 1, at 297. Immordino *supra* note 3, at 629. Freestone and Hey *supra* note 1, at 3. Segger and Gehring *supra* note 1, at 292. Applegate S, 'The Taming of the precautionary principle' (2002) 27 Wm. & Mary Environmental L. & Policy Rev. 14, 17. Kiss A, 'The Rights and Interests of Future Generations and the Precautionary Principle', in Freestone and Hey *supra* note 1, at 27. Holder J and M Lee, *Environmental Protection, Law and Policy* (Cambridge: CUP, 2007, 2nd Edition) 21. Cheyne I, 'Gateways to the Precautionary Principle in WTO Law' (2007) *Journal of Environmental Law* 1–18, 5.

7 Adopted at the United Nations Conference for the Environment and Development UN Doc. A/CONF.151/5/Rev.1, 13 June 1992.

8 *Contra* Wingspread Statement on the Precautionary Principle drafted and finalized at a conference at the Wingspread Conference Center, Racine, Wisconsin, 23–25 January 1998 at <http://www.gdrc.org/u-gov/precaution-3.html> (Accessed 19 April 2008).

9 Weiss *supra* note 1, at 141.

no scientific uncertainty does *not* mean that *no* measures should be taken.[10] The principle does not compel action, set forth positive obligation, require intervention or tell us what should be done.[11] 'Failure to take action against [a] threat may be defended on other grounds' as Principle 15 acknowledges by reference to cost-effective measures.[12] The principle does not set specific standards.[13] Rather it is a guide for discourse and decision-making which leaves the discretion of the policy to the decision-makers.[14] It can help to legitimise and de-legitimise certain approaches to protect against risks.

The precautionary principle is a trade off among a set of available alternatives, which can also carry risks. It is not risk free and is a choice among other policies that decision-makers may use. In this way, the precautionary principle is a political decision framed within what a society may deem appropriate levels of risks.[15] It is a decision between limiting actions in the present against constraining choices in the future that may carry risks to the environment or human health. By this criteria, it is an intergenerational principle.[16]

Moreover, the precautionary principle only permits action, and 'reminds legislators that they cannot wait for proof of a cause-effect linkage between a given substance, process or activity and environmental harm before acting to reduce or eliminate the risk of this harm'.[17] However, stronger versions of the precautionary principle such as the Wingspread Statement require action.[18] It states that,

> When an activity raises threats of harm to human health or the environment, precautionary measures should be taken even if cause and effect relationships are not fully established scientifically . . . The proponent of the activity, rather than the public, should bear the burden of proof.[19]

This means that uncertainty justifies action unlike Principle 15.[20] It requires prohibition of an activity feared to be risky, until the proponents of that activity can

10 Stone C, 'Is There a Precautionary Principle?' (2001) 31 *Environmental Law Reporter* 10790.

11 Wiener *supra* note 2, at 603. Cheyne I: 'Risk and Precaution in World Trade Organisation Law' (2006) 40(5) *Journal of World Trade* 837–864, 843–844, 'The Precautionary Principle in EC and WTO Law: Searching for a Common Understanding' (2006) 8 *Environmental Law Review* 257–277, 258. Weiss *supra* note 1, at 141. Ellis J, 'Overexploitation of a valuable resource? New literature on the precautionary principle' (2006) *European Journal of International Law* 445–462, 446.

12 Ellis *supra* note 11.

13 Cheyne *supra* note 11. Ellis, *supra* note 11.

14 Cheyne *supra* note 11.

15 Cheyne 'The Precautionary Principle in EC and WTO Law: Searching for a Common Understanding' *supra* note 11, at 258. O'Riordan and Cameron *supra* note 1, at 12.

16 Alder and Wilkinson *supra* note 2, at 150. Boissier M, 'Pondering the Precautionary Principle' (2003) 70 *Joint Bone Spine* 318.

17 Ellis *supra* note 11, at 446.

18 Weiss *supra* note 1, at 140.

19 Wingspread Statement on the Precautionary Principle *supra* note 8.

20 Wiener *supra* note 2, at 606.

demonstrate it poses no unacceptable risk. The burden of proof shifts to the proponents of the activity.[21] This emphasises that until an activity is shown to carry negligible risks to the environment or human health, proponents are disallowed from engaging in that activity.[22] However, given that nothing can be proven safe, scientifically, and what counts as safe is subjective, this version of the precautionary principle may prompt policy paralysis or over regulation.[23]

Whatever its formulation I can surmise three salient constituent features of the precautionary principle in environmental law. These are that action precedes scientific certainty, the principle does not require concrete recommendation of action against the potential risk, and consequences of inaction against a potential risk could lead to irreversible or serious damage to the environment or human health. With these features in mind, I can now examine the arguments put forward for the incorporation of the precautionary principle in WTO law.

5.2 The gateway approach for the incorporation of the precautionary principle into WTO law

Given that I have already discussed the ideas of gateways in chapter 3, the purpose of this section is to recap them here specifically for the discussion on the precautionary principle. Ilona Cheyne, in an intervention on how to think about and account for the interaction between WTO law and precautionary principle, states that a gateway is a 'provision [in the WTO Agreement] that allows non-trade principles or concepts to be introduced into the WTO Agreement'.[24] In advancing her argument for the incorporation of international law in WTO law, Cheyne states that gateways incorporate concepts, principles, norm or values from different international legal systems into the WTO legal system.[25]

Having an understanding of the meaning of gateways, the next question is what is the rationale or basis for gateways. Put differently, I am trying to figure out on what premise does the gateway approach rest and operate. Why are international trade law scholars arguing for gateways in WTO law to incorporate the precautionary principle? Cheyne suggests that gateways address 'one of the persistent problems of the WTO' which she believes is the 'need to find an appropriate balance between trade rules and environmental protection measures'.[26] This would mean that gateways are a practical tool to balance competing interests of 'trade and' by incorporating those competing interests into WTO law. By incorporating

21 Ibid.

22 Cameron *supra* note 4, at 46.

23 Alder and Wilkinson *supra* note 2, at 166–167. Weiner *supra* note 2, at 606.

24 Cheyne, 'Gateways to the Precautionary Principle in WTO Law' *supra* note 6, at 1–18, 1–2.

25 Cheyne *supra* note 6, at 1–2. Similarly, see Pauwelyn J, 'Cooperation in Dispute Settlement', in Cottier T, J Pauwelyn and E B Bonanomi, *Human Rights and International Trade* (Oxford: OUP, 2005). Pauwelyn argues that there are 'avenues' or 'ways' in which the WTO could 'integrate' human rights.

26 Cheyne *supra* note 6, at 1.

external international law into WTO law, Cheyne is implying that there can be a balance of the tensions, or interests between the fragmented and overlapping areas of international law.[27] The other related implication is that gateways can impose coherence in international law by providing for the incorporation of external international law into WTO law.[28] Incorporationists appear to suggest that we can address fragmentation by the 'technique of a single, coherent' system of law.[29]

The argument in favour of gateways to incorporate external international law into WTO law appears to arise from the need to avoid creating small isolated pockets of international law which could contradict the perceived unity of international law by promoting conflicting judicial decisions.[30] Essentially gateways are just a way to account for the process of how norms move from being outside a system to inside that system. As such, the idea can usefully remind us of the input-output of norms within a system. By definition, the rationale of gateways suggests that the WTO can incorporate external international law, as long as the correct gateway provision into WTO law can be found.

In the next section, I examine the notion of precaution, in the texts of the SPS Agreement, which Cheyne claims can incorporate the precautionary principle in WTO law. This forms the basis for my discussion on how I suggest that the principle is (re)constructed into a trade law variable, and the basis on which to rethink the approach of gateways which I return to, before the conclusion of this chapter.

5.3 Overview of the SPS Agreement

The focus of the WTO is to eliminate tariffs and quantitative restrictions, through obligations of non-discrimination and non-protectionism.[31] In their domestic market, WTO Members could use non-tariff barriers (NTBs) such as product standards and testing requirements, ban products, or impose certain quality controls on the import of a product from another Member on the basis that the product can cause harm to their environment, or to the health of their population. This could affect trade in that it directly bans or indirectly frustrates the process of trade. The internal regulations put in place by the importing Member could potentially create more favourable trading conditions for the product of the importing Member than for the product of the exporting Member. *Prima facie* the internal regulations of the importing Member would be a violation of national treatment, WTO/GATT[32]

27 See chapter 3 for a full discussion on gateways.

28 Pauwelyn J, 'Bridging Fragmentation and Unity: International Law as a Universe of Inter-Connected Islands' 905–916, 905.

29 Koskenniemi M and P Leino, 'Fragmentation of International Law? Postmodern Anxieties' (2002) 15 *Leiden Journal of International Law* 553–579, 556–557.

30 See also chapter 1.

31 See chapter 4 for discussion on the purpose of WTO law.

32 GATT is the General Agreement on Tariffs and Trade 1947 that was the predecessor to the WTO. Upon the formation of the WTO in 1994, the GATT 1947 became a part of WTO law, referred to as WTO/GATT when identifying texts that were originally GATT 1947 but now part of the WTO.

Article III, in that it may be applied in a manner to the domestic product to protect domestic production[33] or accords more favourable treatment to a domestic product than the imported product.[34] National treatment enshrines the principle of non-discrimination in that whatever treatment is afforded to a domestic product must be afforded to a like or similar imported product. WTO/GATT Article III embodies the principle on two levels.

The first targets discrimination at the level of the process of 'importation' of products and the regulations required should not afford protection to domestic production of a similar or like product.[35] The second targets the discrimination that could be afforded by an importing Member to a domestic product by that Member's unfavourable use of its internal taxes and regulations which may be required for sale when the 'imported' product is in the Member's market. The aim is that internal taxes and regulations should not afford more favourable conditions to a domestic product than would be to a like or similar imported product.[36] Instead of genuinely protecting the health of their consumers or the environment from harm, the importing Member may be using its internal regulations as a form of NTB to offer disguised protection to a domestic product and producer, and so thwart the efforts of trade (exportation) by another Member.

In the Uruguay Round that established the WTO, NTBs were therefore a focus, and agreements were introduced to target and reduce them.[37] These agreements

33 Article III:1 (national Treatment on Internal Taxation and Regulation) of WTO/GATT notes that: 'The contracting parties recognise that internal taxes and other internal charges, and laws, regulations and requirements affecting the internal sale, offering for sale, purchase, transportation, distribution or use of products, and internal quantitative regulations requiring the mixture, processing or use products in specified amounts or proportions, *should not be applied to imported or domestic products so as to afford protection to domestic regulation*.' [My emphasis in italics.]

This Article targets discrimination at the level of the 'importation' of products, and the regulations required for that process which should not afford protection to domestic production of a similar of like product.

34 Article III:4 states that: 'The products of the territory of any contracting party imported into the territory of any other contracting party shall be accorded *treatment no less favourable* than that accorded to like products of national origin in respect of all laws, regulations and requirements affecting their internal sale, offering for sale, purchase, transportation, distribution or use. The provisions of this paragraph shall not prevent the application of differential internal transportation charges which are based exclusively on the economic operation of the means of transport and not on the nationality of the product.' [My emphasis in italics.]

This Article targets the discrimination and protectionism at the level of the 'imported' product and the internal taxes, regulations that may be required for internal sale, and which should not afford more favourable conditions to a domestic product, not afforded to a like or similar imported product. Further, Article III is connected to Article I (Most Favoured Nation Status) through a reference in Article I to paragraphs 2 and 4 of Article III.

35 Appellate Body Report, *Japan – Taxes on Alcoholic Beverages*, WT/DS8/AB/R, WT/DS10/AB/R, WT/DS11/AB/R, adopted 1 November 1996, 18.

36 Appellate Body Report, *Canada – Certain Measures Concerning Periodicals*, WT/DS31/AB/R, adopted 30 July 1997, 19.

37 Lowenfeld A F, *International Economic Law* (Oxford: OUP, 2002) 323. Marceau G and J Trachtman, 'The Technical Barriers to Trade Agreement, the Sanitary and Phytosanitary Measures Agreement and the General Agreement on Tariffs and Trade: map of the World Trade

were introduced to supplement the general requirements of WTO/GATT Article III and to curb abuses that could result in a violation of that Article, and thereby the core of the WTO/GATT rules to prohibit discriminatory and protectionist trade practices.[38] These include the SPS Agreement.[39] The focus of the SPS is to provide a detailed regime for the regulation of food safety, and human, animal and plant health standards, because such regulations have the potential to be used for protectionism, contrary to WTO/GATT Article III, with potentially adverse effects to trade in food stuff and agricultural goods.[40] The SPS Agreement is primarily an elaboration of WTO/GATT Article XX (b).[41] The SPS Agreement states that SPS measures, which 'conform to the relevant provisions of the SPS Agreement', shall be 'presumed to be in accordance with GATT in particular Article XX (b).[42] Article XX (b) allows Members to adopt measures that are normally inconsistent with WTO/GATT provisions such as Articles I and III if those measures are genuinely aimed at protecting human health and the environment, and are not disguised restrictions and discriminations on trade.[43]

5.3.1 *Compliance with WTO/GATT is not necessarily an SPS defence*

Despite the fact that the SPS Agreement is an extension of WTO/GATT rules on non-discrimination and an elaboration of Article XX(b), this should not obscure

Organisation Law of Domestic Regulation of Goods' (2002) 36(5) *Journal of World Trade* 811–881, 813–815. Lester S and B Mercurio et al. *World Trade Law: Text, Materials and Commentary* (Oxford: Hart Publishing, 2008) 557.

38 Ibid.

39 Agreement on Sanitary and Phytosanitary Measures (available at www.wto.org). For a brief and good overview of the SPS Agreement, see Thorn C and M Carlson, 'The Agreement on the Application of Sanitary and Phytosanitary Measures and the Agreement on Technical Barriers to Trade' (2000) 31 *Law and Policy in International Business* 841.

40 Trade in food is estimated at between US$300 and 400 billion. See United Nations Food Agricultural Organisation <http://www.fao.org/docrep/w9114e/W9114e06.htm> Also see: Peel J, 'A GMO by Any Other Name … Might Be an SPS Risk!: Implications of Expanding the Scope of the WTO Sanitary and Phytosanitary Measures Agreement' (2006) 17 *The European Journal of International Law* 1009–1031, 1013–1014. Ministerial Declaration on the Uruguay Round, September 20, 1986, Part I, Sec. D Agriculture (iii).

41 The preamble of the SPS Agreement notes in setting out that agreement that it is 'desiring therefore to elaborate rules for the application of the provisions of GATT 1994 which relate to the use of sanitary and phytosanitary measures, in particular the provisions of Article XX(b)'.

42 Article 2.4.

43 Article XX (General Exceptions) states that: 'Subject to the requirement that such measures are not applied in a manner which would constitute a means of arbitrary or unjustifiable discrimination between countries where the same conditions prevail, or a disguised restriction on international trade, nothing in this Agreement [WTO/GATT] shall be construed to prevent the adoption or enforcement by an contracting party of measures:

(b) necessary to protect human, animal or plant life or health [Article XX(b)].

See: Appellate Body Report, *United States – Standards for Reformulated and Conventional Gasoline*, WT/DS2/AB/R, adopted 20 May 1996, 24. Appellate Body Report, *United States – Import Prohibition of Certain Shrimp and Shrimp Products*, WT/DS58/AB/R, adopted 6 November 1998, paras158, 159.

the autonomous nature of the agreement.[44] Article XX(b) is construed as an exception to be used when a measure is found inconsistent with WTO/GATT rules on non-discrimination. The adjudicating bodies have turned to the SPS Agreement without establishing prior breach of the WTO/GATT. This means that compliance with WTO/GATT is not a defence under the SPS Agreement.[45] The practice of the adjudicating bodies on the SPS Agreement in *Australia – Salmon* and *EC – Hormones* are good examples of this.[46]

In *Australia – Salmon*, Canada disputed Australia's SPS measure to prohibit the importation of fresh, chilled or frozen salmon from Canada.[47] Australia defended this on grounds that it was necessary to prevent the introduction of diseases that could potentially affect the salmon industry and large species of the domestic salmon population. The Appellate Body (AB) found that the SPS measure was inconsistent with scientific risk assessment as stipulated by the SPS Agreement.[48] Australia could have attempted to defend its requirement of heat treatment for imported salmon and not its own domestic salmon on the basis that it was not in breach of WTO/GATT Article III because the heat-treated salmon and the non-heated-treated salmon would not be 'like products'.[49] The key for the application of WTO/GATT Article III is that the products must be like,[50] or directly competitive or substitutable products.[51] Otherwise, no unfavourable treatment could be inferred, as the two products would not be competing in the same market and trade space. However, as to the autonomous nature of the SPS Agreement from WTO/GATT, in *Australia – Salmon* a breach of GATT did not have to be established as the case was directly considered under the SPS Agreement. This means that there was no chance for a WTO/GATT Article III defence and a possible Article XX(b) or (g) exception if the measure was found to be in violation of Article III.[52]

44 Scott J, *Commentary on the Sanitary and Phytosanitary Measures Agreement* (Oxford: OUP, 2007) 9–10. Kalderimis D, 'Problems of WTO Harmonisation and the Virtues of Shields over Swords' (2004) 13 *Minnesota Journal of Global Trade* 305–335, 337.

45 Kalderimis *supra* note 44, at 337–338.

46 Kalderimis *supra* note 44, at 337–338. Scott, *supra* note 44, at 9–10. See: Panel Report, *EC Measures Concerning Meat and Meat Products (Hormones), Complaint by Canada*, WT/DS48/R/CAN, adopted 13 February 1998, modified by Appellate Body Report, WT/DS26/AB/R, WT/DS48/AB/R paras 8.41–8.42. Panel Report, *Australia – Measures Affecting Importation of Salmon*, WT/DS18/R and Corr.1, adopted 6 November 1998, modified by Appellate Body Report, WT/DS18/AB/R, paras 8.38–8.39.

47 Appellate Body Report, *Australia – Measures Affecting Importation of Salmon*, WT/DS18/AB/R, adopted 6 November 1998 (hereinafter *Australia – Salmon*).

48 See sections 5.3.5 and 5.5.4 for further discussion.

49 Kalderimis *supra* note 44.

50 Appellate Body Report, *European Communities – Measures Affecting Asbestos and Asbestos-Containing Products*, WT/DS135/AB/R, adopted 5 April 2001, paras 91–92 (hereinafter *EC – Asbestos*).

51 Appellate Body Report, *Korea – Taxes on Alcoholic Beverages*, WT/DS75/AB/R, WT/DS84/AB/R, adopted 17 February 1999, paras 114–115, 120. Appellate Body Report, *United States – Transitional Safeguard Measure on Combed Cotton Yarn from Pakistan*, WT/DS192/AB/R, adopted 5 November 2001, paras 96–98.

52 Article XX (General Exceptions) states that: 'Subject to the requirement that such measures are not applied in a manner which would constitute a means of arbitrary or unjustifiable discrimination

In *EC – Hormones*, the US challenged the EC SPS measure to prohibit the importation of beef treated with bovine growth hormones (BGH).[53] The prohibition also extended to domestic use of BGH, as well as the sale of meat from animals treated with BGH. *EC – Hormones* went directly to the SPS Agreement because there is no need to establish compliance with WTO/GATT first. The EC was not able to resort to Article XX(b) as an exception to the non-discrimination rules of WTO/GATT Article III and XI, which it would have likely violated. The EC measure failed under the SPS not because of its trade restrictive character but because it did not comply with the stipulations of the SPS Agreement for the measure to be supported by risk assessment.[54] As with *Australia – Salmon*, because there is no need to establish an initial violation under WTO/GATT, the SPS Agreement appears as an autonomous agreement, though part of WTO law. This limits the availability of WTO/GATT Article XX as a defence against violations of the WTO treaty once a breach of the SPS Agreement is established, even if Members have a right to directly take SPS measures, as I discuss in the next section.

5.3.2 The 'right' to take an SPS measure

As the SPS Agreement is an autonomous agreement from WTO/GATT, it establishes the 'right' of Members to 'take' SPS measures 'necessary for the protection of human, animal or plant life or health'.[55] This right to take SPS measures is significant, as it appears to mean that Members can set their own level of protection.[56] The right to take an SPS measure in determining levels of protection appropriate to a Member is however not absolute or unquestionable,[57] as it concerns the consistency of the measure and, overall, must not bei unjustifiable or discriminatory against trade.

between countries where the same conditions prevail, or a disguised restriction on international trade, nothing in this Agreement [WTO/GATT] shall be construed to prevent the adoption or enforcement by any contracting party of measures:

(g) relating to the conservation of exhaustible natural resources if such measures are made effective in conjunction with restrictions on domestic production or consumption [Article XX (g)].'

53 Appellate Body Report, *EC Measures Concerning Meat and Meat Products (Hormones)*, WT/DS26/AB/R, WT/DS48/AB/R, adopted 13 February 1998 (hereinafter *EC – Hormones*).

54 See sections 5.5.6 and 5.6 for further discussion.

55 Article 2.1.

56 See Scott *supra* note 44, at 35–40. See also Annex A(5) of the SPS Agreement. The concept of an appropriate level of protection appears in the SPS Agreement, Article 3.3, 4.1, 5.5 and 5.6. See: *EC – Hormones supra* note 53, at para 172. Panel Report, *Japan – Measures Affecting Agricultural Products*, WT/DS76/R, adopted 19 March 1999, modified by Appellate Body Report, WT/DS76/AB/R, para 8.81. *Australia – Salmon supra* note 47, at para 199. Also, addressing the same point of a Member to set their own level of protection concerning Article XX(b), see *EC – Asbestos supra* note 50, at para 168.

57 *EC – Hormones supra* note 53, at paras 173, 175–176. *Australia – Salmon supra* note 47, at paras 205–206. Desmedt A, 'Proportionality in WTO Law' (2001) *Journal of International Economic Law* 456, 458.

The right is contingent upon what I can identify as several other factors in the SPS Agreement. The measure must not be 'inconsistent with the provisions' of the SPS Agreement.[58] It shall be 'applied only to the extent necessary to protect human, animal, or plant life or health'.[59] In this application, the measure has to be 'based on scientific principles'.[60] Further, and in connection with this requirement the measure cannot be 'maintained without sufficient scientific evidence'.[61] This appears as part of the balance the SPS Agreement attempts to strike between what can often be the competing interests of trade and protecting the life and health of humans, animals or the environment.[62]

Members can take an SPS measure but they must ensure that the measure does not 'arbitrarily or unjustifiably discriminate between Members where identical or similar conditions prevail'.[63] The SPS measure shall not also be 'applied in a manner which would constitute a disguised restriction on international trade'.[64] The right to take an SPS measure thus 'seems to have somewhat of a political element, designed to present the Agreement as respecting the protection of human, animal or plant life or health. [Whereas] in truth the SPS Agreement is no different from other WTO Agreements, in that Members must act consistently with the obligations' of the WTO.[65]

5.3.3 Definition and coverage of an SPS measure

An SPS measure can be identified by two requirements. The first is that the measure must be formally identified as an SPS measure. The second is that it may directly or indirectly affect international trade.[66] This is indicative of the broad

58 Article 1, last part of the sentence.

59 Article 2.2, first part of the sentence. Panel Report, *European Communities – Measures Affecting the Approval and Marketing of Biotech Products*, WT/DS291/R, WT/DS292/R, Corr.1 and Add. 1, 2, 3, 4, 5, 6, 7, 8, 9, adopted 21 November 2006, para 7.3392 reads Article 2.2 as comprising three 'distinct' obligations to be satisfied. See also Scott *supra* note 44, at 84.

60 Article 2.2, second part of the sentence.

61 Article 2.2, third part of the sentence also provides an exception provided for in Article 5.

62 *EC – Hormones supra* note 53, at para 177.

63 Article 2.3, first sentence. *Australia – Salmon Panel supra* note 46 at para 199 broke this down into three cumulative elements that had to be satisfied to find a violation of Article 2.3. These were

1. the measure discriminates between the territories of Members other than the Member imposing the measure or between the territory of the Member imposing the measure and that of another Member
2. the discrimination is arbitrary and unjustifiable
3. identical or similar conditions prevail in the territory of the Members compared.

64 Article 2.3, second sentence.

65 Lester and Mercurio *supra* note 37, at 559.

66 Article 1.1 See: Panel Report, *EC Measures Concerning Meat and Meat Products (Hormones), Complaint by Canada*, WT/DS48/R/CAN, adopted 13 February 1998, modified by Appellate Body Report, WT/DS26/AB/R, WT/DS48/AB/R, para 8.39. Panel Report, *EC Measures Concerning Meat and Meat Products (Hormones), Complaint by the United States*, WT/DS26/R/USA, adopted 13 February 1998, modified by Appellate Body Report, WT/DS26/AB/R, WT/DS48/AB/R, para 8.36.

scope of the SPS Agreement to tackle NTBs.[67] The requirement for a measure to be an SPS measure means that it must fall into one of the categories set out in Annex A.1 of the SPS Agreement. These are 'any measure applied':

(a) to protect animal or plant life or health within the territory of the Member from risks arising from the entry, establishment or spread of pests, diseases, disease-carrying organisms or disease-causing organisms;
(b) to protect human or animal life or health within the territory of the Member from risks arising from additives, contaminants, toxins or disease-causing organisms in food, beverages or feedstuffs;
(c) to protect human life or health within the territory of the Member from risks arising from disease carried by animals, plants or products thereof, or from the entry, establishment or spread of pests; or
(d) to prevent or limit other damage within the territory of the Member from the entry, establishment or spread of pests.

> Sanitary or phytosanitary measures include all relevant laws, decrees, regulations, requirements and procedures including, *inter alia*, end product criteria; processes and production methods; testing, inspection, certification and approval procedures; quarantine treatments including relevant requirements associated with the transport of animals or plants, or with the materials necessary for their survival during transport; provisions on relevant statistical methods, sampling procedures and methods of risk assessment; and packaging and labelling requirements directly related to food safety.

Establishing whether a measure falls within one of these categories can be considered the first step to making the SPS Agreement applicable to a dispute within the WTO.[68] This signifies that, to a large degree, the concept of an SPS measure is 'functionally determined' in that it is defined to protect one of the limited ranges as listed in Annex A.1.[69] The categorisation of Annex A.1 is not to be taken lightly. It has implications for determining whether a measure will attract the jurisprudence of the SPS Agreement, the Agreement on Technical Barriers to Trade (TBT Agreement) or other parts of the WTO/GATT treaty.[70] The category under which a measure falls determines whether it will be considered an SPS measure according to Annex A.1.[71] The seriousness that a

67 Kalderimis *supra* note 44, at 337, Scott *supra* note 44, at 25–27.

68 See Peel *supra* note 40, at 1011–1012. Pauwelyn J, 'The WTO Agreement on Sanitary and Phytosanitary (SPS) Measures as Applied in the First Three SPS Disputes: EC – Hormones, Australia – Salmon and Japan – Varietals' (1999) *Journal of International Economic Law* 641, 644.

69 Scott *supra* note 44, at 12.

70 Take for example that Article 4.1 of the SPS Agreement states that 'Nothing in this Agreement shall affect the rights of Members under the Agreement on Technical Barriers to Trade with respect to measures not within the scope of this Agreement.' This means that measures not found within the scope of the SPS Agreement can then be considered under the TBT Agreement.

71 See Panel Report, *Australia – Measures Affecting Importation of Salmon*, WT/DS18/R and Corr.1, adopted 6 November 1998, modified by Appellate Body Report, WT/DS18/AB/R, para 8.34.

categorisation of an SPS measure can pose is appreciated in consideration of *EC – Biotech*.[72]

In the dispute *EC – Biotech*, the US charged that several EC Members prohibited the marketing and sale of biotech or genetically modified (GM) products, even though the EC had approved procedures for the import and marketing of these products in the EC. The EC applied a moratorium for the approval of GM products between 1998 and 2003, effectively prohibiting the import and sale of GM products in the EC. In this time, the EC adopted legalisation requiring the labelling and traceability of GM products, from which point when the legislation came into force in April 2004, GM products were allowed in the EC market. The case is as much about the violation of WTO law as it is about the internal conflict in the EC between Members who 'remain hostile to the use and sale of GM products in their national markets on environmental and consumer choice grounds' and those who do not.[73]

The Panel was established in 2003 and with regard to the dispute arising under the SPS Agreement. The Panel using the 'ordinary meaning' of the terms of Annex A expanded the interpretation of the nature of SPS risks.[74] This effectively widens the scrutiny of the SPS Agreement on environmental, health and agricultural measures related to food products.[75] The Panel stated that the phrase 'animal or plant life or health' in Annex A was 'meant to be comprehensive in coverage'.[76] This meant that the term risk to 'animal of plant life or health' could involve assessment of GM crops on micro-flora and micro-fauna. For example, insects may be indirectly affected by GM products if they consume the pollen of a GM plant.[77] The Panel also noted that the 'risks arising from' in Annex A were 'broad and unqualified' because there was 'nothing' in Annex A 1 (a) that potential risks had to cause the 'direct or immediate result, e.g. the spread of pest'.[78]

The Panel's reasoning extends the definition of an SPS measure, which also extends the coverage and depth, for what measures come under the SPS Agreement. In light of this, SPS measures would not be limited to a direct causation of risk but if a chain of causation can be shown to link the product or activity with a risk then it seems as if it would be an SPS measure.[79] As discussed above, the SPS Agreement as autonomous from the WTO/GATT already limits the availability of WTO/GATT defences. There is also an apprehension that a broadening of the definition of an SPS measure would mean that measures that are precautionary in nature and not normally covered by the SPS Agreement would now come

72 See chapter 2 for further discussion of *EC – Biotech*.

73 See Cheyne I, 'Life after the WTO Biotech Products Panel Report' (2008) 10 *Environmental Law Review* 52. See also Baughen S, *International Trade and the Protection of the Environment* (London: Routledge-Cavendish, 2007) 73–77.

74 See chapter 2.

75 Ibid.

76 *EC – Biotech supra* note 59, at para 7.219.

77 Ibid, para 7.220.

78 Ibid, paras 7.225–7.226.

79 Peel *supra* note 40, at 1022–1023.

under the scrutiny of the Agreement. Essentially those genuinely precautionary SPS measures that may have once eluded the discipline of the SPS Agreement could now come under the review of the Agreement. With no breach of WTO/GATT having to be established, which would make Article XX defences available to a Member, the SPS Agreement in carrying a strong scientific requirement in its texts and practice may not augur well for the precautionary principle (as fully discussed in sections 5.3.5, 5.4 and 5.5.1).

5.3.4 Harmonisation of international standards and the SPS Agreement

Different Members have different SPS standards, which mean that the SPS Agreement operates against a background of regulatory heterogeneity and diversity for regulation of protection against risks in the categories as identified above in Annex A.1.[80] Against this and the potential for these different standards to be NTBs, the SPS Agreement, apart from elaborating the non-discrimination rule and the right of Members to take SPS measures, aims to reduce 'regulatory heterogeneity which can act as a form of trade barrier' and be an 'extra costs to importers.'[81] The SPS Agreement does this by promoting the harmonisation of standards for Members to use when implementing SPS measures.[82]

Harmonisation appears as a voluntary process where Members are encouraged to harmonise on 'as wide as basis as possible' and to 'base' their SPS measures on international standards.[83] It also appears as an 'incentive'[84] as Members 'may choose' to establish an SPS measure that is based on relevant international standards, but may not necessarily adopt all of the features of that standard.[85] If Members conform their SPS measures to these harmonised international standards the SPS measure in question would be found 'necessary to protect human, animal or plant life or health' and consistent with the SPS Agreement.[86] In this view, harmonisation may appear somewhat more as a strong 'incentive' than as voluntary.[87]

80 Fisher E, *Risk Regulation and Administrative Constitutionalism* (Oxford: Hart Publishing, 2007) 179. Scott *supra* note 44, at 243–279 *passim*.

81 Fisher *supra* note 80, at 179. Also Fisher notes: Sykes A, 'The Limited Role of Regulatory Harmonisation in International Goods and Services Markets (1999) 2 *Journal of International Economic Law* 49.

82 Preamble to SPS Agreement which states 'Desiring to further the use of harmonised sanitary and phytosanitary measures between Members, on the basis of international standards, guidelines and recommendations developed by the relevant international organisations…'.

83 Article 3.1. See *EC – Hormones supra* note 53, at paras 102, 171, 172, 165–169. For further discussion on Article 3.3 see section 5.5.6.

84 *EC – Hormones supra* note 53, at para 102.

85 Ibid, at paras 171, 163.

86 Article 3.2. See: *Australia – Salmon (Panel) supra* note 47, at para 7.11.

87 Matsushita M, T J Schoenbaum, P C Mavroidis, *The World Trade Organization: Law, Practice, and Policy, Second Edition* (Oxford: OUP, 2006) 503. *EC – Hormones supra* note 53, at para 107 notes that 'The presumption of consistency with relevant provisions of the SPS Agreement that arises under Article 3.2 in respect of Members that conform to international standards may well be an

Given that a key aim of the SPS Agreement is to harmonise SPS standards, the process is not left to chance. The SPS Agreement makes provision for the formation of an SPS Committee, which is to 'monitor the process of international harmonisation and coordinate efforts in the regard with the relevant international organisations.'[88] Members are also encouraged to 'play a full part within the limits of their resources in the relevant international organisations.'[89] In addition to direct provisions that encourage harmonisation, the SPS Agreement also makes allowance for the use of similar standards that may prevail between Members. Members 'shall accept' the SPS measure of another Member as equivalent even if the measure is different from their own.[90] This is conditional upon both Members trading in the same product, and the exporting Member being able to 'objectively' demonstrate to the importing Member that the SPS measure achieves the importing Member's level of SPS protection.[91] Members are encouraged to enter into bilateral and multilateral agreements when they recognise the equivalence of SPS measures between or among them, respectively.[92]

Together, these directives are indicative of the purpose of the SPS Agreement to encourage by incentive[93] and suggest ways to harmonise.[94] This is to reduce regulatory heterogeneity and the chances of NTBs that violate the non-discrimination of WTO/GATT law, while allowing Members to pursue SPS measures with levels of protection they deem appropriate.[95] The SPS Agreement attempts to reconcile the harmonisation of SPS standards and the 'right' of deference to Members to be able to take what they deem as appropriate levels of protection for human health, animal or plant life in their territory against harm from products imported from other Members.[96]

5.3.5 The scientific requirements of the SPS Agreement

In line with the approach that a Member has a right to take SPS measures, the SPS Agreement allows Members desirous of a higher level of protection to depart from

incentive for Members so to conform their SPS measures with such standards. It is clear, however, that a decision of a Member not to conform a particular measure with an international standard does not authorise imposition of a special or generalised burden of proof upon that Member, which may, more often than not, amount to a penalty.'

88 Article 3.5.

89 Article 3.4.

90 Article 4.1, first sentence.

91 Article 4.1, second sentence.

92 Article 4.2.

93 Article 3.1, Article 3.2.

94 Article 3.4, 3.5, 4.2.

95 *EC – Hormones supra* note 53, at para 177. 'The ultimate goal of the harmonisation if SPS measures is to prevent the use of such measures for arbitrary or unjustifiable discrimination between Members or as a disguised restriction on international trade, without preventing Members from adopting or enforcing measures which are both necessary to protect human life of health and based on scientific principles and without requiring them to change their appropriate level of protection.'

96 Fisher *supra* note 80, 178–179.

the harmonised standards. Members may 'introduce or maintain' SPS measures which result in higher levels of protection than would be achieved from relevant international standards.[97] The burden of proof is on the complaining Member to demonstrate that the measure of the defending Member cannot be scientifically justified and thus may prove inconsistent with the SPS Agreement.[98] The right of a Member to introduce an SPS measure like that which allows a Member to take higher levels of protection than those required by the harmonised standards of the SPS Agreement is contingent upon certain factors. The right is not an absolute one.[99] The higher levels of protection are applicable 'if there is scientific justification [for the measure] or as a consequence of the level of . . . protection a Member determines to be appropriate in accordance with' the risk assessment procedures[100] of the SPS Agreement.[101] The SPS Agreement specifies the 'process for setting SPS measures'.[102] Members are required to undertake a risk assessment,[103] which takes into account 'available scientific evidence',[104] and 'relevant economic factors',[105] as well the 'objective of minimizing negative trade effects.'[106]

The measure must also avoid being 'arbitrary and discriminatory',[107] or a 'disguised restriction on trade',[108] and be 'no more trade-restrictive than required' to achieve the appropriate level of protection, taking into account technical and economic feasibility.[109] There is also allowance, where 'relevant scientific evidence is insufficient', for a Member to 'provisionally adopt' SPS measures'.[110] This is conditional on the 'basis of available pertinent information' and Members must also 'seek to obtain additional information necessary for a more objective' risk assessment, and review of the SPS measure within a 'reasonable period of time'.[111]

97 Article 3.3. *EC – Hormones supra* note 53, at para 172 notes that it is an autonomous right and not an exception from a general obligation under Article 3.1.

98 *EC – Hormones supra* note 53, at para 165. Cheyne I, 'Risk and Precaution in World Trade Organization Law' (2006) 40(5) *Journal of World Trade*, 837, 847.

99 See section 5.3.4 for further discussion.

100 Article 5: Assessment of risk and determination of the appropriate level of sanitary or phytosanitary protection.

101 Article 3.3.

102 Fisher *supra* note 80, at 177.

103 Article 5.1. See: *EC – Hormones supra* note 53, at para 181. Panel Report, *Australia – Measures Affecting Importation of Salmon – Recourse to Article 21.5 of the DSU by Canada*, WT/DS18/RW, adopted 20 March 2000, paras 7.68–7.70, 7.41. *Australia – Salmon supra* note 47, at para 121. *Japan – Agricultural Products II supra* note 56, at para 112.

104 Article 5.2.

105 Article 3.5 These are the potential damage in terms of lost of production or sales in the event of entry, establishment or spread of pests or disease; the costs of control or eradication in the territory of the importing Member, and the relative cost-effectiveness of alternative to limiting risks.

106 Article 5.4.

107 Article 5.5.

108 Article 5.5.

109 Article 5.6.

110 Article 5.7.

111 Article 5.7.

This is significant because it provides the exception to the stipulation in the SPS Agreement, as discussed earlier, that Members are not to maintain an SPS measure without sufficient scientific evidence.[112]

Science permeates the obligations of the SPS Agreement in determining whether an SPS measure is violating the principles of WTO/GATT to prohibit restrictions on trade. In order for the importing Member to use its domestic SPS measure, which may restrict trade, the Member has to show the necessity of that measure. The scientific requirements of the SPS Agreement then stipulate that the SPS measure be based on and not maintained without scientific evidence.[113] This is except where scientific evidence is insufficient,[114] at which point the importing Member can take the SPS measure provisionally but has to review it based on scientific risk assessment.[115] The importing Member may also conform to an international SPS standard which is based on science.[116] If the Member wishes to use a higher standard than the international standard, the Member needs to use science to justify the SPS measure.[117]

The Agreement uses science as a central tool to distinguish between legitimate and disguised restrictions of trade applied as regulations for the protection of public health or the environment.[118] It is the only part of WTO law which imposes the obligation on Members to base their measures on scientific evidence. This is regardless of whether the measures violate the non-discrimination of WTO/GATT.[119] There is a reason for this. Consider that the non-discrimination rules of WTO law may appear as a less strong standard for differentiating between legitimate and protectionist trade measures, given that the WTO has seemingly exhausted its coverage of non-discrimination, whether *de jure* or *de facto*, as far as possible.[120] The creative ability of governments to come up with new NTBs is endless. While the effect of NTBs on trade is clear, they usually do not fit within

112 There is a connection between Articles 2.2 and 5.7.

113 Article 2.2.

114 Article 5.7.

115 Article 5.7.

116 Article 3.1.

117 Article 3.3.

118 Thomas D, 'Where's the Beef? Mad Cow and the Blight of the SPS Agreemnt' (1999) 32 Vand. J. Transnational Law 492. McNeil D, 'The First Case under the WTO's SPS Agreement: the EU Hormone Ban' (1998) 39 Va. J. International Law 94. Grosko *supra* note 3, at 310. Stonehouse P, 'Review of WTO and Environmental Issues' (2000) 13 *Journal of Agricultural and Environmental Ethics* 131.

119 *EC – Hormones supra* note 53, at para 193. *Japan – Agricultural Products II supra* note 56, at para 84. In agreement see Bevilacqua D, 'The International Regulation of Genetically Modified Organisms: Uncertainty, Fragmentation, and Precaution' (2007) *European Environmental Law Review* 314–336, 322. Howse R and P Mavroidis 'Europe's Evolving regulatory strategy for GMOs, The Issue of Consistency with WTO Law: Of Kine and Brine' (2000) *Fordham International Law Journal* 314.

120 Howse R, 'Democracy, Science and Free Trade: Risk Regulation on Trial at the WTO' (2000) 98 Mich. L. Rev. 2330, 2332–2333. For example see: Appellate Body Report *Canada – Certain Measures Affecting the Automotive Industry*, WT/142/AB/R. Panel Report *Indonesia – Certain Measures Affecting the Automotive Industry*, WT/DS54/R.

the traditional categories of import or internal restraints that non-discrimination cover.[121] In this way, the reason for scientific requirement of the SPS Agreement is apparent. If an SPS measure supposedly aimed at protecting human health or the environment restricts trade and 'there is no scientific evidence of any danger to be avoided or any reduction in risk' as a result of the SPS measure, then the 'suspicion arises that the measure is disguised protectionism'.[122] The scientific requirements of the SPS Agreement are used to prevent disguised restrictions on international trade.

However, as discussed in the next section, the scientific requirement can create hurdles for what may be genuine SPS measures to protect human health and the environment. More specifically, I suggest that there is an epistemological break between what is a precautionary measure in the SPS Agreement and what is generally understood as precautionary in environmental law. This means that the nature of precaution in the SPS Agreement is a variable of trade law, which is at variance with the broad features of the precautionary principle. In this section, I stated what the SPS Agreement is, and discussed the permeation of science as a tool in that Agreement to set the bar for legitimate and illegitimate trade barriers. This puts me in a position to present an account of the SPS Agreement, highlighting where in the texts a precautionary measure may be relevant and which texts *prima facie* appear as concessions to the precautionary principle. This is also to provide the basis for the discussion on the practice of the adjudicating bodies on the precautionary principle in section 5.5. At that moment I can consider the SPS Agreement and the practice of the adjudicating bodies through the lens of constrained openness, which would suggest that the precautionary principle is not incorporated but (re)constructed as a variable of trade law.

5.4 The precautionary principle and the texts of the SPS Agreement

The purpose of this section is to discuss the way that the precautionary principle is expressed in the texts of the SPS Agreement. From that I draw some preliminary conclusions as to the difference between the precautionary principle and how the SPS Agreement textually addresses the precautionary principle, which I further examine in detail in section 5.5.

The precautionary principle does not appear, directly or indirectly, in the texts of the SPS Agreement or anywhere else in WTO law. That is the reason some proponents argue that there are gateways in the SPS Agreement through which to incorporate the principle into WTO law.[123] If it were felt that the principle was

121 Jackson J H, W Davey and A Sykes, *Legal Problems of International Economic Relations, Fourth Edition* (Minnesota: West Group Publishing, 2002) 420–412.

122 Sykes A, 'Domestic Regulation, Sovereignty, and Scientific Evidence Requirements: A Pessimistic View' (2002) 3 Chi. J. International Law 354.

123 See section 5.2 and chapter 3 for further discussion.

already established in WTO law, as it is recognised in international environmental law,[124] any argument to incorporate it into WTO law would be *non sequitur*. The SPS Agreement 'reflects' the principle, because of the right of Members to introduce measures and set their threshold of protection against risk from harm.

Though the principle may not be a direct part of WTO law, what makes the discussion about the principle interesting and relevant is that the SPS Agreement is formulated to address the management of risks. This is in order to allow Members to introduce what may be trade restrictive measures that seek to protect animal, plant and human life or health. Scientific evidence of the risks is required to justify SPS measures that may be trade restrictive. The precautionary principle (as I discussed in section 5.1) also deals in the same business of managing risk. It provides for the use of measures when there is a lack of full scientific certainty about the threats an action may pose to animal, plant and human life or health. Inaction is not justified because of not having enough scientific evidence. Action is justified even if there is not enough scientific evidence about the risks from a certain action.

The requirement of the SPS Agreement for scientific evidence to justify an SPS measure and consequently the risks 'immediately creates a tension with the precautionary principle, which is invoked precisely in the absence or insufficiency of science'.[125] However, if the importing Member desires a higher level of protection than what is afforded by the international standard it may do so. This means that the importing Member could implement a measure that uses the precautionary principle as the higher standard, which implies action in light of scientific uncertainty. However, the texts of the SPS Agreement may restrict and involve a break between the precautionary principle and how the SPS Agreement addresses precaution. This is because the importing Member must show that the SPS measure, which is restricting trade, is scientifically justified (Article 3.3). This justification is based on risk assessment (Article 5).

When scientific evidence proves to be 'insufficient' to show that the product being limited by the SPS measure is safe or poses little risk, the importing country is allowed to maintain its SPS measure (Article 5.7). This appears concessionary to the precautionary principle, if so more than any other part of the Agreement, because a Member is allowed to take a measure which may be precautionary on the grounds of 'insufficient evidence'. This SPS measure is only temporary on the basis that the importing Member seeks information for a more objective risk assessment and reviews the SPS measure in a reasonable time (Article 5.7). The scientific requirement of this, as with the other texts of the SPS Agreement, challenges the core of the precautionary principle to the point that it can be seen as '*ipso facto* being scientific'.[126]

124 See section 5.1 for further discussion.

125 McDonald J, 'Tr(e)ading Cautiously: Precaution in WTO Decision Making,' in Fisher E, J Jones and R von Schomberg, *Implementing the Precautionary Principle: Perspectives and Prospects* (Cheltenham: Edward Elgar Publishing Ltd., 2006) 160–181, 166.

126 Applegate *supra* note 6, at 53–54. (My emphasis in italics.)

Consider that Principle 15 among other embodiments of the precautionary principle proceeds from the basis of 'lack of full scientific certainty'. This does not demand the demonstration and likelihood of risk but a threat is enough to satisfy the 'risk requirement' for the principle.[127] The use of 'the word "full" implies that there must be a minimum basis – but not a complete assessment – of scientific demonstration'.[128] This is in line with most versions of the precautionary principle[129] which are construed on an 'inadequate (in this case not fully certain) scientific risk assessment'.[130] Whereas the text of the SPS Agreement shows that though a Member has a 'right' to take an SPS measure that is conditioned on the basis of scientific evidence and provisionally if there is 'insufficiency' of scientific evidence.

The requirement of Article 5.7 that the provisional SPS measure be adopted 'on the basis of available pertinent information' appears at odds with the precautionary principle. This implies scientific risk assessment before action can be taken. This is 'of course, not necessarily unreasonable' but it 'reverses to a degree the temporal relationship between information and action that is at the core of the precautionary principle.'[131] The requirement of the SPS Agreement to provide scientific evidence of risks before an SPS measure can be taken in effect effaces the very purpose of the precautionary principle to act in light of uncertainty. It illustrates the difference between how risks are addressed in WTO law, and generally in environmental law.

The argument can be made that it may be normal to act on the basis of known scientific evidence but 'normal' for which system. This takes me back to point I made in chapters 1 and 3 that a system functions based on its internal point of view. So what is understood as a 'normal' course of action in trade law to act based on scientific evidence may not be considered so in environmental law as based on the precautionary principle where to act in light of uncertainty would be 'normal'.

The examination of the texts appear to show that the 'provisions of the SPS Agreement in calling for a firm evidentiary basis for the SPS regulations differ from the more broadly oriented . . . precautionary requirements.'[132] The purpose, design, and function of the SPS Agreement mandate this particular scientific approach. Suggestions that the precautionary principle can be incorporated into WTO law, especially the texts of the SPS Agreement ignore an epistemological break between the precautionary principle as generally understood in environmental law and how the texts of the SPS Agreement construes precaution. What I have shown above is that the disciplines of SPS Agreement appear contrary to the precautionary principle, which I explore in more detail in the next section.

127 Bevilacqua *supra* note 119, at 328.

128 Bevilacqua *supra* note 119, at 328. See also Applegate *supra* note 6, at 51–54.

129 See section 5.1 for further discussion.

130 Bevilacqua *supra* note 119, at 328. See also Applegate *supra* note 6, at 52–53. Peel *supra* note 40, at 1017.

131 Applegate *supra* note 6, at 52.

132 Peel *supra* note 40, at 1012.

In the discussion above, I have suggested that there is a difference between the precautionary principle in texts of WTO law, specifically focused on the SPS Agreement and what exists in environmental law. Up to this point, I have only hinted at what I will make more explicit in the next section, which is that the conceptual framework of constrained openness can provide a prism through which to examine the SPS Agreement, and the practice of adjudicating bodies regarding the Agreement. This raises the critical issue, as proposed in chapters 3 and 4, of the (re)construction of external international law into a variable in the practice of WTO law. In the next section, I will illustrate this (re)construction in the practice of WTO law, concerning the SPS Agreement. The dispute of *EC – Hormones* will be central, as most of the practice as it relates to the precautionary principle developed and evolved from this dispute.

5.5 The (re)construction of precaution as a variable in the practice of WTO law

5.5.1 EC – Hormones *and initial thoughts on (re)construction of external international law*

The earlier and initial position I established in chapter 1 using the rule of recognition to determine that the practice of the adjudicating bodies was that WTO law allows me to examine that practice here on the precautionary principle.[133] The practice of WTO law 'directly' says little about the precautionary principle. Therefore, what can be understood about the precautionary principle comes from how the adjudicating bodies have interpreted the texts of the SPS Agreement, as discussed above in section 5.4.

The first and main case addressing the precautionary principle was *EC – Hormones*. In *EC – Hormones,* the EC in pursuing a ban on hormone treated beef from the US argued that the precautionary principle could override the requirements of WTO law in the SPS Agreement.[134] The EC argued that the precautionary princi-

133 See chapter 1 for discussion on the counter-factual rule of recognition as a method to define WTO las as the practice of the adjudicating bodies. There is a growing body of literature that examines WTO law and EC law with regards to trade and more specifically for what I am discussing here, the precautionary principle. However, for my purposes the focus of this study is on WTO law. For further reading see Scott J, 'International Trade and Environmental Governance: Relating Rules (and Standards) in the EU and the WTO' (2004) 15 EJIL. Cheyne *supra* note 11. McNelis N, 'The Role of the Judge in the EU and WTO. Lessons from the BSE and Hormones Case' (2001) 4 JIEL 189. Scott J and E Vos, 'The Juridification of Uncertainty: Observations on the Ambivalence of the Precautionary Principle within the EU and the WTO' in Joerges C and R Dehouse (eds) *Good Governance in Europe's Integrated Market* (Oxford: OUP, 2002). Weiler J (ed) *The EU and the WTO and the NAFTA* (Oxford: OUP, 2000). de Burca G and J Scott (eds) *The EU and the WTO: Legal and Constitutional Issues* (Oxford: Hart Publishing, 2001). Hancher L, 'EC Environmental Policy – a Pre-cautionary Tale?' in Freestone D and E Hey (eds) *The Precautionary Principle and International Law: The Challenge of Implementation* (Hague: Kluwer Law International, 1996) 187–208.

134 *EC – Hormones supra* note 53. See section 5.4 for discussion on the SPS Agreement.

ple was part of customary international law or a general principle of international law.[135] This would imply that the EC's SPS measure based on the precautionary principle was beyond the reach of the scientific risk assessment of the SPS Agreement, specifically Articles 5.1 and 5.2. The EC was invoking the precautionary principle to override the specific scientific obligations of risk assessment under SPS Article 5.1 and 5.2.[136] The US asserted that the precautionary principle does not represent a principle of customary international law and was rather characterised as an 'approach'.[137] The US also argued that there was no need for the precautionary principle in an effort to be risk averse as the SPS Agreement allowed Members to take their own level of protection.[138] It underlined the EC's use of the precautionary principle 'cannot create risk assessment where there is none nor can the principle create sufficient scientific evidence where there is none'.[139]

The AB in *EC – Hormones* stated that 'the EC did not actually proceed to an assessment, within the meaning of Articles 5.1 and 5.2'.[140] *EC – Hormones* stressed that the status of the precautionary principle in international law was the 'subject of debate among academics, law practitioners, regulators and judges'.[141] It further stated that even while the principle is regarded by 'some as having crystallised into a general principle of customary international *environmental* law' it 'remained unclear whether it had done so as a principle of general or customary international law'.[142] The AB from that reasoning declared that it was not for them to take a 'position' on such an important but abstract question.[143] They found that the principle had 'not been written into the SPS Agreement as a ground for justifying SPS measures that are otherwise inconsistent with the obligations for Members set out in particular provisions of that Agreement.'[144]

The AB in *EC – Hormones* however declared that the principle 'finds reflection' in Article 5.7 of the SPS Agreement, though its relevance was not limited to that Article, and was also observed to be 'reflected' in the sixth paragraph of the Preamble and in Article 3.3 of the SPS Agreement.[145] Given that the principle is merely 'reflected' in the SPS Agreement, the AB in *EC – Hormones* stressed that it does not override specific provisions of the Agreement.[146] This meant that the principle was not part of WTO law, and could not be used to avoid the application of, or be an exception to the SPS Agreement as WTO law. The EC measure to ban hormone treated beef was unsuccessful because the EC failed to satisfy the

135 Ibid.
136 See sections 5.4, 5.3.3, 5.3.5.
137 *EC – Hormones supra* note, 53 at para 43.
138 Ibid.
139 *EC – Hormones* (Panel) *supra* note 46, at para 43.
140 *EC – Hormones supra* note 53, at para 208.
141 Ibid, at para 123.
142 Ibid, at para 123.
143 Ibid.
144 Ibid, at para 124.
145 Ibid.
146 Ibid.

scientific obligations of the SPS Agreement (Article 5.1 and 5.2) for the measure to be based on a risk assessment.

The ruling from the AB in *EC – Hormones* on the precautionary principle was reaffirmed by former appellate body Member, Mitsuo Matsushita, at a roundtable of the American Society of International Law discussing the concerns of the fragmentation of international law.[147] Matsushita observed that the precautionary principle existed in the Cartagena Protocol to cover food safety. Citing this as an example of the principle, he however underscored that the principle was 'not well recognised in WTO law'.[148] He stated that the SPS Agreement contained the precautionary principle 'only in a limited way' and that it could not be applied from the Cartagena Protocol if it would 'de facto overrule WTO Agreements'.[149] This sounds similar to the tone of the ruling of *EC – Hormones* with respect to the precautionary principle, and illustrates with some measure, as discussed in chapters 1 and 3, the internal point of view of WTO law to focus on the operations of trade law, as a self-referential process.[150]

It should also be of no surprise that Matsushita was a Member of the AB that adjudicated *EC – Hormones* and importantly that subsequent decisions by the adjudicating bodies have not generally revised its opinion on the precautionary principle.[151] In fact, the adjudicating bodies have chosen to reiterate the ruling of *EC – Hormones* on the precautionary principle meaning that the practice of WTO law on the principle has remained largely unchanged.[152] Notwithstanding this, I can consider how the practice of WTO law construes precaution, and show the epistemological break between precaution in WTO law and the precautionary principle. The reasoning and results, as discussed below, should be similar to what the examination of the texts yielded above in section 5.4.

What I suggest is that *EC – Hormones* illustrates the (re)construction of precautionary principle as a trade law variable and demonstrates the concept of constrained openness to impose intelligibility on WTO law. If WTO law is seen through the lens of constrained openness, then the practice of WTO law should show that external international law is (re)constructed as a variable of trade law. From this viewpoint the contention in *EC – Hormones* between the US or EU on whether the principle was part of international environmental law or had evolved into a principle of customary international law matters little, because the point remains the same, that the adjudicating bodies have no direct access to it however viewed. As I suggested in chapter 1 and 3, the adjudicating bodies, because

147 *American Society of International Law* 'Proceedings of the 99th Annual Meeting of the American Society of International Law: New World Order or a World in Disorder? Testing the Limits of International Law', WTO Appellate Body Roundtable, 175–187, 184. See also chapters 1, 2 and 3 for discussion on the fragmentation of international law.

148 Ibid.

149 Ibid, 184–185, Former Appellate Body Member James Bacchus who makes a similar point.

150 See chapters 1 and 3, for discussion about the internal point of view.

151 See *EC – Hormones supra* note 53.

152 The most recent example being *EC – Biotech supra* note 59, at paras 7.3060, 7.3065.

they construct reality on the basis of their operations will take their observation of external international law and use it as part of WTO law. In short, external international law is (re)constructed as a variable of trade law and ceases to operate from its own fundamental basis as a constituent of its own legal system. In the next section, I will illustrate this, mainly through examining *EC – Hormones* and other relevant practice to the adjudicating bodies regarding the SPS texts as discussed in section 5.4.

5.5.2 The scientific requirement to maintain an SPS measure

Article 2.2 reads:

> Members shall ensure that any sanitary or phytosanitary measure is applied only to the extent necessary to protect human, animal or plant life or health, is based on scientific principles and is not maintained without sufficient scientific evidence, except as provided for in paragraph 7 of Article 5.

Article 5.1 reads:

> Members shall ensure that their sanitary or phytosanitary measures are based on an assessment, as appropriate to circumstances, of the risks to human, animal or plant life or health, taking into account risk assessment techniques developed by the relevant international organisations.

The Appellate Body in *EC – Hormones* established that Article 2.2 and Article 5.1 must be 'constantly read together' as Article 5.1 is a specific application of the general obligations of Article 2.2.[153] The Panel in *EC – Biotech* reiterates this ruling in *EC – Hormones*, adding that Article 5.1 is a 'specific application of the second and third obligations provided for in Article 2.2'.[154] In order to satisfy the provision of Article 2.2, a measure must be 'based on' appropriate risk assessment as stipulated in Article 5.1.

The AB in *Japan – Agricultural Products II* ruled that sufficiency in Article 2.2 required the existence of an 'adequate relationship between two elements, *in casu*, between the SPS measure and the scientific evidence'.[155] In *Japan– Agricultural Products II*, the US disputed Japan's SPS measure to prohibit the importation of certain fruits as potential carriers of the codling moth disease. Japan had set out guidelines for lifting the probation in 1987 but once the ban was removed, a Member still had to meet additional requirements for approval of additional varieties of the produce being imported.[156] The AB upheld the Panel's finding that Japan's SPS measure requiring different approval for the importation of each fruit variety was

153 *EC – Hormones supra* note 53, at paras 180, 193.
154 *EC – Biotech supra* note 59, at para 7.1439.
155 *Japan – Agricultural Products II supra* note 56, at paras 73–74.
156 This case is also noted in the literature as *Japan – Varietals*.

inconsistent with Article 2.2 which stipulates that measures cannot be maintained without scientific evidence. The adjudicating bodies in *Japan – Agricultural Products II* reinforced the earlier ruling by *EC – Hormones* that Article 2.2 and 5.1 should be read together, and emphasised the two-way nature of the relationship that Article 2.2 included Article 5.1, as well as Articles 3.3 and 5.7.[157]

The AB in *Australia – Salmon* also determined that the general provisions of Article 2.2 would be violated if the specific provisions of Article 5.1 and 5.2 were violated.[158] As had been previously ruled in *EC – Hormones*,[159] the AB in *Australia – Salmon* emphasised that Article 5.1 as informed by Article 2.2 requires that the risk assessment under Article 5.1 'sufficiently warrant' or 'reasonably support' the SPS measure. Accordingly, this means that there is a 'substantive requirement' for a 'rational relationship' between an SPS measure and the risk assessment.[160] The AB in *Japan – Agricultural Products II* also maintained that Article 2.2 required a 'rational or objective relationship between the SPS measure and the scientific evidence'.[161] The obligation that a measure was not to be maintained without sufficient evidence was established in the practice of WTO law to mean that there must be a 'rational or objective' relationship between the SPS measure and scientific evidence.[162]

The practice of WTO law for an SPS measure to bear a rational relationship to scientific evidence and risk assessment appears to contrast with the precautionary principle in environmental law, where the reliance on scientific evidence is met with an 'instruction to act with caution in the face of scientific uncertainty'.[163] The requirement for a rational relationship in the SPS Agreement illustrates how the practice of WTO law, like the texts as examined in section 5.4, is at some variance with the precautionary principle.[164] The argument could be made that there has to be some rational reason to establish a threat of serious or irreversible harm which would make the view that there is some variance between the practice of WTO law and the precautionary questionable. However, that argument would be misplaced in that there is a difference in the outcomes of the rational relationship. For WTO law, the rational relationship asks that the scientific evidence support the need for an SPS measure that prohibits trade. For the precautionary principle the rational relationship would appear to ask that a perceived threat be met with caution in light of scientific evidence being uncertain. Though there has to be a rational relationship between the precautionary measure and the perceived threat, that relationship under the precautionary principle appears to be dictated by uncertainty whereas WTO law requires scientific evidence, even if to show uncertainty.

157 *Japan – Agricultural Products II supra* note 56, at paras 73–74.
158 *Australia – Salmon supra* note 47, at para 8.52.
159 *EC – Hormones supra* note 53, at para 193.
160 Ibid.
161 Ibid at para 73.
162 *Japan – Agricultural Products II supra* note, 56 at paras 73–74.
163 Peel *supra* note 40, at 1017.
164 See section 5.4 for further discussion and generally throughout the chapter.

Further, in *Japan – Apples*, Japan put in a place an SPS measure to protect against the possible spread of the disease 'fire blight' from apples imported from the US.[165] The SPS measure banned the importation of the fruit from places where blight was found to be present. Other conditionalities of the measure imposed geographical restrictions, periodic inspection of orchards and requirements for the transport of products.[166] The potential risk from blight varies across differing hosts, and Japan sought to take a precautionary approach. Japan argued that its SPS measure was 'reasonable as well as scientific because it derived from perspectives of prudence and precaution'.[167] This was, as Japan contended, because its own approach was premised on 'the fact that the pathways of . . . transmission of the bacteria are still unknown in spite of several efforts to trace them'.[168]

The AB in *Japan – Apples* concurred with the preceding Panel that Japan's SPS measure was 'clearly disproportionate' to the risks as related to the 'requirement of a rational or objective relationship between an SPS measure and the scientific evidence'.[169] The AB in *Japan – Apples* added that 'total deference to the finds of national authorities would not ensure an objective assessment' and for these reasons the adjudicating bodies are not 'obliged to give precedence to the importing Member's approach to scientific evidence and risk when analysing and assessing scientific evidence'.[170] This practice of WTO law on the matter of the precautionary principle is at odds with the principle. In WTO law, if there is no scientific evidence to justify and support an SPS measure, then the Member cannot maintain or adopt that measure, except under Article 5.7, which has it own set of conditionalities as discussed in section 5.4. The adjudicating bodies focus on the operations of the WTO as centrally concerned with trade. This is a critical indication that the SPS Agreement is not about health or environmental protection *per se* but is centrally aimed at the use of science as a means to distinguish between legitimate and illegitimate SPS measures that protect health or the environment, and in doing so may negatively affect trade. The point emphasised by the AB is that the risk assessment under the Articles 5.1 and 2.2 requires that measures must not be maintained without sufficient evidence. This was 'intended as a countervailing factor in respect of the right of Members to set their appropriate level of protection'.[171] The AB argued that this was 'essential for the maintenance of the delicate and carefully negotiated balance in the SPS Agreement between the shared, but sometimes competing, interests of promoting international trade and of protecting the life and health of human beings.'[172]

165 Appellate Body Report, *Japan – Measures Affecting the Importation of Apples*, WT/DS245/AB/R, para 14.
166 Ibid.
167 Ibid, at para 150. (Quotation marks suppressed.)
168 Ibid.
169 Ibid, at paras 147, 163–164. (Quotation marks suppressed.)
170 Ibid, at paras 165–167.
171 Ibid, at para 177.
172 Ibid.

As the AB in *Japan – Apples* points out, even if I accept that a Member can use an SPS measure that is precautionary in approach, that Member still has to fulfil the core of the SPS Agreement. That is, the measure must be specific to the risks being protected against, and bear a rational relationship with the scientific evidence. If it cannot meet the disciplines of the SPS Agreement, no matter how precautionary an SPS measure is, the practice appears to demonstrate at this stage that it would not pass the disciplines of the SPS Agreement. This is an indication that not only does WTO law function according to its own operations, to prohibit disguised or other restrictions on trade, but that on encountering external international law, that law is understood through the operations of WTO law. In effect, the precautionary nature of an SPS measure has no independent and direct application in WTO law, which would explain and as I suggested underline the (re)construction of it as a variable of WTO law.

5.5.3 The two different definitions and evidentiary standards of risk assessment

As discussed above, the practice of WTO law on establishing a rational relationship between an SPS measure and scientific evidence directs a strong inclination towards science, which appears contrary to a precautionary approach, which emphasises the lack of scientific certainty. Article 5.1 in obliging Members to base their SPS measure on scientific risk assessment underscores this point. According to *EC – Hormones*, 'risk assessment is a scientific process aimed at establishing the scientific basis' for an SPS measure.[173]

Risk assessment is a 'process characterised by systematic, disciplined and objective enquiry and analysis'.[174] There are two definitions of risk assessment found in Annex A of the SPS Agreement.[175] These state that risk assessment is the 'evaluation of the likelihood of entry, establishment or spread' and the 'evaluation of the potential for adverse effects on human or animal health arising'.[176]

The first definition of risk assessment concerning the spread of pests and disease involves an evaluation of the likelihood, or probability of entry, establishment and spread of pests and diseases.[177] The AB in *Australia – Salmon* stated that the risks could either be qualitative or quantitative and that there was 'no requirement' for this definition of 'risk assessment to establish a certain magnitude or threshold level of degree of risk'.[178] However, the AB later stated that they would still have to find that the risk assessment met the meaning as in Article 5.1.[179] This indicates the underlying requirement for scientific evidence to justify SPS measures by risk

173 *EC – Hormones supra* note 53, at para 187.
174 Ibid.
175 SPS Agreement Annex A, para 4 *supra* note 56.
176 Ibid.
177 *Australia Salmon supra* note 47, at paras 123–124.
178 Ibid, at para 124.
179 Ibid, at para 126.

assessment, which is at variance with the precautionary principle as discussed in section 5.1.[180]

Additionally the first definition involves an evaluation of 'associated potential biological and economic consequences'.[181] In elaborating on those factors, Article 5.3 only accounts for economic risks.[182] In reviewing the import ban of the SPS measure by Australia of fresh, chilled, and frozen salmon, the AB in *Australia – Salmon* stated that Australia did not meet the standards of risk assessment by not adequately evaluating the biological and economic consequences of the potential diseases.[183] The latter is a kindly reminder that the SPS Agreement is about trade. The operations of the adjudicating bodies directed by the Agreement focus on how SPS measures constrain trade and, if the measure is genuinely protecting human health whether, such constraints should be allowed. There is also the possibility that expressing risks in economic terms could make it somewhat difficult for precautionary measures, if the potential threat has to be realised in economic terms.[184] Precaution would have to be (re)constructed as a variable of trade and be given an economic value. This would make it more likely for risks that can be directly translated into a commercial and trade value to pass the SPS Agreement.[185] I can then realise that through the lens of constrained openness, the practice of the adjudicating bodies is at variance with the precautionary principle in that instead of not justifying action in light of lack of full scientific certainty, the use of precaution here would justify action on the basis of an economic and trade loss. The AB in *Australia – Salmon* does not engage with the precautionary principle directly, and instead takes the issue of risk and represents it not as based on a precautionary approach but a matter for trade.

Precaution has been turned into a variable of trade, as part of the operations of WTO law. This is not to suggest that the concept of constrained openness can direct or predict the outcomes of the practice of WTO law, with regard to external international law. More subtly, and perhaps more importantly, it is simply a basis from which I can rethink the interaction between WTO and external international law.

In assessing the second definition of risk assessment, the AB in *EC – Hormones* concurred with its preceding Panel that interpreting risk assessment under Annex 4 for 'evaluation of the potential for adverse effects on human or animal health

180 See also section 5.5.1 for further discussion.

181 SPS Agreement Annex A, para 4 *supra* note 56.

182 McDonald *supra note* 125, at 169. Article 5.3 states that: 'In assessing the risk to animal or plant life or health and determining the measure to be applied for achieving the appropriate level of sanitary or phytosanitary protection from such risk, Members shall take into account as relevant economic factors: the potential damage in terms of loss of production or sales in the event of entry, establishment or spread of a pest or disease; the costs of control or eradication in the territory of the importing Member; and the relative cost-effectiveness of alternative approaches to limiting risks.'

183 *Australia Salmon supra* note 47, at paras 128–138.

184 MacDonald *supra* note 125, at 169.

185 Ibid.

arising' is a two-step process. The first is to identify the 'adverse effects on human health (if any)' and secondly, 'if such adverse effects exist, evaluate the potential or probability of occurrence of such effects'.[186] *EC – Hormones* did not set a requirement for a 'minimum degree of risk' in the second definition of risk assessment as it related to the 'potential' health threats to humans or animals.[187] This may accord with the 'idea that the amount of evidence required should be lower where risks are very serious of irreversible harm',[188] but critically it also reflects a bias in Annex A in favour of human health over animal and plant life.[189]

Combined with the fact that Article 5.3 does not impose the evaluation of economic factors and focuses on potential and not likely risk, this bias also implies that there is a more onerous risk assessment process imposed in relation to the first definition of risk to protect environment, as opposed to human or animal health.[190] The damage that could result from a threat to the environment may directly be negative to human or animal health, so in this regard the higher standard of evidence required for the first definition of risk appears at odds with the precaution precautionary. In fact, as discussed above, these factors appear to point to a (re)construction of the very core of that principle on economic and trade terms to make use of it in WTO law, to differentiate between trade restricting legitimate and illegitimate SPS measures.

5.5.4 The scientific risk assessment requirement of Article 5.1 and its relationship to Article 5.5

The requirement of Article 5.1 that SPS measures be 'based on' risk assessment does not set a minimum procedural requirement for the risk assessment process as the AB in *EC – Hormones* observes. The AB determined that 'based on' meant 'a certain objective relationship between two elements, that is to say, to an objective situation that persists and is observable between an SPS measure and a risk assessment'.[191] The scientific justification requirement of Article 5.1 to be 'based on' risk assessment allows science to be used in the SPS without being decisive.[192] Since

186 *EC – Hormones supra* note 53, at para 183.

187 *EC – Hormones supra* note 53, at para 183. SPS Agreement Annex 4, para 4 *supra* note 56. McDonald *supra* note 125, at 169.

188 McDonald *supra* note 125, at 169.

189 McDonald *supra* note 125, at 169. See SPS Agreement Annex 4, para 4 *supra* note 56. This may however reflect a more general tendency in the practice of WTO law to favour human health over other concerns, as for example between *EC – Asbestos supra* note 50 and Appellate Body Report, *Korea – Measures Affecting Imports of Fresh, Chilled and Frozen Beef*, WT/DS161/AB/R, WT/DS169/AB/R, adopted 10 January 2001. The former case was able to pass WTO law, because it involved protecting human health against risk from cancer causing asbestos, and the latter failed because the matter seemed of less consequence in protecting consumer concerns. See Desmedt *supra* note 57, at 465.

190 MacDonald *supra* note 125, at 169.

191 *EC – Hormones supra* note 53, at paras 189–190. Also see *EC – Hormones* fn 207.

192 Howse *supra* note 120, at 2341.

there is no threshold of scientific certainty because of the 'based on' risk assessment requirement, the scientific justification of the SPS refers to the role of science in the democratic process of risk regulation and not to a level of scientific certainty below which democratic judgements about risk are illegitimate.[193]

Additionally, the 'based on' provision allows other non-scientific factors to come into play. The AB in *EC – Hormones* ruled that Members had a 'certain degree of flexibility in meeting the requirements of Article 5.1'.[194] Following on from this it stated that the list of factors for risk assessment in Article 5.2 is not exhaustive. The AB in *EC – Hormones* emphasised that risks under Article 5.1 should not be only confined to those ascertainable in a science laboratory, but actually risk that affected human health in the 'real world where people live and work and die'.[195] This broad interpretation of risk assessment looks as if it can 'virtually' allow the use precautionary measures in that countries can choose the level of protection they desire.[196]

However, the use of non-scientific factors in the risk assessment may be 'ultimately irrelevant' because in the end they cannot override the meaning of 'sufficient scientific evidence', and the rational relationship between an SPS measure and the requirement for scientific evidence.[197] The AB in *EC – Hormones* leaves the non-scientific factors, which are part of the exhaustive lists 'to be considered in the determination of appropriate levels of protection and choice of measure'.[198] Additionally, the ruling by *Australia – Salmon* that a 'finding of inconsistency with Article 5.1 is an appropriate warning signal for a disguised restriction on international trade'[199] shows that for an SPS measure to be precautionary and not based on scientific risk assessment appears less than likely. The AB in *Australia – Salmon* connects Article 5.1 with Article 5.5. The relevant part of Article 5.5 reads that,

> With the objective of achieving consistency in the application of the concept of appropriate level of sanitary or phytosanitary protection against risks to human life or health, or to animal and plant life or health, each Member shall avoid arbitrary or unjustifiable distinctions in the levels it considers to be appropriate in different situations, if such distinctions result in discrimination or a disguised restriction on international trade.[200]

193 Ibid.
194 *EC – Hormones supra* note 53, at para 129.
195 *EC – Hormones supra* note 53, at para 187.
196 Quick R and A Blunther, 'Has the Appellate Body Erred? An Appraisal and criticism of the ruling in the WTO Hormones case' (1999) JIEL 625–626.
197 McDonald *supra* note 125, at 177.
198 McDonald *supra* note 125, at 171.
199 *Australia – Salmon supra* note 47, at para 166.
200 The rest of Article 5.5 reads as follows: 'Members shall cooperate in the Committee, in accordance with paragraphs 1, 2 and 3 of Article 12, to develop guidelines to further the practical implementation of this provision. In developing the guidelines, the Committee shall take into account all relevant factors, including the exceptional character of human health risks to which people voluntarily expose themselves.'

In what can be seen as a reinforcement of the use of science as a tool to distinguish between legitimate and illegitimate trade restrictive SPS measures, the AB in *EC – Hormones* ruled that Article 5.5 has to be 'read in the context of the basic obligations contained in Article 2.3'. This required that an SPS measure 'shall not be applied in a manner which would constitute a disguised restriction on international trade'.[201] Together with the ruling by the AB in *Australia – Salmon*, this is an indication of the use of science in the SPS Agreement, and the basis of the Agreement as part of WTO law to prohibit restrictions on trade. The practice of WTO law, on the scientific risk assessment, if viewed from constrained openness would suggest that the adjudicating bodies make sense of the precautionary principle through their own operations.

5.5.5 Insufficient evidence, showing uncertainty and the provisional SPS measure of Article 5.7

EC – Hormones declared that the precautionary principle was reflected in Article 5.7.[202] Article 5.7 reads:

> In cases where relevant scientific evidence is insufficient, a Member may provisionally adopt sanitary or phytosanitary measures on the basis of available pertinent information, including that from the relevant international organisations as well as from sanitary or phytosanitary measures applied by other Members. In such circumstances, Members shall seek to obtain the additional information necessary for a more objective assessment of risk and review the sanitary or phytosanitary measure accordingly within a reasonable period of time.

When a Member has determined that scientific evidence is insufficient, subsequent to satisfying Article 2.2 and Article 5.1, the Member according to Article 5.7, first sentence, may 'provisionally' adopt an SPS measure 'on the basis of' available pertinent information. The reading of Article 5.1 as informed by Article 2.2 creates a sequence of activities that may trigger Article 5.7. The SPS Agreement requires that actual uncertainty must be shown under Article 2.2 and Article 5.1 before precautionary measures can be applied under Article 5.7. Thus, when an SPS measure is found consistent with Article 5.7, it is not found in violation of Article 2.2.[203]

Additionally the Member must seek, according to the second sentence, to obtain additional information necessary for a 'more' objective assessment of risk and 'review' the SPS measure within a 'reasonable time period'. *Japan – Agricultural Products II* confirmed this reading of Article 5.7, establishing that the four criteria

201 *EC – Hormones supra* note 53, at paras 238, 212.
202 *EC – Hormones supra* note 53, at para 124.
203 Panel Report, *Japan – Measures Affecting Agricultural Products*, WT/DS76/R at para 8.48.

covered in the first and second sentence of Article 5.7 were cumulative and had to be equally satisfied in order to avoid inconsistency with Article 5.7.[204]

The notion of precaution in Article 5.7 assumes that a precautionary SPS measure does not remain indefinitely precautionary. Japan's SPS measure failed not because it was precautionary but because it did not satisfy the obligation under Article 5.7, second sentence, to review the measure within a reasonable time-period. The AB in *Japan – Agricultural Products II* concludes that Members determine the specific method of collection for the additional information in order to continue the provisionally adopted precautionary measure.[205] A Member however does not escape risk assessment. A Member can turn to Article 5.7 because of insufficient information to carry out an initial risk assessment. The additional information gathered within a reasonable time-period as stipulated by Article 5.7 'must be germane' to conducting a more objective risk assessment.[206]

Japan – Agricultural Products II was further instructive in that it emphasised that the time-period for the review of an SPS measure would be determined on a case-by-case basis. This was to be tempered by the difficulty in obtaining information and the characteristics of the SPS measure.[207] The risk assessment process may be postponed but it is not cancelled under the SPS Agreement. This 'precludes permanently precautionary measures that are based upon irreducible uncertainty, converting precaution into a postponement principle.'[208] Article 5.7 does not relieve a Member from having to conduct scientific risk assessment to show actual harm.[209] 'A *mere hunch* is insufficient'.[210] The relationship between Article 2.2 and Article 5.7 creates a situation where Article 5.7 appears as an 'exception' according to Article 2.2.[211] Thus, Article 5.7 forms a core part of, and operates as a 'limited exemption' to Article 2.2.[212] As *Japan – Agricultural Products II* articulated, 'Article 5.7 operates as a qualified *exemption* from the obligation under Article 2.2 not to maintain SPS measures without sufficient scientific evidence. An overly broad and flexible interpretation of that obligation would render Article 5.7 meaningless.'[213]

'Insufficient scientific evidence' delineates when a Member may turn to Article 5.7. The 'absence of adequate risk assessment under Article 5.1 is thus a prerequisite for recourse to Article 5.7'.[214] Article 5.7 is not directly triggered by scientific uncertainty, as typically expected of the precautionary principle outside of the SPS Agreement, but by scientific evidence which reveals itself insufficient. As the AB in

204 *Japan – Agricultural Products II supra* note 56, at para 89.
205 Ibid, at para 92.
206 Ibid, at para 92.
207 Ibid, at para 93.
208 McDonald *supra* note 125, at 172.
209 Applegate *supra* note 6, at 52.
210 Weiss *supra* note 1, at 152 [my emphasis]. He noted that it was called a 'super situation' in the words of the EC brief for the *EC – Hormones* case.
211 *Australia – Salmon (Panel) supra* note 47, at paras 8.27, 8.48.
212 Scott *supra* note 44, at 113.
213 *Japan – Agricultural Products II supra* note 56, para 80 (my emphasis in italics).
214 Scott *supra* note 44, at 113.

Japan – Apples states, the application of Article 5.7 is 'triggered not by the existence of scientific uncertainty, but rather by the insufficiency of scientific evidence'.[215] In underlining the point, the AB further noted that the 'text of Article 5.7 is clear: it refers to cases where relevant scientific evidence is insufficient, not to scientific uncertainty. The two concepts are not interchangeable. Therefore, I am unable to endorse Japan's approach of interpreting Article 5.7 through the prism of scientific uncertainty.'[216] Based on this ruling the role of risk assessment as construed in Article 5.1 is not reduced or escaped in Article 5.7. Though the AB states that Article 5.7 could address situations where there was little scientific evidence to execute an adequate risk assessment or available scientific evidence does not resolve the matter.[217] As Scott states 'risk assessment may yield uncertain results, but still measure up as a risk assessment within the meaning of Article 5.1'.[218] The understanding of 'without sufficient evidence' in Article 2.2 seems to imply 'lack' of evidence and 'not broad' uncertainty. This suggests that the scientific risk assessment must still show that some degree of uncertainty exists.

Viewed through the lens of constrained openness, I can see this as a move away from the core understanding of precautionary action directed by scientific uncertainty and not just on the insufficiency of scientific risk assessment, as set out in Article 5.7.[219] Moreover, it is an illustration of the epistemological break between the precautionary principle, generally construed in environmental law, and as it would be (re)constructed in WTO law. Turning to Article 5.7 is a secondary action to the primary one of satisfying the requirements of Article 2.2, which is to ensure an SPS measure that prohibits trade is based on scientific risk assessment as stipulated by Article 5.1. 'Precaution is admitted only after and upon an inadequate risk assessment phase.'[220] If sufficient information (Article 2.2) is available 'based on' a risk assessment 'appropriate to the circumstances' (Article 5.1), then the notion of precaution in the SPS Agreement (Article 5.7) is not applicable.

In *EC – Hormones*, as was the case in *Japan – Agricultural Products II*, the SPS measure failed not because of its precautionary nature *per se* but because of a failure to satisfy the obligations of the SPS Agreement. In the case of *EC – Hormones*, the EC ban on hormone treated beef from the US was unsuccessful because the EC failed to satisfy the requirements of Article 5.1 and Article 5.2 for the measure to be based on risk assessment.[221] The EC invoked the precautionary principle to override its obligation under Article 5.1 and 5.2. The AB countered that 'the EC did not actually carry out an assessment, within the meaning of Articles 5.1 and 5.2'.[222] The EC insisted that its SPS measure was not 'provisional' within the boundaries of Article 5.7 but

215 *Japan – Apples supra note 165*, at para 184.
216 Ibid, at para 184.
217 *Japan – Apples supra note 165*, at para 185. See Scott *supra* note 44, at 115–116.
218 Scott *supra* note 44, at 116. See also *EC – Biotech supra* note 59, at para 7.3240.
219 Applegate *supra* note 6, at 51, Peel *supra* note 40, at 1017.
220 Bevilacqua *supra* note 119, at 326.
221 Dobos *supra* note 1, at 391. Weiss *supra* note 1, at 152.
222 *EC – Hormones supra* note, 53 at para 208.

'definitive'. The EC consequently argued that the precautionary principle was part of customary international law or a general principle of international law, thereby meaning that its SPS measure based on the precautionary principle was beyond the reach of the scientific risk assessment of Article 5.1 and 5.2. In retort, the AB in *EC – Hormones* stressed that the precautionary principle could not override Articles 5.1 and 5.2, because there was 'no clear textual directive' for the precautionary principle in the SPS Agreement.[223] In other words, *EC – Hormones* reveal the operational parameters as set out in the SPS Agreement on which the use of precaution is acceptable. In the case of *Japan – Agricultural Products*, the SPS measure failed because Japan failed to review the measure within what the adjudicating bodies had considered a reasonable time-period, as stipulated in Article 5.7.[224]

Understanding the SPS measure of the EC in *EC – Hormones* through constrained openness, the EC would have had to put forward the precautionary principle in accordance with the operations of WTO law. It missed that chance by declaring its measure as definitive and not applicable to provisional status of SPS measures under Article 5.7.[225] The EC would have been required to undertake further scientific risk assessment regarding the specific effects of growth hormones in beef, as a potential risks to harm human health. If challenged by the US and Canada, the EC would appear to carry out the review within the time the Panel was requested and when the SPS Agreement came into force, which was less than one year apart.[226] However, as Lowenfeld writes,

> The restrictions enforced by the European Community on hormones in beef had been in effect in one form or another for close to two decades, and could hardly be considered provisional measures. Thus it was relatively easy for the Appellate Body to decline to apply the precautionary principle in the Beef Hormones [*EC – Hormones*] case, without making a general pronouncement on the issue.[227]

Article 5.7 does not appear to embody the language of the precautionary principle as construed in section 5.1, to be found in environmental law. Nevertheless, being the 'qualified exemption' to Article 2.2, as declared by *Japan – Agricultural Products II* could provide some leeway for use of a precautionary SPS measure. This is if the SPS measure satisfies the scientific requirements of the SPS Agreement. Though in effect this would mean that the measure turns out to be preventive rather than a precautionary because the preventive principle encompasses cautious measures based a probable risk, while the precautionary principle is based on uncertainty implying the possibility of a risk.[228]

223 *EC – Hormones supra* note 53, at para 208.
224 *Japan –Agricultural Products II supra* note 56, at para 93.
225 Quick and Bluthner *supra* note, 196 at 625.
226 Lowenfeld *supra* note 37, at 327.
227 Ibid.
228 Bevilacqua *supra* note 119, at 327 fn 90.

Having looked at the practice of WTO law regarding precaution, I can reasonably conclude at this point that the adjudicating bodies do not recognise the application of the precautionary principle in WTO law. The argument could be made that a Member could apply precautionary measures as an appropriate level of protection based on risk assessment. The measure could also take into account non-scientific considerations provided there was a rational relationship between the measure and the risk assessment according to the SPS Agreement. Even if I concede to this argument, that does not mean that the adjudicating bodies are applying the precautionary principle. The practice shows that the adjudicating bodies observe the existence of the principle, or the idea of precaution but this is based on their operation, which is to prohibit Members from erecting arbitrary, disguised or other barriers to trade. The practice shows that if the precautionary measure a Member wishes to use fits within the operations of WTO law, it is more likely to pass the strictures of the SPS Agreement than a measure a Member bases on the precautionary principle.

5.5.6 The right of a Member to set a higher level of SPS protection, standard of review and Article 3.3

Article 3.3 states that,

> Members may introduce or maintain sanitary or phytosanitary measures which result in a higher level of sanitary and phytosanitary protection than would be achieved by measures based on the relevant international standards, guidelines or recommendations, if there is scientific justification, or as a consequence of the level of sanitary or phytosanitary protection a Member determines to be appropriate in accordance with the relevant provisions of paragraphs 1 through 8 of Article 5. Notwithstanding the above, all measures which result in a level of sanitary or phytosanitary protection different from that which would be achieved by measures based on international standards, guidelines or recommendations shall not be inconsistent with any other provision of this Agreement.

EC – Hormones states that, as with Article 5.7 and the preamble to the SPS Agreement, Article 3.3 reflect the precautionary principle because it 'recognise[s] the right of Members to establish their own appropriate level' of SPS.[229] This is an indication of the deference that the WTO shows to the Members in setting their own levels of protection. Moreover, it is part of the issue of standard of review.[230] That is, 'whether and to what extent' the adjudicating bodies 'should respect' an SPS measure, 'although they would prefer a different factual conclusion or legal

229 *EC – Hormones supra* note 53, at paras 123–125.

230 For comprehensive study, see Oesch M, *Standard of Review in WTO Dispute Settlement Resolution* (Oxford: OUP, 2003).

interpretation'.[231] In other words, standard of review is about the adjudicating bodies 'second-guessing' the measures of Members, which are under dispute as alleged violations of WTO law.[232]

In effect, this would call into question the autonomy of a Member to decide what level of protection is appropriate against risk of harm to their health or environment. This can be situated within a broader debate about the interaction between international law and domestic law, and the growing interdependence of States, which is also compounded by the fragmentation of international law.[233] These are political and legal hot-button issues about the sovereignty of the State in a globalised political and economic market place that has even led some commentators to speak of the retreat or decline of the state as the centre of international legal and political affairs.[234] However, here I specifically focus on examining the issue of standard of review as it plays out in the practice of the SPS Agreement. The extent to which, under Article 3.3, Members can adopt higher levels of SPS protection than international standards as an indicator of the precautionary principle in WTO law will be considered. This is in relation to the way in which the adjudicating bodies address risk assessment in the practice of WTO law.

The AB in *EC – Hormones* stated that under Article 3.3 the right of a Member to establish its own level of protection is an autonomous right and not an exception to the obligation of Article 3.1 to harmonise SPS measures as far as possible.[235] The ruling not only provides discretion to Members in managing their risks,[236] but also appears *prima facie* to swing open the doors in the WTO to the precautionary principle. Added to this the AB did not attribute, like its preceding Panel, a protectionist intent on the EC SPS measure that banned the import of hormone treated beef.[237] The AB deferred to the EC because the documentation that came before and accompanied their SPS measure showed the 'clear depth and extent of the anxieties experienced' by the EC regarding the general scientific studies on the carcinogenic effects of growth hormones. [238] *EC – Hormones* did not find that the SPS measure was arbitrary or a disguised restriction on trade.[239] Based on this, Cheyne asserts that at this stage of risk management the precautionary principle 'should be largely immune from external review'.[240] It is hardly surprising that she also suggests that Article 3.3 provides for a gateway to incorporate the precautionary principle in WTO law.[241]

231 Oesch *supra* note 230, at 13–14.

232 Croley S and J Jackson, 'WTO Dispute Procedures, Standard of Review, and Deference to National Governments' (1996) 90 *American Journal of International Law* 193–213, 194.

233 Ibid. See also chapters 1, 2 and 3 for discussion on the fragmentation of international law.

234 See, for example, Strange S, *The Retreat of the State: The Diffusion of Power in the World Economy* (Cambridge: CUP, 1996).

235 *EC – Hormones supra* note 53, at para 172.

236 Thomas *supra* note 118, at 510.

237 *EC – Hormones supra* note 53, at paras 245–246.

238 Ibid.

239 Ibid.

240 Cheyne, 'Risk and Precaution in World Trade Organization Law' *supra* note 11, 843.

241 See section 5.2 and chapter 3 for further discussion.

In upholding the discretion of countries to set their own level of protection, the *Japan – Agricultural Products II* Panel stressed that it was up to the Member to determine its appropriate level of SPS protection, in accordance with Annex A.5, which defines the appropriate level of protection as the level deemed appropriate by the Member.[242] Likewise, *Australia – Salmon* emphasised that an adjudicating body could not question the level of protection of an SPS measure deemed appropriate by a Member. By this ruling, the AB stated that Article 11 or any other provision of the DSU did not support a standard of review or second-guessing of a Member's SPS protection.[243] Article 11 stipulates that a Panel should make an objective assessment of the case and the facts surrounding that case with regard to conformity with the relevant covered agreements. The level of protection was the prerogative of the Member concerned, and thereby the Panel could not substitute its own reasoning about the implied level of protection that a Member expresses.

The AB in *Australia – Salmon* further implied that a Member could set their level of risk at 'zero risk'.[244] The AB in *EC – Hormones* made a distinction between risks as part of risk assessment under Article 5.2 and the determination of the 'appropriate level of protection' under Article 5.6 that allows Members to set their level of risk at zero. It asserted that risk in the risk assessment must be ascertainable risk and not be a 'theoretical uncertainty'.[245] This does not mean that a Member cannot set their level of protection at zero as the AB further underscored, but it correlates to Article 5.7 that some uncertainty to use precaution has to be shown.[246] Article 3.3 may be viewed as a form of precaution because it allows Members to set higher SPS protection than what is available internationally.

Furthermore, Article 3.3 carries no explicit requirement to defend a measure as 'necessary' as would be under Article XX(b).[247] Article 3.3 thus appears less stringent that Article XX(b) in allowing a measure to protect the environment or human health to pass, though it may be trade restrictive. The practice not only signals the deference or a margin of discretion to the Members to set their own

242 *Japan – Agricultural Products II (Panel) supra* note 56, at para 8.81.

243 *Australia – Salmon supra* note 47, at para 199. This was part of the cumulative three-prong test by *Australia – Salmon* as to whether a violation of Article 5.6 of the SPS Agreement had occurred in that SPS measures are not trade restrictive if it is reasonably available taking into account technical and economic feasibility; achieves the Members' appropriate level of SPS protection and is significantly less restrictive to trade than the contested SPS measure.

244 Pauwelyn *supra* note 68, at 652. Desmedt *supra* note 57, at 456.

245 *EC – Hormones supra* note 53, at para 186.

246 See sections 5.5.4–5.5.6 for further discussion.

247 For further discussion see Panel Report, *United States – Section 337 of the Tariff Act of 1930*, BISD 36S/345 at para 5.27 [hereinafter *US – Tariffs*] 5.26–5.27. Panel Report, *United States – Restrictions on Imports of Tuna*, BISD 39S/155, not adopted, report circulated on 16 August 1991 paras 5.27–5.28. Panel Report, *United States – Restrictions on Imports of Tuna*, DS29/R, not adopted, report circulated on 16 June 1994 paras 5.34–5.36. Appellate Body Report, *European Communities – Measures Affecting Asbestos and Asbestos-Containing Products*, WT/DS135/AB/R, adopted 5 April 2001 paras 67–68. *Korea–Beef supra* note 189, at paras 64–67. (This case addresses Article XX(d) but is relevant to understanding the necessity tests.)

levels of protection,[248] but at the very least suggests that there is room for precautionary measures in the SPS Agreement. It is not difficult to see how Article 3.3 could attractively look like a gateway for the incorporation of the precautionary principle.[249]

However, if I take a deeper look at the practice of WTO law surrounding Article 3.3 through the lens of constrained openness, it reveals a different picture. As part of the self-referential operations of WTO law, the deference to nations to set their levels of SPS protection appears not as a gateway to incorporate external international law, but more plausibly correlates with the right of Members to take necessary measures to protect human, animal, plant life or health as stipulated in Article 2.1 of the SPS Agreement.[250] Moreover, *EC – Hormones* stated that the 'right of a Member to define its appropriate level of protection is . . . not an absolute or unqualified right'.[251] There appear to be two optional conditions of Article 3.3 that a Member can introduce an SPS measure with a higher level of protection than international standards if there is scientific justification 'or' in accordance with scientific risk assessment of Article 5. However, the AB in *EC – Hormones* appears to have effectively transformed the options of the 'or' into an 'and' by stating that the 'scientific justification' of the first option under Article 3.3 is part of the nature of risk assessment required in Article 5.1 and defined in paragraph four of Annex A of the SPS Agreement.[252] Therefore, even though Members can take measures that are higher than international standards, which indicate a leeway to the precautionary principle, because an SPS measure still faces the strict scientific requirements of Article 5, the nature of the precautionary measure would be somewhat ineffectual.

The conclusion I draw at this point is that the practice seems to show that a Member has a right to take an SPS measure and set their level of protection. This is not directly second-guessed by the adjudicating bodies but the practice appears to show that because of the discipline of the scientific requirements of the SPS Agreement it may be done indirectly. Take for instance the matter of minority and majority scientific opinion that Members may use to set their levels of protection. In *EC – Hormones* the majority of the studies showed that there was no convincing evidence that hormone treated beef consumed by humans increased their risks of cancer.[253] The AB in *EC – Hormones* noted that a Member was not obliged to follow what may constitute a majority opinion which implies that risk assessment could use both the majority and minority scientific opinions.[254] However, the SPS

248 Oesch *supra* note 230, at 137.

249 See Cheyne in section 5.2 and chapter 3.

250 Matthee and Vermersch *supra* note 1, at 65.

251 *EC – Hormones supra* note 53, at para 173.

252 *EC – Hormones supra* note 53, at para 175. See Schoenbaum T, 'International Trade in Living Modified Organisms', in Francioni F, *Environment, Human Rights and International Trade* (Oxford: Hart Publishing, 2001) 27–38, 31.

253 *EC – Hormones supra* note 53, at 206.

254 *EC – Hormones supra* note 53, at para 178.

Agreement may dictate a contrary result. The structure and design of the SPS Agreement to prohibit restrictions on trade, by using science to distinguish between legitimate and illegitimate SPS measures, means that whatever the evidence to support that measure, it must show a reasonable relationship between the measure and risk assessment. As *EC – Hormones* states,

> By itself, [divergent scientific opinion from the mainstream] does not necessarily signal the absence of a reasonable relationship between the SPS measure and the risk assessment, especially where the risk involved is life-threatening in character and is perceived to constitute a clear and imminent threat to public health and safety. Determination of that the presence or absence of that relationship can only be done on a case-to-case basis, after account is taken of all considerations rationally bearing upon the issue of potential adverse health effects.[255]

When *EC – Hormones* showed deference to nations, because of the operations of WTO law to prohibit restrictions on trade, such deference was not unqualified, as to allow precautionary measures without the basis of scientific evidence. 'The prerogative of . . . WTO Members in choosing their level of protection should not be *overestimated*. It does not represent a *carte blanche* for legitimising SPS measures.'[256] Such caution is informed by *Australia – Salmon*, which declared that the level for protection was the prerogative of Members, but it demonstrated that the AB could determine the level of protection for a Member if the Member failed to do so or did so imprecisely.[257] *Australia – Salmon* stopped short of constructing an obligation for Members to determine positively their level of protection, though asserting that an implicit obligation exists in the SPS Agreement.[258]

However, Desmedt urged that a Member could limit intervention from the adjudicating bodies by explicitly determining its level of protection. Though, as he noted, the practice of WTO law as in *Korea – Beef* demonstrates that such a determination may still be rejected because the level is inconsistent with the measure being pursued by the Member.[259] Desmedt observed that though the AB in *Korea – Beef* had emphasised that WTO Members had a right to determine their levels of enforcement and protection it was not 'hesitant to reject the truthfulness of Korea's stated level'.[260] This was in contrast with the cautious reliance the adjudicating bodies seem to take towards Australia's stated level of SPS protection in *Australia – Salmon*, despite its condemnation of the measure at stake.[261] It may appear that the deference of the adjudicating bodies not to second-guess the SPS

255 Ibid.
256 Desmedt *supra* note 57, at 458 [my emphasis].
257 *Australia – Salmon supra* note 44, at paras 205–206.
258 Ibid at 205–206.
259 Desmedt *supra* note 57, at 458. See *supra* note 189.
260 Desmedt *supra* note 57, at 465.
261 Ibid at 465.

measure or evidence of that measure is more sympathetic for measures to protect human health than for measures to protect consumer interests as was the case in *Korea – Beef*.

EC – Hormones stated that the standard of review is 'neither de novo review as such nor total deference but rather the objective assessment of the facts' according to the adjudicating bodies.[262] There is deference *so as long as* it conforms to the SPS WTO law. This may be considered second-guessing.[263] It is up to Members to choose what level of protection they deem appropriate and thus it seems that this approach would be able to accommodate a precautionary level. Nevertheless, that SPS measure will only be valid according to, as I have examined, requirements of scientific evidence, specificity of the measure to the risk, and demonstration of a reasonable relationship between the measure and the scientific evidence. This second-guessing for an SPS measure to meet requirements of scientific risk assessment, which are contrary to the precautionary principle as I have examined earlier, would make the likelihood that Article 3.3 is a gateway to incorporate the principle somewhat less straightforward than incorporationist such as Cheyne envisaged.[264] The point, as explored more fully in the next section, is that even if *prima facie* the SPS Agreement looks like it could be a getaway to incorporate the precautionary principle, examining the issue through the lens of constrained openness, I can rethink how external international law comes into WTO law. It may not be a matter of incorporation, but as I have discussed, the (re)construction of external international law into a variable of WTO law.

5.5.7 Returning to EC – Hormones*: (re)constructing precaution into a trade law variable*

EC – Hormones underscores that there is no particular methodology for carrying out a risk assessment.[265] It however added that, though general studies of risk assessment were relevant, they were not 'sufficiently specific' to the potential risks in the dispute.[266] *Japan – Apples* supported this point in stating that the risk assessment 'must consider a specific agent or pathway' of the risks.[267] It referred to and concurred with *EC – Hormones* that the scientific evidence the EC used was 'general' in that it had not evaluated 'the carcinogenic potential of those hormones when used *specifically* for growth promotion purposes'.[268] The EC, based on several

262 *EC – Hormones supra* note 53, at para 117. (Quotation marks suppressed.)

263 Osech *supra* note 230, at 140. Janow M, 'Commentary on McNeil' Paper' in Cottier T and P Mavrodis (eds) *The Role of the Judge in International Trade Regulation: Experience and Lessons for the WTO*, World Trade Forum Vol. 7 (Michigan: University of Michigan Press, 2003) 248.

264 See Section 5.2 and chapter 3 for further discussion.

265 *EC – Hormones supra* note 53.

266 Ibid, at para 200.

267 *Japan – Apples supra* note 165, at paras 202–204. Panel Report, *Japan – Measures Affecting the Importation of Apples*, WT/DS245/R, adopted 10 December 2003, upheld by Appellate Body Report, WT/DS245/AB/R para 8.92.

268 *EC – Hormones supra* note 53, at para 199 (original italics).

scientific studies regarding hormones, prohibited from the US imports of meat and meat products derived from cattle to which either natural or synthetic hormones were administered. This was in order to protect human health from risks, for which there was a lack of full scientific certainty.[269] *EC – Hormones* stated that the evidence from the scientific studies must 'sufficiently warrant – that is to say, reasonably support – the SPS measure at stake'.[270] In assessing if the EC's evidence in the scientific reports warranted a ban on hormone treated beef from the US, the AB concurred with the preceding Panel that the reports used by the EC showed that use of the hormones at issue for growth promotion purposes is 'safe'.[271] The AB stated that the scientific evidence submitted by the EC showed the growth hormones to be safe if administered in accordance with the requirements of good veterinary practice.[272]

EC – Hormones expressed that risk assessment could be either mainstream or minority scientific opinion.[273] However, it ruled that the 'single divergent opinion expressed by Dr Lucier is not reasonably sufficient to overturn the contrary conclusions reached in the scientific studies referred' to by the EC, which were that the hormones were 'safe'.[274] These studies did not refer '*specifically* to residues of the hormones in meat from cattle to which hormones had been administered for growth promotion'.[275] The AB stated that the EC relied on these scientific reports which related to 'carcinogenic potential of the entire *categories* of hormones, or of the hormones at issue in *general*'.[276] The contention by *EC – Hormones* was that the studies did not evaluate the carcinogenic potential of the hormones to cause cancer when 'specifically' used for growth promotion purposes, and the 'specific potential' that could arise from its presence in food, and 'more specifically' in meat or meat products.[277] *Japan – Apples* contextualised that point:

> Indeed I am of the view that, as a general matter, 'risk' cannot usually be understood only in terms of the disease or adverse effects that may result. Rather, an evaluation of risk must connect the possibility or adverse effects with an antecedent or cause. For example, the abstract reference to the 'risk of cancer' has no significance, in and of itself, under the SPS agreement; but when one refers to the 'risk of cancer from smoking cigarettes', the particular risk is given content.[278]

269 Ibid, at paras 192–209.
270 Ibid, at para 193.
271 Ibid, at para 196.
272 Ibid, at para 206.
273 Ibid, at para 194.
274 Ibid, at para 197.
275 Ibid, at para 197.
276 Ibid, at para 199.
277 Ibid, at para 199.
278 *Japan – Apples supra* note 165, at para 202, fn 372.

The AB in *EC – Hormones* concurred with the preceding Panel that the studies were 'insufficient to support' the SPS measure to ban hormone treated beef from the US. This is because the scientific risk assessment studies put forward by the EC and opinion of individual scientists (such as Dr Lucier) showed the 'existence of the general risk of cancer' but did not 'focus on' and 'address' the 'particular kind of risk here at stake'.[279] That risk being the 'carcinogenic or genotoxic potential of the residues of those hormones found in meat derived from cattle to which the hormones had been administered for growth promotion purposes – as is required by paragraph 4 of Annex of the SPS Agreement.'[280] *EC – Hormones* concluded that the 'general studies' were 'relevant but do not appear to be sufficiently specific to the case at hand'.[281]

What is most striking about this ruling apart from the emphasis by the AB that the risk assessment must pointedly and specifically relate to the risk the SPS measure is targeted to, is footnotes 180 and 181 in which the AB noted that the minority scientific opinion of Dr Lucier was not specific to the risk being assessed. In footnote 180, the AB noted the opinion of Dr Lucier at a joint meeting of scientific experts as set out in paragraph 819 of the Annex to the US and Canada Reports that,

> For every million women alive in the United States, Canada [and] Europe today, about 110, 000 of these women will get breast cancer. This is obviously a tremendous public health issue. Of those 111, 000 women [to] get breast cancer, maybe several thousand of them are related to the total intake of exogenous [hormones such as] oestrogens from every source, including eggs, meat, phyto-oestrogens, fungal oestrogens, the whole body burden of exogenous oestrogens. And by my estimates one of those 111,000 would come from eating meat containing oestrogens as growth promoter, if used as prescribed.[282]

The AB concludes at footnote 182:

> Assuming that Dr. Lucier's estimate is realistic, it is *noteworthy* that there could be up to 371 persons who, under conditions identified by Dr. Lucier, would get cancer in the Member States of the European Union. The total population of the Member States of the European Union in 1995 was 371 million.[283]

According to this, *EC – Hormones* appears to imply, even if not their intention, that if the risk assessment was correct, then potentially 'up to' 371 women would get cancer out of a population of 371 million, which could mean that the risks to

279 *EC – Hormones supra* note 53, at paras 199–200.
280 Ibid, at para 200.
281 Ibid, at para 200.
282 Ibid, at para 198, fn 181.
283 Ibid, at para 198, fn 182 (my emphasis in italics).

such a small section would not justify the precautionary measure to inhibit the operation of the market.[284] The EC ban on hormone treated beef from the US affected US exports to the lucrative EC market.[285] As Anne Orford points out, if we translate the ruling that the AB made regarding the women in footnote 182 into 'language of international economic law', the AB was 'providing instruction to Member states in how to decide in a way that is responsible to the market in accordance with the dictates of their obligations under WTO agreements'.[286] In light of this ruling, as I discussed earlier, the right of Members to take whatever SPS measure they deemed appropriate seems somewhat misplaced. This is because the SPS measure will always be subject to the scrutiny of its restrictiveness on trade. In effect the SPS measure, even though protecting against risk from harm to human health, animal or plant life, is construed as part of and in accordance with WTO law. The SPS measure, I recall, as *EC – Hormones* spelt out, could not override the specific obligations of the SPS Agreement and WTO law which was to prohibit restrictions on trade.

Seen through the lens of constrained openness, the ability and 'responsibility' to take SPS measures appears 'not owed to the women of footnote 182'.[287] Nor is it owed, as *EC – Hormones* has stated in asserting that scientific risk assessment is broader than 'theoretical uncertainty', to those who 'live and work and die' in the country.[288] The right and the responsibility of a Member to take an SPS measure appears constrained by the SPS Agreement[289] and by extension WTO law, as external international law is (re)constructed as variables of WTO law. The operation of WTO law to prohibit restrictions on trade as the basis of a free market 'becomes the singular other whose demand' has to be fulfilled by a Member.[290] As Mike Feintuck states, an 'emphasis on market mechanisms may well serve to challenge the effective application of any precautionary approach at the international level, as illustrated by the recent dispute between the EU and the United States of America in relation to hormone-treated beef.'[291]

Consider that Article 5.6 stipulates that Members must ensure that SPS measures are 'not more trade-restrictive than required to achieve their appropriate

284 Orford A, 'Beyond Harmonisation: Trade, Human Rights and the Economy of Sacrifice' (2005) 18 *Leiden Journal of International Law* 179–213, 191.

285 Mavroidis P, 'The Trade Disputes Concerning Health Policy Between the EC and the US', in Petersmann E and M Pollack, *Transatlantic Disputes: The EU, the US and the WTO* (Oxford: OUP, 2003) 233–245, 235, 237. In upholding the US claim, the EC failed to bring its measure in line, and the US was allowed to take $191 million worth in countermeasures against the EC.

286 Orford *supra* note 284, at 198.

287 Orford *supra* note 284, at 198.

288 *EC – Hormones supra* note 53, at paras 187, 208.

289 Orford *supra* note 284, at 198.

290 Ibid.

291 Feintuck M, 'Precautionary Maybe, but What's the Principle? The Precautionary Principle, the Regulation of Risk, and the Public Domain' (2005) 32(3) *Journal of Law and Society* 371, 373. See also Salmon N, 'A European perspective on the precautionary principle, food safety and the free trade perspective of the WTO' (2002) *European Law Review* 137, 146–150. Matthee and Vermersch *supra* note 1, at 61.

level' of SPS protection, taking into account technical and economic feasibility.[292] The AB in *Australia – Salmon* concurred with its preceding Panel, and later *Japan – Agricultural Products II* agreed, that there was a three-prong cumulative test to establish inconsistency with Article 5.6.[293] The three elements of the test under Article 5.6 were that another SPS measure is reasonably available taking into account technical and economic feasibility achieves the Member's appropriate level of protection and is significantly less restrictive than the SPS measure contested. Given the cumulative nature of the test, if any one of the elements was not fulfilled, the disputed SPS measure would be found to violate Article 5.6.[294] This would mean that a Member would have to show that all three elements of the test were fulfilled 'in order to discharge of its initial burden of proof' in Article 5.6.[295]

In considering *EC – Hormones* through the lens of constrained openness, I can see how the practice of WTO law shows that the issue of risk assessment and precaution is presented in WTO law as a WTO variable, as it relates to the disturbance that a ban on hormone treated beef would cause to trade. The WTO adjudicating bodies did not find the EC measure was precautionary within the meaning of the SPS Agreement, and more specifically ruled that the EC did not provide a risk assessment as directed by the SPS Agreement. The consideration of potential risk was assessed as a variable of WTO law. Given that the risk of harm was to a small number of people as compared to the larger number of people who were safe, the AB appears, though one would suspect it was not their intention, to implicitly deem that the 'deaths of this [small] number of women would not justify enacting measures that could constrain the operation of the market or inhibit progress towards economic integration',[296] The SPS measure was not upheld because the risk assessment could not show a reasonable relationship between the SPS measure and the risks the measure targeted, according to the SPS Agreement.

Seeing the practice of WTO law on the precautionary principle through the lens of constrained openness does not in any way suggest that the framework can always put forward single answers. As stated in the Prologue and in chapters 1 and 3, I am not looking for a single correct answer or truth of any kind, but I am more interested in laying some groundwork to rethink WTO law and its interaction with external international law. In this chapter, I applied constrained openness to the practice of WTO law, to show that the WTO does not simply and statically incorporate external international law, with the precautionary principle as the example. Whether constrained openness produces an answer is somewhat less important than if it can help show the nuances of how external international law is applied by the WTO adjudicating bodies.

292 Article 5.6 notes that it functions 'without prejudice' to Article 3.2 which stipulates that when SPS measures conform to international standards, they shall be deemed necessary to protect human, animal or plant life or health.

293 *Australia – Salmon supra* note 47, at para 194. *Japan – Agricultural Products II supra* note 56, at para 95.

294 *Australia – Salmon supra* note 47, at para 194.

295 *Japan – Agricultural Products II (Panel) supra* note 56, at para 8.72. See also Scott *supra* note 44, at 159.

296 Orford *supra* note 284, at 191.

5.6 Rethinking the incorporation of the precautionary principle in WTO law

In this chapter I have considered through the lens of constrained openness that WTO law does not simply incorporate external international law but engages in a process of (re)construction of that law into a WTO law variable. Having done this, I can now return to Cheyne's claims, which I discussed in section 5.2 of this chapter (and in chapter 3) that the precautionary principle is incorporated into WTO law through gateway provisions in the SPS Agreement. Cheyne makes four different interchangeable claims for the interaction between WTO law and the precautionary principle. These are that the principle is 'introduced'[297] 'incorporated',[298] 'reflected'[299] and 'accommodated'[300] in WTO law. I shall examine each conceptually, and then compare those broad claims that the precautionary principle is incorporated into WTO law to what I suggest through the lens of constrained openness is the (re)construction of the precautionary principle as a WTO law variable.

Firstly, Cheyne argues that a gateway provision in WTO law can 'act' as a means by which the WTO can incorporate its 'own' version of the precautionary principle.[301] According to her, this constitutes 'a sui generis application in trade law'.[302] If, as Cheyne argues, WTO law in incorporating the precautionary principle as an external norm creates a WTO law version of that external international law, or that WTO law has its own version, then the WTO would not have incorporated the external norm. By her own definition, which seems incongruous to her purpose for gateways to incorporate external international law, the external norm would never come into WTO law. The reason as Cheyne herself states is that WTO law would already have its own version of that norm.

Secondly, Cheyne suggests that a gateway exists when the adjudicating bodies 'accommodate' external norms, which is to locate the meaning of WTO law in state practice outside WTO law.[303] This meaning of a gateway works only if I presuppose that the adjudicating bodies can in essence make room for these external norms, by adding them to WTO law. If the WTO adds that law, what is its relationship to WTO law? Is WTO law displaced, or can other law exist unchanged alongside WTO law in the WTO? The question may be asked, what if WTO law recognises external international law as relevant to interpret the meaning of WTO law? Then WTO law has already (re)constructed that external international law as a variable of WTO it has found useful to understanding WTO law.

Thirdly, Cheyne also argues that if an external norm is found to be 'reflected' in WTO law it is 'another gateway provision in the sense that it incorporates'

297 Cheyne, 'Gateways to the Precautionary Principle in WTO Law' *supra* note 6, at 1–2.
298 Ibid, at 5–7.
299 Ibid, at 11.
300 Ibid, at 11.
301 Ibid, at 5.
302 Ibid.
303 Ibid, at 11.

that norm. She notes that this gateway could allow a wide range of principles and measures into WTO law.[304] Cheyne also links reflection with incorporation. However, the terms are not necessarily interchangeable. Reflection does not signify incorporation. For example, B can look similar to, or have a similar effect to A but that does not tell us that B has been incorporated into A. Even if I assume that A could incorporate B, does B remain the same or does it change? Consider the precautionary principle, which Cheyne argues, is incorporated into WTO law through gateways. The examination above of the same texts and practice that Cheyne engages with shows how in addressing the precautionary principle the meaning, status and understanding of the precautionary principle in environmental law is not incorporated directly into WTO law. The WTO interprets external international law by reference to itself, and the precautionary principle has no direct effect in WTO law. There is an epistemological break between the precautionary principle in environmental law and the notion of precaution in WTO law. As stated earlier, and a point which Cheyne supports, to 'constitute legal conditions' for the use of the most typical version of the precautionary principle in Principle 15 does not require measures to be provisional and supported by a review programme.[305] However, in the WTO these criteria are legal requirements for the use of precautionary measures.

As I have demonstrated, SPS measures must be based on scientific principles, not maintained without sufficient scientific evidence, provisionally adopted and the measure must be reviewed using objective risk assessment within a reasonable time-period. Cheyne is correct to argue that 'As a result the version of the precautionary principle contained in Article 5.7 must be applied in the context of the SPS and subject to its conditions. In particular, the right to introduce provisional measures is excluded if sufficient evidence exists to make an adequate assessment of risks.'[306] Additionally, she writes that the 'obligation to seek further scientific evidence and to carry out regular reviews *is not* part of the precautionary principle as generally expressed, for example, in the Rio Declaration'.[307] I agree with this, but it seems incongruent with Cheyne's notion of gateways. This is because the principle as expressed in WTO law, as I demonstrated above, is not the precautionary principle as expressed in environmental law, which Cheyne claims is incorporated into WTO law.

In arguing for the incorporation of the precautionary principle she unwittingly concedes that it is actually (re)constructed as I suggest. She writes that 'The Appellate Body has . . . treated the provisions that reflect the precautionary principle as internal rules for the purposes of interpretation, with virtually *no* reference to *external* norms'.[308] There is, as constrained openness suggests, an epistemological

304 Ibid, fn 32.
305 Ibid, at 5.
306 Ibid.
307 Ibid (my emphasis in italics).
308 Ibid, at 17.

break, and a (re)construction of how the WTO goes about assessing the principle as a WTO law variable, through reference to itself.[309]

By suggesting that there are identifiable gateways for the incorporation of the precautionary principle in WTO, Cheyne conceals what the WTO may actually be doing, which is a dynamic process of reconstructing external norms. Rather than facilitating the spread and use of the precautionary principle, the gateway approach may be somewhat hampering that process which constrained openness suggests is not an incorporation of the principle but a (re)construction of the principle. Constrained openness reveals these nuances and calls for us to rethink the notion that the WTO can incorporate external international law, and instead forces us to pose the opposite question. The question is not about the capacity of the adjudicating bodies to apply external international law, but whether they can or actually do so.

5.7 Conclusion

The main aim of this chapter was to assess the applicability of constrained openness as a lens and show its relevance to make sense of the interaction between WTO law and external international law. It did this by examining the practice of WTO law in relation to a specific example of external international law, that is, the precautionary principle. I concluded that the precautionary principle in environmental law is not the same notion of precaution that is exhibited in the texts or the practice of the SPS Agreement. The approach that the principle is incorporated into WTO law through gateways in the SPS Agreement appeared as a somewhat inadequate explanation of the interaction between WTO law and external international law. However, because the focus was specifically related to SPS Agreement, I am not imputing broad generalisations about WTO law. I am making a more reticent assertion. That is the illustration of the SPS Agreement and the precautionary principle, understood through constrained openness, provides a basis on which to rethink how WTO law interacts with external international law. Principally the WTO does not incorporate external international law, but is cognitively open to that law and through its own operations. Having examined a specific example of the interaction between WTO and external international law, I continue in chapter 6 to demonstrate constrained openness by examining more broadly the practice of WTO law regarding other examples of external international law.

309 See chapter 3.

6 Examples of interaction between WTO law and external international law

6.0 Introduction

In chapters 1–4 I developed the theory of constrained openness, premising that WTO law constructs its own reality from an internal point of view, the consequence of which is the (re)construction of external international law. On this basis I argued that external international could not be directly incorporated into WTO law. In chapter 5, I examined a specific example of how WTO law interacts with external international law using the precautionary principle. This chapter continues with that theme of applying constrained openness to WTO law by examining general examples. The aim of this chapter, as in chapter 5, is not to test the theory of WTO law but to use the theory as a lens through which we can understand WTO law. In this chapter, I juxtapose the three models of WTO law as a limited domain, open and privileged as to each other and constrained openness. This does two things. Firstly, this chapter provides a demonstration of the conceptual structure of the debate I discussed was occurring among the three models, in chapter 4. Secondly, and more importantly, it provides an evidentiary basis by which I can assess the models and constrained openness as it relates their capacity to make sense of five examples of practice between WTO and external international law. The five examples of practice I examine include a bilateral agreement, an agreement between the WTO and an international organisation, 'law not contracted out from', international environmental law to define WTO law, and a potential cross dispute with another trade panel, NAFTA. The structure of the chapter is as follows. Each examination will begin with an overview and discussion of the dispute between WTO law and the external international law. This is followed by commentary, case analysis and summary on the dispute as to each models of WTO law (see chapter 4) compared to each other and to constrained openness. In the final case analysis, drawing on an actual case, I hypothesise a case with each model as an adjudicating member. This assessment will provide the basis from which to return to the discussion of reflexive strategies to indirectly influence WTO law (see chapter 3), as a better way to think about how WTO and external international law interact.

6.1 A bilateral agreement: *EC – Poultry*

In *EC – Poultry*, the dispute over the application of international law in the WTO was about a bilateral agreement between Brazil and the EC to govern a tariff quota for frozen poultry. Brazil argued that the bilateral Oilseeds Agreement governed its tariff quota with the EC. The EC argued Schedule LXXX under WTO law regulated the quota.[1] Under Schedule LXXX Brazil only got a percentage of the tariff quota, on a shared Most-Favoured-Nation (MFN) basis with other WTO members, as opposed to the more lucrative bilateral Oilseeds Agreement. Brazil argued that the tariff-rate quota of the EC should have been allocated exclusively to Brazil.[2]

The AB examined whether the Panel 'erred' in its interpretation of the relationship between Schedule LXXX under the 1994 WTO Agreement and the Oilseeds Agreement negotiated under Article XXVIII of GATT 1947 (as part of a resolution of the 1990 *EEC – Oilseeds*[3] dispute).[4] The question before the AB was whether the application of the Oilseeds Agreement (hereinafter Oilseeds) could overrule WTO law in Schedule LXXX. In other words, could the Oilseeds constitute the basis by which the adjudicating bodies determined the legality of the EC tariff-rate quota on frozen poultry to Brazil, as opposed to Schedule LXXX, that is, WTO law? The AB agreed with the Panel that there was no need to examine the Oilseeds, as it was not a covered agreement, in the definition of Article 1 of

1 Jackson J, W Davey and A Sykes, *Legal Problems of International Economic Relations* (St. Paul, MN: West Group, 2002, Fourth Edition) 340, states that in 'order to apply tariffs, a nation needs a complex set of regulations, including a detailed list of goods indicating the tariff for each product' which is a tariff schedule. For further reading on tariffs and schedules, see generally Chapter 8 (Tariffs and Customs Rules) 338–386. See also Appellate Body Report, *Argentina – Measures Affecting Imports of Footwear, Textiles, Apparel and Other Items*, WT/DS56/AB/R and Corr.1, adopted 22 April 1998, DSR. This case highlighted that WTO Members must not exceed their tariff binding but may vary their tariff type in their schedules. The United States claimed Argentina violated GATT Article II:3 which, the US asserted, prohibited Members from altering their method of tariff calculation from what was set out in their Schedule. Argentina was applying specific tariffs when it had bound itself to ad valorem tariffs. Argentina underscored that a Member was free to choose the method of calculation for their tariff provided that the maximum level of protection specified in that Member's tariff binding is not exceeded. The Panel found for the United States on the grounds that Members may not alter their method of calculation. The Appellate Body, however, agreed with Argentina that a Member is free to choose the method of calculation, provided that the tariff binding specified in that Member's Schedule is not exceeded. However, Argentina lost the case because having introduced no ceiling or cap to the tariff level, they could not ensure that the equivalent ad valorem tariff would not be exceeded.

2 Appellate Body Report, *European Communities – Measures Affecting the Importation of Certain Poultry Products*, WT/DS69/AB/R, adopted 23 July 1998 [hereinafter *EC – Poultry (AB)*]. Panel Report, *European Communities – Measures Affecting the Importation of Certain Poultry Products*, WT/DS69/R, adopted 23 July 1998, modified by Appellate Body Report, WT/DS69/AB/R [hereinafter *EC – Poultry (Panel)*]. See also: Trachtman J, 'Case Note: EC-Communities – Measures Affecting the Importation of Certain Poultry Products' (1998) 9(3) *European Journal of International Law* 551.

3 Panel Report, *European Economic Community – Payments and Subsidies Paid to Processors and Producers of Oilseeds and Related Animal Proteins*, BISD 37S/86 adopted 25 January 1990, and DS28/R adopted 31 March 1992.

4 *EC – Poultry (AB) supra* note 2, at para 76.

the DSU.[5] Article 1 of the DSU states that the 'rules and procedures' of the DSU apply to disputes on the 'covered agreements' which are listed in Appendix 1 and Appendix 2 of the Agreement Establishing the WTO (the WTO Agreement). The Panel questioned the relevance of the Oilseeds, based on the terms of reference for WTO Panels to examine the covered agreements.[6] The AB in referring to a previous ruling in *EC – Computer Equipment*[7] stressed that Schedules were part of WTO law.[8] It stated that,

> Schedule LXXX is annexed to the Marrakesh Protocol to the General Agreement on Tariffs and Trade 1994 (the "Marrakesh Protocol"), and is an integral part of the GATT 1994.[9] As such, it forms part of the multilateral obligations under the WTO Agreement. The Oilseeds Agreement, in contrast, is a bilateral agreement negotiated by the European Communities and Brazil under Article XXVIII of the GATT 1947, as part of the resolution of the dispute in *EEC – Oilseeds.*[10] As such, the Oilseeds Agreement *is not a 'covered agreement'*[11] within the meaning of Articles 1 and 2 of the DSU.[12]

The AB found that Schedule LXXX was a covered agreement, in contrast to the Oilseeds. It decided, categorically, that 'Schedule LXXX, rather than the Oilseeds Agreement [contained] the relevant obligations to the European Communities under the *WTO Agreement.* Therefore, it was Schedule LXXX, rather than the Oilseeds Agreement, which forms the legal basis for this dispute.'[13] Moreover, it also decided that because Schedule LXXX as WTO law defined the legal basis for

5 *EC – Poultry (AB) supra* note 2, at para 79. *EC – Poultry (Panel) supra* note 2, at para 196.

6 Article 7 of the WTO Dispute Settlement Understanding (DSU) sets down the terms of reference for a Panel. It states that, 'Panels shall have the following terms of reference unless the parties to the dispute agree otherwise within 20 days from the establishment of the panel:

To examine, in light of the relevant provisions in (name of the covered agreement(s) cited by the parties to the dispute), the matter referred to the DSB by (name of party) in document . . . and to make such findings as will assist the DSB in making the recommendations or in giving the rulings provided for in that/those agreement(s).'

EC – Poultry (Panel) supra note 2, at para 196. The Panel noted that, '. . . the issue of the relevance of the Oilseeds Agreement in this case as a preliminary question . . . has to be addressed before the examination of substantive claims.'

7 Appellate Body Report, *European Communities – Customs Classification of Certain Computer Equipment*, WT/DS62/AB/R, WT/DS67/AB/R, WT/DS68/AB/R, adopted 22 June 1998, para 84: 'A Schedule is made an integral part of the GATT 1947 by Article II:7 of GATT 1994. Therefore, the concessions provided for in that Schedule are part of the terms of the treaty. As such, the *only* rules, which may be applied in interpreting the meaning of a concession, are the general rules of treaty interpretation set out in the Vienna Convention.' WTO/GATT Article II:7 stated that, 'The Schedules annexed to this Agreement are hereby made an integral part of Part I of this Agreement.'

8 *EC – Poultry (AB) supra* note 2, at para 82.

9 Original footnote 27: Article II:7 of the GATT 1994.

10 Original footnote 28: Adopted 25 January 1990, BISD 37S/86; and DS28/R, 31 March 1992.

11 My emphasis in italics.

12 *EC – Poultry (AB) supra* note 2, at para 79.

13 Ibid, at para 81.

the dispute, then recourse to the VCLT (Article 59.1 or 30.3)[14] as advocated by the EC to invalidate the Oilseeds was in effect irrelevant. The EC argued that either Article 59.1 or 30.3 of the VCLT should have defined the relationship between the Oilseeds and Schedule LXXX.[15] VCLT Article 30.3 incarnates the *lex posterior* principle and incorporates Article 59.1 by reference, which states that a 'treaty shall be considered as terminated if all the parties to it conclude a later treaty relating to the same subject-matter'.[16] The EC contended on these grounds that Schedule LXXX would supersede and terminate the Oilseeds because Schedule LXXX was a 'conscious act' of a treaty later in time to clarify the Oilseeds.[17] The EC further argued that through Article 30.3 the earlier in time treaty, the Oilseeds, could only apply to the extent that its provisions were compatible with the later in time treaty, Schedule LXXX.[18] Either way, the EC was arguing that the Oilseeds was invalid based on these particular provisions of the VCLT.

However, the Panel stated that it could not 'summarily dismiss the significance of the Oilseeds in the interpretation of Schedule LXXX by recourse to the public international law principles embodied in the Vienna Convention.'[19] The AB found no 'reversible error' in the manner in which the Panel addressed the relationship between the Oilseeds and Schedule LXXX because the Oilseeds was not a covered agreement and could not form the legal basis of the dispute.[20] The AB continued that reasoning and dismissed the EC arguments on a similar basis declaring that it was 'not necessary' to have 'recourse' to Articles 59.1 and 30.3 of the VCLT, as the basis to determine the validity of the Oilseeds.[21] Marceau argued that the adjudicating bodies are 'certainly prohibited' from reaching a conclusion on the violation of external law as VCLT Articles 30 and 59 would dictate, because their mandate is limited to examining the violation of WTO law.[22] She noted that the adjudicating bodies are 'restrained' by DSU Articles 19.1 and 3. According to DSU Article 19.1, the adjudicating bodies decide on the inconsistency of a measure according to a 'covered agreement'. The recommendation of the adjudicating body to the Member in a dispute is to bring its measure into 'conformity' with the covered agreement at issue and not with international law.[23]

14 Article 30 (3) states that, 'When all the parties to the earlier treaty are parties also to the later treaty but the earlier treaty is not terminated or suspended in operation under article 59, the earlier treaty applies only to the extent that its provisions are compatible with those of the later treaty.' See chapter 2 for further discussion.

Article 59 (1) states that, 'A treaty shall be considered as terminated if all the parties to it conclude a later treaty relating to the same subject matter . . .'

15 *EC – Poultry (AB) supra* note 2, at paras 38–40; *EC – Poultry (Panel) supra* note 2, at paras 26–29.

16 See chapter 2, for further discussion.

17 *EC – Poultry (AB) supra* note 2, at paras 39–40.

18 Ibid, at para 40.

19 Ibid, at para 207.

20 Ibid, at para 85.

21 Ibid, at para 79.

22 Marceau G, 'Conflicts of Norms and Conflicts of Jurisdictions: The Relationship between the WTO Agreement and MEAs and other Treaties' (2001) 35(6) *Journal of World Trade*, 1081, 1103.

23 Ibid.

DSU Article 3 contains extensive assertions that the adjudicating bodies cannot add to or diminish the WTO rights and obligations of WTO Members. Marceau asserted that the adjudicating bodies could examine external international law and applicable law between Members in a dispute. However, she stated that they do not have the 'constitutional capacity' accorded by the DSU to decide that external international law can supersede the WTO treaty. This would be adding to or diminishing the rights and obligations of WTO Members as expressed in DSU Articles 3 and 19.[24] The adjudicating bodies can only rule on WTO law. Accordingly as in *EC – Poultry*, the adjudicating bodies would not use VCLT Articles 30 and 59 over WTO law to determine the validity of the Oilseeds.

In not having recourse to VCLT Articles 30.3 and 59.1, the AB however did not wholly dismiss the use of the VCLT.[25] It noted that the Oilseeds was still relevant to the dispute given the 'close connection'[26] between it and Schedule LXXX. The AB extended the Panel's reasoning, noting that the Oilseeds was 'negotiated within the framework of Article XXVIII of GATT 1947 with the authorisation of the CONTRACTING PARTIES'. The AB stated that the Oilseeds 'may serve as supplementary means of interpretation of Schedule LXXX pursuant to Article 32 of the Vienna Convention, as it is part of the historical background of the concessions of the European Communities for frozen poultry meat.'[27] What is noteworthy about *EC – Poultry* is that the AB subsequently did not apply the Oilseeds as supplementary or subsidiary to Schedule LXXX.[28] Given that reports of the adjudicating bodies are only binding on parties of the particular dispute, the Panel considered the Oilseeds as far as it could clarify the obligations in Schedule LXXX between Brazil and the EC.[29] The AB decided that the Oilseeds was subject to VCLT Article 31(1) as noted in DSU Article 3.2.[30] This is a 'representative example of how the formal treatment of certain rules of international does not necessarily correspond with the substantive treatment of these rules in the

24 Marceau, *supra* note 22, at 1104.

25 Van Damme I, 'What Role is there for Regional International Law in the Interpretation of WTO Agreements', in Bartels L and F Ortino, *Regional Trade Agreements and the WTO Legal System* (Oxford: OUP, 2006) 570.

26 *EC – Poultry (Panel) supra* note 2, at 201. *EC – Poultry (AB) supra* note 2, at para 77 quotes the *EC – Poultry (Panel)* on this point.

27 *EC – Poultry (AB) supra* note 2, at para 83.

Article 32 of the VCLT states that, 'Recourse may be had to supplementary means of interpretation, including the preparatory work of the treaty and the circumstances of its conclusions, in order to confirm the meaning resulting from the application of article 31, or to determine the meaning when the interpretation according to article 31:

(a) leaves the meaning ambiguous or obscure; or
(b) leads to a result which is manifestly absurd or unreasonable.'

For further discussion see Chapter 2.

28 Van Damme *supra* note 25, at 570.

29 Ibid, at 569–570.

30 *EC – Poultry (AB) supra* note 2, at para 209.

interpretation' by the adjudicating bodies.[31] The overall decision of the AB appeared to dismiss recourse to VCLT Articles 59 (1) and 30 (3) as potentially determining the substantial outcome of the dispute.[32] The AB stated that the Oilseeds was not a covered agreement. The AB however noted the potential of the Oilseeds as an interpretative aid through VCLT Article 31 by which to apply WTO law.

6.1.1 Case commentary: **EC – Poultry**

Proponents of Model I, WTO law as a limited domain, view *EC – Poultry* as nothing short of a victory for the model.[33] This means that the WTO adjudicating bodies only apply WTO law as in the covered agreements. Trachtman stated that *EC – Poultry*, '. . . has wide international legal implications, and refutes arguments made by some scholars[34] that WTO dispute settlement resolution may apply other law other than WTO law.'[35] Additionally he noted that the WTO adjudicating bodies have limited jurisdiction and the WTO is not a court of general jurisdiction.[36] Trachtman emphasised that *EC – Poultry* was a 'critical jurisprudential point that will have *long* and *loud* repercussions'. This is because he argued that its 'logical implication' is that international law cannot be 'directly' considered by the adjudicating bodies 'if it authorises or requires an action that otherwise violates WTO obligations'.[37] Similarly, Marceau asserted that the Oilseeds, which was negotiated under the auspices of GATT, can be a useful tool of interpretation, but 'cannot be enforced by the adjudicating bodies unless explicitly provided for in the

31 Van Damme *supra* note 27, at 570.

32 *EC – Poultry (AB) supra* note 2, at para 81.

33 Trachtman J: 'The Jurisdiction of the WTO' (2004) 98 ASIL Proc. 139, 141. The same comment was repeated in: 'Jurisdiction in WTO dispute settlement' in Yerxa R and B Wilson (eds) *Key Issues in WTO Dispute Settlement: The First Ten Years* (Cambridge: CUP, 2005) 137, 140. 'Case Note: EC-Communities – Measures Affecting the Importation of Certain Poultry Products' *supra* note 2, at para 3a.

34 Trachtman 'Jurisdiction in WTO dispute settlement' in Yerxa R and B Wilson *supra* note 33, at 136 writes that, 'There is overwhelming evidence that the mandate to the WTO dispute settlement panels and Appellate Body is to apply as substantive law only WTO law: the covered agreements. In fact, the only argument to the contrary asks that we ignore the textual evidence and infer jurisdiction. Rather, they are courts of limited jurisdiction that are not permitted to exceed their mandates.' Regarding arguments that are to the contrary, he footnotes Joost Pauwelyn (*Conflict of Norms in Public International Law: How WTO Law Relates to Other Rules of International Law* (Cambridge: CUP, 2003) and *Panel Report Korea – Procurement*.

35 Trachtman: 'Case Note: EC-Communities – Measures Affecting the Importation of Certain Poultry Products' *supra* note 2, at para 3a; 'The Domain of WTO Dispute Resolution' (1999) 40 Harv. Int'l L.J. 333–377, 342; 'The Jurisdiction of the WTO' *supra* note 33, at 141; 'Jurisdiction in WTO dispute settlement' in Yerxa R and B Wilson *supra* note 33, at 140.

36 Ibid. See also Marceau G: 'A Call for Coherence in International Law' (1999) 33(5) JWT 87–152, 110. 'Conflicts of Norms and Conflicts of Jurisdictions: The Relationship between the WTO Agreement and MEAs and other Treaties' (2001) 35(6) *Journal of World Trade* 1081–1131, 1102. 'WTO Dispute Settlement and Human Rights' (2002) 13 *European Journal of International Law* 753–814, 776.

37 Trachtman 'Case Note: EC-Communities – Measures Affecting the Importation of Certain Poultry Products' *supra* note 2, at para 4.

WTO'.[38] This means that for a proponent of closure, external law referenced in the treaty can serve as a point from which international law is applicable in WTO law. In that the international law would be 'enforced through the WTO provisions' and 'within the WTO [legal] system'.[39] However, international external law, not referenced in WTO law, is only applicable as reference material because, as Trachtman alsonotes, the 'competence' of the WTO tribunals is limited to the 'covered agreements'.[40] In addition to being reference material, Marceau proposed that the Oilseeds could be applicable through VCLT Article 31(3)(c) which stated that account is taken of 'any relevant rule of international law applicable in the relations between parties'.[41] She however stressed that external international law is still not enforceable and only serves the 'purpose of interpreting' WTO law.[42]

Pauwelyn, as a chief proponent of Model II, WTO law as open, supported the ruling in *EC – Poultry*, though he disagreed with the assessment from the proposition of closure that it means the domain of WTO law is limited. In *EC – Poultry*, the Oilseeds was submitted by Brazil as a claim and not a defence. For Pauwleyn, 'the answer to such requests is *obvious*: only those GATT rules that were incorporated into WTO covered agreements (including member-specific schedules of concessions) can be subject of claims before a panel.'[43] This is in keeping with his view and similar to closure that claims in the WTO are limited to WTO law. However and contrary to closure, Pauwelyn has argued that defences can be based on international law.[44] He therefore proposes that the Oilseeds submitted as a defence and not a claim could have prevailed over Schedule LXXX.[45] However, for closure, Oilseeds either as a defence or claim would not have changed the conclusion of *EC – Poultry* because in their view the WTO can only apply WTO law. Through the lens of closure, WTO law could apply the Oilseeds but only as an aid to interpretation but not directly in WTO law as the Oilseeds would not satisfy the requirement to be WTO law as; a covered agreement, external law referenced in WTO law, or as an exception under WTO/GATT Article XX.[46]

38 Marceau, 'A Call for Coherence in International Law', *supra* note 36, at 111. Brackets removed and my emphasis in italics.

39 Marceau, 'A Call for Coherence in International Law', *supra* note 38, at 112. See also Trachtman: 'The Domain of WTO Dispute Resolution' *supra* note 35, at 342–344.

40 Trachtman: 'The Domain of WTO Dispute Resolution' *supra* note 35, at 342; 'The Jurisdiction of the WTO' *supra* note 35, at 135–140; 'Jurisdiction in WTO dispute settlement' in Yerxa R and B Wilson *supra* note 36, at 141. See also chapter 4.

41 Marceau, 'A Call for Coherence in International Law' *supra* note 36, at 119. For further discussion on this, see chapter 2.

42 Marceau, 'A Call for Coherence in International Law' *supra* note 36, at 125.

43 Pauwelyn, J: *Conflict of Norms in Public International Law: How WTO Law Relates to Other Rules of International Law* (Cambridge: CUP, 2003) 478. My emphasis in italics. 'The Role of Public International Law in the WTO: How Far Can We Go?' (2001) 95(3) AJIL 535–578, 567–568.

44 Ibid.

45 Pauwelyn: 'The Role of Public International Law in the WTO: How Far Can We Go?' *supra* note 43, at 568; *Conflict of Norms in Public International Law: How WTO Law Relates to Other Rules of International Law supra* note 43, at 478–479.

46 Trachtman 'The Domain of WTO Dispute Resolution' *supra* note 35, at 342. For further discussion see chapter 4.

Bartels as a proponent of Model III, WTO law as privileged, contended that 'despite what the Appellate Body said' it was because of the conflicts clause inferred in DSU Articles 3.2 and 19.2 that Schedule LXXX prevailed over the Oilseeds.[47] In his view, Schedule LXXX did not prevail because the Oilseeds was a 'non-covered agreement' but because of the conflict clause in DSU Articles 3.2 and 19.2 that no agreement shall 'add to or diminish the rights or obligations' of Members.[48]

6.1.2 Case analysis: EC – Poultry

The first and probably the obvious *prima facie* point in *EC – Poultry* is the conclusion of the adjudicating bodies that the Oilseeds was not a covered agreement. The Oilseeds therefore could not constitute the basis of the decision in WTO law, as a claim against a violation of WTO law.[49] Pauwelyn, a proponent of WTO law as open, acknowledges this point before re-conceptualising the case to argue 'what would happen if' the Oilseeds was proposed as a defence against a violation of WTO law. The fact is that the AB did not use the Oilseeds to interpret Schedule LXXX, which it defined as a covered agreement within the meaning of its own law, principally DSU Article 1. The AB did not apply or enforce the conditions of the Oilseeds, in order to ascertain the validity of WTO law. Instead, the AB used WTO law to ascertain the legal validity of the Oilseeds in WTO law. Even if not a covered agreement, the AB emphasised that the Oilseeds could not be the basis to determine the WTO legality of a Member's action under WTO law. This is because the Oilseeds was not part of the decisions, procedures and customary practices, which can guide the interpretation of WTO law under Article XVI:I[50] of the WTO Agreement.[51] Nevertheless, from examining the dispute in the preceding section, the AB declared that the Oilseeds could serve as a part of the history of Schedule LXXX for supplementary interpretation through VCLT Article 32.

This brings me to the second and probably less obvious point in *EC – Poultry* which is that the AB ruled on the functioning of the VCLT, as whether it could be a basis to invalidate the application of the Oilseeds in WTO law. The VCLT, though external law, is referenced in WTO law through DSU Article 3.2, unlike the Oilseeds. In addition, where the two differ is that the VCLT is procedural in nature and the Oilseeds is substantive. *EC – Poultry* apart from shedding insights

47 Bartels L, 'Applicable Law in the WTO Dispute Settlement Proceedings' (2001) 35 JWT 499–519, 509.

48 Ibid.

49 *EC – Poultry (AB) supra* note 2, at paras 79–81. *EC – Poultry (Panel) supra* note 2, at para 196.

50 Marrakesh Agreement Establishing the WTO Article XVI:I states that, 'Except as otherwise provided under this Agreement or the Multilateral Trade Agreements, the WTO shall be guided by the decisions, procedures and customary practices followed by the CONTRACTING PARTIES to GATT 1947 and the bodies established in the framework of GATT 1947.'

51 *EC – Poultry (AB) supra* note 2, at para 80. *EC – Poultry (Panel) supra* note 2, at 207.

on how the WTO interacts with external international law also provides insights into how the adjudicating bodies address the nature different types of external international law.

The AB appeared to have addressed three counts of international law in *EC – Poultry*. Firstly, the AB dismissed the application of the Oilseeds Agreement to WTO law.[52] Taken on its own as the straightforward outcome of the dispute, this makes it somewhat hard to deny that the proposition of Model I, WTO law as limited domain, is correct: the WTO can only apply WTO law. Secondly, the AB also dismissed the VCLT as a means to determine the validity of the Oilseeds.[53] The AB had to address the potential use of the VCLT to validate the application of substantive external law which was the Oilseeds over WTO law. Thirdly, the AB used the VCLT as a basis by which the Oilseeds could serve as supplementary law to the dispute.[54] This appears more of a procedural point regarding the use of the VCLT in this case to allow the application of substantive external law, the Oilseeds as supplementary law to WTO law. The VCLT was not under direct consideration in this case. However, the manner in which the AB applied the VCLT as external international law presents insight into how the WTO applies external law that is referenced and not referenced WTO law. Models I and II seem to neglect this point in addressing the case.

Using my theory of constrained openness, I can put forward an interpretation of *EC – Poultry*. Constrained openness suggests that WTO law cognises or recognises external international law through its own law. This means that external law is not directly relevant as external international law on its own terms but only to the aims and terms of WTO law.[55] Consider that the adjudicating bodies in *EC – Poultry* in addressing the VCLT do not seem to apply it directly in WTO law, even though the VCLT, as proponents of Model I (WTO law as limited domain) would argue, is referenced in WTO law.[56] According to constrained openness WTO law does not directly engage with external international law but engages with itself about what that external law could mean and where it may be relevant to WTO law. Using constrained openness it appears that the adjudicating bodies in this case refer to the VCLT in accordance with WTO law as expressed in DSU Article 3.2.[57] To be more specific neither Panel nor AB refer directly to the VCLT but refer to the 'customary rules of interpretation of public international law', as DSU Article 3.2 stipulated.[58] It appears that the VCLT, like the Oilseeds, has no standing as law on its own accord in WTO law as WTO law does not directly apply external law. From this case, the manner in which WTO law engages with

52 *EC – Poultry (AB) supra* note 2,, at para 81.
53 *EC – Poultry (AB) supra* note 2 at. para 81, 83. *EC – Poultry (Panel) supra* note 2, at 209.
54 *EC – Poultry (AB) supra* note 2, at para 83.
55 See chapters 3, 4 and 5.
56 Trachtman 'The Domain of WTO Dispute Resolution' *supra* note 35, at 343.
57 *EC – Poultry (Panel) supra* note 2, at para 209. *EC – Poultry (AB) supra* note 2, at para 81.
58 Ibid.

external law, namely the Oilseeds and VCLT, appear to be based on WTO law. WTO law in using the Oilseeds does not use the VCLT as external law to validate it but uses it own WTO law, DSU Article 3.2 to propose the potential use of the Oilseeds as supplementary law. On the VCLT, the adjudicating bodies use the VCLT not as an independent source of law to validate WTO law but according to WTO law in the DSU Article 3.2. In *EC – Poultry*, the VCLT appeared useful, only in providing the adjudicating bodies with procedural rules, albeit important ones, on which the WTO law is silent as it cannot cover every eventuality and circumstance. On the basis of constrained openness I would argue that the AB seemed to accept the procedural role of the VCLT to make WTO law operate but rejected the VCLT as a means by which substantive law (Oilseeds) could be applied over WTO law (Schedule LXXX).

6.1.3 Summary: EC – Poultry

The AB categorically stated there was no recourse to the VCLT to dismiss the application of the Oilseeds. It already had access to WTO law in DSU Article 1 and Schedule LXXX that provided the legal basis for determination of the dispute.[59] In *EC – Poultry*, the AB dismissed the specific provisions of the VCLT Article 59.1 and 30.1 that would allow substantive external law to be the legal basis to determine the validity of WTO law. In doing this, the AB applied WTO law to determine WTO law as the 'covered agreement' as set out in DSU Article 1. It proceeded to apply WTO law in Schedule LXXX to determine the dispute. The AB used WTO law to determine the interaction between the Oilseeds as external international law and Schedule LXXX as WTO law.

Using constrained openness *EC – Poultry* appeared to conclude that the interaction between WTO law and external law was not governable in a 'substantive' way by the VCLT or by the Oilseeds but by WTO law. The AB also strongly suggested in this dispute that the VCLT could serve in a 'procedural' manner in the dispute to make the Oilseeds relevant as part of the history of the dispute. However, the AB did not apply the Oilseeds as supplementary law to WTO law. As constrained openness would show, WTO law in *EC – Poultry* appeared cognitively open to external international law but only through its own substantive WTO law. This appears reasonably evident if I consider that even if the Oilseeds Agreement could form supplementary law to the WTO law by means of the VCLT; this dispute suggested that such a determination would not be made on the grounds of the VCLT but on the terms of WTO law. The adjudicating bodies in *EC – Poultry* do not appear as closure would argue to only apply WTO law. However, they also do not appear to support the point of openness that all external law is potentially applicable in the WTO as defences. The practice proves more nuanced than Models I (limited domain) and II (open) can account for, as further examinations of the practice of WTO law indicate.

59 *EC – Poultry (AB) supra* note 2, at para 81. *EC – Poultry (Panel) supra* note 2, at 207.

6.2 An agreement between a WTO Member and an international organisation: *Argentina – Textiles and Apparels*

In *Argentina – Textiles and Apparels*, the adjudicating bodies faced the question of whether an agreement between the International Monetary Fund (IMF) and Argentina could allow Argentina to violate its WTO/GATT obligations.[60] The US asked the Panel to consider whether Argentina charged tariffs in excess of its bound rates (provided for in Argentina's Schedule LXIV) regarding certain imports of textiles, apparel, footwear and other items.[61] The US also queried the legality under WTO law of a 3 per cent (ad valorem) statistical tax on imports from all WTO Members except those that were members of the regional trading bloc MERCOSUR, to which Argentina was also a member.[62] Argentina argued that the tax was designed to finance the collection by Argentine customs of statistical information on imports and exports. The US claimed that Argentina was violating its bound rates by charging in excess of those rates, as well as imposing a 3 per cent statistical tax. Argentina claimed the imposition of the statistical tax was because of an agreement between Argentina and the IMF. As the Panel stated,

> Argentina *stressed* that the statistical tax was a commitment entered into by Argentina vis-à-vis the IMF. At the same time, Argentina had *equivalent obligations* as a Member of the WTO primarily under Article VIII GATT 1994[63]

60 Panel Report, *Argentina – Measures Affecting Imports of Footwear, Textiles, Apparel and Other Items*, WT/DS56/R, adopted 22 April 1998, modified by Appellate Body Report, WT/DS56/AB/R.

61 Panel Report, *Argentina – Measures Affecting Imports of Footwear, Textiles, Apparel and Other Items*, *supra* note 60, at para 1.1. For further discussion of facts of the case see paras 2.1–2.21 esp. 2.19 addressing the matter of the statistical tax.

62 *Argentina – Textiles and Apparels (Panel) supra* note 60, at para 2.14.

63 Article VIII (Fees and Formalities connected with Importation and Exportation) states that,

> '1 (a) All fees and charges of whatever character (other than import and export duties and other than taxes within the purview of Article III) imposed by contracting parties on or in connection with importation or exportation shall be limited in amount to the approximate cost of services rendered and shall not represent an indirect protection to domestic products or a taxation of imports or exports for fiscal purposes.
> (b) The contracting parties recognize the need for reducing the number and diversity of fees and charges referred to in subparagraph (a).
> (c) The contracting parties also recognize the need for minimizing the incidence and complexity of import and export formalities and for decreasing and simplifying import and export documentation requirements.
> 2. A contracting party shall, upon request by another contracting party or by the CONTRACTING PARTIES, review the operation of its laws and regulations in the light of the provisions of this Article.
> 3. No contracting party shall impose substantial penalties for minor breaches of customs regulations or procedural requirements. In particular, no penalty in respect of any omission or mistake in customs documentation which is easily rectifiable and obviously made without fraudulent intent or gross negligence shall be greater than necessary to serve merely as a warning.

> and Article V:1 of the WTO Agreement.[64] If the assertions of the United States regarding a violation of Article VIII were true, Argentina would find itself involved in a conflict of cross-conditionalities, since Argentina might find itself in a situation where it would be prevented from fulfilling its IMF commitments if it were obliged to fulfil its WTO commitments. Conversely, the continued implementation of its IMF commitments could place it in a position incompatible with its obligation under the WTO.[65]

The Panel faced the following questions: 'Is an ad valorem statistical tax of 3 per cent imposed on imports compatible with Article VIII?' and 'What effect, if any, does Argentina's relationship with the IMF have on the answers to the above question?'[66] The Panel found from the evidence Argentina presented that the three per cent statistical tax was not compatible with Article VIII especially given countries in the regional trading bloc MERCOSUR of which Argentina was a member were exempt from the tax. Therefore, the basic principle of WTO/GATT, the Most Favoured Nation status was not being satisfied, as members of MERCOSUR were being afforded a tax exemption on importation while other WTO Members, in this dispute the US, were not afforded the same exemption.

The Panel found that Argentina was not required to meet commitments to the IMF, as Argentina argued based on its 'Memorandum of Understanding' with the IMF.[67] Argentina did not state that the IMF 'actually' required it to implement the statistical tax but was arguing that the Memorandum of Understanding and declarations between the WTO and IMF[68] should be considered integral in deciding the dispute.[69] The Panel in a decision upheld by the AB stated that,

4. The provisions of this Article shall extend to fees, charges, formalities and requirements imposed by governmental authorities in connection with importation and exportation, including those relating to:

   (a) consular transactions, such as consular invoices and certificates;
   (b) quantitative restrictions;
   (c) licensing;
   (d) exchange control;
   (e) statistical services;
   (f) documents, documentation and certification;
   (g) analysis and inspection; and
   (h) quarantine, sanitation and fumigation.'

64 Article V (Relations with Other Organizations) states that, '1. The General Council shall make appropriate arrangements for effective cooperation with other intergovernmental organizations that have responsibilities related to those of the WTO.'

65 Ibid, at 3.277. My emphasis in italics.

66 Ibid, at 6.72.

67 Ibid, at para 3.278.

68 Ibid, at para 3.279.

69 Ibid, at 3.286. See also Appellate Body Report, *Argentina – Measures Affecting Imports of Footwear, Textiles, Apparel and Other Items*, WT/DS56/AB/R and Corr.1, adopted 22 April 1998, DSR, para 65.

> . . . although [Argentina] does not argue that it is required to impose this specific tax [the statistical tax] in order to meet its commitments to the IMF, Argentina argues that the tax should be found to comply with Article VIII, if necessary through a less strict application of the requirements of Article VIII of GATT that was adopted in the Customs Users Fee. We find *no exception* in the WTO Agreement that would excuse Argentina's compliance with the requirements of Article VIII of GATT. Moreover, we see *nothing* in the Agreement between the IMF and the WTO, the Declaration in the Relationship of the WTO with the IMF and the Declaration on the Contribution of the World Trade Organisation to Achieving Greater Coherence in Global Economic Policymaking that suggests that we should interpret Article VIII as argued by Argentina.[70]

On appeal, Argentina asked the AB to consider whether the Panel erred in failing to 'take into account' Argentina's obligation under the agreement with the IMF in its interpretation of WTO/GATT Article VIII.[71] Argentina was not appealing the finding of the Panel that the statistical tax violated WTO/GATT Article VIII. It argued that the Panel failed to account for Argentina's IMF obligation to implement the statistical tax contained in a 'Memorandum on Economic Policy' between Argentina and the IMF.[72]

The AB agreed with the Panel's ruling that Argentina failed to show it had a 'legally binding commitment' to the IMF that would conflict with or 'supersede' fulfilment of its obligations in WTO/GATT Article VIII.[73] In extending the Panel's ruling, the AB observed that the provisions of GATT 1947 on the IMF, unless specified in the covered agreements, should govern the interaction between the IMF and the WTO.[74] The AB stated that,

> The Agreement Between the IMF and the WTO . . . *does not* modify, add to or diminish the rights and obligations of Members under the WTO Agreement, nor does it modify individual States' commitments to the IMF. It *does not provide any substantive rules* concerning the resolution of possible conflicts between obligations of a Member under the WTO Agreement and obligations under the Articles of Agreement of the IMF or any agreement with the IMF. However, paragraph 10 of the Agreement Between the IMF and the WTO contains a direction to the staff of the IMF and the WTO Secretariat to consult on 'issues of *possible inconsistency* between *measures under discussion*'.[75]

70 *Argentina – Textiles and Apparels (Panel) supra* note 60, at para 6.79. My emphasis in italics.

71 *Argentina – Textiles and Apparels (Panel) supra* note 60, at para 2.19. *Argentina – Textiles and Apparels (AB) supra* note, 69 at paras 13–16.

72 *Argentina – Textiles and Apparels (AB) supra* note, 69, at paras 65–66.

73 *Argentina – Textiles and Apparels (AB) supra* note, 69, at paras 68–70.

74 Ibid, at para 73.

75 Ibid, at para 72. Original italics in the last sentence. Other emphasis in italics suppressed. My emphasis in italics in second sentence.

Further, the AB asserted that nothing in the agreement between the IMF and the WTO 'justifies' that a Member's commitments to the IMF prevail over WTO law.[76] It was also careful to emphasise that its decision was based on the Declaration on the Relationship of the WTO with the IMF. The AB was examining rules beyond the immediate purview of the covered agreement. The IMF rules and the Declaration on the Relationship between the WTO and the IMF, though a legal instrument in WTO law, is not part of the covered agreements of WTO law that the adjudicating bodies can adjudicate, as defined by DSU Article 1. The AB pointed out the provisions of the covered agreements in relation to the IMF that permit an exception as a violation of WTO obligations. These were WTO/GATT Articles XII, XIV, XV and XVIII. Since no such exceptions were to be found under WTO/GATT Article VIII, Argentina's violation of Article VIII could not be maintained in accordance with the WTO's covered agreements.

The interaction for the AB between the WTO and IMF was governed by the covered agreements. The AB upheld the Panel's ruling that nothing in the agreements between the WTO and IMF modified Argentina's WTO obligations under WTO/GATT Article VIII. As in *EC – Poultry*, in *Argentina – Textiles and Apparels*, independent external international rules such as the IMF obligations appear unable to justify a violation of WTO law. Discussing *Argentina – Textiles and Apparels* from my theory of constrained openness as will be further discussed in section 6.2.2, what was significant as an indication of the cognitive openness of WTO law in this case is that the AB accessed the IMF rules, which are outside the immediate preview of the covered agreements of WTO law.

6.2.1 *Case commentary:* Argentina – Textiles and Apparels

Trachtman (Model I) argued that the limited role of the WTO to only apply WTO law is confirmed by *EC – Poultry* and 'supported' by *Argentina – Textiles and Apparels*, which in his view 'suggest[ed] that a purported agreement between Argentina and the IMF would not modify WTO obligations'.[77] Trachtman further contended that the AB appeared 'unwilling' to take account of the potential conflict between WTO law and international obligations such as IMF obligations as in *Argentina – Textiles and Apparels*.[78]

Contrarily, Pauwelyn (Model II) argued that the AB in *Argentina – Textiles and Apparels* did not limit itself to the 'four corners' of the covered agreements. Thus in his view if there was a conflict of obligations, external law applicable as a defence may prevail over WTO law.[79] Pauwelyn criticised the decision of the AB for allowing only those provisions identified as exceptions within WTO law as a basis from

76 Ibid, at para 70.

77 Trachtman, 'The Domain of WTO Dispute Resolution' *supra* note 35, 342–344.

78 Trachtman J, 'Case Note: Argentina – Measures Affecting Imports of Footwear, Textiles, Apparel and Other Items' (1998) 9(3) *European Journal of International Law* 551–552, para 4b.

79 Pauwelyn, 'The Role of Public International Law in the WTO: How Far Can We Go?', *supra* note 43, at 569.

which to allow the violation of WTO law in fulfilment of an IMF obligation.[80] He further criticised the AB for not finding whether the IMF rules such as the memorandum was 'part of the WTO covered agreements' but rather assessing the IMF memorandum against the WTO rules to consider which rule should prevail.[81] However, Pauwelyn noted that the conclusion the AB reached in *Argentina – Textiles and Apparels* is 'fully warranted and supports' his view of the interaction between WTO law and international law because the AB 'does not limit its examination to WTO covered agreements'.[82]

Bartels (Model III) appeared to synthesise Models I and II in assessing *Argentina – Textiles and Apparels.* He asserted that the adjudicating bodies can recognise instruments other than the covered agreements.[83] This position sounds similar to the Model II (WTO law as open) in that a conflicting obligation may influence and even prevail over a WTO obligation. However, Bartels appeared forced to the other side of the argument, and ends up near to Model I (WTO law as limited domain) in that he also asserted that the adjudicating bodies may have gone 'too far' in 'admitting the possibility' that a conflicting obligation under the IMF could modify Argentina's WTO obligations. He makes this assertion based on his conflicts clause that WTO obligations should prevail over external obligations, except to the extent that the obligations 'shed light' on the scope of the Member's obligations.[84]

6.2.2 Case analysis: **Argentina – Textiles and Apparels**

Pauwelyn (Model II) claimed that *Argentina – Textiles and Apparels* showed that the AB did not limit itself to the four corners of the covered agreements, because the AB examined the IMF rules and the Declaration on the relationship between the WTO and the IMF, which are not covered agreements. In contrast, Trachtman and Marceau (Model I) purport that the AB applies only WTO law and stays within the four corners of WTO law, to borrow Pauwelyn's phrase.

However, taken conceptually, none of the models appears to hold if I turn to their merits. The point that makes them sound becomes the point of weakness that makes them vulnerable to the contrary model. So for Pauwelyn, as much as *Argentina – Textiles and Apparels* was about the adjudicating bodies showing that they were not limited to the four corners, it was also, as Trachtman said, about the WTO showing it only applies WTO law. The problem with each model is that it misses the view of the other model.[85] As with *EC – Poultry*, Bartels' (Model III) amalgamation of Trachtman (Model I) and Pauwelyn (Model II) is somewhat weak because

80 Ibid.
81 Ibid, at 596.
82 Ibid, at 596.
83 Bartels *supra* note 47, at 505.
84 Ibid, at 508.
85 See chapter 4 for discussion on the structural nature the debate among the models.

the counter model of each is evident. The result would be vulnerable to attacks from both sides.

Constrained openness may offer a more nuanced model in that instead of trying to find a middle ground between Model I (WTO law as limited) and Model II (WTO law as open), as argued in chapter 4, we make use of both models. WTO law is open but only on the basis on its limited domain. In other words, WTO law constructs its reality from its own operations as WTO law. This suggestion of constrained openness appears to be borne out by *Argentina – Textiles and Apparels* in that WTO law is limited but that does not mean it is hermetically sealed from the influence of external international law. The implication of viewing WTO law, more specifically *Argentina – Textiles and Apparels*, through the lens of constrained openness is that WTO law may not communicate directly with external international law but communicates by reference to its own WTO law.

Consider that the AB examined the IMF rules which are outside of WTO law in order to come to a decision about their relevance to understanding WTO law. WTO law appeared not to have direct access to the IMF rules but did have access to its understanding of what those rules meant for WTO law. The AB then seemed to be cognitively aware and open to the IMF rules that Argentina purported to have based its decision about WTO law but in examining those rules used WTO law. The IMF rules had no direct application in WTO law and were relevant in as much as the AB was not going to use those rules to change or modify WTO law.

6.2.3 Summary: Argentina – Textiles and Apparels

The WTO is not limited to the four corners of the covered agreements. The adjudicating bodies went beyond the covered agreements in exploring the IMF rules and the Declaration between the IMF and WTO which were not part of the covered agreements. To believe as Pauwelyn (Model II) did that this is evidence that the WTO is not limited in its application of law to the covered agreements seemed reasonable. However, Pauwelyn appeared to miss the point, which closure underscored, that the adjudicating bodies stated that in the event of a conflict the IMF obligations could not modify the WTO obligations.[86] Conversely, proponents of Model II (WTO law as a limited domain) in arguing that *Argentina – Textiles and Apparels* underscored that the WTO only applies WTO law miss the critical part of the decision that Model I (WTO law as open) brought somewhat into view. That is, and more correctly described is that WTO law is cognitively open to external international law.

Argentina – Textiles and Apparels was a soft dispute, as Argentina could not prove or did not directly assert that it implemented the statistical tax because of its IMF obligation. The point to take away from this dispute as viewed through the lens of constrained openness is that WTO law is open to external international law

86 *Argentina – Textiles and Apparels (AB) supra* note 69, at para 72. *Argentina – Textiles and Apparels (Panel) supra* note 60, at para 6.79.

beyond the four corners of the covered agreements. However, the importance of constrained openness is to understand the nature of how WTO law is cognitively open to external international law. The argument I put forward is that openness, as to *Argentina – Textiles and Apparels*, appeared conditioned by the covered agreements (WTO law) in the articulation by the adjudicating bodies that external law was not going to modify the obligations of Members of the WTO legal system.

6.3 Law 'not contracted out from': *Korea – Government Procurement*

In *Korea – Government Procurement*, the Panel asserted that the relationship between WTO law and external law as customary international law was 'broader' than the specific articulations of DSU Article 3.2, which direct the adjudicating bodies to use the customary rules of interpretation to clarify the provisions of the WTO. The Panel appears to take this decision based on Article 3.2 which specifically refers to the rules of customary interpretation of international law, generally seen as the VCLT and no other rules.[87] However, the Panel was faced with what they characterised as an 'unintended gap' in WTO law on error in treaty formation. The Panel saw it as necessary to fill this gap with external law in order to adjudicate on the case before them.[88]

The Panel, in a footnote, noted that they saw 'no basis' for 'an *a contrario* implication that rules of international law other than the rules of interpretation do not apply'.[89] The Panel asserted that DSU Article 3.2 addressed this issue because reliance on negotiating history was seen as inconsistent with the customary rules of interpretation.[90] The assertion by the Panel appeared to support the view of Model II (open) that the adjudicating bodies have to apply external international law to the extent not contracted out from by WTO law.[91] However, for proponents of Model I (limited), Article 3.2 is a signal that the adjudicating bodies can only apply WTO law or external law referenced in WTO law that would for them essentially make it WTO law.[92]

The application of external international law however, seems contingent on the fact that external international law should not conflict with WTO law.[93] Prior to *Korea – Government Procurement*, the Appellate Body in *US – Gasoline* made a similarly telling point that WTO law was not to be 'read in clinical isolation from public international law'.[94] Though having similar overtones that WTO law is somehow part of international law, the seminal point is what *US – Gasoline*

87 See chapter 2.
88 Panel Report, *Korea – Measures Affecting Government Procurement*, WT/DS163/R, adopted 19 June 2000, para 7.101.
89 Ibid, at para 7.96 (footnote).
90 Ibid.
91 See Pauwelyn *supra* note 43.
92 See for further discussion, chapter 4.
93 See discussion on *Argentina – Textiles and Apparels* in this chapter.
94 Appellate Body Report, *United States – Standards for Reformulated and Conventional Gasoline*, WT/DS2/AB/R, adopted 20 May 1996, 15–16.

and *Korea – Government Procurement* highlight about the role of external international law in WTO law. From the discussion above, we are aware that for *Korea – Government Procurement*, the interaction between WTO law and external international law was *broader* than the scope of DSU Article 3.2. The Article stated that the WTO treaty was to be interpreted using the 'customary rules of interpretation', which are embodied in the VCLT to 'clarify' WTO law.[95] For *US – Gasoline*, Article 3.2 reflected that the WTO was not clinically isolated from international law. Taken together, both cases appear as a continuum if not an articulation of the same position that WTO law is part of international law. *US – Gasoline* signals that Article 3.2 reflects a broader purpose for the WTO to be part of international law. *Korea – Government Procurement* signals that because of the use of Article 3.2 to correct the historically faulty use of treaty interpretation by the adjudicating bodies, the Article reflects the broader application of external international law in WTO law. Some may argue that this analysis conflates *US – Gasoline* and *Korea – Government Procurement*, in that the cases addressed different purposes of external international law respectively, as directly applicable and for interpretative purposes. This critique misses an important point, which we have already mentioned (see chapter 4) but deserves a reiteration here: the distinction between jurisdiction, applicable law and law for interpretative, purposes is somewhat ineffectual. Of course, on the face of it, I do not deny the value in being able to point to a difference between the law the adjudicating bodes will enforce as part of a claim and the law that is applicable to determine the law that will be enforced. Such a distinction can be a useful marker in delineating different types of external international law as for example, substantive and interpretative. However, even if you have the distinctions, all the law is still external as to application by the adjudicating bodies in WTO law. The distinction is a convenient short-hand for telling us where the law ends up in the WTO adjudicative process but it does not tell us how any of this happens. In effect the distinction for our purposes here becomes somewhat ineffectual, as it does not address the nature and purpose of WTO law or how the adjudicating bodies should respond to external international law. Moreover as to constrained openness, it matters little whether the external international law has been enforced or interpreted because whatever the action, WTO law still constructs its own reality, so that external international law only has significance as to the purpose of WTO law (see chapters 3 and 4).

6.3.1 Case commentary: **Korea – Government Procurement**

Korea – Government Procurement like all the cases discussed thus far attracts the diverging views of Model I (WTO law as a limited domain) and Model II (WTO law as open). Pauwelyn (Model II) asserted that the WTO treaty 'need not refer explicitly to or confirm all other potentially relevant rules of international law . . . [because]

95 See chapter 2 for further discussion.

such reference or confirmation occurs automatically as a result of the simple fact that the DSU was created and continues to exist in the wider context of international law.'[96] In his view, all law that the WTO has not contracted out from remains active and available for application as a 'fall back' to general international law.[97] His point is that international law 'does not suddenly evaporate when WTO claims are transferred to a WTO panel.'[98] Similarly, Bartels' (Model III, WTO law as privileged) suggested that when there is 'settled' law on a matter, that is, law not contracted out from, that law should bind WTO law.[99] He found support for his position in the decision by the Panel in *Korea – Government Procurement* that the interaction between WTO law and customary international law was broader than Article 3.2 of the DSU. In his view, customary international law was applied to the extent that the WTO did not 'contract out' from it.[100]

However, Trachtman (Model I) retorted that the only two views that stand contrary to his view that the WTO should only apply WTO law, were that of what he obviously believed was the misguided Panel in *Korea – Government Procurement* and that of Pauwelyn.[101] Conversely to Pauwelyn, Trachtman thus contended that the 'default rule' in international law is 'auto-interpretation' in that countries are not held to have accepted a law without their consent.[102] He further underscored that Pauwelyn neglected an important point that the WTO is not a general court of jurisdiction, competent to apply 'all' international law.[103] Therefore, according to Trachtman 'international law tribunals are authorised only to (1) hear cases and (2) apply law pursuant to their specific, positive mandates. They are not implicitly courts of general jurisdiction either as to the cases they can hear or as to the law they can apply.'[104] Marceau added that the WTO should not enforce non-WTO law by 'providing remedies for breaches of public international law' as this would burden the multilateral trading system.[105]

96 Pauwelyn, 'The Role of Public International Law in the WTO: How Far Can We Go?' *supra* note 43, at 561–562.

97 See chapter 4 for further discussion.

98 Pauwelyn: *Conflict of Norms in Public International Law: How WTO Law Relates to Other Rules of International Law supra* note 43, at 478–479. 'The Role of Public International Law in the WTO: How Far Can We Go?' *supra* note 43, at 567–568 specifically 562.

99 Bartels *supra* note 47, at 516.

100 *Korea – Government Procurement supra* note 88, at para 7.96. My emphasis in italics.

101 Trachtman, 'Jurisdiction in WTO dispute settlement' in Yerxa R and B Wilson (eds) *supra* note 33, at 136. Also McRae D, 'Claus-Dieter Ehlermann's presentation on "The Role and Record of the Dispute Settlement Panels and the Appellate Body of the WTO" ' (2003) JIEL 709–717, 713.

102 Trachtman 'Jurisdiction in WTO dispute settlement' in Yerxa R and B Wilson (eds) *supra* note 33, at 139. See also chapter 4 for further discussion.

103 Trachtman, 'Domain of WTO Dispute Resolution' *supra* note 35, at 338.

104 Trachtman: 'Book Review of Conflict of Norms in Public International Law: How WTO Law Relates to Other Rules of International Law by J Pauwelyn' (2004) 98 AJIL 855–886, 858. 'The Jurisdiction of the WTO' *supra* note 33, at 140. 'Jurisdiction in WTO dispute settlement' in Yerxa R and B Wilson (eds) *supra* note 33, at 136

105 Marceau, 'A Call for Coherence in International Law' *supra* note 36, at 111.

6.3.2 Case analysis and summary: Korea – Government Procurement

If we take Trachtman's (Model I) view, it appeared that the Panel in *Korea – Government Procurement* over-stepped its mandate in stating that the WTO was broader than the treaty. WTO law is a limited court that has a mandate driven by the agreed provisions of its treaty. However, Pauwelyn (Model II) holds the converse point, underlined by *Korea – Government Procurement*, that the WTO is broader than the treaty in that as a system of international law, it will have to interact with external international law, which is not directly part of the WTO legal system. It may also be faced with points of law that are not contained within its treaty because a treaty cannot contain 'all' textual support for the practice of the law. That said, a closer look at *Korea – Government Procurement* does not provide evidence to support the views of either Pauwelyn or Trachtman. As with the practice of WTO law examined in the preceding sections, each model often appears to tell only part of the story.

The Panel in *Korea – Government Procurement* did make the assertion that the interaction between WTO law and external international law was broader than the articulation of DSU Article 3.2. As discussed in chapter 2 and 4, WTO law applies external procedural rules such as the VCLT, which DSU Article 3.2 references, in order to apply its own WTO law. The law the WTO has not contracted out from will apply but only within the operations of WTO law, as I would argue using constrained openness. To take the point on its own that WTO law applies to law not contracted out from, as Pauwelyn did, as a description of the interaction between WTO law and external international law, I think is somewhat inadequate. Viewed through the lens of constrained openness, the Panel went on to make a very important characterisation that external international law not contracted out from does apply but only to the extent that there is 'no conflict or inconsistency' or some part of the 'covered agreements' that 'implies differently'.[106] In other words, the WTO appears cognitively open to external international law but only in terms of its own WTO law.

6.4 International environmental law to define WTO law: *US – Shrimp*

In *US – Shrimp*, the AB on appeal from Thailand, India, Malaysia and Pakistan was faced with the application of WTO/GATT Article XX (g)[107] to allow a unilateral US ban on shrimp that were not caught using methods that pro-

106 *Korea – Government Procurement supra* note 88, at para 7.96.

107 This states that, 'Subject to the requirement that such measures are not applied in a manner which would constitute a means of arbitrary or unjustifiable discrimination between countries where the same conditions prevail, or a disguised restriction on international trade, nothing in this Agreement shall be construed to prevent the adoption or enforcement by any contracting party of measures:

(g) relating to the conservation of exhaustible natural resources if such measures are made effective in conjunction with restrictions on domestic production or consumption;'

tected turtles, as an exception to WTO/GATT Articles I, XI and XIII.[108] To determine the meaning of the term 'natural resources' in Article XX (g), the AB reasoned that the term was not static but evolutionary. It stated that it was 'pertinent to note that modern international conventions and declarations make frequent references to natural resources as embracing both living and non-living resources.'[109] What is important for the discussion here is that in defining the term natural resources, the AB referred to a number of conventions and declarations. These included the 1982 United Nations Convention on Law of the Sea (UNCLOS),[110] Convention on Biological Diversity,[111] Resolution on Assistance to Developing Countries adopted in conjunction with the Convention on the Conservation of Migratory Species of Wild Animals[112] and the Convention on International Trade in Endangered Species of Wild Fauna and Flora (CITES).[113] Moreover, the AB turned to CITES to emphasise its position that turtles were a natural exhaustible resource, as they were in Appendix I of CITES which includes species threatened with extinction.[114]

The other use of external treaties by the AB was to assess whether the US policy of banning shrimp caught using methods that harmed turtles was being applied in an unjustifiably discriminatory manner that upsets or prohibits trade. The assessment was to ascertain whether the US had genuinely pursued across-the-board negotiations with the appellees before implementation of the ban that restricts

108 Article I:1 (General Most-Favoured-Nation Treatment) states that, 'With respect to customs duties and charges of any kind imposed on or in connection with importation or exportation or imposed on the international transfer of payments for imports or exports, and with respect to the method of levying such duties and charges, and with respect to all rules and formalities in connection with importation and exportation, and with respect to all matters referred to in paragraphs 2 and 4 of Article III,* any advantage, favour, privilege or immunity granted by any contracting party to any product originating in or destined for any other country shall be accorded immediately and unconditionally to the like product originating in or destined for the territories of all other contracting parties.'

Article XI:1 (General Elimination of Quantitative Restrictions) states that, 'No prohibitions or restrictions other than duties, taxes or other charges, whether made effective through quotas, import or export licences or other measures, shall be instituted or maintained by any contracting party on the importation of any product of the territory of any other contracting party or on the exportation or sale for export of any product destined for the territory of any other contracting party.'

Article XIII:1 (Non-discriminatory Administration of Quantitative Restrictions) states that, 'No prohibition or restriction shall be applied by any contracting party on the importation of any product of the territory of any other contracting party or on the exportation of any product destined for the territory of any other contracting party, unless the importation of the like product of all third countries or the exportation of the like product to all third countries is similarly prohibited or restricted.'

109 Appellate Body Report, *United States – Import Prohibition of Certain Shrimp and Shrimp Products*, WT/DS58/AB/R, adopted 6 November 1998, para 130.

110 Ibid.

111 Ibid.

112 Ibid.

113 Ibid, at para 132.

114 Ibid.

trade.[115] The AB looked to the Inter-American Convention for the Protection and Conservation of Sea Turtles, with the conclusion that it provided evidence that an alternative course of action besides the ban was 'reasonably' open to the US for securing the policy of protecting turtles.[116] The Inter-American Convention for the Protection and Conservation of Sea Turtles provided two purposes for the AB, as evidence of the efforts by the US to negotiate an international treaty and as an interpretative element in assessing whether the US sought less trade restrictive measures using WTO/GATT Article XX.[117] Van Damme argued that *US – Shrimp* seemed to confirm that the Inter-American Convention for the Protection and Conservation of Sea Turtles was used by AB as a supplementary means of interpretation as within VCLT Article 31.[118] This would be similar to the AB in *EC – Poultry*, where the AB declared that the Oilseeds could serve as a supplementary means of interpretation. Like *EC – Poultry*, the external law – in *US – Shrimp* the Inter-American Convention for the Protection and Conservation of Sea Turtles – was not directly applied in the WTO or applied independently of WTO law.

6.4.1 Case commentary: **US – Shrimp**

US – Shrimp addressed external law in three ways. Firstly, external law was used to define the term 'natural resources' in WTO law. Secondly, external law was used to determine the status of turtles as endangered within the term natural resources. Thirdly, external law was used to assess how justifiable the discrimination of the US policy was in banning shrimp caught using methods that harmed turtles, by comparing it to other available measures. Conspicuous is the use by the AB of external treaties to which not all the WTO Members in the dispute were parties.[119] The AB was not using external international law on which it could base its decisions but it was demonstrating the broad reach of that external law beyond WTO Members having to be party to the particular law for it to be considered in a dispute. There is some parallel to *Argentina – Textile and Apparels* in that the AB in that case in looking at the IMF declarations reached beyond immediate WTO law as the covered agreements. Using constrained openness *US – Shrimp*, like *Argentina*

115 Ibid, at para 162.

116 Ibid, at paras 167–171. See also Panel Report, *United States – Import Prohibition of Certain Shrimp and Shrimp Products – Recourse to Article 21.5 of the DSU by Malaysia*, WT/DS58/RW, adopted 21 November 2001, upheld by Appellate Body Report, WT/DS58/AB/RW paras 12–129.

117 *US – Shrimp supra* note 109, at paras 167–171. In agreement, Van Damme *supra* note 25, at 570–571.

118 Van Damme *supra* note 25, at 570–571.

119 For example the Convention on the Conservation of Migratory Species of Wild Animals (1979) was ratified by India and Pakistan but Malaysia, Thailand and the US were not parties to the Convention. Also the Convention on Biological Diversity was ratified by India, Malaysia and Pakistan but Thailand and the US had signed but not ratified. See *US – Shrimp supra* note 109, at paras 111, 113. Also see Panel Report, *European Communities – Measures Affecting the Approval and Marketing of Biotech Products*, WT/DS291/R, WT/DS292/R, Corr.1 and Add. 1, 2, 3, 4, 5, 6, 7, 8, 9, adopted 21 November 2006 at para 7.94 refers to this point as a basis to make use of external law. For further discussion see chapter 2, section 2.7.

– *Textiles Apparels*, demonstrates that WTO law is cognitively open and the argument that this openness is conditioned on and by the operations of WTO law is not a suggestion that WTO law functions in isolation from international law. Constrained openness is an argument that WTO law will interact with external law but only on the basis of the closure of its own law. The point is that in *US – Shrimp* the AB did not independently apply any of the external treaties it used to define WTO law. The adjudicating bodies did not provide or perform any assessment of the merits or demerits of the environmental treaties it used. Like *EC – Poultry* and *Argentina – Textiles and Apparels*, the adjudicating bodies seemed to use international external law in the WTO only to the extent that it was not in conflict with WTO law. Importantly, international external law was not independently applied, but only to further the operation of the WTO to be able to reach credible decisions in its dispute settlement process, as to its purpose in liberalising trade.

The procedural use of international external law in *EC – Bananas* is similar to *US – Shrimp* but diverges somewhat in that *EC – Bananas* addressed the use of external international law that was referenced in WTO law.[120] *EC – Bananas* is significant as it raises the issue of international law that is 'referenced' in a WTO obligation to define the focus of that WTO obligation.[121] In *EC – Bananas*, pursuant to WTO/GATT Article IX of the Agreement establishing the WTO, the European Community (EC) adopted a waiver, the Lomé waiver under WTO law. The waiver was part of the Lomé Convention, which was to guarantee duty-free market access for bananas from the African-Caribbean-Pacific group (ACP) to the EC market.[122] The EC argued that the Panel should defer to the EC interpretation of the Lomé Convention. The Panel however examined the Convention under the claim that a reference to the Convention in the Lomé waiver under WTO law made the matter a WTO/GATT issue.[123] The Panel stated that, in not deferring to the EC interpretation of the Lomé Convention they had 'no alternative but to examine' the Lomé Convention for *themselves* 'in so far as' it was necessary to interpret the Lomé waiver which was part of WTO law.[124] In appealing the Panel's decision before the AB, the EC again argued that the Panel should have deferred to the 'common EC and ACP views on the appropriate interpretation of the Lomé Convention'.[125] The AB noted that this assertion by the EC was 'without merit'.[126]

120 Appellate Body Report, *European Communities – Regime for the Importation, Sale and Distribution of Bananas*, WT/DS27/AB/R, adopted 25 September 1997 paras 164–188.

121 Marceau 'A Call for Coherence in International Law' *supra* note 36, at 112–113.

122 The EU Lomé Convention gave preferential treatment to the ACP which means African, Caribbean and Pacific countries. The Lomé Agreement expired in 2000 and was replaced by the Cotonou Agreement which will expire in 2020 (February). For further information see http://ec.europa.eu/development/geographical/cotonouintro_en.cfm.

123 Panel Report, *European Communities – Regime for the Importation, Sale and Distribution of Bananas*, WT/DS27/R/ adopted 25 September 1997, modified by Appellate Body Report, WT/DS27/AB/R para 7.98.

124 Ibid.

125 *EC – Bananas (AB) supra* note 120, at para 167.

126 Ibid.

Like the Panel, the AB did not defer to the EC and ACP views to interpret the Lomé Convention, nor consider the practice of the EC and ACP concerning the Lomé Convention.[127] The AB agreed with the Panel stating that 'We, too, have no alternative' but to examine the Lomé Convention.[128] The approach of the adjudicating bodies in *EC – Bananas* was similar to the Panel in *EC – Poultry*. In defining the 'global annual tariff quota' in the Oilseeds the Panel ruled that the various agreements submitted by Brazil 'do not constitute conclusive evidence to the effect that the particular terms used in the Oilseeds Agreement must be read the way claimed by Brazil'.[129]

In *EC – Bananas* the AB appeared not to strictly use the Lomé Convention to clarify or define terms in WTO law but to set out that the interpretation of the Convention was required because of a 'reference' to the Lomé Convention in the Lomé waiver which made the Convention a 'GATT/WTO issue.'[130] However, Van Damme said, 'it is not entirely clear' what the adjudicating bodies meant by the Convention being a GATT/WTO issue.[131] The Lomé waiver is part of WTO law pursuant as discussed above to Article IX but that does not make the Lomé Convention part of WTO law. The adjudicating bodies seemed to reason that because the Lomé waiver was part of WTO law and the Lomé Convention was part of the Lomé waiver, then the Lomé Convention was matter they could consider in their decision-making. Van Damme argued that the line of reasoning of the AB to examine the Convention could imply that it can interpret an international treaty referred to in WTO law without prejudice to the corresponding institutions of that treaty.[132] She concluded that this would bring the WTO dispute settlement system close to acting as a global treaty interpreter.[133]

However, viewing *EC – Bananas* through the lens of constrained openness, I think, shows that even if the adjudicating bodies examine external international law, it does not mean it has applied or incorporated that law in the WTO. As Marceau argued, the adjudicating bodies were 'obligated' to 'examine' the Lomé Convention because it was referred to in the Lomé waiver under WTO law.[134] The Panel and the AB did not 'apply' or 'enforce' the provisions of the Lomé Convention so they were not near to making the WTO dispute settlement system a global treaty interpreter. Following the view of constrained openness, that WTO law is cognitively open based on its operations to construct its own reality, the only place for the Lomé Convention seemed to be to determine the scope of the rights and obligations that WTO Members had under the Lomé waiver.[135] I would

127 Oesch M, *Standard of Review in WTO Dispute Settlement Resolution* (Oxford: OUP, 2003) 223.

128 *EC – Bananas (AB) supra* note 120, at para 167.

129 *EC – Poultry (AB) supra* note 2, at para 211. In agreement, Oesch *supra* note 127, at 220.

130 *EC – Bananas (AB) supra* note 120, at para 167. In agreement, Van Damme *supra* note 27, at 571.

131 Van Damme *supra* note 25, at 571.

132 Ibid.

133 Ibid.

134 Marceau, 'A Call for Coherence in International Law' *supra* note 36, at 113.

135 *EC – Bananas (Panel) supra* note 123, at para 7.98, *EC – Bananas (AB) supra* note 120, at para 167.

concede, because of the way the AB reasoned that they had to examine the Lomé Convention, that this procedural role for external law appeared not as clearly spelt out as in *US – Shrimp*.

6.4.2 Summary: US – Shrimp

Both proponents of Model I (WTO law as a limited domain) and Model II (WTO law as open) miss the point in *EC – Bananas* and *US – Shrimp* that, though the AB refers to external international law, it only does so on a procedural basis to support the application of its primary and substantive law, WTO law. It is not a one-dimensional view of being open or closed to international law, but appears as a more dynamic process whereby the adjudicating bodies interact with international law to carry out the aims of the WTO treaty to prohibit trade restrictions. However, on the basis of constrained openness the adjudicating bodies do not appear to directly apply or incorporate that international law as substantive WTO law.

6.5 Potential cross conflict with another trade law system (North American Free Trade Area (NAFTA)): *Mexico – Soft Drinks*

The long-running issue of market access for Mexico's sugar cane to the US and the export of US high fructose corn syrup (an alterative sweetener to cane sugar) to Mexico underlines the dispute of *Mexico – Soft Drinks*.[136] The US and Mexico are both parties to the North American Free Trade Area (NAFTA) and the WTO. Under NAFTA, Mexico in 2000 was unable to obtain a ruling that it was being denied access to the US market[137] because the US blocked the establishment of a NAFTA panel to examine the US quotas on Mexican cane sugar.[138] Following this Mexico imposed antidumping duties against imports of high-fructose corn syrup from the US.[139] The US challenged the duties in the WTO and a Panel ruled that

136 Pauwelyn, 'Adding sweeteners to Soft Lumber: the WTO-NAFTA spaghetti bowl is cooking' (2006) JIEL 197 (hereinafter 'Adding Sweetners . . .'). Davey W and A Sapir, 'The Soft Drinks case: the WTO and regional agreements' (2009) 8(1) *World Trade Review* 5–23. Roessler F, 'Mexico (Tax Measures on Soft Drinks and Other Beverages): prepared for the ALI project on the case law of the WTO' (2009) 8(1) *World Trade Review* 25–30. See Panel Report, *Mexico – Tax Measures on Soft Drinks and other Beverages*, WT/DS308/R, 7 October 2005 [hereinafter, *Mexico – Soft Drinks (Panel)*]. Appellate Body Report, *Mexico – Tax Measures on Soft Drinks and other Beverages*, WT/DS308/AB/R, 6 March 2006 [hereinafter *Mexico – Soft Drinks (AB)*]. For further reading on Free Trade Areas, see generally Kwak K and G Marceau, 'Overlaps and Conflicts of Jurisdiction between the World Trade Organisation and Regional Trade Agreements', in Bartels L and F Ortino, *Regional Trade Agreements and the WTO Legal System* (Oxford: OUP, 2006). Weiler J (ed) *The EU and the WTO and the NAFTA: Towards A Common Law of International Trade* (Oxford: OUP, 2000). Bartels L and F Ortino, *Regional Trade Agreements and the WTO Legal System* (Oxford: OUP, 2006).

137 See Pauwelyn, 'Adding Sweeteners . . .' *supra* note 136. Davey and Sapir *supra* note 136.

138 Ibid.

139 Pauwelyn, 'Adding sweeteners . . .' *supra* note 136, at 197–201. Davey and Sapir *supra* note 136, at 5–9.

they were be removed. Mexico did so in 2002, at which time it then imposed a 20 per cent tax on soft drinks that used non-cane sugar sweeteners, which is the matter at issue in *Mexico – Soft Drinks*.[140] The 20 per cent tax was imposed on the transfer and importation of soft drinks and on specific services related to transferring and bookkeeping requirements.[141] 'The effect of the tax was to eliminate almost all exports of high fructose corn syrup' from the US to Mexico, of which the US was the main exporter.[142]

The US challenged Mexico's tax measures on the grounds that there were inconsistent with GATT 1994 Article III:2 and 4. Mexico argued that the Panel was to decline jurisdiction and suggest that Mexico and the US submit the dispute to the NAFTA Chapter Twenty Arbitral Panel. The Panel rejected Mexico's argument on the grounds that it had no discretion to decide whether or not to exercise its jurisdiction in a case 'properly before it' and that even if it had, the facts could not justify it declining the case.[143] The Panel stated that it could only have discretion if Panels had freedom to choose from among several options, which were all 'equally permissible in law'.[144] The point is that freedom exists only if a Member did not have the 'legal right to have a panel decide a case properly before it'[145] and as Members do, Panels cannot object to hearing a case. The Panel advanced pursuant to DSU Article 11 that they did not have this freedom, so they had to resolve matters before them to 'secure a positive solution' to disputes. Further to DSU Article 3.2 and 19.2 the Panel stressed that if a Panel did not exercise its jurisdiction it would diminish the rights of the complaining Member under WTO law. And pursuant to DSU Article 23, the Panel said that if a Member considers that any of its WTO benefits have been nullified or impaired as a result of the measures adopted by another Member it had the right to bring the case before the WTO.[146]

Mexico also argued at the Panel that if the Panel declined to reject its jurisdiction, the Panel should find Mexico's measures are justified pursuant to Article XX(d). The Panel rejected Mexico's argument that the taxes could be justified under Article XX(d), which allows Members to maintain measures that are 'necessary to secure compliance with laws or regulations which are not inconsistent with the provisions of GATT'. The Panel ruled that Article XX(d) was concerned with enforcement at a domestic and not an international level. Consequently, as Elena Katselli argues, the Panel did not consider that Mexico's action could be justified under the general law of countermeasures and instead used the ILC's conclusions on countermeasures to determine whether Article XX(d) allowed Mexico to act

140 See *Mexico – Soft Drinks (AB) supra* note 136, at paras 1–8 for a background to the dispute.
141 Ibid.
142 Davey and Sapir *supra* note 136, at 7.
143 See *Mexico – Soft Drinks (AB) supra* note 136, at paras 1–8, esp. paras 4–5.
144 See *Mexico – Soft Drinks (Panel) supra* note 136, at para 7.7.
145 *Mexico – Soft Drinks (AB) supra* note 136, at para 151. *Mexico – Soft Drinks (AB) supra* note 136, at para 7.8.
146 See *Mexico – Soft Drinks (Panel) supra* note 136, at paras 7.8–7.9.

on the grounds it was putting forward.[147] On the issue of countermeasures, the Panel stated that the Draft Articles on Responsibility of States for Internationally Wrongful Acts adopted by the ILC did not address the issue of enforcement, nor is the notion of enforcement used in the Commentary to the articles.[148] It highlighted that paragraph 1 of Article 49 states that an 'injured State may only take countermeasures against a State which is responsible for an internationally wrongful act in order to induce that State to comply with its obligations under Part Two.'[149] The Panel further stated that in the discussions on the formation of the forerunner to the WTO, the International Trade Organisation (ITO), Members were aware of countermeasures but rejected them.[150] The Panel concluded for these reasons that 'to secure compliance' as pursuant to Article XX(d) 'does not apply to measures taken by a Member in order to induce another Member to comply with obligations owed to it under a non-WTO treaty'.[151] As a consequence of the treatment of Article XX(d) Katselli argues that the right of countermeasures in WTO law are 'seriously imperilled'.[152] However, she takes note of DSU Article 23 which underscores countermeasures are not allowed outside of WTO law, but seems to side-step its importance on the basis that countermeasures are available by using Pauwelyn's argument that WTO law is an integral part of international law.[153] There are two criticisms to deploy of this view. First, as much as we can all accept that WTO law is part of international law, this does not in any way mean that somehow all the principles, or even any of them, must be used by WTO law. The fact is that specialist legal systems were formed to remove themselves from some forms of international law. For example DSU Article 23 makes it clear that WTO Members do not have resources to measures outside of WTO law. The second criticism is that *Mexico – Soft Drinks* at no point articulates the view that countermeasures should be available for violations of external international law. In fact the case was pointed in its rejection of the view that defences as to violations of external international law can be mounted through WTO law, which is seemingly what Mexico was trying to do in its long-standing dispute with the US. For the moment it is enough to appreciate that the Panel rejected Mexico's argument for countermeasures on an a view that to decline jurisdiction would diminish the rights of WTO Members to seek redress for alleged violations of WTO law, even if there was a perceived conflict with another system of international law, NAFTA. At no point did the Panel refer to the substantive NAFTA law or any perceived dispute for the purpose of coming to its conclusion, which it did only on the basis of WTO law.

147 Katselli Proukaki E, *The Problem of Enforcement in International Law: countermeasures, the non-injured state and the idea of international community*. (Abingdon: Routledge, 2010) 233.

148 See *Mexico – Soft Drinks (Panel) supra* note 136, at para 8.180.

149 Ibid, at para 8.180.

150 Ibid, at para 8.176.

151 Ibid, at para 8.181.

152 Katselli *supra* note 147, at 233–234, and generally chapter 4.

153 Ibid.

In appealing the Panel's decision, Mexico did so on the grounds that the WTO adjudicating bodies had implied jurisdictional powers where the 'underlying or predominant elements of a dispute derive from rules of international law'.[154] Mexico's argument was that the US's claim that Mexico's tax measures on soft drinks was inconsistent with GATT 1994 Article III were part of a broader NAFTA dispute (as discussed above) on access of Mexican sugar to the US market, which only a NAFTA panel could resolve.[155] The AB however ruled that Mexico identified that there was no legal basis for raising a WTO dispute on the market access claims it was pursing under NAFTA.[156] The fact is that no NAFTA panel had been established to decide the issues Mexico had noted regarding market access.[157] On this basis the AB correctly did not have to express any view as to whether it could have denied jurisdiction.[158] Even if they had to, as to the DSU Article 3.2, they could not determine the rights of external international law, such as NAFTA. There is a distinction to note between, for example, the AB determining the rights of external international law which they are precluded from doing as a limited jurisdiction, and external international law having some strategic influence on the ruling the AB may make in violation of WTO law, which we examine below. On this point, Mexico argued that based on the ruling from the PCIJ in the *Factory at Chorzow* case that the US should not be able to reply on WTO law because of its alleged non-compliance with NAFTA.[159] The passage from the *Factory at Chorzow* case, which Mexico relied on, read that 'one party cannot avail himself of the fact that the other has not fulfilled some obligation . . . if the former party has . . . prevented the latter . . . from having recourse to the tribunal which would have been open to him.'[160] The AB ruled, and here I want to relay the full sentiment of its finding, that,

> Mexico's arguments, as well as its reliance on the ruling in *Factory at Chorzów*, is [*sic*] misplaced. Even assuming, *arguendo*, that the legal principle reflected in the passage referred to by Mexico is applicable within the WTO dispute settlement system, we note that this would entail a determination whether the United States has acted consistently or inconsistently with its NAFTA obligations. We see no basis in the DSU for panels and the Appellate Body to adjudicate non- WTO disputes. Article 3.2 of the DSU states that the WTO dispute settlement system "serves to preserve the rights and obligations of Members under the *covered agreements*, and to clarify the existing provisions of *those agreements*." (emphasis added) Accepting Mexico's interpretation would imply that the WTO dispute settlement system could be used to determine rights

154 *Mexico – Soft Drinks (AB) supra* note 136, at para 10.
155 Ibid.
156 Ibid, at para 11.
157 Ibid, at para 54.
158 Ibid.
159 Ibid, at paras 12, 54–56.
160 Ibid, at para 12, fn. 26.

> and obligations outside the covered agreements. In light of the above, we do not see how the PCIJ's ruling in *Factory at Chorzów* supports Mexico's position in this case.[161]

I think that this paragraph should be read along with paragraphs 54 and 76 as a complete statement as to the AB view that the adjudicating bodies do not adjudicate disputes of external international law. Paragraph 54 reads that,

> Mindful of the precise scope of Mexico's appeal, we express no view as to whether there may be other circumstances in which legal impediments could exist that would preclude a panel from ruling on the merits of the claims that are before it. In the present case, Mexico argues that the United States' claims under Article III of the GATT 1994 are inextricably linked to a broader dispute, and that only a NAFTA panel could resolve the dispute as a whole. Nevertheless, Mexico does not take issue with the Panel's finding that "neither the subject matter nor the respective positions of the parties are identical in the dispute under the NAFTA . . . and the dispute before us." Mexico also stated that it could not identify a legal basis that would allow it to raise, in a WTO dispute settlement proceeding, the market access claims it is pursuing under the NAFTA. It is furthermore undisputed that no NAFTA panel as yet has decided the "broader dispute" to which Mexico has alluded. Finally, we note that Mexico has expressly stated that the so-called "exclusion clause" of Article 2005.6 of the NAFTA had not been "exercised". We do not express any view on whether a legal impediment to the exercise of a panel's jurisdiction would exist in the event that features such as those mentioned above were present. In any event, we see no legal impediments applicable in this case. (Footnotes suppressed)

Paragraph 76 reads that,

> Mexico finds support for its interpretation in the Appellate Body's rulings in US – *Shrimp* and *US – Shrimp (Article 21.5 – Malaysia)*. We fail to see how these rulings support Mexico's position. In those cases, the United States sought to justify its measures under Article XX(g) of the GATT 1994, and the measures at issue were domestic laws and regulations of the United States. The reference to the Inter-American Convention for the Protection and Conservation of Sea Turtles (the "Inter-American Convention") was made in the context of the examination of whether the measures constituted "a means of arbitrary or unjustifiable discrimination between countries where the same conditions prevail" for purposes of the chapeau of Article XX. The United States, in those cases, did not argue that its measures were justified under Article XX(d) because they were intended to secure compliance with the obligations of another Member under the Inter-American Convention. In the present case, Mexico seeks to justify its measures

161 Ibid, at para 56.

> under paragraph (d) of Article XX, and not under paragraph (g). Moreover, Mexico not only refers to the NAFTA in relation to the chapeau of Article XX, but also seeks justification for its measures under paragraph (d) on the basis that they are allegedly intended to secure compliance with the United States' NAFTA obligations. (Footnotes suppressed)

At paragraph 78 the AB stated that,

> Mexico's interpretation would imply that, in order to resolve the case, WTO panels and the Appellate Body would have to assume that there is a violation of the relevant agreement (such as NAFTA) by the complaining party, or they would have to assess whether the relevant international agreement has been violated. WTO panels and the Appellate Body would thus become adjudicators of non-WTO disputes. As we noted earlier [at paragraph 56], this is not the function of panels and the Appellate Body as intended by the DSU.[162]

In summary the decision of the AB seems to make clear that WTO law is a limited jurisdiction. Further, the distinction between the AB having use of external international law and that law having some influence on the decisions of the AB is critical to keep hold of as we continue to discussion the case commentary and analysis. The AB underscored that there was 'no basis' on which they would have to adjudicate an external international law dispute, on the grounds that DSU Article 3.2 only preserves the rights and obligations of WTO Members regarding WTO law.

6.5.1 Case commentary: Mexico – Soft Drinks

Mexico – Soft Drinks has, as would be expected, attracted criticism and support depending on which model commentators adopted either implicitly or explicitly.[163] Trachtman (Model I) has argued that the case 'on first glance' shows that the AB 'definitely rejected the possibility that panels of the AB would apply non-WTO international law'.[164] He supports this view using the statement from the AB that it would see no basis to rule on a non-WTO law dispute and that it was not the function of the adjudicating bodies to do so.[165] Pauweyln (Model II) also reprises his now familiar role, *attack au fer*, stating that *Mexico – Soft Drinks* did not go 'as far as' Trachtman implied.[166] He argued that the AB 'did, indeed, exclude making findings on whether non-WTO agreements (here NAFTA) are violated. Yet, that does not mean that it can never apply non-WTO agreements (or dis-apply WTO rules with reference to such agreements).'[167] Pauwelyn argues that the AB left open

162 Ibid, at para 78.

163 For example, see 'International Economic Law and Policy Blog: Soda Pop!' (Dated 26 March 2006) (http://worldtradelaw.typepad.com/ielpblog/2006/03/soda_pop.html).

164 Ibid.

165 Ibid. Trachtman uses paras 56 and 78 of *Mexico – Soft Drinks (AB)* to support these points.

166 Ibid.

167 Ibid.

the question of whether it can deny jurisdiction on the issue of forum clause shopping regarding NAFTA Article 2005.[168] Perhaps it is not so much that the matter was left open so much as Mexico did not invoke the clause, so the AB did not have to rule on the issue. What is more important is Pauwelyn's claim that the absence of *res judicata* should not 'lead one tribunal to completely ignore the work' of the other.[169] *Res judicata* refers to the preclusion of a claim being brought in a tribunal if the same parties covering the same subject matter have brought the same claim in another tribunal. Additionally he argues that even if *res judicata* is not triggered, double recovery and inconsistent rulings should be still avoided by a WTO panel being 'cognisant' of a NAFTA panel's analysis and vice versa'.[170] Bartels (Model III) argues that the AB decision that it could not rule on non-WTO law along with its point that DSU Article 3.2 serves to protect the rights and obligations of WTO Members under WTO law were 'complete non-sequiturs'. According to Bartels, this was because the AB in ruling on WTO law could still be 'required' to 'determine' 'non-WTO rights and obligations'.[171]

6.5.2 Case analysis: reflexive law and developing strategies for influencing WTO law

The arguments on the way in which the three different models assess the practice of WTO law are by now well known and rehearsed, as is also the argument as to why, using constrained openness, I think they are inadequate. I do not wish in this the final case analysis to go over such well-trodden ground. What I think will be more productive is to examine the conceptual arguments of this case as made by the models, to a logical end, which will reveal the consequences intended or otherwise of the models. In doing so I will imagine that each model is a member of the AB with the case before them, in order to explore the tensions that the three models in a hypothetical situation (with some real antecedents) would bring to bear on WTO law. It is therefore important to set out a background. The facts have been somewhat simplified but are as follows. We have two WTO Members A and B who also belong to another trade organisation, which we can call ZAFTA (this is a fictional free trade association and the acronym does not mean anything). The two Members have a dispute with the potential for adjudication under WTO or ZAFTA law. The dispute is not initiated under ZAFTA because B is blocking the formation of the adjudicating panel as allowed under ZAFTA rules. Member A imposes a heavy tariff on a Member B product so Member B (though blocking a ZAFTA dispute panel) brings a dispute to the WTO with its compulsory and automatic dispute settlement process. Member A claims that the WTO should decline jurisdiction because the dispute should really have been brought under

168 Ibid. (However, note that Mexico had not referred the issue to a NAFTA Panel as it was being blocked by the US.)

169 Pauwelyn *supra* note 60, at 200–202. Davey and Sapir *supra* note 136, at 14–15.

170 Pauwelyn *supra* note 60, at 200–202.

171 See 'International Economic Law and Policy Blog: Soda Pop!' *supra* note 163.

ZAFTA which Member B blocked. As the dispute has been initiated the WTO cannot decline jurisdiction and so is compelled by its rules to examine the matters of the dispute.

Model I adjudicating body member: argues that the WTO adjudicating bodies cannot examine the claims of Member A regarding ZAFTA as it would be asking it to examine external international law. This is on the basis of the limited jurisdiction of WTO law to only address claims made of a violation of WTO law. Therefore the adjudicating bodies do not have the power to examine substantive ZAFTA law to determine if Member A's claim has merit. The only thing the adjudicating bodies can do is to examine the claims Member A makes as to B as regards to a violation of WTO law. The result is that the adjudicating bodies cannot apply or determine the substance of external international law such as ZAFTA, in order to resolve the claims Member A makes as to that external law. In this instance the WTO ignores the external international law.

Model II adjudicating body member: argues that the WTO adjudicating bodies can examine the claims of Member A regarding ZAFTA, because WTO law is part of international law. This gives the adjudicating bodies access to external international law in resolving a dispute on WTO law before them. The adjudicating bodies can therefore determine the substantive terms of ZAFTA in order to resolve the dispute between WTO Members A and B. It also means that in certain cases the adjudicating bodies can decline jurisdiction if a similar case is initiated (or at a stretch is about to be initiated). In this instance, the external international law is effaced into WTO law.

Model III adjudicating body member: argues that the WTO adjudicating bodies can examine external international law. Therefore they can examine ZAFTA as an issue in the claim by Member A. However, the adjudicating bodies will have to privilege the WTO law in the dispute as it is being resolved in WTO law. In doing so, the adjudicating bodies can make a substantive determination of external international law, referring to ZAFTA for the purpose of resolving the dispute. The result is that external international law is applicable in WTO law but cannot be privileged over WTO law. In this instance, the external international law is subjugated, as secondary to WTO law.

According to the discussion above, all three models somehow seem to think that WTO law can directly interact with external international law, either to make a determination that it is not applicable, that it is applicable, or that it is applicable but not privileged over WTO law. Now if we assume, as to constrained openness, that WTO law has no direct access to external international law, that of our fictional ZAFTA, then not only is it unable to make a determination of the merits or otherwise of that law, but there are a three possible outcomes when the two legal systems interact (see chapter 3). Here they are mentioned as the consequences of each model: external international law as ignored, effaced and dominated. Considering these effects, on the basis of constrained openness that a system constructs its reality, brings us back to further application of the idea of reflexive law (see chapter 3). I will discuss this as a way in which the hypothetical adjudicating members could respond to external international law that comes into contact with WTO law. As the discussion on the practice in this chapter and chapter 5 on the precautionary principle has demonstrated, the adjudicating bodies do not directly engage with external international law, and when there is engagement it is for that law to meet the purposes of WTO law with a potential result as one of the three consequences as mentioned above. The question we face is: can the reflexive law element of constrained openness (see chapter 3) be usefully developed as a principle that adjudicating body members can use? Given the nature of the ideas, and given the empirical tradition that envelopes WTO law, it would be easy to dismiss reflexive law element of constrained openness as irrelevant to the way in which the adjudicating bodies should act. Indeed the argument would be that a theory of WTO law is high-minded which does not touch or come close to touching the 'real' practice of WTO law. In fact this is the critique I addressed in the Prologue and return to in the conclusion. As I said then, it is a misconstruction of the role of theory for although a theory may not provide details on how to the adjudicating bodies should respond, it could provide a map to point us in the direction.[172]

The lesson that we drew from reflexive law is not to focus on the substance of the values we want to introduce into WTO law but on the techniques to do so. It is not only about advancing the values but also about using 'sophisticated and flexible strategies' to implement those non-trade values bearing in mind that WTO law, like the systems those values come from, are autonomous of each other in a fragmented legal system. There has not only to be a recognition of this autonomy by the adjudicating bodies but a respect for it because it requires them to function in the fragmented context of international law. It requires, not any greater knowledge on the part of the adjudicating bodies on the substantive elements of external international law, because WTO is court of limited jurisdiction, but knowledge on the functioning of those systems. It is the procedural aspects of external international law that become the focus, not the substantive values and elements of those legal systems, which WTO law has no direct access to at any rate. As there is no direct imposition of external international law, the use of such law must therefore be a matter of strategic intervention. Can this work? Is the indirect approach the way to have external international law influence WTO law? Should the constituents of external legal systems continue banging harder and louder on the legal doors of WTO for recognition and influence in the system?[173]

There is no straightforward answer as different constituents and actors will come to different views on the approach that they should take, and on how the adjudicating bodies should respond to WTO law. However, indirect regulatory influence on WTO law, as the discussion on practice in this chapter and chapter 5 suggests, is more useful than trying to have the adjudicating bodies directly incorporate external international law. The point is that external international legal systems do not force the adjudicating bodies into a regulatory crisis to ignore, efface or dominate external international law. We can now return to the hypothetical case as discussed above, so that Member B in bringing the claim that Member A is

172 Black J, 'Constitutionalising Self-Regulation' (1996) 59(1) *Modern Law Review* 24, 51.

173 Kelly C, 'Power, Linkage and Accommodation: The WTO as an International Actor and its influence over other actors and regimes' (2006) 24 *Berkeley Journal of International Law* 79.

in violation of WTO law, with Member A claiming the basis of substantive external international law that the WTO adjudicating bodies should decline jurisdiction of the dispute. The adjudicating bodies could respond in a similar way as before, not to the substantive claims but with a focus on the strategies that the use of the external international law is trying to achieve. This does not necessarily mean that the external international law will influence WTO law, or more specifically that the adjudicating bodies will take note of the external international law to internalise it as part of WTO law. The point is to increase the chances for influence. The adjudicating bodies may not necessarily make the decision themselves but could with the assistance of constituents involved come to a decision, still a WTO law decision, but one that, if only slightly, widens the base of that decision procedurally.[174] Recently, the *Panel in US – AD/CVD on Products from China* may have come up with way in which we can understand how the adjudicating bodies can respond to external international as an indirect strategic influence. In discussing China's argument that the adjudicating bodies must interpret WTO law [SCM Agreement] in 'conformity with the language and concepts' of the Draft Articles on Responsibility of States for Internationally Wrongful Acts, the Panel stated,

> . . . Rather, in our view, the various citations to the Draft Articles have been as *conceptual guidance only to supplement or confirm, but not to replace, the analyses based on the ordinary meaning, context and object and purpose of the relevant covered Agreements [WTO law]* . . . the exercise undertaken by these panels and the Appellate Body has been to interpret the WTO Agreement on its *own terms*, i.e., on the basis of the ordinary meaning of the terms of the treaty in their context and in light of the object and purpose of the treaty.[175]

As simple as the idea of 'conceptual guidance' may seem, it could hold an important key for how external international law may indirectly and strategically influence WTO law. The result is that external international law is directed towards aiding the understanding and perhaps extension of the terms of WTO law, in its practice by the adjudicating bodies.[176] It is not about trying to fit large chunks of external international law into WTO law on the basis that the adjudicating bodies 'must' examine it in order to assess a claim as a violation of WTO law. Instead the

174 Amicus curiae briefs may be instructive here. For discussion on amicus briefs, see for example: Mavroidis P, 'Amicus Curiae Briefs Before The WTO: Much Ado About Nothing', Harvard Jean Monnet Working Paper 02/01; Umbricht G, An 'Amicus Curiae Brief' on Amicus Curiae Briefs at the WTO' JIEL (2001) 4 (4): 773, Marceau G and M Stilwell. Practical Suggestions for Amicus Curiae Briefs before WTO Adjudicating Bodies' JIEL (2001) 4 (1): 155. See also generally chapter 3 and specifically supra note 38 of chapter 3.

175 Report of Panel, *United States – Definitive Ant-Dumping and Countervailing Duties on Certain Products from China*, WT/DS379/R para 8.87. My emphasis in italics. The Panel goes on to note the circumstances where it has interpreted the Draft Articles on the terms of WTO law. See para 8.88–8.91. See also *EC-Biotech supra* note 119, at para 7.92 for a similar assessment as here.

176 Though as discussion on *EC-Biotech* shows, this too has its dangers in that the extension of 'meaning' can go too far. Indeed the idea is perhaps not to have one approach but engage several at the same time. See chapter 2.

idea could be to direct adjudicating bodies to appropriate external international law that may offer an understanding of WTO law, with the other intention of having that meaning and its attendant value internalised in WTO law. The approach that reflexive law suggests for intervention from one system to another is to be subtle, well structured, flexible and targeted.

6.6 Conclusion

The examination of use made by the three models (limited domain, open and privileged) of the practice of WTO law to support their premises on the interaction between WTO law and external international law raises two important questions. Firstly, is it *necessary* for the WTO to 'incorporate' international law to make use of it in WTO law? Secondly, and possibly the more critical which I have explored throughout the study, *can* WTO law incorporate external international law? The proponents of model I (WTO law as a limited domain) make the argument that the international legal system is probably best seen as a fragmented set of functional differing systems. They argue that international external law is not incorporated into the WTO, unless it is referenced in WTO law. The proponents of Model II (WTO law as open) premise that the use of international law in the WTO is based on its incorporation in that all international law becomes potentially applicable in the WTO by the fact that WTO law is part of international law. International law is perceived as united and homogeneous. What I can garner from this is that the starting point for argument between Model I and II is the need to support or refute the incorporation of international external law in WTO law. If we look at Bartels (Model III), the WTO is somewhat open to external international law that can be brought into WTO law, only that it can not be privileged over WTO law in the WTO legal system.

None of the models explained *how* the WTO incorporated the external international law, and *how* the WTO may actually be applying that external law, or the likely results for WTO law or external international law if the WTO applied or incorporated the external law. The models tell us that the WTO *should* or *should not* be applying external international law, but none defined clearly what WTO law *is* and its purpose. In effect, the models do not give us a rule by which we can identify the legal norms of the WTO in order to observe, classify and evaluate the actual practice of the WTO regarding external international law. The discussion on the practice also showed the pattern, as discussed in chapter 4, of the argument-counter argument between the models, which causes them to miss the critical points in each other.

I think the main point from this chapter is that even if the adjudicating bodies are cognitively open to external law, which I accept, what I realised in this chapter is that this does not 'guarantee' that WTO law 'will be responsive' to that external international law on that laws' terms or it is incorporated into WTO law.[177] The practice shows that WTO law is cognitively open, but only on

177 Perez O, *Ecological Sensitivity and Global Legal Pluralism: Rethinking the Trade and Environmental Conflict* (Oxford: Hart Publishing, 2004) 70.

the basis of its operations (internal point of view) as WTO law (see chapter 1). This makes both Model I (limited domain) and Model II (open) seem inadequate in explaining the interaction between WTO and external international law. It leaves us with constrained openness as a more nuanced understanding of how WTO law interacts with external international law. The aim of this chapter was to further provide evidence of the practical consequences of constrained openness to that of the other models. I did that by examining the merits of the practice of WTO law, and the responses to that practice by the models. I was able to realise that each model appeared to only account for half the merits of the practice, at any one moment. The idea of reflexive law provides what I think to be a more adequate way to perceive the interaction between WTO and external international law, as well as to provide a strategic basis from which to indirectly influence WTO law. In the next chapter 7, I conclude by assessing the consequences of thinking about WTO law using the theory of constrained openness.

7 Conclusion

This study attempted to offer a platform from which to rethink the models that account for the interaction between WTO law and external international law. The dominance of the three models – WTO law as a limited domain, open, or privileged – has at times unintended or otherwise prohibited new ways of thinking about that interaction. The result, which I discussed in chapter 4, is that the models appear to be presented as a choice of one against the other, rather than as a nuanced discussion of how to adequately account for the interaction between WTO law and external law. The purpose of this study has been to create some space among the contending models where I could begin to think differently and in more nuanced ways, about the interaction between WTO law and external law. Different ideas about how WTO law interacts with external law will not necessarily match as shown in the discussions throughout the study. They will disagree about the nature of that interaction itself, as much as the nature of law. No idea can cover every situation or tell the whole story. We must therefore be suspicious of any claims for universality and continually challenge ideas, and not just for the sake of doing so but as part of the process of proper intellectual questioning. To do that it is not simply a matter of pointing out where the disagreements are but it is about using existing dialogues to build and sustain new ideas. It is about reconstructing ideas to make them useful. The effort of the study was to do this. It was about providing a space in which we could debate, reflect and re-tell the stories that existing ideas championed about WTO law. It was not about advocating a grand theory by which I could somehow tell the whole story of WTO law. The study was much more minimalist and reticent.

I think that a criticism of my study may be that in bringing together what might appear as different insights from art, literature, and the sociology of law to form a theory of WTO law, namely constrained openness, I may have oversimplified the very nuances in those insights which I found useful. This would be ironic, given that all the while I claimed that in weaving those insights together I could show that the interaction between WTO law and external internal law was more nuanced than the current models on the matter credited. However, that would not only be too easy a criticism but there is a more relevant objection to such a criticism. As I contended in the Prologue and chapter 1, such criticisms would miss the point of this study in trying to weave together a compelling political argument for why and how I could begin to rethink WTO law. To restate the position at the start of the study in the Prologue, this study is not about making final or total arguments. Indeed, that has been a large part of my criticism of the models that attempted to explain how the WTO interacts with external law, in that they were presented as what seemed as general arguments and to eliminate their counter-argument. The problem however is that each model appeared to contain the counter-argument. The result as discussed in chapter 4 was the emergence of a stalemate, as the debate swung from argument to counter-argument and back to correct perceived limitations in the argument.

The aim of this study was significant not because I intended to use its findings and conclusions to be discussed here to make broader pronouncements about how WTO law works, but because of the exact opposite. I took a more minimalist approach. The methodological and conceptual approaches I have employed in chapters 1 and 3 respectively, and subsequently applied in chapters 5 and 6, cannot be expected to reflect more than the general nature of the debate on the interaction between WTO law and external law. My aim was to bring out a number of subtleties that, when viewed together, are the sum of a persuasive argument which can be used to rethink the interaction between WTO law and external law. Consider, in chapter 4, the characterisation of the polarisation of the debate as between two main models of openness and closure which some may critique as somewhat simplistic. However, the two models principally advocated by Pauwelyn (open) and Trachtman (limited domain) have become what are now the dominant models on how WTO law interacts with external law. In chapter 4 my purpose was to provide a sketch that would discuss the epistemic community that each model formed and the resulting stalled debate. Instead of attempting to propose a middle ground proposition as did Bartels in his idea that WTO law was privileged over external law, this study proposed a re-examination of the assumptions at the heart of debate between openness and closure.

I claimed that the question was *not* about the *extent* to which WTO law can or cannot incorporate external law, but whether WTO law *could* incorporate external law. Changing the assumption that the WTO may not be able to incorporate external law changed the question and allowed me to step away from the augmentative circularity of openness and closure, because I was not looking for the relative importance between the two models, as was the model of WTO law as privileged by Bartels. I was then able in chapters 1 and 3 to create frameworks to impose intelligibility upon the practice of WTO law, which are the events and facts of the debate. This was because, as I argued in the Prologue, these facts do not speak for themselves. In other words, what thinking could I adopt in order to frame the question to inquire into and account for the interaction between WTO law and external law?

The approach of this study has been a plea for circumspection and questioning in assessing how WTO law and specifically the adjudicating bodies define their legal space in relation to external law. I do not suggest that the theory of constrained openness will yield determinate and final answers, but it provides insights into the specific situations I have assessed in this study. For example, in chapter 5, I was able to suggest that the precautionary principle which existed in external law was not the one that the adjudicating bodies of WTO law employed. This prompted the realisation of an epistemological break between the principle *within* and *outside* WTO law. I argued that the WTO adjudicating bodies appear to reconstruct the principle in WTO law to meet expectations of WTO law to prohibit restrictions on trade. The suggestion is that the precautionary principle is not incorporated directly into WTO law and that WTO law interacts with the principle on the basis of the closure of its operations as WTO law. However, that is not to say that the theory of constrained openness applied in other scenarios may yield to such a compelling analysis. That is not the specific point of the study here. What I suggest is that this study can create a space to discuss the interaction between WTO law and external law, free from the back and forth argument–counter-argument of openness and closure.

Therefore, when the theory of constrained openess is applied, as in chapters 5 and 6, to support the view in this study that there was a need and a basis to execute the rethinking of the interaction between WTO law and external law, it is not to suggest it was definitive. The theory contained its own 'penumbra of doubt' in that it has a certain degree of inadequacy to account for all and future practical situations.[1] Constrained openness pointed to a failure of external law to be able to regulate WTO law, in that I have argued that WTO law will reconstruct external law into a variable that makes sense in WTO law. This is a description at a systemic level as stated in chapter 1. As such, I may appear to have minimised or ignored the role of the individual as constituting the adjudicating bodies of WTO law and cast them as inanimate artefacts for communication within and between systems. It could be asked: how can there be a real failure or a weakness of external law on its own terms to be able to regulate or at least influence WTO law, because members of the WTO adjudicating bodies can read, understand and obviously communicate about and with that external law? The retort is, of course, they can. It cannot be forgotten that a system is a collective of individuals, generally embedded in the practice of that system, which makes it possible to perceive the system as a somewhat single coherent entity for purposes of analysis.[2] This is what made it critical to define WTO law, in chapter 3, as the practice of the adjudicating bodies which can be identified as generally coalescing around an internal point of view. Though the focus of this study is at the institutional level, I acknowledge the complex skills of individuals as actors in the adjudication process.[3] Nevertheless, for the approach here to have remained as I intended, that is, minimalist, I do not make any extrapolations from this specific study about the interactions on a systemic level between WTO law and external law to generalise about that role of the individual in that interaction. As I stated in chapter 1 at the start of the study, the aim was to provide a basis to rethink the interaction between WTO law and external law, as a matter of inter-systemic communication.

1 See Hart for use of the term in chapter 1.

2 See chapters 1 and 3, section 3.4 on the internal point of view.

3 See chapter 4.

I submitted three lines of inquiry on which the study was knitted together. This was so I could argue that we needed to and could rethink the way in which we go about understanding the interaction between WTO law and external law. The first was to say that I could define WTO law, so I could know what I was discussing when I employed the term WTO law. That was the methodology in chapter 1. The second was to argue that having defined WTO law, I could think about it and its interaction with external law. I needed some way to understand what was identified as WTO law. That was the theory in chapter 3. The third was to use that theory to evaluate and understand what I had identified as WTO law. That was the analysis of the practice of WTO law in chapters 5 and 6.

The discussion so far has for the most part been a summary of the study, and a reiteration of the ideas contained therein. Knitting the three lines of inquiry of this study together, as realised through chapters 1 to 4, I can now make three points or preliminary findings of what this study has achieved. These points are, however, not a final analysis of WTO law, nor should they be taken as generalisations about how WTO law should or must work to fit this or that model. Based on the study here and the specific examinations of practice of WTO law according to the theory I set up, I have come to the points of analysis I discuss below.

The first is, because there was no Archimedean point of analysis, I needed to employ a theory to determine what I was examining and under what circumstances that examination was going to occur. If there was anything to take away from this approach, it was that in putting forward a theory to determine what WTO law was, I was then able to consistently focus on and analyse what was determined as WTO law. In this case, that was the practice of the judiciary. As discussed throughout the study, especially in the Prologue and chapter 1, we choose what to include and exclude as our analysis. It is through our concepts and methods that we can observe, explain and understand the world around us. Without those meanings and understandings, as discussed in the Prologue, we would be faced with a crisis of meaning as was Alice in Wonderland, Hamlet in the kingdom of Denmark on the death of his father, Dorothy in Oz, and Marco Polo travelling the empire of the Khan. The simple and sometimes overlooked point is that our theories provide us with a way to interpret the world around us. Reality is dependent on the concepts and methods we choose. Select a different theory and the world around us will look different. It is as in the *Wonderful Wizard of Oz*, Emerald City was not green. Its colour depended on whether or not you were wearing the green glasses. Does this mean that there is no reality or we cannot depend on the legal answers that either scholars or judicial officials produce because they are produced from a skewed reality, or rather, from a reality of the actor's choice? The short answer is no. What it does mean is that to understand what those scholars and judicial officials are doing, it is useful to try to understand their theory. But the only way to do that is to actually have a theory of our own, or one that we choose from what is available. On what basis are they engaging with the world around them? There is no single explanation for all things legal. It requires that you develop, as I have done here, your own theory or idea from which you engage with the world of law. Does that make it correct? It is only correct on the terms of its own making. We may all be correct, if only once, within our own theory for explaining how things work. What is probably more important, as I have tried to do in this study, is that the theory (constrained openness) you employ should be as open as possible. It must not only be able to take existing stories and re-tell them, on the basis that new information and ideas made that necessary, but also have the same done to it.

The second point is that even if the overall proposition of constrained openness that I advanced in this study does not hold to broader extrapolations as some critiques may wish it did, as a test of analytical robustness, it has an enduring purpose. That was to show the somewhat unsatisfactory nature of the models of WTO law as: a limited domain (Trachtman), open (Pauwelyn), and privileged (Bartels) in being able to account for and explain the interaction between WTO law and external international law. This study has been an examination of these models and the underlining nature of the debate between them, and the resulting implications of that debate on the interaction between WTO law and external law. I have demonstrated the argument–counter-argument nature of that debate which has resulted in what can be characterised as a mature if not dormant debate. The theory of constrained openness provided insight into that nature and also showed the irrelevance of any model, in that there is nothing that makes one idea more relevant than another or even needed at all.

The third point is that the new approach of constrained openness realises that WTO law is a social construct.[4] The criticism could be made that I conflated the analytical and empirical differentiation of WTO law. The point of the criticism is that the analytical differentiation of WTO law as from other systems of international law could be understood in terms of operational closure but WTO law as empirical differentiation cannot be understood in those same terms. This is 'because the autonomy of societal subsystems operating in the real world is permanently being produced and reproduced by a multiplicity of action elements which are both inside and outside of an analytically defined subsystem.'[5] In other words, systems keep changing. Systems are 'not evolutionary universals, but are historically particular and varying institutions which can be established and changed in different ways.'[6] Therefore, the argument would be that analytically I could construct a theory, as I did using constrained openness, to understand WTO law as a differentiated system of international law but that it would fail to keep track of the constantly changing law. The point would be that my theory would not be able to observe the legal decision-making process of WTO law, as law is not only 'defined as legally right or wrong [but] in reality depends on cultural frameworks, economic calculation, and political power relations'.[7] The point would be that the WTO legal system could be 'separated' from another legal system or other systems

4 See chapter 4. See also Lang A, 'Reflecting on Linkage: Cognitive and Institutional Change in the International Trading System' (2007) 70(4) *Modern Law Review* 523–549.

5 Munch R, 'Autopoiesis by Definition' (1992) 13 *Cardozo Law Review* 1463–1471, at 1463.

6 Ibid, at 1464. See also Lang *supra* note 4 for a discussion on WTO law as socially constructed.

7 Ibid, at 1468.

such as economic or political, but not in an empirical sense as the legal system's autonomy is 'founded' on these cultural frameworks.[8] The difficulty in all of this is in trying to capture something that is constantly changing.

However, what my theory of constrained openness offers is that it is backed by a methodological framework in a counter-factual rule of recognition which allows me to observe WTO law as the empirical practice of the adjudicating bodies. I would tend to agree that by itself, the idea of operational closure though a useful idea may be somewhat inadequate because it could set out an idea of how a legal system could work, but it does not present a tool to tell me what to empirically observe as WTO law. The rule of recognition does that task, and whereas the rule of recognition does not present an idea to understand what was determined as WTO law, the theory does that task. This study has been able to combine two concepts, rule of recognition and operational closure, to overcome the critique of operational closure on which my theory of constrained openness is based, that though it can understand the law analytically, it cannot empirically. Further, constrained openness does not claim to do more than offer a reasonable snapshot of law's moving image. It is an attempt to reconstruct the socially constructed.

In applying constrained openness to understand the practice of WTO law I suggested that the adjudicating bodies reconstruct external law to make sense of it in the context and operations of WTO law. On this basis, WTO law is a special and differentiated system of international law. The differentiation of WTO law would imply that because the WTO was created as part of international law, this does not mean that it could not operate outside the general ambit of international law. Consider that WTO law, though created by international law, is now a legal system and critically a discourse on its own. Take the point that WTO law started to operate on its own and by reference to itself when the 'trade and' debate made sense as an independent discourse. Moreover, it is an implication, as discussed throughout the study, that the WTO had its own legal code of WTO legal/illegal which is separate and distinct to that of other legal systems and discourses. The operational closure of WTO law, as mooted in this study, supported and suggested its specialisation. This takes us back to the starting point and background of this study, the fragmentation of international law.

The fragmentation of international law into specialised systems of law signified the specialisation or functional differentiation of international law. A legal system is able to cognise the environment outside itself by reference to itself, as a constituent of legal experts, born out of the differentiation and specialisation of that area of law from the larger body of international law. This is not an argument for some form of solipsism, however mild. It is more a suggestion that international law is probably a victim of its own success, or perhaps the success of the modernisation of international law that because of the increasing number of specialised legal systems has been a concern for international lawyers. The result is that general international law can not always adequately address or account for the interaction

8 Ibid, at 1468.

between these specialised systems as discussed in this study. This means that the general is displaced for the specialised. The fragmentation of international law is the functional differentiation of international law into specialised areas such as WTO law. The operations of these specialised systems, such as the WTO legal system from the examinations of its practice in this study, do not appear to be externally imposed. WTO law is created as part of the operations of the adjudicating bodies as experts of WTO law as a specialised system of international law. The fragmentation of international law is inescapable in the differentiation of international law into specialised systems.

The purpose of this study has been to set out a new way to think about WTO law and its interaction with external law. This study has been about scouting out new terrain and sketching a map which could be used to guide the development of that terrain. The argument that underlined this study was that it could provide a better understanding of WTO law because it suggested something that the models of openness, closure and privileged did not directly readily do. This was that my study and its ideas were defeasible. My study is open to revision. In the study I asked that arguments that were closed, claimed to explain and account for 'all' situations of WTO law or were presented as fully formulated statements of WTO law, should be resisted. As no arguments are inherent, I believed that I had to be sceptical about categories that appeared fixed. The fact is that WTO law in its formulation and interpretation carries, to borrow Hart's famous formulation, a 'penumbra of doubt', as does the theory I deployed to make sense of WTO law. In applying the theory of constrained openness that systems are open based on their closure, perhaps the best we can do is to realise that paradox can be useful when thinking about the way legal systems interact with each other.

It is apparent that different models will have different approaches for understanding WTO law and its interaction with external law. The case in point, which I discuss in chapters 4 and 6, is that trade lawyers tend to fall into the three broad models, which disagree about how WTO law interacts with external law. To take up either model, as against the other model, I could be seen as absolutist or, the other extreme, solipsist. To not take a side and to argue against the contending model, I would seem relativist as occupying a middle ground. However to take the middle by splitting the difference between the two models, in an attempt to draw the strengths of one side against the weakness of the other, I would potentially create a superficial resolution of the conflict between them. This is an artificial struggle of ideas in that instead of showing the political of contested realities, we end up fighting for a space in the current discourse. The arguments produced are then a perpetuation of the current discourse rather than an attempt or a chance to re-tell the stories. It is easy to choose a side; the more difficult is to show that both sides are entrenched parts of the same argument. This study is about discovering and promoting the nuances in comprehending the interaction between WTO law and external law. It is about realising that the issues of each epistemic community (WTO law as limited, open, privileged) are real enough to them and cannot be made commensurate through a middle ground. To address them I believe there is a need to rethink or reconsider the interaction between WTO law and external law. This may not yield any immediate solutions and may probably make the incommensurability of the problems seem more acute regarding how to think about the interaction between different legal systems. That however should not provide a source of dismay. By providing a new lens through which to think about WTO law, I intend to at least tentatively present a way to begin to prise apart the arguments about WTO law regarding its interaction with external law. This is in order to reveal how the current WTO law discourse thinks about and conceptualises that interaction.

The ideas I suggest are not, nor should they be viewed as, a definitive answer. I believe the challenge is to be the reverse. That is, not brandishing an ultimate answer. It is realising that all ideas are subject to revision, which is an acknowledgement of the dynamics of the discourse of law or for a matter of fact any discourse to change. It is a warning to myself to be sceptical so not to be caught up in models on either side, whether openness or closure, that can dominate how I should see and understand the interaction between WTO law and external law.

Selected bibliography

Journal articles

Abbott K and D Snidal, 'Hard and Soft Law', (2000) 54(3) *International Organisation* 421.

Akehurst M, 'Custom as a Source of International Law', (1974–75) 47 BYIL 1.

Akehurst M, 'Jurisdiction in International Law', (1972–73) 46 BYIL 145.

Alexander K, 'Multi-national Efforts to Combat Financial Crime and the Financial Action Task Force', (2000) 2(5) *Journal of International Financial Markets* 191.

Alston P, 'Resisting the Merger and Acquisition of Human Rights by Trade Law: A Reply to Petersmann', (2002) 13 EJIL 753.

Applegate S, 'The Taming of the Precautionary Principle', (2002) 27 *William and Mary Environmental Law and Policy Review* 14.

ASIL, 'Proceedings of the 99th Annual Meeting of the American Society of International Law: New World Order or a World in Disorder? Testing the Limits of International Law', WTO AB Roundtable, 175–187.

Balkin J, 'Being Just with Deconstruction', (1994) 3 *Social and Legal Studies* 393.

Balkin J, 'Nested Oppositions', (1990) 99 *Yale Law Journal* 1669.

Bartels L, 'Applicable Law in the WTO Dispute Settlement Proceedings', (2001) 35 JWT 499.

Beckett J A, 'Behind Relative Normativity: Rules and Process as Prerequisites of Law', (2001) 12 EJIL 646.

Beckett J A, 'Conflicting Orders: How Peace is Waged', (2007) 20(1) *Leiden Journal of International Law* 281.

Beckett J, 'Countering Uncertainty and Ending Up/Down Arguments: A Prolegomena to a Response', (2005) 16(2) EJIL 213.

Beckett J, 'Rebel Without a Cause? Martti Koskenniemi and the Critical Legal Project', (2006) 7(12) *German Law Journal* 1045.

Bevilacqua D, 'The International Regulation of Genetically Modified Organisms: Uncertainty, Fragmentation, and Precaution', (2007) *European Environmental Law Review* 314.

Bilder R and J Brunnee, 'Book Review of The Precautionary Principle and International Law: The Challenge of Implementation', (1997) AJIL 210.

Black J, 'Constitutionalising Self-Regulation', (1996) 59(1) *Modern Law Review* 24.

Black J, 'Critical Reflections on Regulation', (2002) 27 *Australian Journal of Legal Philosophy* 1.

Bohanes J, 'Risk Regulation in WTO Law: A Procedure-Based Approach to the Precautionary Principle', (2002) 40 *Columbia Journal of Transnational Law* 330.

Boissier M, 'Pondering the Precautionary Principle', (2003) 70 *Joint Bone Spine* 318.

Borgen C J, 'Resolving Treaty Conflicts', (2005) 37 *George Washington Law Review*.

Brietzke P, 'Insurgents in the New International Law', (1994) *Wisconsin International Law Journal* 24.

Brinza D, 'International Trade Dispute Settlement System', (2003) 6(3) JIEL 719.

Broackes J, 'Realism, Scepticism and the Lament for an Archimedean Point: Stroud and the Quest for Reality', (2004) 68 *Philosophy and Phenomenological Research* 415.

Cameron J and K Gray, 'Principles of International Law in the WTO Dispute Settlement Body', (2001) 50 *International Comparative and Law Quarterly* 252.

Carmody C, 'A Theory of WTO Law', (2008) 11(3) JIEL 527–557.

Cass D, 'The Constitutionalisation of International Trade Law: Judicial Norm-Creation as the Engine of Constitutional Development in International Trade', (2001) 12 EJIL 65.

Charney J, 'Is International Law Threatened by Multiple International Tribunals?', (1998) 271 *Recueil des Cours* 101.

Charney J, 'Universal International Law', (1993) 87 AJIL 592.

Charnovitz S, 'The Environment vs. Trade Rules: Defogging the Debate', (1993) 23 *Environmental Law* 475.

Charnovitz S, 'Triangulating the World Trade Organisation', (2002) 96 AJIL 28.

Cheyne I, 'Environmental Treaties and the GATT', (1992) 1 *Review of European Community and International Environmental Law* 14.

Cheyne I, 'Gateways to the Precautionary Principle in WTO Law', (2007) *Journal of Environmental Law* 155.

Cheyne I, 'Life after the WTO Biotech Products Panel Report', (2008) 10(1) *Environmental Law Review* 52–64.

Cheyne I, 'Risk and Precaution in World Trade Organization Law', (2006) 40(5) JWT 837.

Cheyne I, 'The Precautionary Principle in EC and WTO Law: Searching for a Common Understanding', (2006) 8 *Environmental Law Review* 257.

Cover R, 'Foreword: Nomos and Narrative', (1983) 97(4) *Harvard Law Review* 4.

Crawford C, 'Conflicts between the Convention on International Trade in Endangered Species and the GATT in Light of Actions to Halt the Rhinoceros and Tiger Trade', (1995) 7 *Georgetown International Environmental Law Review* 555.

Croley S and J Jackson, 'WTO Dispute Procedures, Standard of Review, and Deference to National Governments', (1996) 90 AJIL 193–213.

Cross F, 'Paradoxical Perils of the Precautionary Principle', (1996) 53 *Washington and Lee Law Review* 851.

D'Amato A, 'Is International Law Really Law?', (1985) 79 *Northwestern University Law Review* 1293.

Dana D, 'Behavioural Economic Defense of the Precautionary Principle', (2003) 97 *Northwestern University Law Review* 1315.

Desmedt A, 'Proportionality in WTO Law', (2001) JIEL 456.

Dobos D, 'The Necessity of Precaution: The Future of Ecological Necessity and the Precautionary Principle', (2002) 12 *Fordham Environmental Law Journal* 384

Dunoff J L, 'Reconciling International Trade with Preservation of the Global Commons: Can We Prosper and Protect?', (1992) 49 *Washington and Lee Law Review* 1407.

Dunoff J L, 'The WTO in Transition: Of Constituents, Competence and Coherence', (2001) *George Washington International Law Review* 979.

Dupuy P, 'International Law: Torn between Coexistence, Cooperation and Globalisation: General Conclusions', (1998) 9 EJIL 278.

Dupuy P, 'Soft Law and the International Law of the Environment', (1991) 12 *Michigan Journal of International Law* 420.

Dyzenhaus D, 'Positivism's Stagnant Research Programme', (2000) 20 *Oxford Journal of Legal Studies* 703–722.

Eckersley R, 'The WTO and MEAs: A Case of Disciplinary Neoliberalism?', (2003) www.utas.edu.au/gov/APSA/REckersleyfinal.pdf (accessed February 2004).

Ehlermann C, 'Experiences from the WTO Appellate Body', (2003) 38 *Texas International Law Journal* 469.

Ehlermann C, 'Reflections on the Appellate Body of the WTO', (2003) 6(3) JIEL 695.

Ehlermann C, 'Six Years on the Bench of the "World Trade Court": Some Personal Experiences as Member of the Appellate Body of the World Trade Organization', (2002) 36(4) JWT 605.

Ehlermann C, 'Tensions between the Dispute Settlement Process and the Diplomatic and Treaty-making Activities of the WTO', (2002) 1(3) *World Trade Review* 301.

Ellis J, 'Overexploitation of a Valuable Resource? New Literature on the Precautionary Principle', (2006) EJIL 445–462.

Ellis J, 'The Precautionary Principle: From Paradigm to Rule of Law', (2000) 2 *International Law FORUM* 127.

Fakhri M, 'Reconstructing the WTO Legitimacy Debates towards Notions of Development', (2009) 5(8) *Comparative Research in Law and Political Economy* 1–25.

Feintuck M, 'Precautionary Maybe, but What's the Principle? The Precautionary Principle, the Regulation of Risk, and the Public Domain', (2005) 32(3) *Journal of Law and Society* 371.

Fisher E, 'Is the Precautionary Principle Justiciable?', (2001) 13(3) *Journal of Environmental Law* 315.

French D, 'Treaty Interpretation and the Incorporation of Extraneous Legal Rules', (2006) 55 *International and Comparative Law Quarterly* 281.

Fry Stephen 'Think of a lobster . . .', Rectorial Address at the University of Dundee, 29 October 1992, 1–26.

Gardner J, 'Concerning Permissive Sources and Gaps', (1988) 8(3) *Oxford Journal of Legal Studies* 457.

Geping R, 'The Law Applied by the WTO Panels', (2003) 17 *Temple International and Comparative Law Journal* 125.

Gold J, 'Strengthening the Soft International Law of Exchange Arrangements', (1983) 77 AJIL 443.

Greenwald J, 'WTO Dispute Settlement: An Exercise in Trade Law Legislation?', (2003) 6(1) JIEL 113.

Grosko B, 'Genetic Engineering and International Law: Conflict or Harmony? An Analysis of the Biosafety Protocol, GATT and the WTO SPS Agreement', (2001) *Virginia Environmental Law Journal* 315.

Guzman A, 'Global Governance and the WTO', (2004) 45 *Harvard International Law Journal* 313.

Hafner G, 'Pros and Cons Ensuing from Fragmentation of International Law', *Michigan Journal of International Law* 849.

Henckels C, 'Overcoming Jurisdictional Isolationism at the WTO-FAT Nexus: A Potential Approach for the WTO', (2008) 19(3) EJIL 571–599.

Hilf M, 'Power, Rules and Principles – Which Orientation for WTO/GATT Law?', (2001) JIEL 118.

Hillgenberg H, 'A Fresh Look at Soft Law', (1999) 10(3) EJIL 499–515.

Hirsch M, 'The Sociology of International Economic Law: Sociological Analysis of the Regulation of Regional Agreements in the World Trading System', (2008) 19(2) EJIL 277–299.

Howse R, 'Democracy, Science and Free Trade: Risk Regulation on Trial at the WTO', (2000) 98 *Michigan Law Review* 2330.

Howse R, 'From Politics to Technocracy – and Back Again: The Fate of the Multilateral Trade Regime', (2002) 96 AJIL 94.

Howse R and P Mavroidis, 'Europe's Evolving Regulatory Strategy for GMOs, The Issue of Consistency with WTO Law: Of Kine and Brine', (2000) *Fordham International Law Journal* 314.

Huntington, S P, 'The Clash of Civilizations?', (1993) 72 *Foreign Affairs* 22.

Immordino G, 'Looking for a Guide to Protect the Environment: The Development of the Precautionary Principle', (2003) 17(5) *Journal of Economic Surveys* 630.

International Centre for Trade and Sustainable Development, *Bridges* 7(6) 2003 (pre Cancun publication) at http://www.ictsd.org/monthly/bridges/BRIDGES7-6.pdf http://www.ictsd.org/monthly/bridges/BRIDGES7-7.pdf (accessed June 2007).

International Centre for Trade and Sustainable Development, *Bridges* 7(7) 2003 (post Cancun publication) at http://www.ictsd.org/monthly/bridges/BRIDGES7-7.pdf (accessed June 2007).

International Centre for Trade and Sustainable Development, *Bridges* 3(8) (pre-Seattle publication) at http://www.ictsd.org/English/BRIDGES3-8.pdf (accessed June 2007).

Jackson J, 'Global Economics and International Economic Law', (1998) 1 JIEL 1.

Jackson J, 'World Trade Rules and Environmental Policies: Congruence or Conflict?', (1992) 49 *Washington and Lee Law Review* 1227.

James C P, 'Seriality and Narrativity in Calvino's *Le città invisibili*', (1982) 97(1) *Modern Language Notes* (Italian Issue) 144.

Kalderimis D, 'Problems of WTO Harmonisation and the Virtues of Shields over Swords', (2004) 13 *Minnesota Journal of Global Trade* 305.

Kammerhofer J, 'The Uncertainty in the Formal Source of International Law Customary International Law and Some of its Problems', (2004) 15(3) EJIL 523.

Keleman R, 'The Limits of Judicial Power: Trade–Environment Disputes in the GATT/WTO and the EU', (2001) 34(6) *Comparative Political Studies* 624.

Kelly C, 'Power, Linkage and Accommodation: The WTO as an International Actor and Its Influence over Other Actors and Regimes', (2006) 24 *Berkeley Journal of International Law* 79.

Kelly J, 'Judicial Activism at the WTO: Developing Principles of Self-Restraint', (2002) 22 *Northwestern Journal of International Law and Business* 353.

Kennedy D, 'The International Style in Postwar Law and Policy: John Jackson and the Field of International Economic Law', (1994–95) 10 *American University Journal of International Law and Policy* 671.

Kennedy K C, 'Resolving the International Sanitary and Phytosanitary Disputes in the WTO: Lessons and Future Directions', (2000) 55 *Food and Drug Journal* 81.

King M, 'The Construction and Demolition of the Luhmann Heresy', (2001) 12 *Law and Critique* 1.

Koskenniemi M, 'Fragmentation of International Law: Difficulties Arising from the Diversification and Expansion of International Law', UN Doc. International Law Commission A/CN.4/L.682 13 April 2006.

Koskenniemi M, 'Hierarchy in International Law: A Sketch', (1997) 8(4) EJIL 566.

Koskenniemi M, 'The Fate of Public International Law: Between Technique and Politics', (2007) 70(1) *Modern Law Review* 1.
Koskenniemi M, 'The Politics of International Law', (1990) 1 EJIL 4.
Koskenniemi M and P Leino, 'Fragmentation of International Law? Postmodern Anxieties', (2002) 15 *Leiden Journal of International Law* 553.
Koskenniemi M, 'The Politics of International Law – 20 Years Later', (2009) 20(1) EJIL 1.
Kramer M, 'The Rule of Misrecognition in the Hart of Jurisprudence', (1988) 8(3) *Oxford Journal of Legal Studies* 401.
Kunz J L, 'Robert Ago's Theory of a Spontaneous International Law', (1958) 52 AJIL 88.
Kunz J L, 'The Nature of Customary International Law', (1953) 47 AJIL 665.
Kuyper P, 'The Law of GATT as a Special Field of International Law', (1994) 25 *Netherlands Yearbook of International Law* 140.
Lang A, 'Reflecting on Linkage: Cognitive and Institutional Change in the International Trading System', (2007) 70(4) *Modern Law Review* 523–549.
Lennard M, 'Navigating by the Stars: Interpreting the WTO Agreements', (2002) JIEL 17.
Lindross A and M Mehling, 'Dispelling the Chimera of "Self-Contained Regimes": International Law and the WTO', (2005) 16(5) EJIL 857.
Luhmann N, 'Law as a Social System', (1989) 83 *Northwestern University Law Review* 136.
Luhmann N, 'Operational Closure and Structural Coupling: The Differentiation of the Legal System', 13 *Cardozo Law Review* 1419.
MacCormick N, 'Reconstruction after Deconstruction: A Response to CLS', (1990) 10(4) *Oxford Journal of Legal Studies* 539.
MacCormick N, 'The Concept of Law and "The Concept of Law"', (1994) 14(1) *Oxford Journal of Legal Studies* 2.
MacCormick N, 'The Ethics of Legalism', (1989) 2(2) *Ratio Juris* 184–193.
McGinnis J, 'The Appropriate Hierarchy of Global Multilateralism and Customary International Law: The Example of the WTO', (2003) 44 *Virginia Journal of International Law* 229.
MacIntyre A, 'Epistemological Crises, Dramatic Narrative and the Philosophy of Science', (1977) 60(4) *Monist* 453.
Maki P C, 'Interpreting GATT Using the Vienna Convention on the Law of Treaties: A Method to Increase the Legitimacy of the Dispute Settlement System', (2000) *Minnesota Journal of Global Trade* 343.
Marceau G, 'A Call for Coherence in International Law', (1999) 33(5) JWT 87.
Marceau G, 'Conflicts of Norms and Conflicts of Jurisdictions: The Relationship between the WTO Agreement and MEAs and other Treaties', (2001) 35(6) JWT 1081.
Marceau G, 'WTO Dispute Settlement and Human Rights', (2002) 13 EJIL 753.
Marceau G and J Trachtman, 'The Technical Barriers to Trade Agreement, the Sanitary and Phytosanitary Measures Agreement and the General Agreement on Tariffs and Trade: Map of the World Trade Organisation Law of Domestic Regulation of Goods', (2002) 36(5) JWT 811–881.
Markey C, 'Calvino and the Existential Dilemma: The Paradox of Choice', (1983) 60(1) *Italica* 55.
Matthee M and D Vermersch, 'Are the Precautionary Principle and the International Trade of Genetically Modified Organisms Reconcilable?', (2000) 12 *Journal of Agricultural and Environmental Ethics* 59.
McBarnet D and C Whelan, 'The Elusive Spirit of the Law: Formalism and the Struggle for Legal Control', (1991) 54 *Modern Law Review* 848.

McLachlan C, 'The Principle of Systematic Integration and Article 31(3)(c) of the Vienna Convention', (2005) 54 *International and Comparative Law Quarterly* 279.
McNeil D, 'The First Case under the WTO's SPS Agreement: The EU Hormone Ban', (1998) 39 *Virginia Journal of International Law* 89.
McNelis N, 'The Role of the Judge in the EU and WTO. Lessons from the BSE and Hormones Case', (2001) 4 JIEL 189.
McRae D, 'Claus-Dieter Ehlermann's Presentation on "The Role and Record of Dispute Settlement Panels and the Appellate Body of the WTO"', (2003) JIEL 709.
McRae D, 'The Contribution of International Trade Law to the Development of International Law', (1996) T-260 *Recueil des Cours* 99.
McRae D, 'The WTO in International Law: Tradition Continued or New Frontier?', (2000) 3 JIEL 27.
Meltzer J, 'Interpreting the WTO Agreements – A Commentary on Professor Pauwelyn's Approach', (2004) 25 *Michigan Journal of International Law* 917.
Montaguti E and M Lugard, 'The GATT 1994 and Other Annex 1A Agreements: Four Different Relationships?', (2000) JIEL 473.
Mullender R, 'Hegel, Human Rights and Particularism', (2003) 30(4) *Journal of Law and Society* 554–574.
Mullender R, 'Human Rights: Universalism and Cultural Relativism', (2003) 6(3) *Critical Review of International Social and Political Philosophy* 70–103.
Mullender R, 'Parliamentary Sovereignty, the Constitution, and the Judiciary', (1998) 49(2) *Northern Ireland Legal Quarterly* 138.
Mullender R, 'Two Nomoi and a Clash of Narratives: The Story of the United Kingdom and the European Union', (2006) 3 *Issues in Legal Scholarship* 9.
Munch R, 'Autopoiesis by Definition', (1992) 13 *Cardozo Law Review* 1463–1471.
Mus J B, 'Conflicts between Treaties in International Law', (1998) XLV *Netherlands International Law Review* 214–217.
Nicholas P, 'Trade Without Values', (1996) *Northwestern University Law Review* 701.
Nichols P, 'GATT Doctrine', (1996) 36 *Virginia Journal of International Law* 379.
Nobles R and D Schiff, 'A Story of Miscarriage: Law in the Media', (2004) 31(2) *Journal of Law and Society* 221.
Orford A, 'A Journal of the Voyage from Apology', (2006) 7(12) *German Law Journal* 993.
Orford A, 'Beyond Harmonisation: Trade, Human Rights and the Economy of Sacrifice', (2005) 18 *Leiden Journal of International Law* 179–213.
Palmeter D, 'The WTO as a Legal System', (2000) *Fordham International Law Journal* 444.
Palmeter D and P Mavroidis, 'The WTO Legal System: Sources of Law', (1998) 92 AJIL 398–413.
Pauwelyn J, 'Bridging Fragmentation and Unity: International Law as a Universe of Inter-Connected Islands', (2004) 25 *Michigan Journal of International Law* 905–916.
Pauwelyn J, 'Enforcement and Countermeasures in the WTO: Rules are Rules – Towards a More Collective Approach', (2000) 94 AJIL 335.
Pauwelyn J, 'How to Win a World Trade Organisation Dispute Based on Non-World Trade Organisation Law? Questions of Jurisdiction and Merits', (2003) 37(6) JIEL 997.
Pauwelyn J, 'Reply to Joshua Meltzer', (2004) 25 *Michigan Journal of International Law* 924.
Pauwelyn J, 'The Jurisdiction of the WTO', (2004) 98 *ASIL Proceedings* 135.
Pauwelyn J, 'The Role of Public International Law in the WTO: How Far Can We Go?', (2001) 95(3) AJIL 535.
Pauwelyn J, 'The WTO Agreement on Sanitary and Phytosanitary (SPS) Measures as

Applied in the First Three SPS Disputes: EC – Hormones, Australia – Salmon and Japan – Varietals', (1999) JIEL 641.

Peel J, 'A GMO by Any Other Name . . . Might Be an SPS Risk!: Implications of Expanding the Scope of the WTO Sanitary and Phytosanitary Measures Agreement', (2006) 17 EJIL 1009.

Perez O, 'Purity Lost: The Paradoxical Face of the New Transnational Legal Body', (2007) 33(1) *Brooklyn Journal of International Law* 1–58.

Priess H J and C Pitschas, 'Protection of Public Health and the Role of the Precautionary Principle under WTO Law: A Trojan Horse before Geneva's Walls?', (2000) 24 *Fordham International Law Journal* 520.

Pulkowski D, 'Book Review of Conflict of Norms in Public International Law: How WTO Law Relates to Other Rules of International Law', (2005) EJIL 153.

Pulkowski D, 'Multiple Perspectives on the Fragmentation of International Law', (2004) Paper presented at the European Society of International Law, 1–6.

Quick R and A Blunther, 'Has the Appellate Body Erred? An Appraisal and Criticism of the Ruling in the WTO Hormones Case', (1999) JIEL 626.

Raban O, 'Dworkin's "Best Light" Requirement and the Proper Methodology of Legal Theory', (2003) 23(2) *Oxford Journal of Legal Studies* 243.

Rasulov A, 'International Law and the Poststructuralist Challenge', (2006) 19 *Leiden Journal of International Law* 799.

Salmon N, 'A European Perspective on the Precautionary Principle, Food Safety and the Free Trade Perspective of the WTO', (2002) *European Law Review* 137.

Sands P D, 'The Greening of International Law: Emerging Principles and Rules', (1994) 1 *Indiana Journal of Global Legal Studies* 297.

Sands P D, 'Whither CITES? The Evolution of a Treaty Regime in the Borderland of Trade and Environment', (1997) 8(1) EJIL 29.

Santillo D, R L Stringer, P A Johnston and J Tickner, 'The Precautionary Principle: Protecting against Failures of Scientific Method and Risk Assessment', (1998) 36(12) *Marine Pollution Bulletin* 939.

Schauer F, 'The Social Construction of the Concept of Law: A Reply to Julie Dickson', (2005) 25(3) *Oxford Journal of Legal Studies* 493.

Schoenbaum T, 'WTO Dispute Settlement: Praise and Suggestions for Reform', (1998) 47 *International Comparative and Law Quarterly* 652.

Scott J, 'International Trade and Environmental Governance: Relating Rules (and Standards) in the EU and the WTO', (2004) 15 EJIL 307.

Segger M and M Gehring, 'The WTO and Precaution: Sustainable Development Implications of the WTO Asbestos Dispute', (2003) 15(3) *Journal of Environmental Law* 292.

Shermer, Michael, 'The Really Hard Science' *Scientific American*. 16 September 2007. Available at http://www.scientificamerican.com/article.cfm?id=the-really-hard-science&ref=rss (accessed on 1 September 2008).

Simma B and A Paulus, 'The International Community: Facing the Challenge of Globalisation', (1998) 9 EJIL 266.

Simma B and D Pulkowski, 'Of Planets and the Universe: Self-Contained Regimes in International Law', (2006) 17 EJIL 483.

Slaughter-Burley A, 'International Law and International Relations Theory: A Dual Agenda', (1993) AJIL 205.

Springer C, 'Textual Geography: The Role of the Reader in *Invisible Cities*', (1985) 15(4) *Modern Language Studies* 289. Steger D, 'The Jurisdiction of the WTO', (2004) 98 *ASIL Proceedings*, 142.

Stone C, 'Is There a Precautionary Principle?', (2001) 31 *Environmental Law Reporter* 10790.

Stonehouse P, 'Review of WTO and Environmental Issues', (2000) 13 *Journal of Agricultural and Environmental Ethics* 121–144.

Sunstein C, 'Beyond the Precautionary Principle', (2003) 151 *University of Pennsylvania Law Review* 1003.

Sunstein C, 'The Idea of a Useable Past', (1995) 95 *Columbia Law Review* 601.

Sykes A, 'Domestic Regulation, Sovereignty, and Scientific Evidence Requirements: A Pessimistic View', (2002) 3 *Chicago Journal of International Law* 354.

Sykes A, 'The Limited Role of Regulatory Harmonisation in International Goods and Services Markets', (1999) 2 JIEL 49.

Symposium: 'Diversity or Cacophony?: New Sources of Norms in International Law', (2004) 25 *Michigan Journal of International Law* 869–878.

Symposium: 'Is the Proliferation of International Courts and Tribunals a Systemic Problem?', (1999) 31(4) *New York University Journal of International Law and Politics* 679.

Tarlock A D, 'Is There a There in Environmental Law?', (2004) *Journal of Land Use and Environmental Law* 251.

Teubner G, 'How Law Thinks: Toward A Constructivist Epistemology of Law', (1989) 23(5) *Law and Society Review* 727.

Teubner G, 'The Two Faces of Janus: Rethinking Legal Pluralism', (1992) 13 *Cardozo Law Review* 1443.

Teubner G, 'Substantive and Reflexive Elements in Modern Law', (1983) 17 *Law and Society Review* 239.

Thomas D, 'Where's the Beef? Mad Cow and the Blight of the SPS Agreement', (1999) 32 *Vanderbilt Journal of Transnational Law* 487.

Thorn C and M Carlson, 'The Agreement on the Application of Sanitary and Phytosanitary Measures and the Agreement on Technical Barriers to Trade', (2000) 31 *Law and Policy in International Business* 841.

Trachtman J, 'Book Review of Conflict of Norms in Public International Law: How WTO Law Relates to Other Rules of International Law, by J Pauwelyn', (2004) 98 AJIL 855.

Trachtman J, 'Case Note: Argentina–Measures Affecting Imports of Footwear, Textiles, Apparel and Other Items', (1998) 9(3) EJIL 551.

Trachtman J, 'Institutional Linkage: Transcending 'Trade and . . .', (2002) 96 AJIL 77.

Trachtman J, 'John Jackson and the Founding of the World Trade Organisation: Empiricism, Theory and Institutional Imagination', (1999) *Michigan Journal of International Law* 175.

Trachtman J, 'The Domain of WTO Dispute Resolution', (1999) 40 *Harvard International Law Journal* 333.

Trachtman J, 'The Jurisdiction of the WTO', (2004) 98 *ASIL Proceedings* 139.

Tribe L H, 'The Curvature of Constitutional Space: What Lawyers Can Learn From Modern Physics', (1989) 103(1) *Harvard Law Review* 1.

Twining W, 'Pericles and the Plumber', (1967) 83 *Law Quarterly Review* 396.

Wai R, 'Countering, Branding, Dealing: Using Economic and Social Rights in and around the International Trade Regime', (2003) 14 EJIL 59.

Weil P, 'Towards Relative Normativity in International Law', (1983) 77 AJIL 413.

Weiler J H H, 'The Rule of Lawyers and the Ethos of Diplomats: Reflections on the Internal and External Legitimacy of the WTO Dispute Settlement', (2001) 35(2) JWT 191.

Weiler J H H and A L Paulus, 'The Structure of Change in International Law or Is There a Hierarchy of Norms in International Law?', (1997) 8(4) EJIL 545.

Weisberg R, 'Autopoiesis and Positivism', (1992) 13 *Cardozo Law Review* 1721.

Weiss C, 'Scientific Uncertainty and Science-Based Precaution', (2003) 3 *International Environmental Agreements: Politics, Law and Economics* 137.
Weiss E, 'Environment and Trade as Partners in Sustainable Development: A Commentary', (1992) 86 AJIL 728.
Williams G, 'Language and the Law', (1945) 61 *Law Quarterly Review* 71.
Williams G, 'Language and the Law', (1946) 62 *Law Quarterly Review* 387.
Wold C, 'Multilateral Environmental Agreements and the GATT: Conflict and Resolution?', (1996) 26 *Environmental Law* 841.
Young M, 'The WTO's Use of Relevant Rules of International Law: An Analysis of the *Biotech* Case', (2007) 56 *International and Comparative Law Quarterly* 907.
Zaring D, 'International Law by Other Means: The Twilight Existence of International Financial Regulatory Organisations', (1998) 33 *Texas International Law Journal* 281.

Books

Akande D, 'International Organisations', in M Evans (ed), *International Law* (London: OUP, 2006).
Akehurst M, *Modern Introduction to International Law*, 7th Edition (Peter Malanczuk) (London: Routledge, 1997).
Alder J and Wilkinson, *Environmental Law and Ethics* (London: Macmillan, 1999).
Allot P, *Eunomia: New Order for a New World* (Oxford: OUP, 2001).
Andenas M and F Ortino (eds), *WTO Law and Process* (London: British Institute of International and Comparative Law, 2005).
Arend A C, *Legal Rules and International Society* (Oxford: OUP, 1999).
Arup C, *The New World Trade Organisation Agreement: Globalising Law through Services and Intellectual Property* (New York: CUP, 2000).
Aust A, *Modern Treaty Law and Practice* (Cambridge: CUP, 2000).
Bankowski Z 'How Does it Feel to Be on Your Own? The Person in the Sight of Autopoiesis', in D Nelken (ed) *Law as Communication* (Aldershot: Darmouth Publishing, 1996).
Baughen S, *International Trade and the Protection of the Environment* (London: Routledge-Cavendish, 2007).
Bayles M D, *Hart's Legal Philosophy: An Examination* (London: Kluwer Academic, 1992).
Beckett J, *The End of Customary Law: A Purposive Analysis of Structural Indeterminacy* (Germany: VDM Verlag, 2008).
Bell S and D McGillivray, *Environmental Law: The Law and Policy Relating to the Protection of the Environment*, 5th Edition (London: Blackstone Press, 2000).
Berlin I, *Four Essays on Liberty* (Oxford: OUP, 1969).
Bernascono-Osterwalder N, D Magraw, M J Oliva, M Orellana and E Tuerk, *Environment and Trade: A Guide to WTO Jurisprudence* (London: Earthscan, 2006).
Birnie P and A Boyle, *International Law and the Environment*, 2nd Edition (Oxford: OUP, 2003).
Borges, J L, 'El jardín de los senderos que se bifurcan' (The garden of forking paths), in *Ficciones*, trans H Temple and R Todd (New York: Grove Press, 1962).
Bos M, 'Will and Order in the Nation-State System: Observations on Positivism and Positive International Law', in R St J MacDonald and D M Johnston (eds), *The Structure and Process of International Law* (Hague: Martinus Nijhoff Publishers, 1983).
Boyle A, 'Soft Law in International Law-Making', in M Evans (ed), *International Law* (London: OUP, 2006).
Brownlie I, *Principles of Public International Law* (Oxford: OUP, 2003).

Brownlie I, *The Rule of Law in International Affairs: International Law at the Fifteenth Anniversary of the United Nations* (Hague: Martinus Nijhoff Publishers, 1998).
de Burca G and J Scott (eds), *The EU and the WTO: Legal and Constitutional Issues* (Oxford: Hart Publishing, 2001).
Calvino I, *Invisible Cities*, trans W Weaver (London: Vintage, 1997; originally published in Italian as *Le città invisibili*, 1972).
Calvino I, *Mr. Palomar*, trans W Weaver (London: Vintage, 1999; originally published in Italian, 1983).
Cameron J, 'The Status of the Precautionary Principle in International Law', in T O'Riordan and J Cameron (eds), *Interpreting the Precautionary Principle* (London: Cameron May, 1994).
Cameron J and J Abouchar, 'The Status of the Precautionary Principle in International Law', in D Freestone and E Hey (eds), *The Precautionary Principle and International Law: The Challenge of Implementation* (Hague: Kluwer Law International, 1996).
Campbell C.M, 'The Career of the Concept', in P Leith and P Ingram, *The Jurisprudence of Orthodoxy: Queens University Essays on H.L.A Hart* (London: Routledge, 1998).
Camus A, *The Rebel* (London: Penguin [1951] 2000).
Carroll L, *Alice's Adventures in Wonderland* (London: Penguin [1865] 1994).
Carroll L, *Through the Looking-Glass and What Alice Found There* (London: Penguin [1872] 2003).
Cass, D Z, *The Constitutionalization of the World Trade Organization: Legitimacy, Democracy, and Community in the International Trading System* (Oxford: OUP, 2005).
Castells M, *The Rise of the Network Society* (Oxford: Blackwell, 2000).
Chang R (ed), *Incommensurability, Incomparability and Practical Reason* (Cambridge, MA: Harvard University Press, 1997).
Charlesworth H and C Chinkin, *The Boundaries of International Law: A Feminist Analysis* (Manchester: Manchester University Press, 2000).
Chen L, *An Introduction to Contemporary International Law: A Policy Oriented Perspective* (New Haven, CT: Yale University Press, 2000).
Coleman J (ed), *Hart's Postscript: Essays on the Postscript to the Concept of Law* (Oxford: OUP, 2001).
Condorelli L, 'Custom', in M Bedjaoui, *International Law: Achievements and Prospects* (Paris: UNESCO, 1991) 180.
Cottier T, J Pauwelyn and E B Bonanomi (eds), *Human Rights and International Trade* (Oxford: OUP, 2005).
Crawford J, *The International Law Commission's Articles on State Responsibility: Introduction, Text and Commentaries* (Cambridge: CUP, 2002).
Crop C, *Marcel Duchamp: Critical Lives*, trans V Rehberg (London: Reaktion Books, 2006).
Darton R, *The Great Cat Massacre and Other Episodes in French Cultural History* (New York: Basic Book, 1984).
Darwin F., *More Letters of Charles Darwin Vol. 1* (New York: D Appleton, 1903).
Demos T J, *The Exiles of Marcel Duchamp* (Cambridge, MA: MIT Press, 2007).
Detter I, *The International Legal Order* (England: Dartmouth, 1994).
Dolin K, *Fiction and the Law: Legal Discourse in Victorian and Modernist Literature* (Cambridge: CUP, 1999).
Dunkley G, *The Free Trade Adventure* (London: Zed Books [1997] 2000).
Durling J and D Hardin, 'Amicus Curiae Participation in WTO Dispute Settlement: Reflections on the Past Decade', in R Yerxa and B Wilson (eds), *Key Issues in WTO Dispute Settlement: The First Ten Years* (Cambridge: CUP, 2005).

Dworkin R, *Law's Empire* (London: Fontana Press, 1986).

Eatwell J and L Taylor, *Global Finance at Risk: The Case for International Regulation* (New York: New Press, 2000).

Einstein A, *Relativity: The Special and the General Theory*, trans R W Lawson (London: Routledge, 2001; originally published 1916).

Endicott T A O, *Vagueness in Law* (Oxford: OUP, 2000).

Ferran E and C Goodhart (eds), *Regulating Financial Services and Markets in the 21st Century* (Oregon: Hart Publishing, 2001).

Fish S, *Doing What Comes Naturally* (Oxford: OUP, 1989).

Fisher E, *Risk Regulation and Administrative Constitutionalism* (Oxford: Hart Publishing, 2007).

Frank H, *On Bullshit* (Princeton, NJ: Princeton University Press, 2005).

Frank H, *On Truth* (London: Pimlico, 2007).

Freestone D and E Hey (eds), *The Precautionary Principle and International Law: The Challenge and Implementation* (London: Kluwer Law International, 1996).

Fukyama F, *The End of History and the Last Man* (New York: Free Press, 1992).

Galligan D J, *Law in Modern Society* (Oxford: OUP, 2007).

Giddens A, *The Consequences of Modernity* (Cambridge: Polity Press, 1990).

Gray J, *Two Faces of Liberalism* (Cambridge: Polity Press, 2004).

Griffen J, 'Incommensurability: What's the Problem?', in R Chang, *Incommensurability, Incomparability and Practical Reason* (Cambridge, MA: Harvard University Press, 1997).

Haigh N, 'The Introduction of the Precautionary Principle into the UK', in J Cameron and T O'Riordan (eds), *Interpreting the Precautionary Principle* (London: Earthscan, 1994).

Hancher L, 'EC Envrionmental Policy – a Pre-cautionary Tale?' in D Freestone and E Hey (eds), *The Precautionary Principle and International Law: The Challenge of Implementation* (Hague: Kluwer Law International, 1996) 187–208.

Hart H L A, 'American Jurisprudence through English Eyes: The Nightmare and the Noble Dream', in *Essays in Jurisprudence and Philosophy* (Oxford: Clarendon Press, 1983).

Hart H L A, *The Concept of Law* (Oxford: Clarendon Press, 1961; 2nd Edition Oxford: OUP, 1997).

Hawking S, *A Brief History of Time: From the Big Bang to Black Holes* (London: Bantam Press, 1988).

Held D and A McGrew (ed) *The Global Transformations Reader: An Introduction to the Globalization Debate* (Oxford: Polity Press, 2000).

Henkin L, *How Nations Behave* (New York: Columbia University Press, 1979).

Higgins R, *Problems and Process: International Law and How We Use It* (Oxford: OUP, 1994).

Hohmann H, *The Precautionary Principle: International Environmental Law: Between Exploitation and Protection* (London: Kluwer, 1994).

Holder J and M Lee, *Environmental Protection, Law and Policy: Text and Materials*, 2nd Edition (Cambridge: CUP, 2007).

Homer, *The Odyssey* (London: Peguin Books, 2003) (original trans E V Rieu, 1946, revised trans D C H Rieu, 1991, 2003.

Huntington S, *The Clash of Civilizations and the Remaking of World Order* (New York: Simon and Schuster, 1998).

Ingman T, *The English Legal Process* (Oxford: OUP, 2006).

Jackson J, 'The Concept of Fact', in P Leith and P Ingram, *The Jurisprudence of Orthodoxy: Queens University Essays on H.L.A Hart* (London: Routledge, 1998).

Jackson J, *The Jurisprudence of GATT and the WTO* (Cambridge: CUP, 2000).

Jackson J, *The World Trade Organisation: Constitution and Jurisprudence* (London: Pinter, 1998).

Jackson J, *The World Trading System: Law and Policy of International Economic Relations* (Cambridge, MA: MIT Press [1989] 1997).

Jackson J, W Davey and A Sykes, *Legal Problems of International Economic Relations*, 4th Edition (St Paul: West Group, 2002).

Jackson, J H, *Sovereignty, the WTO and Changing Fundamental of International Law*, Cambridge, CUP, 2006).

Jackson R, *Fantasy: The Literature of Subversion* (London: Methuen, 1981).

Janow M, 'Commentary on Natalie McNelis' Paper', in T Cottier, P Mavroidis and P Blatter (eds), *The Role of the Judge in International Trade Regulation: Experience and Lessons for the WTO*, World Trade Forum Vol. 7 (Ann Arbor: University of Michigan Press, 2003).

Jennings R, 'The Identification of International Law', in B Cheng (ed), *International Law: Teaching and Practice* (London: Stevens and Sons, 1982).

Judovitz D, *Unpacking Duchamp: Art in Transit* (Berkeley: University of California Press, 1998).

Kant I, 'Idea for a Universal History with a Cosmopolitan Intent' trans., in Humphrey T (ed), *Perpetual Peace and Other Essays on Politics, History and Morals* (Cambridge: Hackett Publishing, 1983).

Kelsen H, *General Theory of Norms*, trans M Hartney (Oxford, OUP, 1991).

Kennealy P, 'Talking About Autopoiesis – Order From Noise', in G Teubner (ed), *Autopoietic Law: A New Approach to Law and Society* (Berlin: Walter de Gruyter, 1988).

Kennedy D, *The Dark Sides of Virtue: Reassessing International Humanitarianism* (Oxford: Princeton University Press, 2005).

Kiss A, 'The Rights and Interests of Future Generations and the Precautionary Principle', in D Freestone and E Hey (eds), *The Precautionary Principle and International Law: The Challenge of Implementation* (Hague: Kluwer Law International, 1996).

Klabbers J, *An Introduction to International Institutional Law* (Cambridge: CUP, 2002).

Koskenniemi M, *From Apology to Utopia: The Structure of the International Legal Argument* (Helsinki: Finnish Lawyers' Publishing Company, 1989).

Kwak K and G Marceau, 'Overlaps and Conflicts of Jurisdiction between the World Trade Organisation and Regional Trade Agreements', in L Bartels and F Ortino, *Regional Trade Agreements and the WTO Legal System* (Oxford: OUP, 2006).

Lester S and B Mercurio et al., *World Trade Law: Text, Materials and Commentary* (Oxford: Hart Publishing, 2008).

Louka E, *International Environmental Law: Fairness, Effectiveness, and World Order* (Cambridge: CUP, 2006).

Lowe V, 'Jurisdiction', in M Evans (ed), *International Law* (London: OUP, 2006).

Lowe V, 'Sustainable Development and Unsustainable Arguments', in A Boyle and D Freestone, *International Law and Sustainable Development: Past Achievements and Future Challenges* (Oxford: OUP, 1999).

Lowe V, 'The Politics of Law-Making: Are the Method and Character of Norm Creation Changing?', in A Boyle and D Freestone (eds), *International Law and Sustainable Development: Past Achievements and Future Challenges* (Oxford: OUP, 1999).

Lowenfeld A F, *International Economic Law* (Oxford: OUP, 2002).

Luhmann N, *Law as a Social System*, trans K Ziegert (Oxford: OUP, 2004).

Luhmann N, 'The Unity of the Legal System', in G Teubner (ed), *Autopoietic Law: A New Approach to Law and Society* (Berlin: Walter de Gruyter, 1988).

MacCormick N, *Legal Reasoning and Legal Theory* (Oxford: Clarendon Press, 1978).

MacCormick N and O Weinberger, *An Institutional Theory of Law: New Approaches to Legal Positivism* (Dordrecht: D Reidel, 1992).

MacCormick N and R S Summers, *Interpreting Statutes: A Comparative Study* (Brookfield, VT: Dartmouth, 1991).

Macintyre A, *After Virtue, A Study in Moral Theory*, 2nd Edition (London: Gerald Duckworth, 1985).

Matsushita M, T J Schoenbaum and P C Mavroidis, *The World Trade Organization: Law, Practice, and Policy*, 2nd Edition (Oxford: OUP, 2006).

Mavroidis P, 'The Trade Disputes Concerning Health Policy between the EC and the US', in E Petersmann and M Pollack (eds), *Transatlantic Economic Disputes: The EU, the US and the WTO* (Oxford: OUP, 2003) 233–245, 244.

McCoubrey H and N D White, *Textbook on Jurisprudence*, 3rd Edition (Oxford: OUP, 1999).

McDonald J, 'Tr(e)ading Cautiously: Precaution in WTO Decision Making', in E Fisher, J Jones and R v Schomberg, *Implementing the Precautionary Principle: Perspectives and Prospects* (Cheltenham: Edward Elgar, 2006).

Mertes T (ed), *A Movement of Movements: Is Another World Really Possible?* (London: Verso, 2004).

Morris P (ed), *The Bakhtin Reader* (London: Edward Arnold, 1994).

North D, *Institutions, Institutional Change and Economic Performance* (Cambridge: CUP, 1991).

Oesch M, *Standards of Review in WTO Dispute Resolution* (Oxford: OUP, 2003).

Oppenheim L, *Oppenheim's International Law*, ed Sir R Jennings and Sir A Watts (Harlow: Longman, 1992).

O'Riordan T, 'The Politics of the Precautionary Principle', in R Harding R and E Fisher (eds), *Perspectives on the Precautionary Principle* (Australia: Federation Press, 1999).

O'Riordan T and A Jordan, *The Precautionary Principle, Science, Politics and Ethics* (London: Centre for Social and Economic Research on the Global Environment, 1995).

O'Riordan T and J Cameron (eds), *Interpreting the Precautionary Principle* (London: Earthscan, 1994).

Pauwelyn J, *Conflict of Norms in Public International Law: How WTO Law Relates to Other Rules of International Law* (Cambridge: CUP, 2003).

Pauwelyn J, 'Cooperation in Dispute Settlement', in T Cottier, J Pauwelyn and E B Bonanomi, *Human Rights and International Trade* (Oxford: OUP, 2005).

Pauwelyn J, 'Remarks at the Fourth Annual WTO Conference', in M Andenas and F Ortino (eds), *WTO Law and Process* (London: British Institute of International and Comparative Law, 2005).

Paz O, *Marcel Duchamp: Appearance Stripped Bare*, trans R Philips and D Gardner (New York: Arcade Publishing, 1990; Original Spanish edition 1978).

Perez O, *Ecological Sensitivity and Global Legal Pluralism: Rethinking the Trade and Environmental Conflict* (Oxford: Hart Publishing, 2004).

Pirsig R, *The Zen and the Art of Motorcycle Maintenance: An Inquiry into Values* (London: Vintage Books [1974] 1999).

Rasch W, *Sovereignty and its Discontents* (London: Birkbeck Law Press, 2004).

Raz J, *The Authority of Law* (Oxford: Clarendon Press, 1979).

Raz J, *The Morality of Freedom* (Oxford: Clarendon Press, 1986).

Reisman M, 'The Concept and Functions of Soft Law in International Politics', in E Bello and B Ajibola (eds), *Essays in Honour of Judge Olawale Elias Vol. 1* (London: Martinus Nijhoff Publishers, 1992).

Rorty R, *Consequences of Pragmatism* (Minneapolis: University of Minnesota Press, 1982).

Sacerdoti G, 'The Role of Lawyers in the WTO Dispute Settlement System', in R Yerxa and B Wilson, *Key Issues in WTO Dispute Settlement: The First Ten Years* (Cambridge: CUP, 2005).

Sands P D, *Principles of International Environmental Law Vol. 1* (Manchester: Manchester University Press, 1995).

Schachter O, 'Non-Conventional Concerted Acts', in M Bedjaoui (ed), *International Law: Achievements and Prospects* (Paris: UNESCO, 1991).

Schoenbaum T, 'International Trade in Living Modified Organisms', in F Francioni (ed), *Environment, Human Rights and International Trade* (Oxford: Hart Publishing, 2001)

Scholte J A, *Globalisation: A Critical introduction*, 2nd Edition (Basingstoke: Palgrave Macmillan, 2005).

Scott D, *Plato's Meno* (Cambridge: CUP, 2006).

Scott J, *Commentary on the Sanitary and Phytosanitary Measures Agreement* (Oxford: OUP, 2007).

Scott J and E Vos, 'The Juridification of Uncertainty: Observations on the Ambivalnce of the Precautionary Principle within the EU and the WTO', in C Joerges and R Dehouse (eds), *Good Governance in Europe's Integrated Market* (Oxford: OUP, 2002).

Searle J, *The Construction of Social Reality* (New York: Free Press, 1995).

Shaw M, *International Law* (Cambridge: CUP, 1997).

Shelton D, 'International Law and Relative Normativity', in M Evans, *International Law* (London: OUP, 2006).

Stiglitz J, *Globalisation and its Discontents* (London: Penguin Group, 2002).

Strange S, *The Retreat of the State: The Diffusion of Power in the World Economy* (Cambridge: CUP, 1996).

Teubner G (ed), *Autopoietic Law: A New Approach to Law and Society* (Berlin: Walter de Gruyter, 1988).

Teubner G, *Law as an Autopoietic System* (Oxford: Blackwell, 1993).

Teubner G and A Febbrajo (eds), *State, Law, Economy as Autopoietic Systems* (Milan: Guiffre, 1992).

Thirlway H, 'The Sources of International Law', in M Evans, *International Law* (Oxford: OUP, 2003).

Thomas J, *Musings on the Meno* (London: Martinus Nijhoff Publishers, 1980).

Titchner M, *British Art Show 6* (London: Hayward Gallery Publishing, 2005).

Titchner M: *IT IS YOU*, ed M. Clarke (Bristol: Arnolfini, 2006).

Titchner M, *Why and Why Not (Vibrations, Schizzes and Knots)* (London: Book Works, 2006).

Toffler A, *Powershift: Knowledge, Wealth and Violence at the Edge of the 21st Century* (New York: Bantam Books, 1991).

Trachtman J, 'Jurisdiction in WTO Dispute Settlement', in R Yerxa and B Wilson (eds), *Key Issues in WTO Dispute Settlement: The First Ten Years* (Cambridge: CUP, 2005).

Trebilcock M J and R Howse, *The Regulation of International Trade*, 3rd Edition (London: Routledge, 2005).

Trouwborst A, *Evolution and Status of the Precautionary Principle in International Law* (London: Kluwer Law International, 2002).

Twining W, *Globalisation and Legal Theory* (London: Butterworths, 2000).

Twining W, *Karl Llewllyn and the Realist Movment* (London: George Weidenfeld and Nicolson, 1973, reprinted with postscript, 1985).

Van Damme I, 'What Role Is there for Regional International Law in the Interpretation of WTO Agreements?', in L Bartels and F Ortino, *Regional Trade Agreements and the WTO Legal System* (Oxford: OUP, 2006).

Ward I, *Law and Literature: Possibilities and Perspectives* (Cambridge: CUP, 1995).

Watts A, 'The Importance of International Law', in M Byers, *The Role of Law in International Politics* (Oxford: OUP, 2000).

Weber M, *The Methodology of the Social Sciences*, trans and ed E A Shils and H A Finch (New York, Free Press, 1949).
Weiler J (ed), *The EU and the WTO and the NAFTA* (Oxford: OUP, 2000).
Wiener J B, 'Precaution', in D Bodansky, J Brunnee and E Hey (eds), *Oxford Handbook of International Environmental Law* (Oxford: OUP, 2007).
Wood M, 'Rule, Rules and Law', in P Leith and P Ingram, *The Jurisprudence of Orthodoxy: Queens University Essays on H.L.A Hart* (London: Routledge, 1998).
Ziegert K A, 'The Thick Description of Law: An Introduction to Niklas Luhmann's Theory of Operatively Closed Systems', in R Banakar and M Travers (eds), *An Introduction to Law and Social Theory* (Oxford: Hart Publishing, 2002).

Index

Note: Page references for cases can be found in the Table of Cases, p.xi.